The Global History Reader

Global history is a fast growing area of historical study. With the acceleration of the age of globalization in the twentieth century, we have been able to view the world across national boundaries. From the speed of electronic communications and the coverage of global news to the proliferation of "ethnic" restaurants, globalization is situated directly in our everyday lives, and affects our perceptions of world events. It also has a major impact on how we should study the history of the world, and this reader of key previously published pieces shows how that can be put into practice.

Drawing together a wide international range of contributors, this groundbreaking work presents an important collection of essays to set globalization in its historical context. Thematic in focus, these essays also draw on perspectives from other disciplines, such as anthropology and development studies. The reader uses global history to view the history of the world through key themes that transcend national boundaries, such as terrorism, the environment, human rights, the information revolution, and multinational corporations.

The Global History Reader is essential reading for all students with an interest in learning more about this definitive new area of historical study.

Bruce Mazlish is Professor Emeritus of History at the Massachusetts Institute of Technology, specializing in intellectual history and global history. **Akira Iriye** is Professor of American History at Harvard University.

The
Global History
Reader

Edited by

Bruce Mazlish and Akira Iriye

Routledge
Taylor & Francis Group

NEW YORK AND LONDON

First published 2005 by Routledge
270 Madison Ave, New York, NY 10016

Simultaneously published in the UK
by Routledge
2 Park Square, Milton Park, Abingdon, Oxon OX14 4RN

Routledge is an imprint of the Taylor & Francis Group

The Dymaxion map appears on the cover courtesy of the Buckminster
Fuller Institute.

Visit their website on www.bfi.org or call toll-free on 800-967 6277.

Typeset in Bell Gothic and Perpetua by
Florence Production Ltd, Stoodleigh, Devon
Printed and bound in Great Britain by
TJ International Ltd, Padstow, Cornwall

British Library Cataloguing in Publication Data
A catalogue record for this book is available from the British Library

Library of Congress Cataloging in Publication Data
Mazlish, Bruce, 1923–
    The global history reader/Bruce Mazlish and Akira Iriye.
        p.cm.
    Includes bibliographical references and index.
    1. History, Modern–20th century.   2. History, Modern–21st
    century.   3. Globalization–History–20th century.   4.
    Globalization–History–21st century.   I. Iriye, Akira.   II. Title.
    D842.M37 2004
    909.82'5–dc22   2004008117

ISBN 0–415–31459–3 (hbk)
ISBN 0–415–31460–7 (pbk)

Contents

Acknowledgments

The authors and publishers wish to thank the following for their permission to reproduce copyright material:

1   Bruce Mazlish, "Comparing Global History to World History," from the *Journal of Interdisciplinary History*, vol. 28, no. 3 (1998), 385–91, 392–3, with the permission of the editors of the *Journal of Interdisciplinary History* and the MIT Press, Cambridge, Massachusetts. Copyright © 1998 by the Massachusetts Institute of Technology and The Journal of Interdisciplinary History, Inc.

2   Michael Geyer and Charles Bright, "World History in a Global Age," from *American Historical Review*, vol. 100, no. 4 (October 1995), reproduced by permission of the American Historical Association.

3   Stephen Kern, *The Culture of Time and Space: 1880–1918*, pp. 65–7, 109–19, 211–19, Cambridge, Massachussetts: Harvard University Press, copyright © 1983 by Stephen Kern. Reprinted by permission of the publisher.

4   Walter A. McDougall, "Technology and Statecraft in the Space Age: Toward the History of a Saltation," from *American Historical Review*, vol. 87, no. 4 (October 1982), reproduced by permission of the American Historical Association.

5   Pierre Lévy, *Cyberculture*, translated by Robert Bononno, University of Minnesota Press, 2001. Copyright 1997 Editions Odile Jacob/Editions du Conseil de l'Europe. English translation copyright 2001 Robert Bonnono. Reproduced by permission of University of Minnesota Press.

6   Monroe Price, *Media and Sovereignty: The Global Information Revolution and its Challenge to State Power*, MIT Press, 2002, reproduced by permission of the MIT Press.

7   William W. Keller and Louis W. Pauly, "Globalization at Bay," from *Current History* (November 1997), reprinted with permission from *Current History* magazine, © 1997 Current History, Inc.

8   Mira Wilkins, "The Historical Development of Multinational Enterprise to 1930: Discontinuities and Continuities," a paper presented at a conference on multinational enterprises, 2000, pp. 1–2, 6–21, 26–8, 30–1, reproduced by permission of Mira Wilkins.

9   Robin Cohen, "Diasporas, the Nation-State, and Globalization," from *Global History and Migrations* by Wang Gungwu (ed.), Westview Press, 1997. Copyright © 1997 by Westview Press, a Member of the Perseus Books Group. Reprinted by permission of Westview Press, a member of Perseus Books, L.L.C.

10 Wang Gungwu, "Migration and Its Enemies," from *Conceptualizing Global History* by Bruce Mazlish and Ralph Buultjens (eds), Westview Press, 1993, reprinted with permission of the author.

11 Saskia Sassen, *The Global City*, 2nd edition, copyright © 2001 Princeton University Press, reprinted by permission of the publisher.

12 Bruce Mazlish, "Consumerism in the Context of the Global Ecumene," unpublished paper, 2001, reproduced by permission of the author.

13 Margaret E. Keck and Kathryn Sikkink, *Activists Beyond Borders: Advocacy Networks in International Politics*, copyright © 1998 by Cornell University. Used by permission of the publisher, Cornell University Press.

14 Lynton Keith Caldwell, *International Environmental Policy: From the Twentieth to the Twenty-First Century*, 3rd edition, copyright © 1996, Duke University Press. All rights reserved. Used by permission of the publisher.

15 Jack Donnelly, *International Human Rights*, 2nd edition, Westview Press 1998. Copyright © 1993, 1998 by Westview Press, Inc. Reprinted by permission of Westview Press, a member of Perseus Books, L.L.C.

16 Louis Menand III, "Human Rights as Global Imperative," from *Conceptualizing Global History* by Bruce Mazlish and Ralph Buultjens (eds), Westview Press, 1993, reprinted with permission of the editor.

17 Akira Iriye, *Global Community: The Role of International Organizations in the Making of the Contemporary World*, University of California Press, 2002. Copyright © 2002 The Regents of the University of California, reproduced with their permission.

18 S. Frederick Starr, "The Third Sector in the Second World," in *World Development*, January 1991, reproduced by permission of Elsevier.

19 Akira Iriye, *Cultural Internationalism and World Order*, pp. 15–29, 1997, reprinted with permission of The Johns Hopkins University Press.

20 Ulf Hannerz, "The Withering Away of the Nation? An Afterword," from *Ethnos*, Routledge, 1993, www.tandf.co.uk, reproduced by permission of Taylor & Francis.

21 John Joyce, "The Globalization of Music," from *Conceptualizing Global History* by Bruce Mazlish and Ralph Buultjens (eds), Westview Press, 1993, reprinted with permission of the editor.

22 Ulf Hannerz, "Scenarios for Peripheral Cultures," from *Culture, Globalization and the World-System: Contemporary Conditions for the Representation of Identity*, by Anthony D. King (ed.), University of Minnesota Press, 1997, reproduced by permission of the University of Minnesota Press.

23   Erica Barks-Ruggles, "The Globalization of Disease: When Congo Sneezes, Does California Get a Cold?", from *Brookings Review*, vol. 19, no. 4 (Fall 2001), reproduced by permission of The Brookings Institution.

24   Mary E. Wilson, "Travel and the Emergence of Infectious Diseases," from *Emerging Infectious Diseases*, vol. 1, no. 2 (April–June 1995), available from: www.cdc.gov/ncidod/eid/vol1no2/downwils.htm.

25   Bruce Hoffman, *Inside Terrorism*, Columbia University Press, 1998, reproduced by permission of Columbia University Press (US) and the Orion Publishing Group (UK).

26   Lawrence Freedman, "The Third World War?", from *Survival*, vol. 43, no. 4 (Winter 2001–2), reproduced by permission of Oxford University Press.

27   Arjun Appadurai, *Modernity at Large: Cultural Dimensions of Globalization*, University of Minnesota Press, 1996, reproduced by permission of the University of Minnesota Press.

28   Anthony Giddens, *The Consequences of Modernity*, Oxford: Blackwell. Copyright © 1990, Blackwell.

While every effort has been made to trace and acknowledge ownership of copyright material used in this volume, the publishers will be glad to make suitable arrangements with any copyright holders whom it has not been possible to contact.

Introduction

WHAT IS GLOBALIZATION? It is certainly a key word of our times. It is also a relatively new word, dating from sometime in the 1960s–1970s. Its definition is a matter of intense debate, as well it might be. What it stands for defines much of our past, present, and future. As a fact, not just a word, some claim that globalization may have existed as part of the human condition since *Homo sapiens* first emerged, subsequently undergoing many vicissitudes. We are concerned most here, however, with its manifestations in recent times, the background for the emergence of the term. It is this present-day globalization that our reader seeks to make more comprehensible, thus also illuminating any vision we may have about past instances. Because we all live increasingly in this global context, the stuff of our daily lives, it is vital and essential for each and every one of us to understand it in some depth. Hence, all of our readers, at whatever level, are invited to become new historians of globalization.

History is the one perspective that seeks to look at the phenomenon whole, and over the whole of time. Our object is to help our readers unify the various ways of seeing — economic, political, cultural, and so forth — into one connected vision. Of course, one must first look at the pieces in themselves, then see them anew in the light of the larger picture, and then try to assemble, or reassemble, them in the most meaningful ways. Notice we say ways, for there is no one way, no single right "take" on globalization. For one thing, it is not a completed narrative, but a rapidly changing, ongoing process. Nor is it a preordained process, whose end is clearly in sight. And even if we could all agree on exactly what globalization is and where it is going, there would still be the issue of how we feel about it: Do we view it as good, bad, or some mixture thereof?

As the reader will quickly see, we have constructed our book in terms of fourteen clusters. Though clearly not exhaustive, they should give enough of an introduction to their subject matter so as to enable each reader to start making his/her judgment as to what globalization is all about, and to do this in an informed matter, where the first piece of information is that these topics require us to relinquish preconceived notions. Our initial task, therefore, is to approach these chapters with an open and inquiring mind. Our next task is to recognize that they draw us on to further research. In somewhat hyperbolic terms, we are launching ourselves on a quest as exciting in its way as that facing the explorers who began, from the fifteenth century onward, to try to map and understand a dimly glimpsed earth and a new world. We, in our turn, are seeking to represent and comprehend a new space and a global society.

(1)

Let us return to our initial question: What is globalization? We will attempt to say what it is and what it is not. In attempting to define it both positively and negatively, we start with the assumption that it is a contested term. This lack of a single definition may disturb some people. It should not. In fact, like similar over-arching concepts, for example, modernity, globalization derives its meaning from the controversy surrounding it rather than by some a priori, agreed-upon consensus. A changing, many-faceted, historically evolving process, it cannot be captured in a single phrase.

With this understood, we can launch various definitional probes. The most immediate one is to situate globalization in our everyday lives, or what philosophers call our phenomenological existence. We experience it in our daily round in ever-growing fashion. Type an e-mail message, and you realize that it can be sent as rapidly to a friend in India as to one across the street. In computer time they are equally and simultaneously our immediate neighbors. Go out for a meal, and choose from any of a number of "ethnic," i.e. global, restaurants. Turn on the TV and see coverage of a soccer game being viewed by literally billions of others around the globe. Or, more somberly, watch scenes from a war half way around the globe as the events are unfolding. In short, we feel globalization on our pulse. That is one definition: It is a happening occurring in our bodies and minds each day. We must not forget this definition as we proceed to more abstract ones.

Indeed, this underlies one of the most important features of globalization: Its compression of space and time beyond anything previously known. Transactions now can and do take place simultaneously in real time in every space/place in the globe. At which point we must deal with the question: Hasn't the compression of space and time a long history? One can point to the enormous increase in cutting time and moving rapidly across space, for example, in the nineteenth century with the coming of the railroads, the telegraph, the cable system, and at the end of the century the invention of the automobile. Or go back before the industrial revolution and note the use, for example, of semaphores, and before that of smoke signals, and so on. The moral is clear: With globalization we are always talking of changes in intensity and level, and of the synchronicity of developments, all of which have antecedents in earlier times and places. We must always keep an eye on what is new and what is old.

In addition to space/time compression a distinguishing feature of globalization is the increased interconnection and interdependence it brings to humankind. Here are a few riffs on that theme. According to one historian, globalization is "a progressive increase in the scale of social processes from a local or regional to a world level." Such a definition allows us to see that globalization is a thread running through much of world history – and later we will talk of the difference between world and global history – and theoretically can be located in earlier times and places, say the Silk Road of the seventh century connecting Asia and Europe, or the system of trade and cultural exchange that prevailed in the Middle East heartland of the thirteenth century, or the discovery of the globe and its circumnavigation in the time of Columbus and Magellan. These can be seen as previous forms of globalization and also as precursors and even preconditions of present-day globalization.

Our attention here is mainly on that latter phenomenon. Choosing another scholar almost at random, we can follow her as she defines globalization as "a process of increased density and frequency of international or global interactions relative to local or national ones." Its causes are identified as "the increased power of global capital markets; the rise of new information and communication technologies; and the rise of a new hegemon which creates the conditions for increased trade."

If we pursue the phrase "international or global interactions" a new aspect of globalization's definition opens up to us. An international system can only exist when there are nation-states to make it up. Most historians date the coming of both the nation-state (though the latter really doesn't emerge fully until the French Revolution of 1789) and internationalism to the time of the Treaty of Westphalia, in 1648, with its notion of sovereign states, enclosed ideally in inviolable territorial boundaries, regulating their interactions with one another in an international system. For over three hundred years the nation-state has served as the pivot around which modern history has revolved. Only now is it being challenged as no longer capable of handling the changes being brought about by globalization. Thus, an essential part of the definition of present-day globalization is that it represents the transcendence of nation-states, their boundaries, their sovereignty, and calls into question their general competence. In the process, will nation-states disappear? We think not, believing that the nation-state will change drastically, but still persist. One consequence of this part of globalization's definition is that national history itself henceforth can be written effectively only in terms of the impact of global forces upon it.

Another consequence is to see internationalism as intimately tied to nationalism, with internationalism a necessary mechanism with which to regulate the affairs of competing nations. The nineteenth century especially saw an explosion of international agencies and institutions, ranging from an international organization of doctors to an international Postal Union to a Hague conference on international peace. This expansion continued even more vigorously into the next century, marked in noteworthy fashion by first the League of Nations and then the United Nations in the area of world affairs. In this light, we must ask whether internationalism is itself becoming outmoded, its institutions unable to handle the challenges of unregulated globalization, or whether it should be viewed as a predecessor of globalization and now on a continuum with it, or what? In any case, globalization requires us to reexamine our thinking about not only the nation-state but about internationalism.

Congress of Vienna

Returning to the part of the definition that stressed causes, giving prominence to capital markets and new information and communication technologies, we can now try to build upon it an even more extensive and historical definition of globalization. In doing so, we pass resolutely into new global history, or the history that attempts to come firmly to grips with the process of globalization unfolding around us, while acknowledging its roots in the past. Here emphasis is placed on a number of factors or elements that feature prominently in the new globalization.

Among these are the step into space (1957), a stride of incalculable importance, but generally not given the attention it deserves. In one sense, it changed the nature of the human species. In another, it changed our view of ourselves and our planet, now seen from outer space. Closely connected to space exploration is the satellite system that makes possible instantaneous communication, and fast-forwards the space/time compression that we mentioned earlier. Those same satellites have allowed us to see the earth as a whole and to witness the environment and its changes as both a global and a local "happening." They also made possible or at least fostered the growth of multinational corporations (MNCs), whose operations, reflected in their name, transcend national boundaries. These MNCs have not only powerful economic consequences, but cultural ones as well. A seemingly matching development, also abetted by the communication revolution, is the growth of international non-governmental organizations (NGOs), whose rise as the world's conscience and its vehicle for "representing" the peoples of the world has been phenomenal. Of another order is the nuclear power that can overleap the territorial boundaries hitherto thought secure, and introducing a risk – the self-destruction of the human species – previously unthinkable.

These factors, and we need to add many more such as human rights, world music, global consumerism, migrations, terrorism, and so forth, must be seen as interacting in a synchronic and synergistic fashion that makes for the whole we know as globalization. The latter can then be defined as the sum of these parts. More sweeping and more detailed than some of our earlier definitions, this additional delineation nevertheless coexists with them. It has the virtue of also offering us a research agenda, as exemplified in the clusters making up the contents of this reader.

Before leaving this issue of definition, there is one more to be considered. It revolves around the notion of the emergence of a global consciousness. We are conscious, as reflected in the very concept of globalization, of existing on a globe together. In the process we do not lose our sense of nationality, ethnicity, religion, even tribalism, but superimpose on it that of globalism. In so doing, we bring to bear on our existence a new sense of self, a more expanded "self" in more extended connection to "others." We are spinning in unintended fashion to a new identity, a global identity, as befitting our transformed everyday life and our understanding of the transcending processes occurring around and because of us. This final definition of globalization, in the long term, may be the most significant one.

(2)

In defining globalization, it is as important to say what it is not, as to try to say what it is. Many misperceptions surround the subject. It is necessary to clear the decks, so to speak, before we can set forth on our further exploration. Needless to say, every misperception has its grain of truth, not to be thrown out in the thrashing process.

One of the most frequent "definitions" is the one reflected in the comment, "Isn't globalization simply another form of imperialism?" Addressed properly, this challenge becomes a rich opportunity for further understanding. We can ask ourselves whether globalization is a substitute of sorts for the largely Western imperialism of the last century or two, but now in the form of economic domination. This can lead us to ask again whether the essence of globalization is that it brings all peoples into a global society, or at least aims to do so, and thus ideally must be the opposite of imperialism. This still leaves us with the matter of ideal and reality, but at least we are clear about how complex the answer to our question must be. Certainly, old-fashioned imperialism is no longer a possibility; and the presumed new imperialism is contradicted by the very globalization it presumes to forward.

Imperialism in its heyday was closely connected to colonies. It appears that a precondition for the emergence of new globalization has been the dismantling of colonial empires. Former colonies have become independent, and thus able to participate as autonomous agents in the globalization process. Ah, one can say, haven't they simply turned into economic dependencies? Such a charge, of course, returns us to the earlier debate about imperialism. While remnants of dependency exist, along with vast inequalities of power, it can hardly be said that India, for example, is either politically or economically a dependent nation. It is, instead, increasingly interdependent, as are all other nations, in the globalizing society that is developing around us.

Closely related to the definitional oppositions embodied in imperialism and colonialism is the definition of globalization as Americanization. "Isn't globalization simply another term for Americanization?" goes the refrain. Without doubt, the US is a, perhaps the, major power shaping the forces of globalization. Its economic strength is awesome, its cultural impact sometimes overwhelming, its military force truly global in reach. To accept the view, however, that this position of *primus inter pares* equates to "globalization as Americanization" is to buy into the very ideology of those who wish to make over the globe in the image of the US. It is to mistake a power wish for a complicated reality.

In fact, definitions of globalization often reflect partisan positions rather than sustained inquiry. We are brought up short by this fact, and have to add to our previous attempts at definition that globalization is an ideology as well as an idea and an ideal. As an ideology it is promoted most vigorously by those who advocate an unregulated free market. These same advocates "see" globalization as simply an economic matter. But does this not violate all that we have said about globalization as a many-faceted subject, one that must be seen as a whole made up of many parts? In a compelling manner, the Cyclopian gaze of neoclassical economic theory demonstrates a very limited comprehension of globalization itself. It misconstrues a part for the whole.

There are many other misperceptions, or mis-definitions, of globalization that need to be considered. We will add here only a few more, but without discussing them at the same length as the previous items. There is, for example, the reiterated canard that students of globalization present it as deterministic and teleological. Perhaps a few do – some neoclassical economic historians, for example – but the overwhelming number of global historians firmly hold to the position that, while strong currents are pushing the world in a more global direction, the destination is neither fixed nor certain. As in all history, chance, contingency, and agency – what people will actually choose to do – play major roles. Perhaps the canard arises because previous believers in modernization theory, with its presumed inevitability, now advance their ideas under the guise of globalization theory. A more informed grasp of global history, however, should sunder this link.

The charge that globalization is homogenization is another over-simplification. It fits nicely, however, with the belief that globalization is imperialism (in this case, cultural and consumeristic), or equivalent to Americanization. "All the world drinks Coca-Cola (or Pepsi-Cola)," runs the refrain. Watches the same sit-coms, sees the same movies, listens to the same music, etc. This is, of course, partly true, a fundamental aspect of globalization. We must ask ourselves, however, whether all viewers of a sit-com see it in the same way – such a question comes from what is called reception theory – or do they make it part of their own culture? The question is made even more complicated if we look closely at the products being manufactured by the MNCs: More and more they are characterized in terms of small-batch production and the demands of multiculturalism, another aspect of globalization. In short, homogenization is itself not an homogenized concept.

It is, in addition, matched by heterogeneity. Already suggested by the notion of multiculturalism, it is further supported by the extraordinary exchange manifested at the heart of globalization, wherein for every McDonald's outside the US, for example, there are Thai, Chinese, Indian, and other formerly exotic-type restaurants within the country. Individual choice is almost too abundant. In the light of globalization, massification and mass consumerism need to be rethought as mixtures of homogenization and heterogeneity. Defining globalization as increasing homogeneity must be expanded to include increased heterogeneity at the same time.

As is clear, what we are calling misperceptions tend to be half-truthful definitions of globalization. We have tried to offer a number of examples, which will be echoed in the readings. Each reader can add her/his favorite ones to the list. What is important about definitions, and misdefinitions, is that they lead us into further consideration of our subject. They open up avenues of inquiry rather than ending our search. They need to be approached not in black–white terms, but in terms of shadings and balances. The issue is put wrongly when it is stated that globalization is reducible to increased homogenization. Rather we must ask to what extent, in what areas, and in what ways is the statement true. Thus, our definitions of globalization are not to be treated as terminuses but as departure points for a journey into an exciting new space/time-scape.

(3)

Now that we have a feel for the entity we are trying to study we must ask: When did it come into existence? Many people believe that dates and periods are a boring and dispensable part of the effort at understanding the past. We suggest a different conclusion: A definition of a subject such as globalization begs for an assignment in time, dictated by the factors alleged to make up the definition; and, subsequently, a possible modification of the definition in the light of the time line. Dating, in our view, constitutes the love-life of the historian. Or put in less romantic terms, as it is by the eminent ancient historian Thucydides, "Dates and a coherent dating scheme are as essential to history as exact measurement is to physics."

Dates and periods give shape to an otherwise incoherent and chaotic past. They are, needless to say, imposed, not found in the documents; a person living in the Middle Ages was not aware that he/she came after ancient and before modern times. Within the West the great pivotal date lies with the birth of Jesus Christ. It constitutes the hinge by which we swing from BC to AD. Other religions and cultures have different dates. In the global world of today the Christian calendar has come to prevail, although pockets of resistance still exist. An interesting question, of course, is why and how; also how might the triumph of Western periodization be connected to colonialism and imperialism?

Does globalization entail a transcendence of the Christian dating scheme, in the light of multiculturalism? It is hard to see how existing numbers will be discarded – we will probably still "be" in the twenty-first century for almost another ten decades (note that "century" and "decade" are part of our way of dividing up history). Does it make sense now to speak of our entering a "global epoch," whose coming rivals that of the hinge of two thousand years ago? Such a periodization might be as revolutionary as the space/time compression and the other accoutrements of globalization that constitute its coming into being.

The notion of a global epoch can be seen as the largest framing "measurement" for the present-day process, or processes, we seek to study. On a more mundane level, we need to ask when, epochal or not, did this recent phase of globalization first come into being. Here there is much room for fruitful debate, for such dating is intimately linked to what we think the process is about and how it has intimately manifested itself. Did it emerge in the 1950s, the 1970s, or when?

Obviously, we are talking about a cluster of events and factors whose synchronicity and synergy give meaning to the concept of globalization. In the simplest terms, new globalization, the privileged subject of study of new global history, emerged sometime in the period after the Second World War. That war and its first predecessor mark in their name a preliminary step toward globalization. Moreover, in the course of that war, some of the technological predecessors of the space/time compression of which we have spoken make their appearance. Rockets were developed, the nuclear bomb exploded, and the early elements of the computer revolution threw their flickers across the future.

The Second World War also signaled the final end of colonialism, though it would take place sporadically in the course of the next number of decades. As 1945 marked the end of one war, it can be said to mark the beginning of another one: the Cold War. That war, lasting at least until the dissolution of the Soviet Union in 1991, divided the world into spheres of influence, dominated by one or the other superpower. Its passing can be seen as essential for the emergence of a global society.

Yet it is also obvious that the elements of globalization were proceeding apace in the decades of the 1950s and 1960s. Some, such as the launching of Sputnik in 1957 and the subsequent space race, were prerequisites for the stepping past national and earthly boundaries. Others such as the artificial satellites facilitated the extraordinary space/time compression on which we remarked earlier. They also allowed for the first photos, in 1966, from outer space making us acutely aware of being on a spaceship earth. Here on this earth, for example, we could see the environmental threat in global terms.

The satellites also enhanced the ability of multinational corporations to operate beyond national boundaries. In turn, their direct financial investments linked more and more parts of the globe into a single economic system. This system now operates on a twenty-four hour a day trading basis. Among the results have been the homogenization and heterogenization spoken of earlier, the spread of a common consumerism, and the possible cultural hegemony that evokes many protests in various parts of the globe. A matching development, as we noted, has been the rise and extension of NGOs, aided by the same satellites and other elements of the information revolution that have helped the growth of the MNCs.

These are some of the factors that support the claim to date globalization from the 1950s. A comparable list of factors could be compiled – and this is a challenge to our readers – for the 1970s as the decisive time. Or the 1980s, or a later decade? What will become obvious as we attempt this compilation is how particular factors overlap the ten year spans. ARPANET went on line in 1969. The UN conference on the environment was in 1972. That was the year in which terrorism went international with the killing of Israeli athletes at the Olympics. Further dates and events can be added by the attentive reader of the articles that comprise this book.

We can conclude our hints about global dating and periodization by a few comments. The first is that classification by time is a very imprecise "science." Events tumble over and into one another. Most of them are the result of unintended consequences, whose extent is known only later. Our second comment is that, nonetheless, the attempt at dating is necessary and heuristic, to use that fancy word meaning "serving to stimulate investigation." Dating is part of the effort at definition, which itself is also heuristic. Our final comment in this regard is that definition and dating are useful guides as we push further into our exploration of globalization. They are not ends in themselves, but merely essential instruments to aid in our inquiry.

(4)

Hopefully by now the reader will have an idea of many of the questions and elements that go to make up the concept of globalization. As we are using it, the term is understood to mean the history of the world in the age of globalization. As we have seen, while specialists may differ as to when this age, or epoch, began – and some of the essays in this volume will take up that question anew – it seems widely recognized that the history of the twentieth century, especially during its last decades, cannot be understood in the traditional nation-centered framework. This is because so many developments have cut across national and geographical boundaries: communication and information technology, migration (including refugees), global capital markets, the growth of non-governmental organizations, environmental issues, the promotion of human rights, transnational religious and ethnic movements, terrorism, and the like. All these are global forces that have, together with the nation-states, shaped the world as it is today.

Each of these developments, and others, such as culture, consumerism, and disease, will be given detail and depth in the readings that comprise this volume. The purpose of this introduction up to now has been to propose a framework in which to place them. Definition and dating have been the supporting beams on which to erect this edifice. With these in place, much more construction and deconstruction of globalization can now be undertaken. We will not, in fact, undertake that task here, leaving it to our readers as one of their assignments. Instead we will touch in conclusion on two large problems overshadowing our subject. One is the normative aspect, the other is the "working" aspect: How does one "do" global history?

The normative aspect circles around the question of whether globalization is "good" or "bad." Each reader, of course, will make his/her own judgment, but we wish to enter some cautionary remarks. In order to make an informed rather than an ideological decision, we must all come to know much more about the subject itself. Such knowledge is admittedly made difficult by the recent and ever-changing nature of globalization itself. Our reader does not confront a sitting target. Immersion in existing research and much more future research is essential. Indeed, the reader is invited into the circle of researchers. The reward will not be certainty but a sense of clarity in regard to the facts and theories surrounding the subject.

Next, we must remind ourselves of the need for the perspective held out by history, and the possibility it proffers of seeing the phenomenon "whole." One can approve of various aspects of globalization while disapproving of other parts. As in all of life, the trick is in weighing and balancing what we like and dislike. And perhaps recognizing that some of what we like is awkwardly tied to what we don't like. Specifically, we might like some of the cultural consequences of globalization, such as increased cosmopolitanism, while disliking the carriers of that consequence, the MNCs. Or vice versa, i.e. we might like the economic expansion but not the cultural consequence. It would be nice if judgments could be made unfettered by such complicating facets, but, alas, that would be to step out of real life in which parts are more and more interconnected with one another, as in globalization.

Such considerations are not meant to freeze us in indecision, but rather to make us clear about how carefully we must come to our judgments. And also how our own actions will figure in the process of globalization, for we are agents as well as students of the subject. Information and understanding, not celebration or indignation, should be our watchwords as we attempt assessments of globalization.

With these cautions in hand, the topic of anti-globalization can be approached. We need to raise questions about the overall effect of current globalization, for example, on inequality in the world. Is it increasing or diminishing? Has the World Bank and the International Monetary Fund (IMF) with their policies benefited the South as well as the North, and equally so? Or has the gap widened, even though in absolute terms poverty may have diminished across the globe. Fierce battles rage in these matters, with disagreement on the statistics involved as well as on immediate and long-range outcomes.

There is also the danger of conflating the ideal with practice. This might be illustrated, for example, in the case of American economic penetration, wherein the US has sought to woo the globe to its own free trade policies. In theory, a level playing field was to be created. In practice, according to its critics, the US and its supporters force countries across the globe to open their markets – through the IMF, the World Bank, and similar institutions – but then block other countries' exports, especially agricultural products, by using tariffs and subsidies to prevent free and equal access to the domestic market. It is hardly surprising that anti-globalization movements are fueled by this betrayal of globalization's own principles.

On another front, the battle rages in terms of the welfare state. Or, to put it in more neutral terms, the effort by states to provide a safety net for their citizens, and/or to redistribute the unequal gains of globalization. This has been made increasingly difficult by the compulsions of free-trade globalization, forcing nations to compete in the world market by cutting costs in whatever manner necessary, what has been called the race to the bottom. Capital is liquid, and MNCs can threaten to move their money and operations elsewhere. Hardly a new element in economic life – think of baseball teams threatening to move if not given new stadiums, tax breaks, etc. – it has taken on increased velocity in the course of globalization with its negative impact on the welfare state more and more in evidence.

Anti-globalization is clearly a vital part of globalization itself. It is also to be noted that anti-globalization movements avail themselves of the factors of globalization enumerated earlier, ranging from computer and satellite use to the propaganda opportunities provided by TV coverage. Do they threaten the globalization process itself? Inasmuch as that process is multi-causal and multi-faceted, it seems unlikely. Do they serve as a necessary corrective to some of the excesses of completely unregulated capitalism as it takes the form of globalization? A positive answer seems likely. As can easily be seen, judgments about both globalization and anti-globalization, the latter of which is inextricably tied to the former, need to be carefully considered in the light of the information and theorizing to be found in what has been said up to now and in the articles that follow upon this introduction.

(5)

Globalization is clearly a fact of our times. It is best approached, we are arguing, from an historical perspective. Our next question must be: How does one best go about doing it? This requires us to look more closely, as our final task, at the nature of global *history* itself.

After the Second World War, with globalization and its processes vaguely perceived as emerging, the limitations of nation-state history became more and more evident. A reaction set in gradually under the heading of world history. Its intention was to break past the Eurocentrism that characterized history as previously practiced. Thus, its practitioners insisted that surveys of European or Western civilization, as such courses were named, be widened to include sections on Asia and Africa. Not surprising is the fact that many of the pioneers in world history had backgrounds in Asian or African history.

As it sought to define itself, world history at its best became synonymous with the study of particular early transnational phenomena, such as plagues, population movements, and the like. (On most other occasions it settled into the grooves of area studies.) This was in tune with the globalizing tendencies of the actual world around it. The followers of world history, however, were and are inclined to take as their subject the whole of past history. A principle of selectivity generally gets lost in this endeavor. Thus, while world history has had a liberalizing effect, transcending the parochial and the local, it does not stress the thread of globalization per se in its accounts.

One result has been definitional confusion. World history often promotes itself under the rubric of global history. A moment's serious reflection will show that, although they are on a spectrum whereon the two are connected, global history is a separate effort. It focuses on the theme of globalization that runs through the history of the past. It may find that theme in the seventh century or the fifteenth, in Asia or in Europe, or wherever. At that point it studies that example in detail. It may or may not see a tendency or a direction present in these episodes, leading to the globalization of today. In any case, it is open to that possibility (although, as we remarked earlier, a tendency is not a teleology).

It is no denigration of world history, which has its own legitimacy and accomplishments, to separate it out from global history. The latter can then be studied in its own terms. One consequence of this, as we have been trying to show, is that we become aware of the process of globalization taking on an intensity and a consciousness of that intensity in the last half century or so, which is usefully studied under the heading of new global history. Even putting this title aside, it is evident that a new constellation of factors, novel in their depth and degree if not in their nature, has emerged, forming a new "whole." To better understand that constellation, we have suggested dating it in a new manner, calling the resultant period a "global epoch."

The reader is not obliged to accept either the rubric, new global history, or the ambitious periodization incorporated in a global epoch, as she/he voyages into the space and time of present-day globalization. The readings in this volume stand aside from these claims, which have been made with the aim of providing an heuristic frame for what follows. The distinction of global history from world history is a similar attempt at clarification of what is under scrutiny here.

In that same spirit of stretching our imaginations, we want to argue that global history, as we are defining it, is emphatically an interdisciplinary practice. While the historical perspective is central to its mission, global history has an enlarged definition of history that brings under its tent the work of sociologists, anthropologists, political sciences, economic historians, and numerous others. In this same spirit, we are reluctant to view the cultural, the political, the economic, for example, as separate spheres; rather we see every economic development as embedded in culture and politics, and vice versa. Though some observers have fruitfully talked about disjunctions in these spheres we consider it more useful to think about them as coexistent and correlative experiences.

We also want to argue that global history enables us to have a fresh understanding of even conventional topics such as politics and war. One way to look at globalization, for example, is to view it as arising from political struggles as much as from technological and economic developments. Out of the common calamity of world wars, both the first and the second, an unprecedented sense of a shared humanity emerged, and took shape in various political institutions. These, although foreshadowed by the rise of international organizations starting in the nineteenth century, took many and varied shapes – both governmental and non-governmental – by the time of the millennium. Especially in the form of the NGOs the vague outlines of a global civil society suggested the possibilities of non-state political activities, while the UN and other state-based agreements pointed to another, more familiar way of seeking to transcend nation-state boundaries.

As for war, what had become total war now also became global in nature. This development was aided by the information revolution, and not surprisingly, the leader in that revolution was the same as in the military revolution: the United States. By the later twentieth century it alone of the developed nations could be said to have global reach, the ability to deploy military forces anywhere in the world within 24–48 hours. Its only rival, somewhat unexpectedly, and with evident material disproportion, was global terrorism. It too uses the tools of the information revolution and modern technology, as epitomized in the terrorist attacks of September 11, 2001. From this attack has followed the war in Afghanistan and then in Iraq. Some view this latter as a necessary assertion of preemptive war doctrine to defend against terrorism, while others see it as an old-fashioned invasion using the most recent high technology in the service of creating an "American Empire." Global history provides a context for an informed understanding of this war, of terrorism, and of the whole military–political–economic complex of our times.

One further and quite different consequence of globalization, besides giving us greater comprehension of war and peace, may well be the transcending of existing social science disciplines, which have emerged on the basis of the nation-state, itself now being transcended in so many ways. (Let us emphasize once again that the nation-state, nevertheless, will persist and insist on being a part of any future attempt at history.) What made sense as a way of understanding, say, the industrial revolution may no longer be sufficient for the understanding of the information revolution. The working out of these new disciplines, or inter-disciplines, is a part of globalization itself. Their existence and shape will evolve along with the subject of their study.

Putting aside for now this heady prospect, let us ask finally: How do we actually study present-day globalization? What is its documentary basis? How do we break up this protean subject so as to study it in a manageable fashion? What are the topics and the actors to be studied? Such questions point to the understandable anxiety provoked by a process – globalization – which itself is the source of much anxiety. The answers, we believe, are implicit in the readings that follow, and each reader will work out his/her own collection.

For the moment, we would suggest that the choice of documents – the evidence – follows naturally from the choice of topics and actors. If the topic is disease, one will want to look at the global manifestations of it, and scour the medical, the social, and the political literature pertinent to it. The same case holds for, say, migrations or global culture, or human rights. Obviously, as in all such work, selectivity prevails, both as to choice of topic and of subsequent documentation. There is nothing new in this regard when we do global history. The only thing new may be the awareness we bring to our task: an awareness that we ought not to treat the topic in a vacuum but connect it to other aspects of globalization, bringing to bear on our treatment all the potential of an interdisciplinary historical approach.

As for the choice of actors, we must be open to the fact that new ones have entered upon the stage of history. Or at least new ones in the extent of their existence and/or importance. We offer two examples. MNCs can trace their origins to the Dutch and English East India companies of the early 1600s. We can then construct a curve showing their growth until the present, noting along the way that there were about 30,000 in 1960, expanding to about 63,000 in 2000. As we know, their power has also grown almost exponentially. International NGOs demonstrate a similar curve, though starting from a more recent origin. Obviously, these must be studied as our actors in global history. So, too, all of the other subjects-cum-actors treated in our readings.

At all points, we should endeavor to connect the sometimes esoteric facts and the high-flying theories that surround our study with our daily experience of globalization itself. Globalization is happening to *us*. It is not about some foreign "other," but about how that other becomes part of *us* whether we like it or not. And we of that other. Globalization is as much about interconnectedness of our selves as it is about economic and political interdependence. Global history, therefore, is not only about globalization, but also about our new global identities, thrust upon us willy-nilly.

In our effort to comprehend globalization, we must seek "objective" knowledge, to the extent that it is possible. To do so, however, we must also employ "subjective" means in our quest for understanding. The two, object and subject, in fact, go together. To do global history seems to require us to become new historians, or historians of a new type. As we enter upon the readings that follow, we must be prepared to change ourselves as well as our understanding of present-day as well as past globalization. This can be a frightening possibility. We prefer to think of it as an exciting prospect. It is in that spirit that we ask you to approach this book.

Note

The chapters have been edited only for minor, typographical errors. All dates and chronological references appear in the original context in which the articles and/or chapters were written.

PART I

The question of periodization

HISTORY INVOLVES PERIODIZATION; in trying to make sense of the past, historians devise various ways of locating the origins and tracing the development of certain phenomena. For a subject as broad and general as globalization, it is not surprising that many ways of conceptualizing its history have been proposed. Some trace globalization all the way back to the ancient times when humans began establishing connections with one another across distances, whereas others insist that a truly global world has emerged only toward the end of the twentieth century. In between are those who argue that an interconnected world first came into existence after the circumnavigation of the globe in the late fifteenth and the early sixteenth centuries, and those who stress the late nineteenth century as having been of critical importance in bringing about a "global age." Regardless of such disagreement, the controversy shows that scholars have become seriously interested in transcending the nation-centered approach that has characterized most historical writings and in establishing a fresh approach to the past that would pay attention as much to transnational as to national and local developments.

In this section, two essays illustrate how historians seek to establish a chronology of global history. Bruce Mazlish discusses what is new about global, as against world, history and points to the critical importance of the recent decades in that story. Michael Geyer (Professor of History at the University of Chicago) and Charles Bright (Professor of History at the University of Michigan) trace the origins of "globality" to the middle of the nineteenth century and discuss its implications for contemporary history.

Chapter 1

Bruce Mazlish

GLOBAL HISTORY AND
WORLD HISTORY

THE HISTORICAL PROFESSION has been slow to appreciate the importance of globalization. One reason appears to be the confusion caused by the claims of world history, which has been struggling to achieve its own identity. In its fight against more traditional, national approaches, world history has generally seen global history – that is, the study of globalization – as a dilution of its challenge to the establishment. Hence, world historians have tended either to ignore the new global history or to claim that it is already encompassed by what they are doing. Is their response legitimate? What exactly is world history? And what is global history?

World history

World history has accumulated a number of definitions, most of them reflecting different schools of thought. The "Invitation to Membership" of the World History Association (WHA) begins with the statement, "If you teach the whole history of the whole world in nine short months, you know the challenge of planning and organizing a meaningful course in world history." Although adherents of the WHA often deny it, the implication *seems* to be that world history is "the whole history of the whole world," thus offering no obvious principle of selection.

[Jerry] Bentley, the editor of *The Journal of World History*, gives a more limited definition: "My impression is that most participants in the discussion [about the definition of world history] took interactions between peoples participating in large-scale historical processes to be one of the principal concerns of world history." This conception of world history is also vague. For example, would every historian of the Industrial Revolution (even if restricted to one country) – surely, a large-scale historical process – necessarily be a world historian as well, and if not, why not? Bentley continues, "Thus, world history represents (among other things) a dialogue between the past and the present, in that it seeks to establish a historical context for the integrated and interdependent world of modern times."

From Bruce Mazlish, "Comparing Global History to World History," *Journal of Interdisciplinary History*, vol. 28, no. 3 (Winter 1998), pp. 385–91, 392–3.

[William] McNeill is the premier figure of modern world history. He follows, by his own admission, directly in the line of Arnold Toynbee, who inspired him with an ecumenical vision. But McNeill translated this vision into more mundane historical practice. His *Plagues and Peoples* (Garden City, 1976) is intellectual worlds removed from Toynbee's *Study of History* (New York, 1933–54, 10 v). However, although, like Toynbee, McNeill takes civilization as his framework of analysis, he does not construe them as hermetically closed but as open to cultural borrowings.

Ralph Linton and Robert Redfield – anthropologists – also influenced McNeill. From them came his interest in "trans-civilizational encounters," which have shaped his definition of world history as the study of "interaction among peoples of diverse cultures." Long-distance trade, the spread of religions and plague, and a multitude of other trans-civilizational factors have prominent places in McNeill's world history. These concerns are always informed by a biological and ecological awareness that has no precedent in Toynbee's work. Without specifically invoking the theory of evolution, McNeill lives and writes in its environment. The results have been brilliant treatments of processes occurring on a worldwide scale, such as the spread of disease or the emergence of military power.

Other variants of world history exist alongside McNeill's version. The crucial variable is the definition of *world*. Fernand Braudel seemed to have abandoned his fascination with civilizations in favor of "world systems" – that is, worlds constructed by trade and culture. Characteristically, his book *The Mediterranean* (trans. Siäan Reynolds) (New York, 1972) carries the subtitle, *The Mediterranean World in the Age of Philip II*.

Braudel's disciple, [Immanuel] Wallerstein, in *The Modern World-System* (New York, 1976), shows in great detail how the modern commercial and capitalist world came into existence. In similar accounts, of course, Columbus' voyage occupies a central place, adding a New World to an Old one. Wallerstein's emphasis in the second volume is on the seventeenth-century mercantile competition among the Western European nations. His is history in the grand style, but with its feet on the ground (or, perhaps one should say, in the sea).

Carrying the world-system approach even further back in time, [Janet] Abu-Lughod has suggestively argued for an earlier "system of world trade and even 'cultural' exchange." She finds such a system in the period AD 1250–1350, which she designates as a "crucial turning point in history." Though lacking an international division of labor, her system connects disparate areas of the world – Europe, India, and China – through trade between key cities. Applying this approach to even earlier periods, she speaks of the Roman Empire as the "first nascent world system."

What all these variants on world history – McNeill's, Braudel's, Wallerstein's, and Abu-Lughod's – share is a concern with systemic processes and patterns among a wide variety of historical and natural phenomena that affected diverse populations. Compared with earlier ecumenical histories, they are less keen about making predictions, and about tracing the course of civilizations through fixed cycles. In addition, though forced to rely heavily on secondary accounts, they stay close to the scholarship of ordinary historians, offering strictly secular accounts (even of religion). In short, these accounts are serious attempts to treat historical phenomena that arise on a world scale. And it is at this point that the meaning of the term "world" becomes especially crucial. It is the point at which a possible transition to global history occurs.

Global history

As with the competing definitions of world history, obfuscation also enters into the differences between world and global history. In the foreword to a series edited for the American Historical Association – "Essays on Global on Comparative History" – [Michael] Adas announced a "'new' global or world history which differs in fundamental ways from its predecessors." That difference, for Adas, led to virtually a paraphrase of McNeill's version. Adas' series included not only an account of Abu-Lughod's thirteenth-century world system, but also such essays as "The Columbian Voyages" and "Gender and Islamic History." It offered serious and worthwhile contributions to world history but unthinkingly misappropriated the title "Global History," which needed to be defined afresh in its own proper terms. Even McNeill realized that something unprecedented was in the works, commenting, "I suspect that human affairs are trembling on the verge of a far-reaching transformation," which he compared to the importance of the agricultural revolution.

We encounter the same intuition in an important article by [Michael] Geyer and [Charles] Bright, the very title of which, "World History in a Global Age," indicated the tenuous transition taking place. In their words,

> What we have before us as contemporary history grates against the familiar explanatory strategies and analytic categories with which scholars have traditionally worked. . . . This is a crisis, above all, of Western imaginings, but it poses profound challenges for any historian: the world we live in has come into its own as an integrated globe, yet it lacks narration and has no history. . . . The central challenge of a renewed world history at the end of the twentieth century is to narrate the world's past in an age of globality.

Our "imaginings" must leap from world history to global history. In making this jump, a look at the etymology of the words, *world* and *globe*, is helpful. Words are *not* just what individuals say they mean; they have a historical nature. *World* comes from the Middle English for "human existence"; its central reference is to the earth, including everyone and everything on it. Worlds can also be imaginary, such as the "next world," meaning life after death, or they can designate a class of persons – the academic world, for instance. For many, the discovery of the New World marked the advent of world history. More recently, a first, a second, and a third world have been discerned, demarcating different levels of development.

Such usage ill accords with the term *global* (one cannot substitute New Globe for New World in 1492, or third globe for third world today). It occupies a different valence, deriving from the Latin, *globus*, the first definition of which is "something spherical or rounded," like a "heavenly body." Only secondarily does the dictionary offer the synonym *earth*. *Global* thus points in the direction of space; its sense permits the notion of standing outside our planet and seeing "Spaceship Earth." (Incidentally, *earth* is a misnomer for our planet; as is evident from outside space, our abode is more water than earth.) This new perspective is one of the keys to global history.

What are the other keys? These we can determine by dividing the definition of global history into two parts. The first focuses on the history of globalization; that is, it takes existing processes, encapsulated in the "factors of globalization," and traces themes far back in the past as seems necessary and useful. The second signifies processes that are best studied on a global, rather than a local, a national, or a regional, level. The second definition is a continuation of much that is to be encountered in McNeill's variation of world history, except that it begins in the present, openly acknowledging its informed global perspective.

The first part of the definition – the history of globalization – is both the heart and the novelty of global history, deciding the initial field of study and raising the questions: What is involved in globalization? And what are the factors at work in our contemporary "world"? An early attempt to answer them (by this author) stated,

> The starting point for global history lies in the following basic facts of our time (although others could be added): our thrust into space, imposing upon us an increasing sense of being in one world – "Spaceship Earth" – as seen from outside the earth's atmosphere; satellites in outer space that link the peoples of the earth in an unprecedented fashion; nuclear threats in the form of either weapons or utility plants, showing how the territorial state can no longer adequately protect its citizens from either military or ecologically related "invasions"; environmental problems that refuse to conform to lines drawn on a map; and multinational corporations that increasingly dominate our economic lives.

Among other "basic facts of our time" that could be added to this list are global consumerism (obviously related to multinationals), human rights, the displacement of an international political system by a global one (the Geyer–Bright article cited earlier is especially strong in this regard), the globalization of culture (especially music, as fostered by satellite communications), and so forth. What is essential to note is the synergy and synchronicity of these various factors – their unprecedented interaction with one another, in ever-increasing extent and force, notwithstanding the origin of them all in a differentiated past. Globalization is the sum of their combined presences. It is a reality that now affects every part of the globe and every person on it, even though in widely differing local contexts. In fact, one could say that much of global history has necessarily to devote itself to studying the factors of globalization in relation to a "local" reality, which can take many forms.

The practitioners of global history – as in, say, artificial-intelligence studies – include adherents of both a strong and a weak interpretation. The former are convinced that globalization is ushering in a new global *epoch*, which replaces existing attempts to construct such periods as the postmodern or the postindustrial. The adherents of the weak interpretation abstain from diversionary schemes, and are content to study the globalization process without further claims. For those who see globalization as introducing a new period, the issue of when the global epoch "began" is worth considerable attention (analogous to the issue of when modern history began). Some opt for the 1950s and others for the 1970s (I place myself in the epochal camp, and opt for the later time). This argument turns on the question of when enough synergy and synchronicity arises to justify the launch of a new periodization.

Behind this argument is a conviction that time and space have been compressed in an unprecedented fashion. The roots of this compression reach far into the past. The development of sea vessels, from sail to steam, cutting distance and duration, forms one thread in this account. The invention of the telegraph, the laying of cables, the introduction of the telephone, and then of radio communication represent another wave of enormous changes. Now, satellites, with the aid of computer link-ages, allow simultaneous communication between any spot on the globe – 1 billion people watched the first step on the moon on their television sets – and they can go from one end of the globe to the other in less than a day. It should also be noted that with globalization has come the adoption of a uniform calendar.

Another major thread to follow is mapping. Since the fifteenth century, Ptolemaic maps have guided the opening of a new world, in which half of a previously unknown globe spun into perspective. Yet, forgotten in this burst of vision was the fact that large areas of that globe were still "dark." Parts of Africa remained unmapped until the end of the nineteenth century, and the poles were not adequately explored until recent expeditions. Only in our time has the globe come to be more or less fully known (including the depths of its seas). We have even seen it from outside, as one of the many spherical bodies in space. Our map of the globe must now take its place as part of the mapping of outer space. [. . .]

Needless to say, the course of this globalization is not foreordained: Global history is not Whiggish. Or, more to point, the shape it will take cannot be predicted. Like most historians, global historians are aware of the contingency and uncertainty of human affairs; they are not practicing ecumenical history. Nor are they practicing world history in the primitive sense of "the whole history of the whole world." Rather, global historians, or at least historians of globalization, are trying to establish a more deliberate research agenda. They know that each of the factors of globalization requires rigorous empirical study, and that new actors will increasingly occupy the center of the historical stage – non-governmental organizations (NGOs) – such as human rights and environmental groups, which are almost equivalent in importance to nation-states (of the 100 entities possessing the largest gross domestic products (GDPs), 49 are multinationals); and the United Nations (UN), in all its aspects, but especially its nascent military role.

Although global history is mainly transnational in its subjects of study, it would be a grave error to neglect the study of the nation as well. National history merits reexamination in light of how the forces of globalization have affected the nation-state, and vice versa. Nations will not be going away. They are still the preferred settings for large numbers of people to organize on behalf of common ends: protection of territory and property, economic production, and – last but not least – group identity. The literature of the subject is vast. In short, global history, though it seeks to transcend national history, is engaged nevertheless with the nation-state as a major actor on the international and global scene.

The main focus of world history, as opposed to global history, has been civilizations. But as global historians are well aware, civilizations do not send up rockets, operate television networks, or organize a global division of labor. Empires, the carriers of civilizations in the past, are no more; they have been replaced by nation-states (more than 180 as of this writing and counting). Hence, global history examines the processes that transcend the nation-state framework (in the process, abandoning the centuries-old division between civilized and uncivilized, and ourselves and the "other"; "barbarians," that is, inferior peoples, no longer figure in global history, only momentarily less developed peoples).

Chapter 2

Michael Geyer and Charles Bright

WORLD HISTORY IN A GLOBAL AGE

THE PROCESS OF GLOBALIZATION was not simply an acceleration along a continuum of European expansion but a new ordering of relations of domination and subordination among all regions of the world. This fact captures the revolutionizing quality of the European departure at mid-century. Unlike other regions in crisis at the mid-century passage, Europe alone resolved its regional crisis by turning outward, externalizing its quest for solutions in projections of power over-seas, and it did so not by conquests in the old manner of empire building, through spatial expansion and occupation, but in a new effort, with new capabilities, to syn-chronize global time and coordinate interactions *within* the world. This development – the metaphors matter here: this was no longer quite a "thrust" or a "projection" of force but an exercise in "webbing" or "enveloping" – was sustained by new tech-nologies, especially the telegraph and, later on, radio and telephones, but it was fully articulated in transnational regimes of power made possible by the formation of com-munications-based systems of control (the gold standard, the global deployment of maritime force, or the futures markets) that began to envelop the world in global cir-cuits of power by the end of the century. These systems of control, which prolifer-ated throughout the long twentieth century, were the key that enabled a "new" European imperialism to exploit the self-improving strategies of all other regions, adapting the dynamics of competitive interaction among regions to move beyond mere extensions of power "over" others to the direct, sustained organization "of" oth-ers in global regimes of control. In this way, the European–Atlantic world became "the West" and gained its status as the centering axis of an integrating world.

As the dynamics of regional crisis drove Europe outward along externalizing paths, European initiatives collided, overlapped, and interacted with the dynamics of parallel crisis in other regions, and with strategies of competitive self-improvement that were devised to shore up regional power and to fend off or contain external pressures. Historiographic attention focuses on East Asia, but elements of these strug-gles can be observed in the Indian, Persian, Arab, African, and Latin American worlds as well. As regional power centers moved to defend autonomy, Europeans found in

From *American Historical Review*, vol. 100, no. 4 (October 1995), pp. 1047–60.

these self-improvement efforts the pathways and the allies for further and deeper intervention. This was a profoundly disruptive, extremely violent, and often callous process, but it was never simply the plunder of compradors. Instead, Western expansionism picked up and amplified regional and local processes of self-mobilization, permeating and transforming them in the course of using them. The projections of Western power were thus locally articulated as self-mobilizations and absorbed into the very fabric of local affairs – causing wider ramifications of change, much of it beyond the view let alone the control of European powers, but also beginning processes of utterly dependent integration that deepened as self-improvement strategies took hold.

Global integration was thus not a set of procedures devised in the West and superimposed on the rest as if a compliant world waited for its victimization, but, for this very reason, neither was global integration flatly or consistently rejected. Rather, integration was carried forward asymmetrically and unevenly, on a global scale. India and Egypt, as well as Argentina, China, Persia, and Africa, became victims of Western expansionism and of outright aggression. But imperialism was also able to exist because Indians, Egyptians, Argentines, Chinese, Persians, and Africans helped make it happen, and not simply as lackeys and dupes but by pursuing strategies of renewal that synchronized in the web of European-dominated global regimes. Running at full tilt themselves, they engaged Western powers in complex patterns of collaboration and resistance, accommodation and cooptation, as they tried (often against great odds but also, we may add, with remarkable success) to reproduce and renew local worlds, using imperialists to shore up or to create positions of power, using sites of indigenous power to make deals, using the European and American positions as interlopers in order to selectively appropriate the ways of the conquerors to local ends. In this way, *they* were the ones to produce the resources for global integration, creating in the process a more integrated world, albeit not exactly as Western imperialists had intended. Global integration was built with this kind of labor.

The surpluses of this labor forged an ever tighter (if always competitive and contested) concentration of power within the West. That is, military power was projected everywhere, but nowhere was it more concentrated and lethal than within the European region. State power was extended as colonial regimes throughout Africa and Asia, even as state power became concentrated and coordinated in Europe. Western communication and transportation systems reached into every corner of the world, yet nowhere were the linkages denser or their impact more far-reaching than in the European–Atlantic region. Industrial goods were available and traded everywhere, but both trade and production were most heavily concentrated and grew most rapidly in the core region. The intensification and concentration of capitalist production went hand in hand with its global extension, binding the world together in tighter, if always uneven and unequal, global circuits of power, capital, and culture.

Within this integrating world, Europeans and Americans increasingly drew the lines of demarcation that defined an emergent global center over and against the rest. Global integration entailed a spatial reorganization of human and capital mobility that came to the fore in a rush of imperial imaginings by travelers, expatriates, civil servants, and armchair enthusiasts. These were elaborated into universal knowledge in a set of new imperial sciences: geography, ethnology, and biology

"global integration"

being pioneer disciplines of the day. It was also toward the end of the nineteenth century that barriers were erected to control the movements of non-European peoples and a more rigid racial "others," not only in colonial and semi-colonial environments but very much at the centers of power as well. Racism became deeply entrenched in legal, social, and cultural practices. This division of people underwrote a new global division of labor that separated, worldwide, capital-intensive industrial production from handicrafts and extraction, agriculture from industry, and was further reinforced by new procedures for allocating and controlling the movement of wealth, grounded in the international acceptance of the gold standard and of financial rules enforced, primarily, by the Bank of England. Across an integrating world, new lines of segregation and distinction were thus drawn and powerfully imagined in racialist world views that set the white European–Atlantic region and its dispersed settlements around the world apart from the rest and ensured their privilege.

The deepening chasms that divided an increasingly integrated world, together with the proliferating distinctions between "us" and "them" that were handed down as social sciences (modern/traditional, advanced/backward) and constituted Western discourse about the rest, swallowed up the older, enlightened imagination of "humanity" that had previously informed world history narratives. As difference and distinction grew within an integrating world, the overarching simplicities of universal history were supplanted by naturalized histories of the "rest" – studied as the grand traditions of world civilizations in the humanities – and by a specialized and instrumental knowledge about progress – pursued as development and modernization theories in the social sciences. The West (in fact, a few core European states, subsequently enlarged to a European–North Atlantic world and only belatedly extended to the Pacific rim) *gained* in this process a new intellectual identity as a discrete region. Europe was constituted as the West in the context of forging a unified, scientific narrative for an integrating world. This was, one might add, a secular West that in the science of modernizing the world found a counter to and a strategy for surpassing its older religious identity as the site of (Latin) Christianity in juxtaposition, internally, to Judaism and, externally, to Islam. That Islam became a powerful and modernizing global imagination in its own right during the course of the long twentieth century (and not merely in the last two decades or so) is commonly forgotten.

The paradigm of global modernization was powerful knowledge with an unequivocal vision of the world to come. It underwrote a new narrative of world history, which left behind the pieties of Enlightenment thought. This history of a world being integrated predicted, first, that in dominating the world through its mastery of the technical and material means of global integration, the West would actually control the world and be able to shape the course of global development, and, second, that in shaping the world, the West held secure knowledge, positive empirical proof in its own development, of the direction and outcome of world history. The world would become more like the West in a protracted process of modernization, and, as the rest of the world moved toward uplift and progress, the division between "the West" and "the rest" would diminish.

It did not happen this way. First, efforts to establish global order proved notoriously unstable and short-lived. The two most powerful ventures, the *pax britannica* in the first half and the *pax americana* in the second half of the long twentieth century, came and went quickly as world-ordering efforts. Neither was able to transform a staggering superiority of force into lasting political order – that is, into a consensual global politics as opposed to domination and the threat of violence. This proved to be the single most abiding limitation on the West's ability to realize global control. Second, it did not happen this way because Western mastery of the powers of production and destruction (and of the scientific knowledge that underwrote it) never imparted a sure capacity to shape and mold the world into a homogenous global civilization. What Western exertions produced instead was a disorderly world of proliferating difference, a world in which the very production of difference was lodged in the processes of globalization that the West had presumed to control. Even where difference was partially overcome by non-Western efforts to emulate and surpass Western productivity – a path taken by Japan and, later, others in the northeast Asian region, for example – the power of the Western narrative, with its presumption of control and its racist exclusions, masked emergent dynamics of integration.

Thus not only did the destination remain cloudy but emergent realities in the global age ground powerfully against available images and expectations – creating a profound dissonance and proliferating fissures in the narration of the present. These are the signatures of accelerated times or, as Jacob Burckhardt called them, "world historical crises." This is, or should be, an exhilarating moment for historians, for it is now possible to set the *res gestae* of the origins of our actually existing world against the predictions and expectations of the past – no longer in order to announce the pending unification of the world or to criticize explanations and ideologies heretofore used but to account for the world as it is. Narrating world history in our global age means taking seriously (rather than fleeing from) the present. And it means recovering the spirit and intent of historical inquiry, as it is practiced in archival research, and adapting this to the task of writing contemporary history. For the basic operation of any modern *Historik* consists in teasing out the fissures and tensions between what happened (in as much as the sources allow us to tell) and what is said to have happened (in the lore, ideologies, imaginings, and general assumptions of contemporaries and memorialists). For modern historians, archival research is "investigative" practice. It is in applying these procedures to the present condition that we can begin to explore the question of endings.

There are many aspects of the contemporary world that offer examples of narrative fissure, where the course of events disrupted expectations. Examining how these reversals came about, how the emergent condition of globality grated against the expectations or desires of available world views, can give insight into key aspects of twentieth-century development and pose the crucial problems for closer study. We choose four paradigmatic arenas, partly to demonstrate the procedure but also to suggest the tensions that run through processes of globalization. Rather than seeing them strictly in a dialectic of "the global" and "the local," which belatedly has become quite fashionable, we would rather see these tensions as arising out of worldwide processes of unsettlement (the mobilization of peoples, things, ideas, and images and their diffusion in space and time) and out of the often desperate efforts both locally (by communities of various kinds) and globally (by regimes of varying composition and reach) to bring them under control, or, as it were, to settle them. The outcome of these processes is a radically unequal but also radically de-centered world.

One of the most peculiar reversals of expectation that runs through the history of globalization concerns the expansion of industrial forms of production and destruction. The simultaneous process of diffusion and concentration of industrial capabilities was intimately associated with the project of subordinating the world to, and centering it on, the West. Integrating the rest into the economies of the West and subordinating non-Western warfare to Western command and control were key elements of modernization theory and of expectations about how global integration would proceed. Yet the diffusion of industrial production has actually eroded the boundaries of a global division of labor that, at the beginning of the century, delineated centers and marked them off from peripheries. The spread of industrial production to enclaves and export platforms (as, for example, in the Philippines) or the encapsulation of whole societies in processes of industrialization (as in the Republic of Korea) has, in recent years, shattered the fragile unity of the Third World. Rather than integrating regions and nations into a world economy of uplift, the progress of industrialization has re-segmented and re-divided the world, creating islands and belts of rapid and intense development beside productive waste-lands – not just "out there" in Kinshasa, Dacca, or Rio de Janeiro but also in Liverpool, Detroit, and Los Angeles. Not only have the wastelands grown in tandem with expanding productivity, in a checkerboard of poverty and affluence, but the proceeds of industrialization, everywhere, have been turned to the production of violence. Despite the enormous concentration of violence in the two world wars and the nuclear stand-off between the United States and the Soviet Union in this century, the proliferation of small wars and major massacres – and the general diffusion of violence not controlled by any center of power – has been unprecedented in our time. And again, these wars – occurring underneath, in between, and in conjunction with the grand confrontations – do not simply happen out there, in rickety "Third World nations" (and when they do, they produce industrial-scale violence, as in the Middle East), they also occur as "low-intensity" violence in the West, in the former Yugoslavia and on the streets of North America. The mobilization of production and destruction thus turns out to be a globally unsettling process of unprecedented dimensions.

A second reversal of expectations concerns the constitution of regimes of order in a unifying world. At the beginning of the century, it seemed that empires would be the main agents of political order in the world and that corporate forms of capital would play analogous roles in ordering the world economy The rivalry of empires set the rules of international relations, while the competition of monopoly firms, governed by the rules of the gold standard and subsequently by Bretton Woods, set the terms of survival for business. The notions of "great powers" and "global companies" assumed a centering of politics and economics in Western forms and practices and carried as well the undertone of an omniscient "brain" or "overmind" that understood and ordered the whole. None of this has survived the actual integration of the world. Instead of institutions that preside over the whole and guarantee a regime of order in the manner of secular universal monarchies, we face a proliferation of largely anonymous transnational practices, carried on in international organizations and networks of exchange, in banking and commerce, in information and communication, and, not least, in the interactions of states. The best scholarship on this matter coheres around metaphors of movement, flow, circuitry, following people, goods, and images in motion and seeking to specify the structural practices and imaginary "(land)scapes" that are created by and that sustain this movement. Thickets of rules and regulations, most of them instrumental and self-made, as well as institutional structures, hold the myriad of transactions together, but these are not centrally administered, nor do they have more than limited accountability. They have hardly any publicity. Organized in information corridors and segmented circuits or webs of exchange, enormously powerful, they slip our conceptual grasp because they are so unlike the images associated with global forms of order and settlement at the beginning of our century. It is not world government but regimes of mostly private regulations and practices that maintain and service the process of globalization. They may look brand-new, but, in fact, they have a history that accompanies the process of globalization from its beginning.

Migration, our third aspect of globalization, has also undergone dramatic reversals. The long twentieth century began with a massive out-migration of Europeans to the Americas, North and South, and in lesser numbers, to Africa, Asia, and Oceania. This movement was conceived both as an orderly expansion and as a way of maintaining order within Europe, because its population remained one of the most dynamic well into the nineteenth century. Such emigration was closely associated with efforts to organize the overseas world in ways that sealed off "native" populations in enclaves or compartments, when their reproduction served the extended family of Europeans. The global imaginings that were associated with these migratory processes have all been dashed. Not only has the direction of migration been dramatically reversed, as the industrial nations become host to growing numbers of the world's poor, but the gaps between the West and the rest, once established by distance, are now transmogrified into transnational circuits of culture and exchange, wherein migrants move back and forth across borders (physically and by fax), keeping close touch with the "home" and combining appropriated images and practices with a continuously renegotiated "authenticity." This process, combined with the slow dismantling of regimes of ethnic and racial segregation in industrial societies such as South Africa and the United States, has led to the collapse of the once-policed compartments of cultures and contributed to the formation of what Carol Breckenridge has called crossover "public cultures": new mass markets for contested and mediating terrains in the formation of communal and national identities. Again, the marketing of identities is not a new phenomenon. Moreover, its study has been ill-served by the single-minded concentration on the connection between the printing press and imagined communities, which is, as far as the twentieth century is concerned, an anachronistic assessment of what has happened. The fact that these markets are frequented by religious fundamentalists (the Ayatollah Khomeini's famous audio tapes) as much as by secular capitalists (Coca-Cola), by producers of Hindu devotionals (with a huge market in East Africa), and by Brazilian, Mexican, or Taiwanese purveyors of soap operas (favorite pastimes in states of the former communist empire), as well as Hollywood conglomerates, should lay to rest the obsessive fear of homogeneity that has lately become a speciality of French intellectuals in their campaign against Americanization. These public spaces of identity have led to a certain euphoria, especially among a younger generation of scholars. But if the balance of global development points toward an irreversible mixing of cultures and peoples, the cautious historian will also want to recall the staggering costs in ethnic violence and genocide that have accompanied the recurring efforts to salvage purity and authenticity in the face of global unsettlement.

A final arena in which the reversal of expectations helps illuminate patterns of globalization concerns the nation-state. Throughout the long twentieth century, the worldwide mobilization of peoples and resources and their channeling into transnational networks of exchange were effected by, and contained within, emergent state structures. States flourished in the context of globalization, a fact that must qualify much of the commonplace concern about global integration and transnational regimes threatening the integrity or autonomy of the state. They did so because the condition of globality has always been organized locally, in one place after the other, according to particular circumstances and conditions that happen to obtain. No matter how powerful or abstract the networks of global exchange or how remote their nodes of control, each transaction needs articulation in some particular place, in some meaningful idiom, under specific circumstances; processes of globalization must come to ground in concrete social, cultural, and political contexts that move people to purposeful ends and thus allow them, in some fashion, to represent themselves. In the twentieth century, states have sought, in their own interests and in the promotion of national development, to negotiate these connections; indeed, it was the (relative) success of the state in managing the linkages with an integrating world that allowed "national" politics to flourish. This is why states have grown in tandem with globalization, but it is also where powerful questions arise: for the process of global integration, while not destroying states, has had a tendency to bypass politics, short-circuit the formation of national agendas, and challenge the capacity of the state for political self-organization, that is, to constitute the nation and organize complex social relations. The result of this development is not only growing disillusionment with politics, worldwide, but the proliferation and strengthening of family and kinship networks and, more generally, of identity-based (ethnic or religious) communities as substitutes for national politics in much of the world. These go together with the proliferation of export platforms, para-states, "private" (family-based) states, and state satrapies. Here we find the key questions requiring closer examination for the whole of the long twentieth century – not in the collapse of the state but in the uncertainties of nations and in the crises of politics as popular representation.

By charting these reversals, in which the course of global development disrupts expectations and settled narratives, we find the crosscurrents and fissures that define the parameters of a century of global development. The processes of globalization have promoted social fragmentation and disassociation, just as the struggles to define community and defend it in the context of social dissolution have necessitated coming to terms with global integration. Increasingly over the course of the twentieth century, struggles for autonomy have turned into contestations over the *terms* of global integration – not over whether the world should move together but by whom and under what terms the identities of individuals, social groups, and entire societies should be defined. As this point is reached and passed again and again, the former center loses particularity; the more globalization proceeds, the less any region or society can pretend to control the struggle over the terms of integration. Thus we arrive at the end of the twentieth century in a global age, losing our capacity for narrating our histories in conventional ways, outward from one region, but gaining the ability to think world history, pragmatically and realistically, at the interstices of integrating circuits of globalizing networks of power and proliferating sites of localizing politics. This is the new condition of globality.

"The infinite lies outside of experience and experience is the sphere of history." At the end of the twentieth century, we encounter, not a universalizing and single modernity but an integrated world of multiple and multiplying modernities. As far as world history is concerned, there is no universalizing spirit, no *Weltgeist*, to be re/presented working its way out in history. There are, instead, many very specific, very material and pragmatic practices that await critical reflection and historical study. At the same time, there is no particular knowledge to be generalized or built up from these discrete practices into a general theory or global paradigm. Rather, there is general and global knowledge, actually in operation, that requires particularization to the local and human scale. Fundamentally, then, our basic strategies of historical narration have to be rethought in differentiations that have come into play. Lacking an imagination capable of articulating an integrated world of multiple modernities, globality is enveloped in an eerie silence, which, however, cannot mask its powerful effects; and contestations over the terms of globalization, lacking a language that can accommodate, even facilitate, difference, turn into implacably hostile rejections of otherness.

A reversal of this silence entails, above all, thinking and narrating the history of *this* existing world and how it has come about. This project must proceed with an understanding that, unlike the systems builders of the European past, who visualized the world and thought world history long before they could possibly experience the world as a whole, we contemporaries of the late twentieth century experience the world long before we know how to think it. The aim of this world history becomes a dual one: to shatter the silence surrounding global practices, by tracking them, describing them, and presenting them historically and, at the same time – recognizing with Georg Simmel that, in an integrated world, we encounter only more strangers – to facilitate public cultures as the free and equal marketplace of communicating among the many voices of different histories and memories. The practice of world history in this conception does not refuse or jettison the findings of world-systems theories or of a comparative history of civilizations, inasmuch as they survive a rigorous critique and shed their respective nostalgias for autonomous regions and essentialist civilizations. But the practice of world history in a global age does not reconfigure the field in which these paradigms are deployed. It proceeds from the recognition that the trajectory of this world cannot be extrapolated from anyone's particular past, because globality is without precedent in any one specific society, religion, or civilization – although it is not without precedent in more syncretistic ages and spaces. In recognizing that global development in the twentieth century has broken through all historiographic conventions, historians must attempt to find a representation of the world as the field of human contestation in which the histories of the world are mixed together, but societies and peoples are not thereby transformed into one, or even made more alike.

But here we confront a startling new condition: Humanity, which has been the subject of world history for many centuries and civilizations, has now come into the purview of all human beings. This humanity is extremely polarized into rich and poor, powerful and powerless, vociferous and speechless, believers and non-believers. There are clusters of dense interaction and clusters of loose and distance encounters. There are liminal zones and there are areas of devastation – wastelands both in the actuality of the present moment and in lingering memory. This humanity, in short, does not form a single homogenous civilization. But in an age of globality, the humanity that inhabits this world is no longer a universalizing image or a normative construct of what some civilization or some intellectuals would want the people of this earth to be. Neither is this humanity any longer a mere species or a natural condition. For the first time, we as human beings collectively constitute ourselves and, hence, are responsible for ourselves.

This condition of globality can no longer be represented by notions of earth/nature or cosmos/world picture, as has been the case in the past. Instead, this condition of globality is the integrated global space of human practice. As a consequence, humanity no longer comes into being through "thought." Rather, humanity gains existence in a multiplicity of discrete economic, social, cultural, and political activities. In the past, such humanity has been the dream of sages and philosophers and, not to be forgotten, of gods, but now it has become the daily work of human beings. This daily work needs imagination. To this end, world history makes explicit and visible – it traces – both practices of global regimes and the imbrication of local communities. Its task is to make transparent the lineaments of power, underpinned by information, that compress humanity into a single humankind. And it is to make accessible to all human beings the diverse human labors, splintered into so many particularities that go into creating and maintaining the global condition. This conclusion underscores both the promise and the challenge of the twentieth century as an age of world historical transition – that, in forging a world in which "humanity" has become a pragmatic reality with a common destiny, we do not arrive at the end of history. World history has just begun.

PART II

Time and space

NOWHERE IS GLOBALIZATION more dramatically demonstrated than in the technological innovations that have continued to narrow distances among various parts of the world – and between the earth and other planets. Starting in the nineteenth century, such innovations as the railway, the steamship, the automobile, and the airplane have drastically reduced the time to reach geographical destinations, while the telephone, the telegram, and the computer have brought individuals into virtually instant communication with one another. The result has been the creation of an interconnected world and the awareness that we all live on the "spaceship earth."

Stephen Kern (Professor of History at Ohio State University) calls the late nineteenth-century phase of this technological revolution a "culture of time and space." People's attitudes toward time and space changed within the span of a few decades, something that had profound cultural implications. These innovations, at the same time, transformed political, diplomatic, and strategic affairs among nations and gave rise to the question whether technological globalization would ultimately serve the interests of the whole humankind.

Walter McDougall (Professor of History at the University of Pennsylvania) puts that question in the context of the space age that dawned in the 1950s. The spacecraft, he notes, is closely linked to statecraft, and only a wise use of the new space technology by nations would ensure a healthier future for the whole world.

Chapter 3

Stephen Kern

THE CULTURE OF TIME AND SPACE

O N THE NIGHT OF APRIL 14, 1912, the largest moving structure ever built, the *Titanic*, steamed at a recklessly high speed into an ice field in the North Atlantic. The first officer recalled that the sea was especially calm and so that night there were no "ice blinks" – flashes of light given off when waves splash against icebergs and illuminate their crystallized surfaces. Visibility was further reduced by fog. At 11:40 P.M. a lookout suddenly spotted an iceberg dead ahead. The ship turned sharply and, as it scraped by, was opened up like a tin can with a gash below the water line three hundred feet long. The captain determined that they were going to sink fast and at 12:15 A.M. ordered his wireless operator to send the distress call. Within a few minutes the airwaves were rippling with signals as over a dozen ships became aware of the disaster. This was simultaneous drama on the high seas, driven by steam power and choreographed by the magic of wireless telegraphy.

Ten ships heard the call from over a hundred miles away and remained in contact but were too distant to help, as were also the *Hellig Olav* at 90 miles and the *Niagara* at 75 miles. The *Mount Temple* was 50 miles away but had to move slowly through the ice fields. The *Carpathia* at 58 miles was the first to arrive, but not until almost two hours after the *Titanic* went down with 1,522 passengers. Another ship, close enough to have saved all the passengers, was not in wireless contact. The *Californian* was approximately 19 miles away, but its wireless operator had hung up his earphones for the night about ten minutes before the *Titanic* sent out its first CQD. Two watchmen on the deck of the *Californian* saw the rockets that the *Titanic* fired but could not figure out what they meant or convince their captain to pull anchor and find out. What the eyes and ears of man could not perceive the wireless could receive over vast distances and through darkness and fog.

The operator on the *Carpathia* got the call for help when he put on his earphones to verify a "time rush" (an exchange of time signals with a neighboring ship to see if their clocks agree). At 1:06 A.M. he heard the *Titanic* tell another ship coming to help, "Get your boats ready; going down fast on the head." The world began to get

From Stephen Kern, *The Culture of Time and Space: 1880–1918* (Harvard University Press, 1983), pp. 65–7, 109–19, 211–19.

news of the disaster at 1:20 A.M., when a wireless station in Newfoundland picked up the message that the *Titanic* was sinking and was putting women off in boats. Shortly after that hundreds of wireless instruments along the Atlantic coast began to transmit and the airwaves became jumbled in confusion. The *Titanic*'s wireless had a range of only 1,500 miles, so signals to Europe had to go first to New York and then across the ocean by cable; still, by early morning the entire world was privy to news of the disaster.

To one of the survivors in a life boat it seemed as if the stars above saw the ship in distress and "had awakened to flash messages across the black dome of the sky to each other." The communication that he imagined between stars was accomplished on a lesser scale between the ships at sea by wireless. On April 21, the *New York Times* commented on its magical power.

> Night and day all the year round the millions upon the earth and the thousands upon the sea now reach out and grasp the thin air and use it as a thing more potent for human aid than any strand of wire or cable that was ever spun or woven. Last week 745 [sic] human lives were saved from perishing by the wireless. But for the almost magic use of the air the *Titanic* tragedy would have been shrouded in the secrecy that not so long ago was the power of the sea . . . Few New Yorkers realize that all through the roar of the big city there are constantly speeding messages between people separated by vast distances, and that over housetops and even through the walls of buildings and in the very air one breathes are words written by electricity.

An editorial in the *London Times* of April 16 noted the expanded range of experience made possible by the wireless.

> The wounded monster's distress sounded through the latitudes and longitudes of the Atlantic, and from all sides her sisters great and small hastened to her succor. . . . We recognize with a sense near to awe that we have been almost witness of a great ship in her death agonies.

An officer of the American Telephone and Telegraph Company praised the communication that made it possible to follow the rescue. The telephone and wireless, he wrote, "enabled the peoples of many lands to stand together in sympathetic union, to share a common grief." William Alden Smith, the Michigan senator who chaired an exhaustive inquiry into the sinking, as part of his summary of those hearings before the United States Senate on May 18, 1912, referred to the new sense of world unity that required worldwide safety regulations. "When the world weeps together over a common loss," he said, "when nature moves in the same directions in all spheres, why should not the nations clear the sea of its conflicting idioms and wisely regulate this new servant of humanity?" Although the wireless had been used before to save lives at sea, this rescue effort was particularly highlighted because so many were aware of the tragedy: the survivors watching from life boats, the wireless operators in distant places, and the frustrated seamen in the rescue ships. [. . .]

In 1897 Germany embarked on a policy of *Weltpolitik* and began to build a battle fleet to challenge British control of the seas. That same year the German passenger steamer *Kaiser Wilhelm der Grosse* took away from the British Cunard Line the Blue Riband for the fastest Atlantic crossing. In 1903, with its national prestige at stake, the British government subsidized the construction of a vessel capable of reaching twenty-five knots and beating the German record. The Cunard yards produced the *Mauretania*, which regained the Blue Riband in 1907 and retained it for twenty-two years. The White Star Line that designed the *Titanic* hoped to surpass all rivals in speed and luxury. As several expert mariners testified at the British inquiry into her sinking, the pressure to keep to schedule obliged many captains to steam at recklessly high speeds though fog and ice. One survivor commented that the public demanded more speed every year and refused to patronize the slower lines. A bishop in Chicago condemned the "insane desire" for excessive speed on both land and sea. Another critic observed a "mania for speed and smashing records." In a letter to the London *Daily News and Leader* George Bernard Shaw criticized the captain of the *Titanic* for deliberately steaming into an ice field at full throttle, and Joseph Conrad wrote an angry article in the *English Review* predicting more irresponsibility in the future when steamships could plow across the ocean in all weather at forty knots.

The arrogance of large ocean liners, their pursuit of speed records at risk of life, was the subject of *Futility* (1898), a novel of uncanny prevision. It is a story about the largest craft afloat, a symbol of modernity that incorporated the knowledge of "every science, profession, and trade known to civilization." The designers had discovered how to close compartments automatically in case of collision, and the ship was advertised as "practically unsinkable" and carried as few life boats as law would permit. The owners announced that it would steam at full speed in all weather. The first night out it cut another ship in two, and the man on watch insisted on reporting all he knew in the hope of ending "this wanton destruction of life and property for the sake of speed." The name of the ship was *Titan*.

The sinking of the *Titanic* was but the most tragic consequence of speed made possible by a broad technological revolution that also affected how people traveled to work and how fast they worked when they got there, how they met each other and what they did together, the way they danced and walked and even, some said, the way they thought. There was no question that the pace of life was greatly accelerated, but there was sharp debate about the meaning and value of speed.

The German historian Karl Lamprecht observed that in the last decades of the nineteenth century there was a sharp rise in the domestic production and importation of pocket watches (he estimated 12 million imported watches for a German population of about 52 million). At the same time people began paying specific new attention to short intervals of time – "five-minute interviews, minute-long telephone conversations, and five-second exchanges on bicycles." The new profusion of watches was a response to, as well as a cause of, a heightened sense of punctuality in this period, especially in urban centers. In an essay on "The Metropolis and Mental Life" (1900), Georg Simmel commented on the impact of the "universal diffusion of pocket watches" in accelerating modern life and instilling a sense of punctuality, calculability, and exactness in business transactions as well as human relations.

The bicycle was about four times faster than walking and warnings were issued about getting "bicycle face" by moving against the wind at such high speeds. Its design made the bike difficult to ride, but this became easier after 1886 when the wheels were made of equal size, and more comfortable in 1890 with pneumatic tires. In America, Sylvester Baxter observed that the bicycle "quickened the perceptive faculties of young people and made them more alert." A French critic attributed the excitement of cycling to the sheer pleasure of movement, enhanced by a sense of mastery over the environment. The popular French writer Paul Adam wrote that it created a "cult of speed" for a generation that wanted "to conquer time and space."

A penetrating evaluation of its impact on human sensibilities and social relations was made in 1898 by Maurice Leblanc in a novel about cycling, *Voici des ailes!* On its title page is a drawing of a bare-breasted woman with an unbuttoned chemise trailing down over her belt, hair streaming in the wind, strings flying free from her wrists, pedaling a winged bicycle, all of which suggests the sexual, social, and spatial liberation that the two married couples of the book experience during a bicycle tour. The first day out Pascal observes to his friend Guillaume that nothing evokes the idea of speed more than the humming spokes of a bicycle. On the road the couples feel a new rhythm of movement, a unique sense of penetrating the surrounding world as their senses open to new parts of the terrain. They experience a new sense of time, as if they were moving through a dream rather than the French countryside. Social restrictions loosen when they address each other by first names. Sartorial and sexual liberation begins when Pascal's wife unbuttons her blouse and bathes her neck and shoulders in a public fountain. The next day both women appear without corsets. Later they strip off their blouses and cycle bare-breasted, and eventually the bonds of marriage break down as the couples exchange spouses and finish their tour re-paired.

Pascal comments on the dimensions of experience opened up by the bicycle. Steam and electricity only serve man, but the bicycle alters his body with a faster pair of legs. "This is not two different things like man and horse. There is not a man and a machine. There is a faster man." Speeding along he finally declares his love for Guillaume's wife and shouts "we have wings" – to escape the narrow spatial framework of their former city lives, the constricted social world of their ill-suited marriages, the physical confinement of corsets and tight clothing, and the emotional restrictions of their sexual mortality.

The automobile captured the imagination in the 1890s and became a major means of transportation in the first years of the twentieth century. In France there were about 3,000 automobiles in 1900 and about 100,000 by 1913. Between 1896 and 1900 at least ten journals about "automobilism" appeared, all attentive to the ever breaking speed records, which by 1906 had exceeded 200 kilometers per hour. Commenting on its impact the French novelist Octave Mirabeau mixed metaphors as rapidly as the movement of his subject – the mind of modern man. Under the impact of the automobile it has become an "endless race track." "His thoughts, feelings, and loves are a whirlwind. Everywhere life is rushing insanely like a cavalry charge, and it vanishes cinematographically like trees and silhouettes along a road. Everything around man jumps, dances, gallops in a movement out of phase with his own."

In England the Highways and Locomotives Act of 1878 required that any vehicle using public roads be preceded by a man on foot and not exceed a speed of four miles per hour. This law was abolished by another of 1896 that opened public roads to the faster "light locomotives," but as the number of traffic accidents rose opposition mounted. In 1903 the *Daily Telegraph* campaigned for a new speed limit, about which C.S. Rolls protested: "Our hereditary instincts are shocked at seeing anything on the road faster than a horse, but as our senses become educated we shall recognize the fact that speed of itself is not dangerous but the inability to stop is dangerous." Parliament was not fooled by such doubletalk and in 1904 imposed a limit of 20 miles per hour on public highways, 10 miles per hour if required by local authorities. During the next year 1,500 motorists were charged with reckless driving. The number of traffic fatalities in London increased from 769 in the period 1892–6 to 1,692 in the period 1907–11. In April 1914, when a child was killed by the chauffeur-driven car of Hildebrand Harmsworth, son of the famous newspaper magnate Lord Northcliffe, public outrage peaked. Annoyances and inconveniences of car travel were substantial. The dust that trailed behind autos engulfed pedestrians and cyclists and ruined the crop of lettuce farmers. And since the dust *was* the road there were complaints from taxpayers. In *The Condition of England* of 1909, C.F.G. Masterman hissed his protest about automobiles that "scramble and smash and shriek all along the rural ways."

Nothing moved faster than the electricity that raced through conduits, powering motors and accelerating a variety of activities. The first electric tram was put into operation by Werner Siemens in Berlin in 1879; the first one in America ran between Baltimore and Hampden in 1885. They sashayed about the inner city like those that marked the regular pace of public time in Bloom's Dublin. The electrified London underground was completed in 1890, and in the following decade there was a proliferation of electric rails everywhere. In the United States the 1,261 miles in 1890 increased to 21,290 miles by 1902. Visitors to the 1900 World Exhibition in Paris were impressed by the new Otis escalator and a moving pavement designed by the French that portended faster pedestrian traffic. The telephone accelerated business transactions and enabled Wall Street to become a truly national financial center by increasing the liquidity of securities and the speed of fund raising. J.P. Morgan averted a financial panic in 1907 when, over the telephone, he extended $25 million credit to several major banks threatened with excessive withdrawals. The great generating station that opened in Niagara Falls in 1895 converted the rush of water into an even faster rush of electrical current that transformed the pace of life and, some speculated, the very processes of life. An article in the *Fortnightly Review* proposed that electricity might accelerate the growth of crops and increase agricultural yield. This theory was elaborated upon by the Belgian chemist Ernest Solvay in a lecture at the opening of his Institute of Physiology in Brussels. Enthusiasm for this theory peaked with the work of the Nobel Prize winning chemist Svante Arrhenius, who tested the effect of electrical stimulation on the growth of children. He placed one group in schoolrooms with wires carrying high-frequency alternating current. After six months the "electrically charged children" had grown twenty millimeters more than those in the control group. The "magnetised teachers" reported that "their faculties were quickened." While some researchers tried to use electricity to accelerate the processes of life, others used it to speed up death; in 1888 New York passed a law substituting death by electricity for hanging. In 1890 the New York prison authorities first used the "electric chair" to execute a convicted murderer, although it proved to be far less speedy than expected. The first charge of current failed to kill the man, and after some delay a second charge was given. When it was all over eight minutes had elapsed, the victim was covered with blood from cuts sustained at the points of contact with the circuitry, the District Attorney was in tears, one witness had fainted, everybody was horrified, and a reporter for the *New York Times* wrote that it had been a "revolting spectacle," "far worse than hanging."

The technology of speed affected newspaper reporting and modified the language of journalistic communication. On February 12, 1887, a reporter for the *Boston Globe* used a telephone for the first time to report a speech made by Graham Bell in Salem, Massachusetts; and in 1880 the *London Times* installed a direct telephone line to the House of Commons to gain 45 minutes in the reporting of late night debates for their morning edition. Robert Lincoln O'Brien noted in an essay of 1904 on "Machinery and English Style" that the telegraph came into ever greater use as the need for fast reporting increased. Because economy of expression produced monetary savings, reporters were inclined to write their stories with the fewest possible words. The telegraph also encouraged the use of unambiguous words to avoid any confusion, and the language of journalism came to be more uniform as certain words came into more frequent use. Adverbial phrases at the beginning of a sentence were especially "dangerous," because they might be confused with the preceding sentence, and writers used the simplest syntax. Information tended to be written with a minimum of punctuation. "The delicacy, intricacy, nuance of language is endangered by the wires," O'Brien concluded, as the need for speed, clarity, and simplicity shaped a new "telegraphic" style. No doubt Hemingway's simplification of the English language was in part a consequence of his experience as a foreign correspondent, obliged to prepare his articles for transmission over the Atlantic cable.

Factory work was accelerated by applying Frederick W. Taylor's "scientific management," which he first conceived in 1883. Taylor observed skilled workers and determined the exact series of elementary operations that make up their job, selected the quickest series, timed each elementary operation with a stop-watch to establish minimum "unit times," and reconstructed jobs with composite times as a standard. Although there was nothing new about cracking the whip, scientific management was, as the name implied, scientific, or at least systematic, and avoided the caprice of a foreman's shifting moods. Wages were raised as workers approached their maximum efficiency rate, and those who fell short of a minimum rate were discharged. One of Taylor's reports shows the kind of psychological harassment caused by this systematic speedup:

> it was found necessary to measure the output of each girl as often as once every hour and send a teacher to each individual who was falling behind to find what was wrong, straighten her out, and encourage her and help her to catch up.

He began to publicize his methods in 1895 stressing that workers complete jobs in the shortest possible time. The following year a Massachusetts builder, Sanford Thompson, devised a "watch book" with stop-watches concealed in the cover, so that they could be operated without the worker's knowledge. Taylor disapproved of "spying" because it undermined the mutual commitment to speed and efficiency between worker and management that he thought essential, but he conceded that some workers object to being timed, and for them concealment might be necessary.

Taylor's disciple, Frank B. Gilbreth, applied the methods of scientific management to work in space. A "motion study" of bricklaying in 1909 enabled him to devise an adjustable scaffold for piling up bricks that tripled worker output. He conducted research by means of "cyclegraphs" produced by attaching small electric lights to the body and making photographic time exposures of motions that appeared as continuous white lines. These made it possible to see the path of a motion and reconstruct it in three dimensions with a stereoscopic light. For more precision he adapted a motion picture camera to take "chronocyclegraphs," which would show "the paths of each several motions made by various parts of the body and their exact distances, exact times, relative times, exact speeds, relative speeds, and directions." In an article on scientific management of households Gilbreth boasted that with chronocyclegraphy "we can now for the first time record the time and path of individual motions to the thousandth of a minute." His wife, Lillian, who collaborated with him, conceived of a new managerial position – the "speed boss" – whose job was to demonstrate to a worker how a task is to be done in the specified time. But not all was rush, work, and profit. The Gilbreths also sought to reduce worker fatigue, and their book on that subject stressed the need to offset the dreariness of factory routine by providing a certain number of "Happiness Minutes" for the workers: They concluded with the uplifting thought that "the good in your life consists of the quantity of 'Happiness Minutes' that you have created or caused."

Scientific management, the motion studies of Muybridge and Marey, early cinematography, Cubism, and Futurism reflect aspects of each other across the cultural spectrum like images in a house of mirrors. As the Cubists broke up and recreated bottles and guitars, Gilbreth broke down and reconstructed work processes. He made wire models of workers' movements from cyclegraphs similar to the wire-and-plaster models of birds in flight that Marey made from chrono-photographs. Gilbreth's use of successive photographs to analyze motion derived from Muybridge's serial photographs of a galloping horse. Muybridge later used the technique to capture the grace of a woman stooping to pick up a basket; Gilbreth applied it to improve the speed of workers picking up bricks. Cinema was the technological link: Muybridge and Marey were searching for a way to make moving pictures; Gilbreth used the motion picture camera to make chronocyclegraphs; the term for a film's composition – "montage" – is the French word for the assembly of a product from "Cubist Cinema"; and the Futurists were inspired by its suggestion of new possibilities for a kinetic visual art. Marcel Duchamp observed that "the whole idea of movement, of speed, was in the air," and acknowledged that his *Nude Descending a Staircase* was inspired by chronophotographs and motion pictures. The cinema reproduced the mechanization, jerkiness, and rush of modern times.

The very name of the new medium identified its effect – moving pictures. The turning projector supplied movement of images on the screen. In 1896 one of Lumiere's cameramen, M.A. Promio, hit upon the idea of taking pictures from a moving boat along the Grand Canal of Venice. With creative editing action could move as fast as it did in Griffith's last-minute rescues or at a more leisurely pace in cuts between widely separate pales. The story could change settings as rapidly as the interval between frames, and since in the early movies the picture was taken at 16 frames per second and projected at 24, the actors themselves seemed to hurry across the flickering screen. The cinematograph so exaggerated the quickness of movement that some actors moved more slowly than they would in real life in order to give the final result a normal tempo. One critic explained that the decline in the popularity of the theatrical melodrama, which relied on a fast pace to sustain interest, was caused by competition with the cinematograph, which could intensify action and present it much more rapidly than was possible on the stage. "The swiftness develops the breathlessness and excitement [that] the melodrama proper fails to evoke." Some film makers intentionally accelerated motion for special effects: Flowers boiled out of buds in seconds, and the metamorphosis of a caterpillar into a butterfly could be compressed from weeks into minutes. Cinematic coverage was greatly accelerated in 1911 when a special express train outfitted with a dark room was used to develop and transport a film of the investiture of the Prince of Wales at Carnarvon at four o'clock in the afternoon and have it ready for public viewing in London at ten o'clock that night.

These "rushes" dazzled audiences. Erwin Panofsky concluded that the basis for enjoyment of moving pictures was not the subject matter "but the sheer delight in the fact that things seemed to move." The early viewers were fascinated by any simple moving subject: Niagara Falls, horses jumping hurdles, workers emerging from a factory, a train pulling into a station. Some inexperienced viewers would duck in their seats to avoid an approaching train. Already in 1899 the Kinetoscope made its way into a novel, as Frank Norris's McTeague was "awestruck" at an approaching cable car on the screen.

The French Cubist painter Fernand Léger identified the effect of the cinema and of technology in general on the aesthetic sensibilities of artists and the viewing public. In 1913 he observed that life was "more fragmented and faster-moving than in previous periods" and that people sought a dynamic art to depict it. Cinema and color photography have made it unnecessary to paint representational and popular subject matter. "The few working class people who used to be seen in museums, gaping in front of a cavalry charge by M. Detaille or a historical scene by M.J.P. Laurens, are no longer to be seen; they are at the cinema." Evolution of the means of locomotion has affected the way people see and the art they like: "A modern man registers a hundred times more sensory impressions than an eighteenth-century artist." The view through the door of a moving railroad car or the windshield of an automobile is fragmented, although at high speeds it becomes continuous the way continuity is created out of a series of stills by the cinema. Léger responded to these new dynamics with paintings that incorporated machine-like elements in figure studies and landscapes – one can almost hear the clanging of machinery in his art. [. . .]

On October 2, 1872, some members of the exclusive Reform Club of London were playing a game of whist in front of a fire and debating the chances of a bank robber's making a successful escape. The engineer, Andrew Stuart, maintained that they were good. One of the directors of the bank, Gauthier Ralph, disagreed. A description of the robber had been sent to agents all over the world, and so, "Where could he possibly go?" Stuart replied, "I don't know about that, but the world is big enough." "It was once," said another gentleman in a low voice. Ralph agreed and pointed out that one could now go around the world "ten times more quickly than a hundred years ago."

Another member reported that a new section of the Great Indian Peninsular Railway had opened recently, and according to a calculation in the *Morning Chronicle*, a man could, if he made all the right connections, travel around the world by rail and steamer in eighty days.

They continued to debate the feasibility of actually making such a trip, when, without interrupting his play, the soft-spoken man who first alluded to the shrinking size of the earth brought the discussion to a head around 7:00 P.M. by wagering the others 20,000 pounds that he could tour the world in eighty days or less. He proposed to leave on the Dover train at 8:45 that night, but first insisted on finishing the hand. At 7:25 Phileas Fogg, having won twenty guineas, left the Reform Club and prepared to begin his tour of the world with his French servant Passepartout.

The hero of Jules Verne's classic, *Around the World in Eighty Days* (1873), embodied all the self-assuredness and extravagance of the British Empire. The source of his wealth was a mystery, and he used it to indulge tastes acquired during extensive travels. The ice at the Reform Club was "brought at great expense from the American lakes" to keep his drinks fresh. He was polite, taciturn, and punctual – a perfect gentleman whose life style would have pleased Samuel Smiles. He awoke, dressed, breakfasted, and continued his routine throughout the day according to a strict timetable – habits that served him well in the course of his race around the world. His elegant home at Savile Row was outfitted with the most precise new electric clocks and had electric bells and speaking tubes to facilitate instantaneous communication between master and servant. The dash of his successful journey appealed to the masses who quickly made the book an international bestseller. With Fogg and Passepartout they could vicariously race against time and conquer space.

The book was a mixture of fact and fantasy, a compendium of global travel that was actually taking place, and an inspiration for others to follow. Although Verne never admitted to having a specific model for this hero, two men might well have been. In 1870 the Boston businessman George Francis Train almost toured the world in eighty days. Two years later another American businessman, William Perry Fogg, published a book called *Round the World* that chronicled a slower 1869 tour. It is most likely that Verne got his eighty-day timetable from one that appeared in the *Magasin pittoresque* in March of 1870, made after the completion of the Suez Canal, the American Transcontinental Railway, and the Trans-Indian Peninsular Railroad.

The fame of Verne's novel made eighty days the time to beat. The first to do it was the American journalist Nellie Bly, who in 1889–90 took seventy-two days. Geroge Train got it down to sixty days in 1892. With improvements in travel, scheduling facilitated by the introduction of world Standard Time, and the invention of the telephone and wireless, the time required to circumnavigate the globe was progressively reduced, and by the turn of the century the hope was to cut Fogg's time in half. When officials from several European countries and China met in 1902 to schedule a railroad journey from Paris to Peking, they also announced that they had "resolved the problem of traveling around the world in forty days." The novel projected a new sense of world unity that became ever sharper in the decades that followed as the railroad, telephone, bicycle, automobile, airplane, and cinema revolutionized the sense of distance.

Railroads were not new, but around the turn of the century their hold on political, military, economic, and private life tightened as the railroad networks thickened. In the metaphorical language of the naturalistic novel, the railroad took on sinister meanings. In Zola's *The Human Beast* (1890)

> it was like a huge body, a gigantic being lying across the earth, his head in Paris, his vertebrae all along the line, his limbs stretching out into branch lines, with feet and hands in Le Havre and the other terminals.

A stranglehold of iron tentacles on farmers is the central image of Frank Norris's *The Octopus* (1900), and the entire San Joaquin Valley was in its grip:

> From Reno on one side to San Francisco on the other, ran the plexus of red, a veritable system of blood circulation, complicated, dividing, and reuniting, branching, splitting, extending, throwing out feelers, off-shoots, taproots, feeders – diminutive little bloodsuckers that shot out from the main jugular and went twisting up into some remote county, laying hold upon some forgotten village or town, involving it in one of a myriad branching coils, one of a hundred tentacles, drawing it as it were, toward that center from which all this system sprang.

The railroads ended the sanctuary of remoteness. Wheat farmers were sucked into the mainstream of national and international markets by railroads that united the land masses to sea lanes in a single commercial unit.

In the complex interaction between need and technological intervention, it is difficult to identify one or the other exclusively as causal. The railroad responded to economic need and in turn had an enormous impact on economic life. In a similar manner electronic communication related to the creation of worldwide markets. The telegraph, like the railroad, was a product of the early nineteenth century, but the telephone was unique to the last quarter of the century and greatly expanded the range, mobility, and contact points between which messages could be sent, drawing millions of people into an instantaneous communications network. The French were suspicious of the telephone at first and by 1898 had only 31,600 telephones. The more enterprising British had 600,000 in operation by 1912 when the government took control of the system. In Germany there was faster growth. In 1891 there were 71,000 telephones in use, and 1,300,000 before the war. According to one report, over 2.5 billion separate calls were placed in Germany in 1913. The telephone was most enthusiastically received in the United States, where there were 10,000,000 in operation by 1914. Assuming the same ratio of calls per telephone and doubling the figure to allow for the two parties, it can be estimated that in 1914 telephone lines in the United States were used approximately 38 billion times.

Bismarck was the first political leader to grasp the value of long-distance telephone communications. He saw its unifying potential as early as 1877 when he ran a line over 230 miles between his palace in Berlin and his farm at Varzin. By 1885 there were 33 cities linked directly with Berlin. The Russians were quick to perceive the telephone's military use; in 1881 they established a commission to explore the potential and three years later opened a direct line between Moscow and St. Petersburg. The first international line was set between Paris and Brussels in 1887, and overseas telephony began in Europe with the laying of the first underwater telephone cable between England and France in 1891. Long distance service in the United States was inaugurated with the opening of the New York-to-Chicago line in 1892, and by 1915 the first coast-to-coast line opened between New York and San Francisco. The "annihilation of distance" was not a science-fiction fantasy or some theoretical leap of physicists; it was the actual experience of the masses who quickly became accustomed to an instrument that enabled them to raise money, sell wheat, make speeches, signal storms, prevent log jams, report fires, buy groceries, or just communicate across ever increasing distances. An article of 1905 reported that "there are sections where chicken stealing has become a lost art, because the rural telephones make it possible to block every avenue of escape as soon as the crime is discovered." Chicken thieves or Verne's hypothetical bank robber found that the annihilation of distance just increased the space crooks had to go to make their getaway.

Telephony expanded lived space too. "The telephone changes the structure of the brain. Men live in wider distances, and think in larger figures, and become eligible for nobler and wider motives," wrote one social observer. Conversations whet the appetite for visits. Proust felt both a sense of closeness and separation from telephone conversations. In a letter of 1902 he related how he had spoken to his mother just after she lost her parents, and

> suddenly her poor shattered voice came to me through the telephone stricken for all time, a voice quite other than the one I had always known, all cracked and broken; and in the wounded, bleeding fragments that came to me through the receiver I had for the first time the dreadful sensation of all things inside her that were forever shattered.

In *Remembrance of Things Past* he translates this experience into a conversation between Marcel and his grandmother and speculates on the essence of telephone communication. It is an "admirable sorcery," which brings before us,

> invisible but present, the person to whom we have been wishing to speak, and who, while still sitting at his table, in the town in which he lives . . . in the midst of circumstances and worries of which we know nothing, but of which he is going to inform us, finds himself suddenly transported hundreds of miles.

The telephone operators are "priestesses of the Invisible" who bring us the sound of "distance overcome." But the voice of his grandmother also gave Marcel a premonition of an "eternal separation." Her voice was not only distant, but also cut off from the rest of her being – the movements of her body, her facial expressions, the sounds and smells and touches that had competed the *mise-en-scène* of prior conversations. This truncated, abstract individual became a symbol of his own isolation and of the eternal separation that awaits everyone in death.

The distance was also useful to buffer the intensity of face-to-face encounters. Telephone conversation allowed men to take liberties with operators that they would never think of taking in person. Men courted women on the telephone; some even proposed marriage. The telephone also made possible a dispersion of business activity. While in the mid-century company offices were usually located on the premises of factories, around the turn of the century they began to move into urban centers. Central offices began to cluster in New York in the 1880s and in London in the early twentieth century. Telephones also enabled businessmen to get out of cities and run their affairs from the country. An article in *Scientific American* in 1914 titled "Action at a Distance" pointed to the problem of urban congestion and looked forward to a time when the telephone and a picture phone (yet to be invented) would allow business to be conducted at a distance from cities. Telephone connections could have a dual impact. They could disperse business from single-trade neighborhoods or concentrate it. The telephone permitted businessmen to buy and sell from afar without leaving their "territory" and forced them to reach out further. It brought people into close contact but obliged them also to "live in wider distances" and created a palpable emptiness across which voices seemed uniquely disembodied and remote.

The bicycle created another set of distancing effects. In 1893 a new American bicycle cost between $100 and $150. In 1897 it averaged around $80, but by 1902 mass manufacturing had driven the price down to anywhere from $3 to $15, well within the range of the working classes. The "bicycle boom of the 1890s" enabled more and more people to travel freely. In *Voici des ailes!* Leblanc's hero Pascal expressed his exhilaration over the new command of space: "The stifling limits of the horizon are destroyed and nature is conquered." Guardians of morality warned that women were taking advantage of the new mobility afforded by the bicycle and more of them were venturing farther from their homes unchaperoned. The bicycle also bridged social space. One snob writing in the *Fortnightly Review* in 1891 conceded that it was possible for an individual to cycle "without imperiling his or her social status." But the peril was implied with his reassurance that in Dublin, where it was customary for everybody to cycle together, the upper classes "never feel their gentility offended by breathing the same air as the shop-boy from the neighboring grocers." An article in the *Minneapolis Tribune* in 1895 was more positive about the "most democratic of all vehicles" that allowed all ranks to entertain themselves in the same fashion. Another journalist was carried away with praise for the "revolutionary" impact of the bicycle – that "great leveler" and instrument of social equality. Joseph Bishop praised the bicycle for compressing social distances and making it easier for the sexes to meet on a common ground. Bishop also noted the expanded radius of travel and the growing popularity of suburban tours that were "unconsciously but surely bringing city and country into closer unions." His observation that the bicycle had expanded the radius of the social circles from two or three miles to ten or twenty was echoed in similar assessments (for longer distances) about the automobile after the turn of the century.

One early motor-car enthusiast, Alfred Harmsworth, explained in 1902 how the automobile was going to extend social life in the country by making it possible to visit someone 25 miles away without having to arrange a change of horses as would have been necessary ten years earlier. Before the automobile, anyone living more than 8 or 10 miles away was "beyond calling distance." Recalling his childhood, Siegfried Sassoon wrote: "Dumborough Park was 12 miles from where my aunt lived . . . My aunt was fully 2 miles beyond the radius of Lady Dumborough's 'round of calls.' Those 2 miles made the difference, and the aristocratic yellow-wheeled barouche never entered our white unassuming gate." Stefan Zweig observed that

> The mountains, the lakes, the ocean were no longer as far away as formerly; the bicycle, the automobile, and the electric train had shorter end distances and had given the world a new spaciousness. . . . Whereas formerly only the privileged few had ventured abroad, now bank clerks and small trades-people would visit France and Italy.

In *La Morale des sports* (1898) Paul Adam elaborated on the new automobilism. Driving builds skills that require sustained attention and quick responses over large distances. The ease and frequency of traveling engenders an exchange of ideas, stimulates the intellect, breaks up prejudices, and diminishes provincialism. Writing in that same year Henry Adams brooded about the conquest of space as well as time by automobiles that could unite the widely scattered monuments of the past such as the cathedral at Chartres and enable him to pass "from one century to another without a break." Proust made a similar observation. Before the war many people had speculated that speedy railway travel would kill contemplation, but, he observed, "the car has taken over its function and once more deposits tourists outside foreign churches." However, Proust preferred the railroad. Travel by car was "more genuine" because it allowed one to remain in closer intimacy with the earth and traverse space as a continuum, while trains jumped from station to station and made the difference between departure and arrival as intense as possible. Railway travel was like a metaphor in that it "united two distant individualities of the world, took us from one name to another name." Train travel was one clue to the recapture of time lost. His most famous definition of art centered on the way metaphor united the "distant individualities" of experience:

> Truth – and life too – can be attained by us only when, by comparing a quality common to two sensations, we succeed in extracting their common essence and in reuniting them to each other, liberated from the contingencies of time, within a metaphor.

In Verne's story the earth remained the same size throughout the duration of Phileas Fogg's tour; in Proust's, distances contracted and expanded through the mediation of consciousness. Verne used technology to get his hero around the world in eighty days, while Proust used it to illustrate the kinds of spatial and temporal leaps that the mind makes uncontrollably and incessantly. Fogg could plan when he would depart and make connections en route, while Marcel had to wait for involuntary memories to start his journeys and then watch the myriad places in his memory rush past in a flash. Ortega commented on this unique sensitivity to space when he wrote that Proust had invented "a new distance between ourselves and things" – a distance modified by attention and imagination, by love and desire. In the forty years that elapsed between the publication of Verne's travel story and the publication of the first volume of Proust's novel, the sense of distance in literature had been transformed by more than new means of transportation and communication. For Proust, as for Joyce, travel took place in the mind as much as in the world, and distances depended on the effect of memory, the force of emotions and the passage of time.

The cinema made two unique contributions to the sense of distance in the visual arts with the close-up and the quick cut. The first dramatic use of a close-up was in the last scene of Porter's *The Great Train Robbery* (1903), when the screen is filled with the gun barrel of an outlaw firing point-blank at the audience – a symbol of the explosive impact of the entire medium as well as this technique. Five years later Griffith used the close-up in an adaptation of Tennyson's *Enoch Arden* about a man marooned on an island. In one scene Griffith filled the screen with the face of Annie Lee brooding about her long-lost husband and immediately after cut to her husband alone on the island. The combination of the intimate close-up and quick cut across the ocean shocked the early cinema audiences, but the scene was effective and illustrated how to create new distances and the emotions suggested by them. In 1916 Hugo Münsterberg interpreted the close-up as a device of the cinema to recreate the way the mind selects important objects and fixes on them. If a camera points out that a locket is hung on the neck of a stolen child, it is not necessary to tell the audience that everything will hinge on it when the girl grows up. The close-up increased the size and significance of certain objects, made the audience feel closer to them, and gave film makers one more technique to render the varying lived distances of experience.

Chapter 4

Walter A. McDougall

TECHNOCRACY AND STATECRAFT IN THE SPACE AGE

THE "SPACE AGE," born with the first artificial earth satellites in the autumn of 1957, is already twenty-five years old. The origins of space technology have passed into contemporary history even as the Space Shuttle, the European rocket *Ariane*, permanent Soviet space stations, and the prospect of space-based laser weapons open a second Space Age of ineffable potential. What is the Space Age? Did *Sputnik I* mark the beginning of a distinct period in the history of human institutions and collective behavior? These questions matter at a moment in history when our societies, politics, economies, and diplomacy are wrenched by perpetual technological revolution.

The prima facie case is impressive for marking the technological turning point of the mid-twentieth century at the birth of the Space Age. The first Sputniks seemed to overturn the foundations of the post-World War II international order. They promised imminent Soviet strategic parity, placed the United States under direct military threat for the first time since 1814, triggered a quantum jump in the arms race, and undermined the calculus on which European, Chinese, and neutralist relations with the superpowers had been based. The space and missile challenge was then mediated by massive state-sponsored complexes for research and development, in the United States and throughout the industrial world, into institutionalized technological revolution and, hence, accelerating social, economic, and perhaps cultural change. Space technology altered the very proportions of human power to the natural environment in a way unparalleled since the spread of the railroads. Machines can now travel, deal destruction, store and transmit information, observe and analyze the earth and universe at orders of magnitude beyond what was possible before 1957. Virtually every field of natural science has leapt forward or been transformed on the strength of space-based experimentation and data. Sputnik would seem to qualify as a historical catalyst.

Has similar distinctly Space Age change occurred in domestic and international politics? The explosion of science and technology and its impact on society in the

From Walter A. McDougall, "Technology and Statecraft in the Space Age: Toward the History of a Saltation," *American Historical Review*, vol. 87, no. 4 (October 1982), pp. 1010–11, 1023, 1037–40.

1960s inspired numerous suggestions that this was so. John K. Galbraith and Daniel Bell wrote of the postindustrial age, Charles S. Maier of an age in which intense political exploitation of collective human thought replaced that of raw materials and labor. Even Soviet theorists adopted the phrase "scientific and technological revolution" as a stock description of the post-Sputnik world, in which capitalism itself altered its laws and Leninist doctrine was modified to include science as a "direct productive force." The four realms most often cited as the loci of revolutionary change in the Space Age are (1) international politics, (2) the political role of science and scientists, (3) the relationship of the state to technological change, and (4) political culture and values in nations of high technology. This essay describes the literature on the impact of space technology in these four realms and proposes some hypotheses for future inquiry. Its findings suggest that those who speak of the revolutionary consequences of space and related technologies and those who belittle their impact both exaggerate the reality. For the history of the relationship of politics and technology is evolutionary. Since the 1860s governments have steadily increased their interest in the direct fostering of scientific and technological progress. But within that evolution Sputnik triggered an abrupt discontinuity, a saltation that transformed governments into self-conscious promoters, not just of technological change but of perpetual technological revolution. This change above all defines the Space Age as a historical period and helps explain what most alert undergraduates would attest: that history, in our times, is speeding up. [. . .]

"The horror of the twentieth century," wrote Norman Mailer, "was the size of each new event, and the paucity of its reverberation." *Sputnik I* was truly the shot heard 'round the world and its international effects were manifold; but it did not alter the nature of the international system. The national state remained supreme, cooperation remained a muted form of competition, and military rivalry incorporated the strategic canopy of orbital space. The international imperative stimulated the rapid development of space technology, but it was not in turn transformed by it. When President Johnson, for instance, sent to world heads of state in December 1968 the famous photograph from *Apollo 8* of the gorgeous blue earth rising beyond the rim of the moon, "There came a response from Hanoi, from Ho Chi Minh, thanking me." Surely, wrote Arthur C. Clarke, this was the best example "of the way space can put our present tribal squabbles in their true perspective." Perhaps – but the war continued unabated. [. . .]

There *is* such a thing as the Space Age – defined by the discontinuous leap in public stimulation and direction of research and development. Its ramifications have only just begun and they are already obliging us to set aside categories of political and economic history that have served more or less effectively for the whole industrial age. But have these phenomena and the existence and promise of ever more futuristic technology altered the bedrock of cultural values among nations? Is the advent of space flight capable, as Tsiolkovsky dreamed, of elevating mankind spiritually? Romantics after 1957 harbored such hopes. There was a certain symmetry in the notion that mankind's escape from the world itself must spawn a global self-consciousness, just as the Age of Discovery sharpened the self-consciousness and self-criticism (as well as hubris) of Europeans. But if space technology permitted some to visualize Spaceship Earth, it led others to see the enemy of cultural values in technology itself. Jacques Ellul argued that technology had so far advanced that politics, economics, and art were not influenced by technique but rather were *situated in* a technical milieu, while a technological morality had long since supplanted inherited values. Space technology is an effervescence of the larger milieu that pre-exists and conditions its relation to modern culture.

Lewis Mumford judged space exploration to be "technological exhibitionism" and the latest expression of the "myth of the machine" that has dominated Western civilization since the twelfth century. Embalming astronauts in an artificial skin and blasting them into infinite vacuums in a skyscraper-tall rocket was for him the analogue to pyramid-building in ancient Egypt. Sociologist Amitai Etzioni also interpreted space technology as the expression of an already flawed society: "Americans are apparently psychologically unready for peaceful coexistence and need to best the U.S.S.R. in everything," while the gigantic instruments that this adolescent insecurity demands only "serve those who seek to preserve the America of yesterday as it is confronted with the problems of tomorrow." For Norman Mailer the American space program belonged to "odorless WASPs," "the most Faustian, barbaric draconian, progress-oriented, root-destroying people on earth." The machine had become art, the astronauts plastic men; and NASA's dubious accomplishment was "to make the moon boring." But Mailer equivocated. "For the first time in history a bureaucracy had committed itself to a surrealistic adventure." He vilified his own abominable army that debauched and dropped out while "they," with cool discipline, "have taken the moon."

These attacks could be matched with enthusiastic affirmations of the space effort and technological revolution from Buckminster Fuller, Krafft Ehricke, James Michener, and others. But whether positive or negative, such comments fall into two groups depending on whether their authors have interpreted the headlong flight of technology in our time as an outside force challenging and perhaps threatening historic culture or as the expression and fulfillment of culture, at least in the West. Is there a process of technological change that operates independently of value systems that would help to explain why Europeans came to explore the world and launch industrialism, or, indeed, why Chinese, Japanese, and Indians are now in such a hurry to get into space? Did Great Britain already have to be a "modern industrial culture" in some way for the factory system to spread, or did the spread of industry help change dominant British values?

We tend instinctively to assume that technological progress is a function of national values. Industrialism is somehow "Western" and the Apollo program very "American." But it is at least possible that our initial impulse is misleading. We also tend to assume that governments devise strategy by identifying their interests abroad and then marshaling the forces required to defend them. In fact, national interests are themselves a function of power – they observedly grow and shrink along with the power potential, not vice versa. Similarly, the values of a given society may be in part a function of that society's power over its environment. Did the apparent power of command technology help to shape social values in the early Space Age? Or did the political decisions giving birth to the Space Age express something deeper and older than Sputnik, NASA, or the Cold War? Must the United States already have been "The Republic of Technology" of Daniel Boorstin's title, or the schizoid cult of hero and machine of John William Ward's intuition of the meaning of Lindbergh's flight, for the space technological revolution to have occurred? Have our inherited values, material or transcendental, fed the geometric expansion of power? And if not, if our once-sovereign culture has become trapped within [Jacques] Ellul's technical milieu, then how did this metamorphosis come about?

In 1957, post-Sputnik American editorials drifted naturally between jeremiads and lamentations of lost technical supremacy. Ten years later the following was overhead at a State Department dinner: "All inventions for a long time will be made in the U.S. because we are moving so fast in technology, and large-scale, organized efforts produce inventions." The eavesdropper was James Webb; the speaker "a Mr. Brzezinski." What had intervened to change a nation's mood was the space technological revolution. Our technological civilization has evolved for centuries. But the international rivalries of our age, culminating in Sputnik, induced a saltation in the politics of technology through the transformation of the state into an active, all-out promoter of technological progress. Alexander Gerschenkron theorized that the more economically backward a country, the more the state must play a role in forcing change. In the current age of perpetual and rapid progress, *all* states have become "backward" on a permanent basis. Hence, the institutionalization of wartime "emergency methods," the permanent suspension of "peacetime" values, the blurring of distinctions between the state and private institutions, and the apparent erosion of cultural differences around the world. History *is* speeding up, and the leading nations justify their ever-accelerating pace of innovation by the need to maintain military and economic security. Yet that very progress may, at times, undermine the values that make a society worth defending in the first place. This, succinctly stated, is the dilemma of the Space Age.

One is tempted to conclude that the creation and use of still more power as a solution to human problems is as vain as the effort of the American tourist to make his English understood by steadily raising his voice. "The worship of technology," wrote William C. Davidson after Sputnik, "has reduced the differences between totalitarian countries and those where human worth and dignity might be expected to find more devoted champions." The fallacy of the early Space Age was that the pursuit of power, especially through science and technology, could absolve modern man from his duty to examine, affirm, or alter his own values and behavior in the first place. The politicians climbed aboard. It was left to Wernher von Braun to admonish "that man raise his ethical standards or perish."

PART III

The information revolution

INFORMATION GATHERING and dissemination are among humans' oldest preoccupations. This is because information is essential to an individual's daily living, but also because, as the saying goes, "knowledge is power." Those with knowledge become experts, sages, even "philosopher kings." For that very reason, those with knowledge and power sometimes seek to control the flow of information. The state, ancient or modern, has funded research, regulated educational systems, and controlled the dissemination of what is considered to be sensitive information, such as military and intelligence data. Subjects and citizens, on their part, have insisted on the right to know.

Information technology was qualitatively transformed after the 1970s, as exemplified by the spreading use of the internet, and new challenges arose to sharing or controlling information. The two essays that follow indicate these aspects of the "information revolution."

Pierre Lévy (Professor of Cyberculture and Social Communication at the University of Quebec) gives a brief history of computer technology after the Second World War and discusses its social and cultural implications.

Monroe Price (Professor of Law at Yeshiva University) adds his perspective by examining how "media globalization" has affected the flow of information throughout the world.

As these essays suggest, the information revolution is a fundamental aspect of global history. The global economy, for instance, cannot function without the instantaneous exchange of information on goods, capital, labor, and markets across national boundaries. Expanding information networks create new social relations that may challenge traditional societies. Or the easy dissemination of information may affect the ways in which wars are fought and terrorist acts organized and carried out. The disparity (the "digital divide") between societies that are capable of utilizing new information technology and those that fall behind might create a serious division in the world. On the other hand, the global dissemination of knowledge through international organizations may create a sense of shared values across nations. No matter how one looks at it, information provides an essential key to understanding the global age.

Chapter 5

Pierre Lévy

CYBERCULTURE

The emergence of cyberspace

THE FIRST COMPUTERS (preprogrammed calculators) appeared in England and the United States in 1945. Initially they were used solely by the military to perform scientific calculations, but civil use expanded throughout the 1960s. Even at this time it was clear that the performance of computer hardware would increase at a steady pace. Yet aside from a handful of visionaries, no one at the time suspected that a general movement toward the virtualization of information would so profoundly affect the fundamental data of social life. Computers were still big calculators, fragile, isolated in refrigerator rooms, into which scientists in white smocks fed punched cards and out of which unreadable lists of data were periodically disgorged. Computer technology was used for scientific calculations, government and business statistics, and large-scale administrative functions (payroll, accounting, etc.).

The turning point occurred during the 1970s. The development and commercialization of the microprocessor (a device for performing logical and arithmetic calculations, lodged on a single small electronic chip) triggered several large-scale economic and social processes. The 1970s gave rise to a new phase of industrial development – robotics, flexible manufacturing cells, numerically controlled machine tools – and saw automation introduced for the first time in the service industries (banking, insurance). Since then the systematic search for productivity gains through the use of electronic devices, computers, and communications networks has gradually taken over all economic activities. This trend continues to this day.

At the same time, a new social movement was taking shape in California. Fed by the ferment of the counterculture, it embarked on the new technological developments and gave rise to the personal computer. From then on, the computer would gradually begin to escape the grasp of business information services and professional

From Pierre Lévy, *Cyberculture* (trans. Robert Bononno) (Minneapolis and London: University of Minnesota Press, 2001), pp. 13–26.

programmers to become an instrument of creation (texts, images, music), organization (databases and spreadsheets), simulation (spreadsheets, decision-making tools, research software), and entertainment (games) in the hands of an ever larger proportion of the population of the developed countries.

During the 1980s, the contemporary horizon of multimedia took shape. Slowly, computer science lost its technological and industrial aspect and began to merge with telecommunications, publishing, cinema, and television. Digitization first became commonplace in music production and recording, but microprocessors and computer memory soon became an integral part of the infrastructure of every field of communications. New kinds of "interactive" messages began to appear: The decade witnessed the arrival of video games, the triumph of user-friendly computing (graphical interfaces and sensorimotor interactions), and the appearance of hyperdocuments (hypertext, CD-ROM).

Toward the end of the 1980s and the beginning of the 1990s, a new social and cultural movement made up of young professionals in large cities and college campuses across America quickly spread throughout the world. Although there was no central controlling body, the various computer networks that had come into existence since the end of the 1970s were joined together, and the number of people and computers connected to this internetwork began to grow exponentially. As with the creation of the personal computer, a spontaneous and unforeseeable cultural current imposed a new direction on technical and economic development. Digital technologies became the infrastructure of cyberspace. The new space served as the locus of communication, sociability, organization, and transaction, as well as a new market for the exchange of information and knowledge.

In this context, technology in and of itself is not very interesting. It is, however, important to outline the major trends in the evolution of contemporary technology before examining the social and cultural mutations that accompany it. Perhaps the most important element in this scenario is the exponential increase in hardware performance (computation speed, storage capacity, bandwidth) combined with continuously dropping prices. At the same time, software has benefited from the conceptual and theoretical improvements that have accompanied the increase in hardware performance. Today software publishers are committed to constructing a work and communications environment that is increasingly transparent and user-friendly.

Projections regarding the social uses of the virtual must incorporate this continuous trend toward ever greater performance, lower cost, and increasing popularity. There is every reason to believe that these three trends will continue in the future. Still, it is impossible to predict the qualitative changes that will accompany these movements or the way in which society will incorporate or inflect them; for at this point, conflict may occur among divergent projects, in which technological, economic, and social forces are indissolubly mixed.

Processing

Information technology encompasses all the technologies that are used to digitize information (input), store it (memory), process it automatically, transport it, and put it at the disposal of an end user, whether human or machine (output). These distinctions are conceptual. The actual hardware and components always combine several functions.

Information-processing units, or processors, which reside on "chips," perform arithmetic and logic calculations on data. They carry out at high speed, and in a highly repetitive fashion, a small number of very simple operations on digitally encoded information. From tubes to transistors, from transistors to integrated circuits, from integrated circuits to microprocessors, extremely rapid advances in information processing have benefited from improvements in circuit architecture, progress in electronics and physics, and applied research on materials. Each year processors become smaller, more powerful, more reliable, and less expensive. This progress, as in the case of computer storage, has been exponential. For example, Moore's law (which has been confirmed over the past twenty-five years) predicts that technological developments will double the number of elementary logical operators on a microprocessor every eighteen months. This results in an almost linear increase in speed and computational power. To illustrate the rate of such growth, consider that the power of today's largest supercomputers will be found in affordable personal computers within ten years.

Storage

Computerized data are generally held in various kinds of storage *media*. Digitized information can be stored on punched cards, magnetic tape, magnetic disks, optical disks, electronic circuits, smart cards, and the biological media. Since the origin of computer technology, storage has evolved toward ever greater capacity, access speed, and reliability as costs have continued to drop.

Progress in computer storage, like that of microprocessors, has been exponential; the space occupied by an 18 MB hard drive on a personal computer in 1983 could hold 10 GB of information in 1993, a thousand-fold increase. This rate of growth has lasted for the past thirty years and looks like it will continue until at least 2010 (the foreseeable horizon).

Between 1956 and 1996, the storage capacity of computer hard drives increased six hundred times, and the density of recorded information by a factor of 720,000. During this same period, the cost of a megabyte of storage dropped from approximately ten thousand dollars to forty cents.

Storage technologies use highly varied materials and processes. Future discoveries in physics and biotechnology, which are actively being pursued in a number of laboratories, may result in advances that are currently unimaginable.

Transmission

Digitized information can be transmitted over almost any imaginable communications channel. Media (disks, diskettes, etc.) can be physically transported by road, rail, boat, or air. But direct, that is, networked, or on-line, connections are obviously faster. Information can be transmitted over conventional phone lines providing it is modulated (using the appropriate analog encoding) when it travels over the telephone network and demodulated (redigitized) when it arrives at a computer or other digital device at the end of the wire. The device that is used to modulate and demodulate digitized information and thus enables communication to take place between computers is called a *modem*. Large, expensive, and slow during the 1970s, since the mid-1990s modems have had a transmission capacity that is greater than that of the average user's telephone line. Now common, modems have been miniaturized and are often integrated in computers in the form of cards or printed circuits.

Information can travel unchanged in digital form over copper coaxial cable, fiber-optic cable, radio waves (electromagnetic waves), or, in the case of the telephone network, by means of telecommunications satellite.

Advances in transmission speed (throughput and reliability) depend on several factors. The first is raw transmission capacity. Here the improvements brought about through the introduction of fiber optics have been spectacular. Research is currently under way in a number of labs on the use of "dark fiber," an optical channel in which a single strand, as fine as a human hair, can handle the US telephone system's entire data stream on Mother's Day (when network usage is highest for the year). Hardware that uses this black fiber would provide a thousand times the current broadcast transmission capacity throughout the entire frequency spectrum.

The second is the capacity to compress and decompress information. Currently, sound and video information consume the greatest amount of bandwidth and storage capacity. Some software programs or compression chips can analyze audio and video, simplifying or isolating the most salient parts of the message, which can be several thousand times smaller than in its original digital form. At the other end of the transmission channel, a decompression module regenerates the audio or video from the description it receives, minimizing the loss of information. By compressing and decompressing messages, we transfer part of the problem inherent in transmission (and storage) to the processing unit, which is becoming faster and cheaper.

The third is the advance in the overall architecture of communications systems. Here the greatest progress has been made in the expanded use of packet switching. Such a decentralized architecture, in which every node in the network is "intelligent," was conceived at the end of the 1950s as a response to the threat of nuclear war. However, full-scale experiments weren't conducted in the United States until the end of the 1960s. With packet switching, messages are cut into small units of equal size, called packets, each of which is provided with a source address, destination address, and position in the complete message. Routers, distributed throughout the network, are able to tread and forward this information. The network can be physically heterogeneous (cables, radio waves, satellites, etc.); routers need only to know how to read the packet addresses and speak the same "language" with one another. If information is lost at some point, routers can request that the missing packets be present. At regular intervals, routers gather information about the state of the network. If there are problems – damage, faults, congestion – packets can take any of a number of different paths, before being assembled at their ultimate destination. This system is particularly resistant to problems on the network because it is decentralized and its intelligence "distributed." As of 1997 it was operational only on certain specialized networks (notably the Internet backbone), but an international communications standard known as Asynchronous Transfer Mode (ATM), which is consistent with packet switching, has been adopted by the International Telecommunications Union (ITU). In the future, ATM will be used for all telecommunications networks and may lead to the use of broadband digital multimedia communication.

We can get some idea of the progress that has been made in transmission speeds from the following figures. Throughout the 1970s, Arpanet (the Internet's predecessor) in the United States could support speeds of 56,000 bits per second. During the 1980s, the network cables used to connect American scientists could transmit 1.5 million bits per second. In 1992 data channels on the same network were able to transmit 45 million bits per second (one encyclopedia every minute). Current research foresees the construction of networks with a bandwidth of several hundred billion bits a second (a large library every minute).

Interfaces

An interface is any device that enables interaction between the universe of digitized information and the ordinary world. Input devices capture and digitize information for further processing. Until the 1970s, the majority of computers were supplied data in the form of boxes of punched cards. Since then we have expanded the possibility of capturing bodily movement and various physical data *directly*: keyboards to enter text and send instructions, mice for manipulating information on computer screens, touch screens, sound samplers, speech recognition software, scanners for images and text, optical readers (bar codes or other information), automatic sensors (data gloves and suits) for capturing the movements of the body, the eyes, brain waves, and nervous system (used in prostheses), sensors for a wide variety of physical measurements, including heat, humidity, light, weight, and chemical properties.

After they have been stored, processed, and transmitted in digital form, abstract models are made visible, descriptions of images are given shape and color, sounds ring through the air, text can be printed on paper or read on-screen, and automations controlled by means of actuators. The quality of the display, or *output*, medium is obviously critical for users of computer systems and, to a large extent, conditions their practical and commercial success. Until the 1970s, most computers had no monitors. The first computer screens could display only monochrome characters (numbers and letters). Today ultraflat color liquid crystal screens are available, and developments are under way to sell systems that can display images in three dimensions.

The evolution of output interfaces has been accompanied by greater resolution and diversification in the modes of communicating information. Aside from the quality of screen graphics, the quality of printed text and graphics has advanced considerably in less than ten years, erasing the distinction between printed text and manuscript and transforming our relationship to the printed document. Most loudspeakers today play music that is stored (and often produced) in digital format, and considerable progress has been made in the field of speech recognition. There have also been improvements in tactile and pro-prioceptive technologies: force feedback on game controllers, joysticks, and other manual controls; the very sensation of smoothness or roughness has helped to enhance the illusion of reality when interacting with virtual worlds.

Two separate research paths are being conducted in parallel for the development of interfaces. One focuses on the immersion of the five senses in increasingly realistic virtual worlds. Virtual reality is used primarily for military, industrial, medical, and urban planning applications. Here the human is asked to cross over to the other side of the screen and interact physically with digital models. The other, known as "augmented reality," populates our natural physical environment with sensors, cameras, video screens, and interconnected intelligent modules. We no longer communicate with a computer by means of an interface but carry out a multitude of tasks within a "natural" environment that supplies us with the various resources for creativity, information, and communication.

Most communications devices (telephones, televisions, photocopiers, fax machines, etc.) contain, in one form or another, an interface with the digital world through which they are interconnected. This is equally true of a growing number of machines, measurement devices, so-called mobile objects (personal digital assistants, cellular phones, etc.), personal transportation vehicles, and so forth. The diversification and miniaturization of interfaces, combined with progress in digitization, are converging toward an extension and multiplication of the number of entry points to cyberspace. [. . .]

Programming

Cyberspace doesn't consist only of hardware, data, and human beings; it is also populated with strange beings, half text, half machine, half actor, half script, known as programs. A program, or software application, is a well-organized series of coded instructions designed to accomplish a particular task on one or more processors. [. . .]

Programs are written in programming languages, which are specially encoded using the instructions that are understood by computer processors. There are a large number of programming languages in existence, each of which is more or less specialized in a certain task. Since the beginning of the computer age, engineers, mathematicians, and linguists have been working to make programming languages more and more like natural language. We distinguish between the esoteric programming languages that are very close to the physical structure of the computer (machine languages, assembly language) and "advanced" languages, which are less dependent on the structure of the hardware and closer to English. These languages include FORTRAN, Lisp, Pascal, Prolog, C, and others. Today some so-called fourth-generation languages can be used to design programs by drawing diagrams and manipulating icons on screen. Companies supply software building blocks that are ready for assembly. In this way, the programmer spends less time coding and more time designing the overall software architecture. Authoring languages enable nonspecialists to perform simple programming tasks and to design multimedia databases and educational software.

Software

Software applications are used by computers to provide specific services to users. I'll give a few canonical examples. Some software programs can automatically calculate employee payrolls for a company; others can prepare customer invoices, manage inventory, and operate machines in real time based on information supplied by sensors. Expert systems can determine the causes of a failure or supply financial advice. As the name indicates, word processors are used to write, modify, and organize texts.

Spreadsheets display columns of numbers, can be used for accounting, and help us make budget decisions. A database manager can be used to enter data in files and retrieve pertinent information based on various input keys, presenting the information to the user from a given point of view depending on need. Drawing software can be used to produce flawless diagrams almost effortlessly. Communications software enables us to send messages and access information stored on other computers. Application software is becoming increasingly open to the personalization of features, without requiring that users learn programming.

Operating systems are programs that manage computer resources (memory, input, output, etc.) and organize the interface between hardware and application software. This application software is not therefore in direct contact with the hardware. Because of this, the same software application can run on different hardware platforms, providing they use the same operating system.

Although not all data are programs, all programs can be considered data: They can be input, archived, and read by computers. And in particular, they can themselves be calculated, translated, modified, or simulated by other programs. Because a program can replace a collection of data that is being translated or processed by another program, successive software layers can exist between the hardware and the end user. The end user communicates directly with the topmost layer and doesn't need to understand the complexity underlying the application he or she is manipulating or the heterogeneity of the network on which he or she is transferring data. In general, the greater the number of software layers, the more the network is "transparent," and the easier it is for us to accomplish human tasks.

From the computer to cyberspace

Today we can freely navigate between software and hardware that was formerly incompatible. Through the adoption of software and hardware standards, the general trend has been toward the development of autonomous virtual spaces for work and communication, increasingly independent of physical media. There has also been an increasing use of standards for describing the structure of text (Standard Generalized Markup Language, or SGML) or multimedia (Hypertext Markup Language, or HTML, HiTime) documents, which enable us to retain information intact in spite of changes in software and hardware. The VRML standard can be used to explore interactive three-dimensional images on the World Wide Web from any machine connected to the network. The increasing use of the VRML standard presages the interconnection of virtual worlds that can be accessed on the Internet and expands the boundaries of a cyberspace that is similar to an immense heterogeneous virtual metaworld undergoing continuous transformation and containing all other virtual worlds.

Long polarized by the "machine," balkanized by software, contemporary information technology – software and hardware – deconstructs the computer and promotes a navigable and transparent communications space based on information. A computer is a particular assemblage of units for processing, transmission, and storage, and interfaces for information input and output. Yet different brands of computer can be assembled from nearly identical components, and computers from the same company can contain parts from very different sources. Moreover, hardware components (sensors, memory, processors, etc.) can be found outside actual computers: smart cards, automatic distributors, robots, motors, household appliances, automobiles, photocopiers, facsimile machines, video cameras, telephones, radios, televisions, and even the nodes of the communications network [. . .] anywhere digital information is automatically processed. A computer connected to cyberspace can use the storage capacity and processing power of other computers on the network (which do the same), as well as remote devices for capturing and displaying information. All computer functions are distributable and, to an ever increasing extent, distributed. The computer is no longer a center but a node, a terminal, a component of the universal computing network. Its atomized functions impregnate every element of the technocosm. Eventually there will be only a single computer, but it will be impossible to locate its boundaries or determine its contour. Its center will be everywhere, and its circumference nowhere. This hypertext computer will be dispersed, living, pullulating, incomplete: cyberspace itself.

Chapter 6

Monroe Price

THE GLOBAL INFORMATION
REVOLUTION AND STATE POWER

IT IS HARDLY NEWS that global information space is being transformed, media structures altered, and the role of the state, simultaneously, redefined. Information, it is said to the point of cliché, is power, and, in an information society, it is a considerable and increasing source of power. While law has been used in the past to protect internal producers of national identity from external competition, the effectiveness of law to achieve that protective umbrella is now under question.

For most of the century, the international order assumed that radio transmissions should be contained primarily within the boundaries so as to assure that these conditions of market division were met and enforced. Over the twentieth century, international regulations and arrangements were built to reinforce the national impulse and to limit broadcasting to indigenous transmissions of good quality within the frontiers of the country concerned. Now, however, the structure of information distribution within a state is so important that other states seek to affect it. That has always been true, to some extent, but expanded trade concerns and global security make it a priority. Economists, political scientists, scholars of cultural studies, and others have all made valuable contributions to a systematic understanding of this process. My effort here is to adapt or suggest several approaches that have not been brought together in the literature of media globalization.

Market for loyalties

I start with an approach I developed in an earlier book, *Television, the Public Sphere, and National Identity*. There I identified a "market for loyalties," in which large-scale competitors for power, in a shuffle for allegiances, use the regulation of communications to organize a cartel of imagery and identity among themselves. Government is usually the mechanism that allows the cartel to operate and is often part of the cartel itself. This market produces "national identity" or "community," to use the

From Monroe Price, *Media and Sovereignty: The Global Information Revolution and Its Challenge to State Power* (MIT Press, 2002), pp. 31–40.

less discriminating Americanism. Management of the market yields the collection of ideas and narratives employed by a dominant group or coalition to maintain power. For that reason alone, control over participation in the market has been, for many countries, a condition of political stability. This market, I contended, has existed everywhere and at all times. What differs in today's market is the range of participants, the scope of its boundaries, and the nature of the regulatory bodies capable of establishing and enforcing rules for participation and exclusion.

The "sellers" in this market are all those for whom myths and dreams and history can somehow be converted into power and wealth – classically states, governments, interest groups, businesses, and others. The "buyers" are the citizens, subjects, nationals, consumers – recipients of the packages of information, propaganda, adver-tisements, drama, and news propounded by the media. The consumer "pays" for one set of identities or another in several ways that, together, we call "loyalty" or "citizenship." Payment, however, is not expressed in the ordinary coin of the realm: It includes not only compliance with tax obligations, but also obedience to laws, readiness to fight in the armed services, or even continued residence within the country. The buyer also pays with his or her own sense of identity.

It is easier to understand the functioning of such a market for loyalties in the traditional context of a single state. One can make the general and expansive claim that much domestic broadcast regulation is an effort, within a society, to maintain or adjust the distribution of power among those who are dominant, with due recog-nition for subsidiary groups. While such legislation is often justified as a means of preserving or strengthening national identity, national identity can be reframed as essentially the set of political views and cultural attitudes that help maintain the existing power structure. Certainly that is often the operational goal (though hardly ever explicitly) of those in control. I have suggested that while there were several ways to define "national identity," including a discovery of the "true" or "historic" national identity of a state, this slightly cynical definition (the construction of the identity by the power structure so as to maintain its power) enhances our under-standing of media legislation by providing an underlying analytic explanation. If familiar regulation of domestic media can be seen, at least in part, as the use of law to reinforce or adjust a political status quo, then much of contemporary national response to media globalization may have a similar explanation. Reregulation or the incentive to change media law and policy occurs, within a state, when the cartel of political allegiances can no longer maintain its position of civil dominance. In that sense the pressures of globalization lead to changes in domestic media laws and structures if either (1) existing domestic broadcasting laws are inadequate at protecting the cartel, or (2) national identity is changing or has changed and legis-lation is necessary to be more inclusive, to legitimate new players, and to protect them, in turn, against unregulated challenge.

Media globalization and new information technologies yield a crisis of domestic law and policy if barriers to entry are lowered for those excluded from the old political cartel, especially if the new entrants could be threats to the control of the *ancien régime*. In response, a government can either redefine the cartel and accommodate new entrants or take effective steps, through law or force, to try to raise the barriers to entry again. "Failed states" or states made to fail by force (Taliban-led Afghanistan, for example) lose control over their media space as force is exerted against them. External entities (corporations, states, and diasporic groups) also participate in the market for loyalties when they advocate the use of technology or international norms to force a state to enlarge the membership of a local cartel.

Media globalization also fosters the reinforcement of power across national lines and the development of international agreements to render new organizations of identity effective. A competition emerges among those who supply different ideologies for command of large-scale sectors. For example, an international cartel could, as a means of shaping a transnational market for loyalties, establish a set of rules on a global level or encourage or impose a set of rules favoring its "products" in the bosom of a significant group of states. Tacit or explicit arrangements among states, or between states and multinational corporates or nongovernment organizations (NGOs), may be designed to affect the nature of a global market in cultural and political attitudes and facilitate the predominance of one ideology or another. Thus, while the apparent determinant of the relationship between regulation and control remains the nation-state, communication avenues in any given state would increasingly be a matter of international action, justified under the aegis of stability, trade, and human rights.

International norms like Article 19 of the Universal Declaration of Human Rights, domestic constitutional rules like the First Amendment in the United States, and regional constraints like the European Convention on Human Rights and the Television without Frontiers Directive in the European Union have a special role in limiting the cartelization of the market for loyalties. These provisions are usually considered curbs on the power of local political cartels to use law and regulation to screen out voices that seek to alter the current power structure, and especially those who seek to use broadcasting despite its power to force such change. Increasingly these norms are used swordlike by those external to the state, often NGOs and media corporations with existing global power, to encourage a more favorable legal regime within a state. To be sure, such expansion often serves the honorable principle of the right to receive and impart information, but it is about the extension of power and influence as well. Less clear is the existence or role of international norms where, in times of conflict, external efforts seek to erase media power in a target state, such as in the Palestinian Authority, Milosevic-controlled former Yugoslavia, or in Afghanistan under the Taliban.

The structure of broadcasting is related to current views on federalism and relative autonomy. In Europe, where there is an effort to build stateless-nations like Catalonia and Scotland, broadcasting policy will, over time, reflect political adjustments. Systems that have been tightly ordered from the center with state control of access to images, state-determined language of the media, and subsidization of emblems of unity will give way to more decentralized methods. In the United Kingdom, as Scottish and Welsh broadcasting become fully autonomous, political devolution is accompanied by devolution in communications structures; Spain and other countries have followed a similar pattern.

The 1989 European Television without Frontiers Directive illustrates the evolution from the long-standing approach of exclusion based on national borders to a more common union that encourages free competition for identity, within the community of members, while seeking to regulate competition, even if mildly, from without. For reasons of trade and regional integration, the mix of information in each member state of the European Union became important to all other members.

In the GATT negotiations of 1994, the European Union did not lower the trade barriers in the film and television industries as in other industries on the grounds that a European cultural space ought to be preserved, strengthened, and protected from the so-called Hollywood influx. Canada, on the one hand, and Malaysia, on the other, are countries with very different traditions that seek to deploy law or utilize law in conjunction with the structure of the industry to control the relationship between images from abroad and from within. Canada does so in a rather open society; Malaysia does so in a society in which televised images from abroad have, traditionally, been tightly controlled.

One can look to other contexts to understand the interaction between globalism and the market for loyalties. Let me turn to the example of India, about which there is a verdant media literature. The effort to control media space domestically has, over the half century since Independence, been maintained through the state's monopoly on terrestrial broadcasting, more expansive a monopoly than in many other states that assert democratic traditions. The rise of foreign satellite channels, distributed by and large through relatively unregulated cable television systems, specifically threatened this enduring practice and possibly the political arrangements that depended on it. In 1997 a report of the Ministry of Information and Broadcasting summarized official views and decried the "adverse impact . . . on Indian values and culture" of the "large number of foreign satellite TV channels beaming their programs over Indian sky." Describing the early moments of the satellite invasion when he was minister of information, P. Unendra said, "A file was put up in the Ministry as to how to counter the satellite invasion. What steps should be taken to stop it? I wrote back saying you cannot stop the sun shining by holding an umbrella. The more you try, the more you encourage people to watch."

Long preoccupied by concerns over the consequences of what might be called an "unbridled" press or a press controlled by entities not, in the historic view, sensitive to the complexities of local conditions, successive governments opposed Western broadcasting influences. India has seen itself as frequently subject to significant security threats from Pakistan (and vice versa). During the 1999 conflict with Pakistan over incursions in Kashmir, the minister of information issued a ban on broadcasting the signal of Pakistan-TV by cable television services on the grounds that India's opponent was spreading misinformation that might lead to disunity within the state. During the same period, Videsh Sanchar Nigam Limited (VSNL), then virtually a monopoly Internet service provider, removed *Dawn*, the Islamabad-based daily, from distribution, probably at the behest of the government. Even after the ban on Pakistan-TV was lifted, the government's right to impose such a ban was generally accepted.

Section 10 of India's draft Broadcast Bill of 1997 embraced a list of concerns that reflected India's history and security consciousness. In a relatively standard list of prohibitions, the statute provided that any license, terrestrial or satellite, would be obliged to ensure that programming would not "offend against good taste or decency." There would be a prohibition on programs "likely to encourage or incite to crime or to lead to disorder or to be offensive to public feeling." Similarly the draft statute included standards requiring that programs reflect India's history and demography. Religious programs were to avoid "improper exploitation of religious susceptibilities" or offending "the religious views and beliefs of those belonging to a particular religion or religious denomination." Statutory standards would require that "due emphasis [be] given . . . to promote values of national integration, religious harmony, scientific temper and Indian culture." Officials were still smarting from fears that international dissension and communal violence might become a significant problem if uncontrolled signals such as news coverage by the BBC, not subject to national censorship, are allowed.

These are a few fragments from a rich history in India. Restraint and restriction are based on the idea of maintaining a democratic state at a time of centripetal forces: national security needs, fears of internal violence because of religious strife, the need to protect morals from forces that endanger cultural traditions, and the need to use media for the balance between the notion of India as a whole and its several parts. The range of justifications for excluding certain entrants into the market is almost as broad as exists anywhere. The prior and existing regime structures reflect the regime's historic ties with Britain and India's periods of neutrality and socialism. The centralized structure and belief in a nation-building purpose in Indian broadcasting demonstrate its British colonial origins. The ideas of control and belief in the instrumentality of the communications system emulate characteristics of socialist neutrality.

Now, internal norms are used by external players to change the mix of voices. A kind of "triumph of capitalism" element characterizes attitudes toward entry, competition, and growth. Human rights ideals have played a part in this trend, specifically in a significant Supreme Court decision that initiated a wholesale review of India's broadcasting laws. Negotiations between Pakistan and India undoubtedly touch on information aspects of conflict and coexistence. Throughout, regulation reflects sensitivity to the relationship between power and the perceived threat of information and images to the maintenance of power. Restraints that control access from groups within the country give way to efforts to restrain, condition, and cushion images and information that come from Pakistan and abroad.

Turkey also provides a dramatic example of the effort to maintain control over competition in the market of loyalties explicitly in the name of national identity. Since the rise of Kemal Ataturk, the Turkish government, at least until the mid-1990s, considered aspects of Islamic fundamentalism a threat to the secular state. Advocates of secularism, and certainly those in control of the state, sought to limit the use of the mass media by competitors for loyalty. The Turkish Radio and Television Authority (TRT) was not only monopolistic, it was in essence the voice of the state, disseminating the unitary ideology and culture of Turkish republicanism. It found itself highly susceptible to government intervention. Charged by statute with "promoting the values of country, unity, republic, public order, harmony, and welfare, and to strengthen the principles of Kemal Ataturk's reforms," TRT has been an instrument for cohesiveness in an environment riven by alternate national identities. When TRT was attacked for broadcasting programs that legitimated Islamic fundamentalism, the government forced the agency's director general to resign.

When threatening broadcasts of radical imams were transmitted by satellite from Germany to Turkey and potentially destabilizing Kurdish-oriented MED-TV broadcasts were transmitted from London to Belgium, the government responded with a variety of legal and political tools. The initial and strong responses included banning programs, regulating satellite dishes and intervening in the countries where the signals were uplinked. Then, however, Turkey took a rather different step.

Largely informally and with a wink of the law, Turkey permitted the expansion of domestic commercial signals, program services that were not threatening politically and often provided by those close to the dominant party. This response was to open the skies, but with much greater influence over what would come into the country.

In the global or regional market for loyalties, Turkey, understanding the importance of a mix of signals entering a country, organized satellite services directed at Turkish-affinity communities in Central Asia. A similar set of circumstances occurred when Turkey succeeded in arranging Turkish-originated programming on cable services in Germany and the Netherlands and other states that housed large numbers of the Turkish diaspora. [. . .] Turkey appealed to domestic and international norms to persuade other countries not to host satellite services aimed at its Kurdish population. Finally the government bolstered its own favored channels to compete for Kurdish favor.

As a way of showing how this process of controlling information or using law works, we can consider the regulation of advertising. In a market for loyalties, advocates for disparate national identities will predictably have different attitudes toward the use of ordinary commercial advertising on television and the kind of Western programming that accompanies it. The preoccupation that governments have long had with limiting advertising messages and excluding competition from commercial broadcasters suggests that the impact of programming on public allegiances yields a substitute for more traditional packages of identity. Advertising can persuade individuals to consume rather than to save and invest, with consequences for particular visions of the public good. In this sense marketers of pure national identities, ideologies that parade as such, compete with sellers of consumer goods, who are trying to impress the citizen with another identity. An individual must decide, at the margin, whether a higher or lower percentage of disposable income should go to the state (in taxes), for education or environmental protection (generosity), or, instead, for personal goods like food or television sets and automobiles. In a poor society, particularly, the impact of an individual's choice may not be measurable in money alone but in his or her contribution to a purer form of sheer human loyalty to the state.

The effect of advertising and of modern Western-style programming in the market for loyalties may, thus, support certain groups and disfavor others. Proponents of some identities recognize the indirect supporting role that the barrage of traditional commercials, for everything from orange juice to computers, might play in connection with their own narrations of future happiness. Parties advocating a more rapid transition to a marketplace economy in states ambitious to increase their gross national product may see the political benefits of a citizenry exposed to a culture of advertising and consumerism because they contain indirect or secondary messages of political significance.

As such, there are assertions of national identity in the interstices of commercials, in their depiction of idealized home life, opportunities to travel, or of a certain idea of traditional family values. "Free and independent media," because of their dependence on advertising, alter citizen priorities as between the state and consumerism. In transition societies, in developing societies, and in societies moving from reliance on public service broadcasting, the inclusion of advertising has cultural and political significance. The most avid proponents of free market television have, consistent with this position, argued that images of Western society, including

Western advertising, are entitled to some of the credit for the fall of the Berlin Wall and the collapse of the Soviet Union. The point here, of course, is not the truth of the claims about the impact of messages, but the perception of that impact and the rhetorical use of it in rendering markets more open or closed.

Advertising may be wholly laudable, it may be the underpinning of independence from state control, it may be liberating for the individual, but it has social and civil consequences. In an analysis that focuses on the state itself, one could say that if the images of consumer society are supportive of the party in power, that could be ground enough for their advocacy of an increase in advertiser-supported broadcasting. If a ruling coalition sees the images of advertising and the narratives of foreign programs as a threat to its continued hold on government, then the often-foreign images are characterized as subversive.

In global environments of negotiated images, the question of whether or how much advertising should be permitted or encouraged is translated into new terms. Advertising is part of a logic of sustainability. If media must be independent of state support in order to be free, then (generally) advertising is necessary for continued existence. Global advocacy of this logic of sustainability is prevalent, yet it contains often unexplained implications for local and general markets for loyalties. Whether a society is closed or open, part of the World Trade Organization or not, interested in the development of human potential or not – these questions themselves have been globalized. Rules about who can speak, who can shape media structures, or what messages course within the society – in short the profile of the market for loyalties – is now a matter for an expanding cartel of state and private interests operating on a more global level.

This argument from the "market for loyalties" approach [. . .] suggests that countries that are in similar geopolitical contexts will take similar approaches to preserving (or modifying) the domestic cartel and employ tools similar to those used elsewhere. Those in charge of the cartel of loyalties would want to find devices to place the power of destabilizing images in what are deemed safe hands. Safe hands might be local hands, corporate hands, or transnational hands; the question would generally be whether those hands are as non-threatening as possible. The rhetoric of broadcasting reform is, almost by definition and except in a few limited instances, different from the substance of broadcasting reform. Few modern and democratic governments or participants in policy making would articulate a policy of regulatory reform saying explicitly that it was designed to keep them in power. An authoritarian society with a monopoly on information that represents itself as an authoritarian society might have little difficulty marrying rhetoric to reality. Threats to the monopoly must be defeated and making that explicit may be part of the ideology of control.

Related to these strategies is the domestication of the global broadcasting entities. More than that, as implied above, some states may prefer global suppliers of news and information because they may be less threatening than home grown opposition channels. The critical theorists, Adorno and Horkheimer, pointed to the political impact of assembly-line, standardized entertainment, the arts, and education. Long before global television, they recognized that a vast industrialized culture industry could benefit a ruling class by separating the masses from critical perspectives and socialist ideas. Blue jeans may be subversive, but they can be less subversive, at least at their introduction in to public consciousness, than an indigenous, dissenting broadcasting regime clawing for increased influence in the society. A media space filled with commercials is thus often preferable, from the perspective of the status quo, to one crowded with opposing alternate identities (say, stations of Islamic fundamentalists in Egypt, Basque separatists in France, or Kurds in Turkey). Commercialization may, in the words of its critics, undermine historic cultures, but be seen as less subversive than destabilizing political messages. In this sense, at least in the short run, the gestation and entry of new and attractive commercial material provides powerful influences against which it may be difficult for competing national identities to emerge.

PART IV

Multinational enterprises

MULTINATIONAL ENTERPRISES, or business organizations that bring technology, capital, and labor from more than one country in order to produce goods and services, are a prominent feature of globalization. It should be recognized that internationalization of economic activities has long existed. International trade is a primary example; it takes advantage of geographical specialization and promotes exchanges of commodities across nations and regions. Moreover, it is possible to find examples from ancient Assyria, Phoenicia, Babylon, Greece, and elsewhere for activities of business people who went abroad and marketed their wares far and wide.

The modern global economy, in contrast, is characterized by organization of production across national boundaries, by the development of a truly global market, and by an international financial system. As Mira Wilkins (Professor of Economics at Florida International University) suggests, modern multinational enterprises had their origins in late eighteenth-century Europe, but a "highly integrated world economy" emerged only at the beginning of the twentieth century and began to penetrate domestic societies. Multinational enterprises became agents of cultural transformation.

A pertinent question in this connection will be the relationship between multinational enterprises and sovereign states. How has the internationalization of banking, manufacturing, and marketing affected national economic policies and priorities? William Keller (Director of the Ridgeway Center for International Security Studies) and Louis Pauly (Professor of Political Science at the University of Toronto) suggest that there always exists some basic tension between the two, while Wilkins points to instances where the state has severely affected the process of economic internationalization through expropriation, protectionism, and war.

Chapter 7

William W. Keller and
Louis W. Pauly

GLOBALIZATION AT BAY

WITHOUT STABLE POLITICAL foundations, markets collapse. Following years of depression and world war, the United States and its allies rebuilt an international economy around this insight. Fifty years later, however, multinational business is often viewed, by proponents and critics alike, as providing more solid foundations for a truly global economy than governments ever could. The common perception today is that political authorities have been relegated to the role of adapting themselves, as well as the societies over which they have receding control, to the convergent logic of an integrated, worldwide technology base, crafted largely by corporations that owe allegiance to no state.

We see things differently. Spreading the benefits of economic development and technological innovation is indeed necessary to make the world a more prosperous place. But the proliferation of multinational firms guarantees no such outcome. Despite intensifying international competition, sometimes accompanied by increases in market concentration, multinationals are not promoting an ineluctable convergence and integration of national systems of innovation, trade, and investment, nor are they forcing deep convergence in the national economies in which they are embedded. They cannot do so because they themselves are not fundamentally converging toward global norms of corporate behavior.

Surface similarities abound. Companies selling goods or services in the same markets do have much in common, and the range of cross-border mergers and acquisitions has broadened significantly in recent decades. But the most strategically important operations of multinationals continue to vary systematically along national lines. The global corporation, adrift from its national political moorings and roaming an increasingly borderless world market, is a myth. States charter multinationals and foster the operating environments in which they flourish. The governments of the states within which most of the world's leading multinationals are based retain the authority to tax, regulate, and otherwise influence business activities.

From William W. Keller and Louis W. Pauly, "Globalization at Bay," *Current History*, November 1997, pp. 370–6.

Different governments apply this authority in different ways. National variations are also apparent in the distribution and redistribution of social costs associated
with explicit and tacit policies. These differences are found even among the United
States, Germany, and Japan, the home states for the majority of the world's leading
multinational firms (and which serve as the principal reference points in our data
analysis and extensive fieldwork). In each case, national political structures continue
to shape the activities that decisively influence the futures of corporations: their
internal governance and long-term financing operations, their most important
research and development programs, and their interrelated direct investment and
intrafirm trading strategies.

In short, at the core of the world's dominant multinationals there is no such
thing as globalization. Instead, the empirical evidence suggests resistance. Most
American multinationals continue to pursue strategies that emphasize short-term
payoffs. German firms continue to focus on a narrow band of industries and a
strategy in which the benefits of new technologies tend to be diffused widely. The
most prominent German multinationals also retain unique relationships with their
local bankers, even as those bankers struggle to create new competitive advantages
in external markets. Japanese multinationals, despite facing extremely difficult
adjustment challenges in the 1990s, continue to depend on long-standing corporate
networks with a distinctly national cast.

No one corporate system is necessarily better than any other; each has its
advantages and drawbacks. Our investigation demonstrates that these structural
differences, which still follow national lines, are not fading away. This conclusion
holds profound implications for the way policymakers, business leaders, scholars,
and the public should think about the changing world economy. At a time when
many critics are seeking points of resistance to pressures associated with globalization, we find systematic national differentiation inside the very corporations thought
to be the harbingers of the new global economic infrastructure.

The appearance of globalization

The nature and extent of structural convergence in the economic realm should be
reflected in the global operations of multinationals. If the global economy is coming
together, the evidence for it should be obvious among the business vehicles that most
prominently appear to be weaving tightening webs of interdependence. Business
leaders certainly speak as if this is the case. From them we constantly hear about the
emergence of global markets, the globalization of industrial sectors, and the potential for stateless electronic commerce – all pointing to the obsolescence of national
economic borders. Ironically, their sharpest critics from the political left agree with
this basic analysis. The difference between them is not descriptive but interpretive.
The end result – one world market – is agreed upon. Where the executives promise
spreading prosperity and hope, however, their critics see catastrophic competition
and the collision of insufficiently controlled market forces.

It is intuitively plausible that a global system of business is emerging.
Increasingly autonomous business enterprises desire ever greater economies of scale
and the product definition required to finance, develop, and exploit new technologies. It is also the case that both capital and technology harnessed by multinationals

are flowing more freely across national borders. Perhaps more plausible is the notion that deep regional integration is driven in large part by the expansion of financial and industrial corporations. As multinationals extend their operations and market access across national boundaries, it would seem that locally minded citizens and policymakers would naturally be pushed to adapt their thinking to a corresponding regional or global logic.

An emerging consensus along such lines seems in view. Multinationals are widely understood to be the most visible elements in a vast process of a political and economic transformation akin to the Industrial Revolution that spawned modern capitalism. The term globalization is commonly invoked to capture the sometimes contradictory elements involved in that process. As one political economist explains it, globalization is moving "the world economy to an even larger structural scale," which entails a more fundamental shift toward "the privatization and marketization" of politics. The result, he contends, is the creation of new centers of power that are "more sovereign than the state."

Derrick de Kerckhove makes the point more poetically, and with considerable license, when he makes the multinational corporation the defining metaphor for a new age: "Multinationals are like the idea of God during the Renaissance. Their center is everywhere and their periphery nowhere." In more passionate terms, a leading social critic depicts such firms as the observable face of "the manic logic of global capitalism." Our analysis, which focuses on the core activities of multinational firms in technology and capital-intensive sectors, suggests something quite different.

Following the state's lead

In theory, technological innovation and the economies of scale it increasingly demands could undermine the established political order. For much of the postwar period, many analysts and policymakers expected the activities of corporations in ever more open markets to promote a gradual convergence of technological capability. In this sense, they anticipated a broad movement of effective decision making on future technological development to increasingly transcend the borders of states.

Dominant models of technological change and economic growth led to the assumption that expanding demand, market liberalization, and open trade would increase the speed and scope of technology diffusion. This process was eventually expected to level the technological playing field among corporations and national governments. International trade and attendant flows of information, largely conducted through corporate channels, would spread the benefits of technological innovation. This would take the form of direct knowledge embedded in the industrial designs of technologically intensive goods and services, production experience, and the migration of scientists and engineers. As a result, many economies would eventually approach or reach technological parity with the dominant economic powers. After a lag reflecting their delayed start, even developing countries could follow if their political authorities pursued policies that converged in the direction of openness and efficient markets.

The technological development and economic growth achieved have been far less than what was expected. Certainly the technology gap between the United States and the other large industrialized nations has narrowed considerably in many industrial sectors, although it appears to be widening with the former Soviet states. Moreover, as the twentieth century comes to a close, several East Asian nations seem to have found a path to rapid economic and technological prowess, even if that path is not yet a smooth one. But the rate and extent of technological leveling has varied greatly across geographic regions and industrial sectors. A deep integration of national systems of innovation has not occurred. New technology, and the information embedded in it, does not flow as easily across national borders and among firms as the model of global convergence would predict.

The ability to develop, adapt, and use new knowledge is not a simple by-product of production. Technological innovation also requires concentrated capital investments in education, human resources, and research and development infrastructure. Our research indicates that the character of corporate and government sponsorship of technology innovation varies markedly, even among the most advanced nations.

Some countries, notably the United States, commit substantial portions of their national income to scientific and technological development, especially in the military field. Others, like Japan, favor investments in broad national technology missions, or investments in the acquisition and diffusion of new commercial technologies. Some promote research directly and aggressively, while others leave more of this activity to the private sector. Some governments regulate competition in ways that inhibit centralization and collaboration, while others encourage concentration and combination in the name of production efficiency.

This persistent divergence in corporate strategy and government policy points directly to the endurance of national systems of innovation and investment. Different methods of organizing the institutions and underlying ideologies that frame the modern state continue to reshape the organization of the multinational companies whose activities often create and sustain national technological competencies. Different ways of arranging the relationship between state and society are mirrored directly in the relationships that drive fundamental corporate operations. In a world where the lion's share of actual technological innovation takes place within corporate networks, the nature of those relationships continues to vary along national lines.

The nationality of multinationals

Once established, of course, the technologies developed by multinational firms tend to spread, largely through licensing agreements and joint ventures, even though they are most often confined within networks of affiliated firms. This is important because a key determinant of the world's future political organization is where technologies will be created, controlled, and deployed. When we look at the multinationals based in the United States, Germany, and Japan, we find distinctive patterns of technological innovation, diverse corporate systems, and different government policies supporting that innovation. In these fundamental areas of corporate activity one can demonstrate convergence only at the margins.

Certainly multinationals change; continuous adaptation to dynamic markets is critical to firm survival. If firms from different countries want to sell similar goods in the same markets, their day-to-day behavior in those markets may often appear quite similar. But for those firms that dominate international markets today, national origins continue to matter in much more fundamental ways. The nationality of firms is not necessarily given by the location of corporate headquarters or the addresses of principal shareholders (although it almost always is). More fundamentally, it is given by history.

The core strategic behavior of multinational firms varies widely. Three main explanations have been advanced to account for this variance. The first sees firm behavior most heavily influenced by the nature of the industrial sector. A second explanation emphasizes the importance of internal influences, such as technological acumen and the maturity of main product lines. The third underlines the essential malleability of the multinational corporation and the determinative influence of the specific environment in which a firm operates (multinationals, for example, are frequently depicted as fluidly adapting themselves to local laws and local tastes in host markets).

We have doubts about all three explanations. The differences in corporate behavior we observe do not correlate with industrial sectors. They are not associated with industrial maturity, and they remain observable even within identical host environments.

No single explanation can capture the essential reality of all firms all the time. The chemical industry, for example, is clearly subject to high transportation costs and particular hazards, which cannot help but influence some aspects of the behavior of chemical companies regardless of nationality. Similarly, firms committed to a particular host market must adapt themselves to that market. In the most fundamental areas of corporate strategy, however, striking differences of an aggregate nature remain. The domestic institutions and ideologies within which companies are most firmly embedded offer the most plausible explanations.

Embedded corporate identity?

The United States, Germany, and Japan – the dominant states within which leading multinationals across a full range of industrial sectors are based – all reduced their own room for policy maneuver in the years following World War II. In short, they sought the benefits promised by intensified international economic interaction. This created the political space within which corporations chartered by them, as well as by other states, flourished. The transformation of many into "multinational" corporations was, in this sense, clearly intended, even if no policy visionary foresaw the outcome precisely. But the multinationalization of firms within this political space did not occur unsystematically. It was less market-driven than state-driven. Variations by industrial sector and product line clearly exist across the world's leading multinationals. More important, however, variations by nationality – thought by many observers to be of receding importance – in fact endure.

A commitment remains in Germany and, especially, in Japan, to resist the merger of unique national values and institutions. That commitment is not necessarily stated in explicit corporate policy, but it is embedded in corporate structure and culture. In other words, compared to many American corporations, German and Japanese firms retain a much clearer sense of their distinct national identities, a clearer commitment to national and regional prosperity in a changing international environment, and a much more realistic sense of the capacity of the rest of the world to adapt to the internal behavioral norms of their homelands.

The difficulty leaders of American multinationals often seem to have with the concept of "national" corporate identity seems peculiarly and typically American. As students of American history might suggest, this is consistent with, and reflective of, a long and much deeper struggle over collective identity and collective interest in a quite exceptional political environment. We make a similar suggestion. The "global corporation" is mainly an American myth.

Consider the different meanings business leaders from different nations associate with the terms "free trade," "deregulation," and even "globalization." In their public pronouncements, and certainly in their private interviews with us, American corporate leaders use these phrases to imply a commitment to more openness and unhindered competition both at home and abroad, as well as a sense of "letting the chips fall where they may." To German and especially Japanese executives, the phrases typically imply a commitment to keeping American and other external markets open to their exports and, increasingly, to their own direct investment in production or distribution facilities. The phrases are not without intellectual content but, in public arenas in Germany and Japan, they seem mainly to have become mantras to ward off any prospect of closure in American markets and, lately, to accelerate adjustments in local labor markets.

Either publicly or privately, German and Japanese corporate leaders rarely imply support for truly laissez-faire policies, the restriction of cartel-like behavior, or other actions that might fully expose their home markets to the bracing winds of global competition. Non-tariff and structural barriers remain, often in subtle forms. Across American, Japanese, and German markets, the shape of basic economic institutions, the actual modus operandi of core industries, the endurance of historical business relationships, and the ideological foundations of those relationships continue to reflect fundamental differences in social values and worldviews.

The phenomenon of corporate multinationalization is essentially a process through which still-national corporations, and the innovation and investment systems in which they remain embedded, are inserted into one another's home markets. Those corporations then adapt themselves at the margins to, for example, make their products and sales operations more consistent with local tastes or to garner some advantage that may prove useful in other markets or back home. But such tinkering at the periphery does not undermine the deep continuities evident, for example, in German accounting and banking systems (even as they are reformed), in the historical drive behind network-based Japanese technology and investment strategies, or in the persistence of institutional disincentives or long-term planning inside American multinationals.

No matter how lustily they sing from the same hymnbook when they gather together in Davos or Aspen, the leaders of the world's great business enterprises continue to differ in their most fundamental strategic visions and objectives. Moreover, they differ systematically in the ways they deal with common challenges, depending on the geographic origins of the companies they represent.

Disciplining the market

Rules that foster mutually beneficial global economic activity emerge when the ideologies and institutional structures that differentiate states are compatible. In the past, this has occurred only with difficulty, especially in periods when no single state or national market has dominated world production and when specific modes of economic interaction have been delimited.

The negotiation of an effective international regime for trade in goods and services, for example, took many decades. It remains imperfect, but a modicum of common national understandings on fair play, appropriate means for redress, and principles by which specific transactions may be judged have now been fairly well specified. The creation of the General Agreement on Tariffs and Trade (GATT) in 1948, and its culmination in the World Trade Organization (WTO) in 1995, depended on painstaking, prolonged, and often difficult political negotiation, not on a market mechanism promoting deep structural convergence.

Barring systemic military instability, the question of whether similar interstate negotiations can craft a solid basis for the deepening interaction of national innovation, investment, and corporate financing systems remains open. Moreover, the parallel convergence of national environmental standards, labor conditions, and competition policies seems light years away. This challenges the optimism of global market devotees who prefer not to confront the interaction of idiosyncratic corporate systems head on. The operations of globe-spanning multinationals do not create automatic or straightforward mechanisms for regime formation; if anything they militate against it. Intensifying cut-throat competition makes enduring national differences in the rules of the game more obvious, not less. It thus renders the need for political negotiation of common understandings on at least the most important rules more, not less, pressing.

In the absence of such intervention in international markets, we will not inevitably enter a world of more perfect competition and more convergent policies. This is ideological bunk. We will more likely end up with sanctuary markets – where leading export industries enjoy an unassailable position in their home base – in some countries and regions, and unacceptable environmental, labor, and human rights standards in others. Under such conditions, inward foreign direct investment is effectively restricted or channeled, and local markets are protected in opaque ways. New forms of corporate networking do not necessarily advance the cause of competitive markets except in rhetorical terms. They may, in fact, foster new forms of cartel-like behavior and tacit market-sharing arrangements. In such a world even the citizens of advanced industrial democracies would rightly begin to ask, "Who makes the rules?"

Although smaller states have often found it more difficult to play by their own rules, today leading industrial states are involved in increasingly intricate negotiation over the rules that govern the future world economy. Certainly questions of grand strategy enter into that negotiation at times. In the main, however, and on the complex agenda posed by the spread of differentially structured multinationals, the negotiation has taken a tacit form. It is an agenda framed by the compatibility or incompatibility of relatively rigid, or slowly changing, national governing structures. Ultimately, domestic politics and international markets cannot easily be disengaged or fully reconciled. Several implications follow.

Our analysis suggests that increasing openness in the corporate markets of leading states must be associated with more deliberate efforts to manage the consequences. Where such efforts fail, measured closure may be a likely response. We see a continuous stream of evidence suggesting that even as tariffs and other barriers to trade are formally dismantled, states remain unwilling to stand idly by when basic corporate, capital, and technological advantages are at risk.

In a recent example, European countries collectively set a floor on the price that foreign producers could charge for DRAM (dynamic random access memory) chips sold in their markets. The policy objective was to give indigenous firms breathing space in an environment widely viewed as hypercompetitive and prone to cycles of excess production. The policy, in short, was designed to preserve in Europe core national economic and technological capacities in a key sector.

The alternative idea – that mobile corporations freed from political interference are arbitraging diverse national interests and forcing a process of convergence or an inevitable trend toward openness – marks, in our view, a road toward political and social instability. Efficient and stable global markets will not likely evolve through the unhindered competition of globe-spanning firms when national institutions and ideologies remain decisive inside those firms. Those institutions and ideologies are not static, but they change only slowly. If they continue to be mirrored inside the world's leading corporations, they will continue to define the limits of a truly global economy more than that economy can redefine them.

If roughly compatible government policies on increasingly complex aspects of corporate life are required to achieve the ultimate objective of a peaceful world where economic prosperity spreads widely, then more effective commercial diplomacy will be required. Markets are a tool of policy, not a substitute for it. Even among multinationals, where cross-national competition is most obvious and most intense, there is no inevitable destination. Japanese, European, and American disagreements on such basic questions as the purpose of corporate growth and technological innovation will not evaporate. And differences on such far-reaching issues as arms exports and the very meaning of international security will persist.

Our research suggests broad differences, even among leading industrial states, on policy fundamentals: the supervision of cartels and other forms of corporate networking, the purpose and direction of national innovation systems, and the nature of the intimate interaction of intrafirm trading and long-term investment strategies. If multinationals reflect such differences in their core structures and strategies, the kinds of nationalist economic policy orientations witnessed early in the twentieth century are not precluded in the modern era of intensifying international competition, only transmuted. The issues thereby raised should not be obscured by the language of globalization.

To put the matter bluntly, power – as distinct from legitimate political authority – may indeed be shifting within different societies, but it is not obviously shifting outward into some supranational corporate ether. Markets or, more precisely, huge, sprawling commercial hierarchies, are not replacing states as the world's effective government, nor are corporations becoming more democratic. Some societies may be structurally better equipped than others to deal with the consequences of such power shifts, but there is little reason to make the challenge more difficult by accepting the conventional corporate line that nothing can really be done because they are "global" phenomena. If certain domestic structures in advanced industrial countries are evolving in ways that make it more difficult to constrain corporate power, they should be adjusted internally.

Such adjustments will likely entail modifying and adapting idiosyncratic state and social structures. Nowhere, for instance, is it written in stone that the short-term interests of corporate shareholders in the United States deserve a higher priority than those of all other corporate stakeholders. But only open and informed national debate over fundamental rules of the American economic system in a new era can lead to a change in the status quo. Similarly, there is no reason why German corporate norms are fixed for all eternity; German citizens themselves are fully capable of reconsidering them, even as deepening regional interdependence encourages adjustments in basic structures of national governance.

The situation would seem quite different, however, for societies not in possession of a large, diversified, and rooted industrial base. From their point of view, power may indeed be shifting in the direction of a few leading states and increasingly concentrated commercial hierarchies durably nested within those states. Such perceptions may help explain the apparently increasing efforts of many smaller countries to negotiate adjustments and seek redress through the World Trade Organization and other multilateral institutions.

There is no doubt that efficiency gains are promised by the integration of national markets. But as those gains are pursued, cross-national and national distributive questions will become more pressing. The strain between the international economic logic of integration and the enduring national logic of political governance will become more obvious. Given scope, nationalist tendencies inherent in the investment, technology, competition, and financial policies that governments of states actually pursue in our time could become increasingly salient.

Notwithstanding the self-assured banter of global market enthusiasts, the possibility of international economic disintegration has not been banished. And the quickest way to make that possibility a reality is to accept the chimerical and too facile notion that intensifying competition among rootless global corporations will inevitably generate a more stable, a more equitable, and a more prosperous world.

Chapter 8

Mira Wilkins

MAPPING MULTINATIONALS

A MULTINATIONAL ENTERPRISE (MNE) is a firm that extends itself over borders to do business outside its headquarters country. It is a firm – as economists define "the firm": an allocator of resources, a producer of goods and services. It is also international: It operates across political boundaries. It has become conventional to use the terms firm, company, corporation, business, and enterprise interchangeably. International, transnational, multinational, and even global are also employed as synonymous – as the modifying adjective. I follow these conventions, albeit my preference is for the designation "multinational enterprise."

For the historian, it is important that firms start and grow. Thus, the initial spread over a border is the beginning of a process. Many firms remain solely domestic. Some spread early in their history over borders. Some enterprises at origin are international. Most have only one home (the headquarters country). Some come to have more than one headquarters – as with Royal Dutch Shell and Unilever. Some never extend beyond a single foreign host country; others remain within a region. Some expand slowly and others rapidly to become truly global: multi-product, multi-process enterprises operating in many countries around the world, horizontally and vertically integrated. By 1930 a number of firms did business – that is, had foreign direct investments – on six continents.

Various ways have been proposed to measure the *extent* of MNE activity. Some scholars have looked at the percentage of business done abroad (certain early, quite small, companies would qualify as being substantial MNEs under this criterion). Others have considered the number of countries in which a firm does business (an enterprise may operate in a few countries but do a large share of its business abroad; by contrast, it may have investments in numerous lands but conduct only a small proportion of its business outside its home nation). Still others have focused on the absolute size of assets or sales or employment or profits outside the headquarters country (a giant firm may have a relatively small percentage of its assets, sales,

From Mira Wilkins, "The Historical Development of Multinational Enterprise to 1930: Discontinuities and Continuities," a paper presented at a conference on multinational enterprises, 2000, pp. 1–2, 6–21, 26–8, 30–1.

employment, or profits represented by affiliates abroad, yet in absolute size its assets, sales, employment, or profit levels in foreign countries could dwarf those of enterprises with far greater percentage involvements). I do not want to fuss with "cut-offs," that is omitting a firm, because it fails to meet a minimum under one or more of these guidelines. Instead, I want to keep these different measures in mind, as I survey the process of internationalization, that is, how firms have evolved over time as they have engaged in business outside their home country. To simplify matters, a firm fits my definition of MNE if it extends itself over borders, internalizing within the firm business in two (including the home) or more locales that are at the time under different sovereignties. Then, later I can discuss the degree or extent of multinational involvement.

Most of the earliest MNEs began with a single operation abroad in a single host location; typically, however, MNEs invest in more than one host country – sometimes gradually, sometimes quickly. What is important about the MNE is that it has a *presence* abroad, however small; it does not merely export to (or through) other unaffiliated firms or to the end-product consumers. The presence is the foreign direct investment. It is also vital that it retains a headquarters at home. The significance of the MNE for the study of world history is that through time the enterprise provides ongoing intra-firm connections, a tissue that unifies on a regular, not one-time, basis. The MNE is not merely a channel for a single transaction, a foreign direct investment, but rather it is an institutional governance structure that serves as a framework for different sorts of interchanges and relationships (including further mobilization of investments, exports and imports, technology, knowledge, and general information transfers, and, most important, management itself). It is, thus, crucial not to focus in on a single function such as foreign direct investment flows, but instead to consider the entire firm as it operates over borders through time. [. . .]

The modern multinational enterprise

During the nineteenth century, there were increasing numbers of businesses over borders (with control maintained in the home country). It was, however, in the last third of the nineteenth century, with and after the transportation and communications revolutions (the spread of railroads, steamships, and cables), that the vast expansion of MNEs could and did occur. "Speed" in delivering goods and information became feasible with the new transportation and communication infrastructure. This made a material difference. Costs fell sharply. Organizational coordination and control within a firm became realizable in ways that in prior years had been inconceivable. The new speed in transactions made possible modern MNEs – businesses that were radically different from their many precursors. [. . .]

[. . .] Many of us in studying the MNE have been immensely influenced by what I call "the American model." In this paradigm, the firm began at home in the domestic market; it developed core competencies; and then typically, if its product was unique, it began to export; its next step was to find foreign agents and then establish foreign sales branches or subsidiaries. If markets abroad were not accessible owing to barriers of trade, to transportation costs, or for other reasons, the firm would start to assemble, pack, bottle, or process abroad and at once or subsequently – at different paces in different markets and in different industries – it would move into manufacturing abroad. It might also integrate backward into raw material at home and/or abroad. As numerous scholars have looked at the evolution of European and then Japanese MNEs, our lens was the American model and the history of many of the European and Japanese MNEs seemed to conform to this pattern of MNE behavior.

This began to trouble me, however, as I studied the history of foreign investment in the United States. My research uncovered many inward foreign direct investments, managed investments, that fit perfectly into the American model, but I also identified managed cattle companies, mining firms, breweries, mortgage providers, and other investments with British parents that failed to conform to the American model – i.e. they had not started with internalized core competencies and extended those competencies abroad, nor was a firm investing in the United States to fill its own supply needs. I unearthed too many exceptions to the American model to see them as merely anomalies. I realized that this matter had bothered John Stopford when in the 1970s he had written on British business overseas. I looked more closely and discovered similar British companies on a global scale and soon I was able to identify comparable French and Dutch business abroad. Meanwhile, others were pointing out that many of the foreign direct investments in Latin America coincided with what I was finding on British-managed investments in the United States. Donald Patterson had compared British and American direct investments in Canada and had seen differences. Jean-François Hennart found the idea useful in discussing British and French investments in tin in Malaya and other foreign investments in tin. Geoffrey Jones would note that the vast expansion of British international banks was not part of the overseas activities of the commercial banks at home, but rather those multinational banks were set up for the specific purpose of doing overseas banking in a particular region. The long and the short of all this was the development of ideas on "the free-standing company," a company that extends over borders but does not grow out of an existing home-based business operation. It seemed very clear that managed investment in foreign countries did not necessarily evolve out of existing business done at home – although it was no accident that MNEs (managed business abroad) came from particular home countries. Also, what became noticeable was that these free-standing companies were in clusters: Since they had not internalized core competencies, they had to draw on the talents of outsiders. Over time, to varying extents, those free-standing companies that survived internalized many of the needed skills. In the exposition below, I will not confine myself to companies that corresponded to the American model, but view the range of types of managed business over borders. What will – and should – become apparent is that there was an immense amount of MNE behavior (managed business over borders) in the late nineteenth and opening third of the twentieth centuries which was highly instrumental in the integration of and in the growth patterns in the world economy. MNEs provided an important institutional structure for the integration of the international economy. What is also evident is that there were a variety of "alliance" relationships that served to enlarge the influence of the MNEs. [. . .]

Basic infrastructure and multinational enterprise – to 1930

In the integration of the world economy in the late nineteenth and early twentieth centuries, MNEs contributed to two fundamental transportation needs: First, there were the pioneer US outward direct investments that arranged transit routes across Nicaragua and Panama (cutting distances) and second, even more significant, there was the Suez Canal Company which, when it opened the canal in 1869, dramatically shrunk the time it took to get between West and East (the distance by sea from London to Bombay was reduced by about 40 percent and from London to Singapore by about 30 percent). Eventually, private enterprise could not put together the resources for the Panama Canal, which was built by the US government and opened in the summer of 1914. The private sector's failure had been what stimulated the US government to step in. The British government invested in the Suez Canal Company, but that venture, with its headquarters in Paris and its administrative office there, remained a private sector-managed foreign direct investment, which lasted until the Egyptians nationalized the canal in the 1950s. The shortening of distances was crucial in the integration of the world economy.

The application of steam to ocean travel in the mid-nineteenth century meant the rise of new steamship companies. These companies typically stationed representatives in ports where they did their principal business. The companies were of many different nationalities – with the British in a dominant position. Steamship companies encouraged new investments in port facilities and docks. Sometimes, they made such investments themselves. Thus, by the outbreak of the First World War, the large German steamship lines owned docks in the United States. A number of British free-standing companies were set up to build docks (and undertake related construction projects) abroad.

Insurance companies organized overseas operations to insure cargos. Marine insurance and fire insurance became associated (warehouses holding goods burned). A formidable number of British, French, German, Swiss, and other insurers established international businesses – initially trade-related and then involved in more extensive multinational business activities. Japanese insurance companies extended abroad, to insure Japanese imports and exports. It seems extraordinary to realize that in 1914 over two-thirds of the policies written on American vessels were by foreign insurers. On the other hand, American life insurance companies were MNEs before the First World War, which had naught to do with trade, but everything to do with the newly-integrated world economy [. . .].

As one applies concepts of MNE to railroads several features become important: (1) the American model, the extension of an existing railroad over borders, does not fare well; while some Canadian railroads stretched over the border into the United States (and vice versa) and there were other cases where existing railroads extended across national frontiers, these were the exceptions; (2) the great British contractors did, however, become MNEs and were instrumental in building railroads outside of their home country; (3) a sizable number of free-standing companies participated in building and running railroads – some with long-lived investments and some rather short; (4) there were railroads that did not have a foreign "parent" but were owned and administered by foreign investors; (5) a number of railroads in "Third World" countries, either at origin or later, came to be associated with particular primary products (for example, bananas with United Fruit); often mining or oil concessions included railroad building, where the railroad concession was acquired by foreign investors with an eye to the development of the primary product; sometimes, a trading company (such as W.R. Grace & Co.) might see the necessity of railroads – and play a role in obtaining their financing abroad; Marc Linder makes the point that many international construction projects were linked with primary product development; (6) on occasion railroad building was connected with iron and steel makers' search for export markets; thus, Krupp obtained a concession to build a railroad in Venezuela in the 1890s; and (7) there were all sorts of sideline activities once railroad building began. Railroad construction companies, for example, often had to develop manufacturing facilities in the country where the line was being built. Railroad building required the mobilization of labor – usually labor that was within the country where the railroad was being built – but sometimes encouraging, directly or indirectly, substantial labor mobility. [. . .]

The first direct communication by cable between London and Paris was in November 1852, through the lines of the Submarine Telegraph Co. and the European and American Telegraph Co. The German Siemens designed and put into operation a Russian telegraph system (in European Russia) between 1852 and 1855; the system was Russian government run. In 1866 an American company financed by British capital was successful in transatlantic cable communication. (Telegraph connections across the United States had been completed in 1861, which had not involved MNEs.) By 1870, the British Indian Telegraph Company of Denmark extended the trans-Siberian line (which had been finished in the late 1860s) from Vladivostok to Shanghai and Yokohama, which system tied in with the cables of the Eastern Extension Company, linking up India with China, Singapore, and Australia. The British led in cable communications. The German MNE, Siemens, was an important participant in laying cables. The British-owned Pender group developed a global business. Cables were vital in moving information. They integrated the world community. By 1914 London and New York were minutes apart. In time, America's role in cables grew in relative importance – especially in Latin America – and in 1920, the Central and South American Telegraph Company became All American Cables; in 1927 International Telephone and Telegraph Corporation would acquire a controlling interest in All American Cables.

Meanwhile in telephones, American MNEs transferred US technology. It was the American-owned Edison Telephone Company that in 1879 began to install, in London, the first European telephone exchange. The involvement (from the 1880s to 1920) by Americans in installing telephone systems abroad brought few rewards to their sponsors. An exceptional success story was in Canada, where in 1880 the American Bell Telephone Company started and initially controlled the Bell Telephone Company of Canada. Yet, American Bell felt that "the whole field is far too large for us to undertake to cover." Its plan was to encourage the involvement of Canadians and Canadian capital. Not only Americans were active in disseminating – through MNEs – telephone operating systems; Germans became very involved (Siemens) as well as Swedes (Ericsson). Gradually, telephone utilities were established – on a global basis. Sometimes, telephone utilities were linked in with waterworks, electric power and light, and electrical tramways. In 1920, when International Telephone and Telegraph Corporation was formed, it expanded worldwide in a dramatic manner. (It acquired Western Electric's international manufacturing operations in 1925 – except for those operations in Canada.) By 1930, I.T.T. operated telephone systems in Spain and in seven Latin American countries (Cuba, Mexico, Peru, Brazil, Uruguay, Chile, and Argentina). That year, it obtained concessions to provide telephone services in Rumania, Turkey, and China.

Also in telecommunications, MNEs introduced radio communication. Before World War I, an affiliate of the British-owned multinational enterprise, Marconi's Wireless Telegraph Company, dominated this sector in the United States. Telefunken, a joint venture between Allgemeine Elekrizitäts Gesellschaft (A.E.G.) and Siemens & Halske, was in 1914 building a high powered wireless station in the United States. Americans were too nationalistic to leave this sector in foreign hands. After the First World War, the US Navy arranged with General Electric for the Radio Corporation of America to take over the Marconi broadcasting facilities. German-built radio stations in the United States were – as a consequence of World War I – never returned to German control. In the 1920s Radio Corporation of America inaugurated long distance wireless communication between the United States, Europe, and Asia. It invested in high power radio stations around the world, from Sweden to Poland, in China, and in Argentina. In other parts of South America it entered into joint ventures with British companies; it did the same in Canada. So, too, large MNEs operating in isolated locations in less developed countries supplied their own facilities; United Fruit, for example, had a radio company as a subsidiary. And then there were the news services – the French predecessor to Agence France Presse (founded in 1835), the British Reuters started in 1851, and the UP (the United Press) organized in 1907. They would use the telegraph and then the radio services to disseminate news on a global basis.

It was not only MNEs in cables, telephones, and radio – and the news services that used these facilities – that contributed to the linking up of communications on a worldwide basis and set the foundations for information to spread more rapidly than ever in history. No medium, until television, did more to unify the world economy than motion pictures – first silent films and later those with sound tracks. In the age of silent film, the key MNE was the French Pathé, which by 1914 had production and distribution outlets in more than forty major cities – in Europe, North and South America, Asia, and Africa. In Europe, Pathé had a presence from London to Moscow; in North America, in New York; in South America, in Buenos Aires; in Asia from Calcutta to Singapore; and in Africa, in Cairo. In the 1920s, when the "talky" replaced the silent film, American movies were marketed internationally by US headquartered MNEs. The effect was dramatic. [. . .]

In addition, and very basic, in the spread of light and power public utilities, an early participant was the Imperial Continental Gas Company, founded in 1825 in the United Kingdom; by 1914, it operated gas (and in certain places also electrical) utilities in Austria-Hungary, Belgium, France, and Germany. In the late nineteenth century and at the start of the twentieth century, MNEs took part in installing and operating electric light and power facilities in urban areas around the world. (This, of course, made it possible to show the movies in the 1920s.) American, Canadian, British, Belgian, German, and Swiss-headquartered MNEs were responsible for electrification's global reach. MNEs in construction and banking provided complementary services – and the electrical manufacturers were involved. The types of and approaches to MNE participation varied. Many of the new power plants provided for urban transportation (traction), as well as heat and light. Financial groups in Belgium moved rapidly from railroads to specializing in tramways and then to more general electrical activities. In Russia, where by 1914 most cities had electricity, non-Russian owned companies owned and controlled about 90 percent of the electrical public utilities.

By the 1920s, the largest new US direct investments abroad were in public utilities. One US headquartered company alone – American & Foreign Power Company – at the end of that decade furnished 90 percent of the electric power in Cuba, 75 percent in Chile, 30 percent in Mexico, 15 percent in Brazil, and 13 percent in Argentina; American & Foreign Power Company also supplied electric power in China and India. By 1930, the Japanese-owned South Manchuria Electric Company (formed in 1926) had taken over many of the power plants, formerly owned by the Japanese South Manchuria Railway Company (the latter had built 12 such facilities between 1914 and 1926).

Coal mining companies did not become multinational. In India, by the early twentieth century, practically the entire capital for its large coal industry was drawn from investors in India. On the other hand, the big coal companies in India do appear to have been of British origin and most of the well-known *trading houses* there did have colliery interests. British steamship companies (the British India Steam Navigation Company) had coal mining interests in Bengal before the First World War. There were coal companies incorporated in South Africa, with London offices, and the majority of ownership in the United Kingdom. Harm Schröter found some German and Belgium free-standing companies in Bohemia before the First World War that were involved in coal production. Much more significant were the Japanese companies that invested in railroads in China, which had major investments in coal. The South Manchuria Railway Company owned coal mines at Fushun and Yentai; in 1930 the Fushun mine was said to be the greatest open cut coal mine in the world. It not only served the railroad, but provided exports to Japan. There were also Japanese coal and iron direct investments in China.

Far more global in their characteristics were the MNE interests in oil. Oil began to take on importance for the world economy in the late nineteenth and early twentieth centuries, even though it was not until the 1960s that oil replaced coal as the world's principal source of energy. Oil was found in commercial quantities in 1859 in Titusville, Pennsylvania. America became the largest producer of crude oil and refiner of oil. In the period covered by this paper, with the exception of a few years around the turn of the century when Russia crude oil output exceeded that of the United States, the United States led the world in crude oil production. From the start, Standard Oil companies were multinational, investing initially in selling and then refining abroad. European capital developed the Russian oil industry. MNEs dominate the narrative on the oil industry. By 1930, the leading companies in this fully internationalized industry were the predecessor of Exxon (Standard Oil of New Jersey), Royal Dutch Shell, and the predecessor of British Petroleum. MNEs invested on six continents in selling, refining, transporting, producing, and exploring. Initially, the international oil companies had served kerosene markets; but with the spread of electrification, they turned to providing the transportation needs (cars, trucks, buses, but also fuel oil for shipping, and oil for tanks, ambulances, and soon airplanes). Oil was used for lubricants and for a wide variety of new purposes. By the late 1920s, the largest oil MNEs were getting involved in petrochemicals.

The provision of transportation, communications, and new energy sources meant a need for trading companies to handle the complexities of international trade. New groups of trading companies had emerged by 1914 to handle the vastly expanded trade. Large general trading companies became experienced in buying and selling different raw materials and manufactured goods; they knew suppliers and markets; they could proctor quality control; and they were able to identify and avoid fraud. In effect their activities cut costs in transactions and aided trade by reducing uncertainties. Indeed, the value of world commerce in primary products and in manufactured articles (measured in current dollars) grew steadily from the mid-1870s to 1929. Throughout these years, the value of international trade in primary products exceeded that in manufactured articles. As the transportation, communication, and energy sectors were developed, there were layered complementary trading arrangements, with trade often internalized within trading companies, and sometimes separate.

Infrastructure needs implied standardized accounting procedures. The principal British accounting firms set up partnerships in the United States, first to audit investments – and then they came to serve the US market. Earlier, we mentioned insurance companies that were involved in financing trade. Many of the international insurance companies penetrated further into countries. In the United States, foreign insurers not only aided trade, but in the 1920s provided other types of insurance services as well.

New international economic relationships, new globalization, required international banking structures. The integrated world economy needed conduits for capital movement. Financial institutions moved monies on an international basis. Banks arranged new issues, pricing them and marketing them. These issues were traded on stock exchanges. By 1914, the London Stock Exchange was an international market – as were the Amsterdam, Paris, Frankfurt, and Berlin exchanges. The New York Stock Exchange was fundamentally a domestic market before 1914 but, in the 1920s, it became an international market. Large German, French, Belgian, and Swiss banks were involved internationally not only as issuers of securities, but as sizable foreign investors. By 1914 most had representation in London. The Deutsche Bank set up certain banks abroad. In the 1920s, stockbrokers became international, providing for global investments.

International trade required financing. International trade is impossible without payments. To carry on such activities, sometimes a little more representation abroad by bankers was required than was the case with the issue of securities. Before 1914, the pound sterling was an international currency and the British dominated the financing of international trade. Just as securities issues brought foreign countries into a global community, so too trade finance linked nations.

International banks also arranged remittances home for immigrants. Italian banks, for example, had representation in Latin America and in the United States – in places where immigrants needed such services. Like securities issues, trade finance, and handling remittances, such functions linked economies, and could be called "shallow" investments.

By contrast, international banks in addition, in certain countries, provided commercial banking services that were of a *domestic* nature, and here the penetration within the domestic economy became deep and pervasive. British overseas banks introduced extensive domestic banking services in many countries; these banks handled both international *and* every-day domestic needs. By the start of the First World War, some 30 British banks owned and ran more than 1,000 branches and offices in six continents. As multinational retail banks in Asia, Africa, the Middle East, and Latin America, British overseas banks were often the first modern banks within the countries where they operated. The impacts varied by nation, but by 1913, for example, three British banks attracted fully a third of the deposits in the entire Brazilian banking system. Banks from various other European countries also expanded into providing domestic banking services abroad. In Brazil in 1913, aside from the three British banks, five French, three German, two Belgian, two Portuguese, and one Argentine bank provided banking services. Richard Tilly describes the role of German overseas banks as "providing credit and payment services to the local merchant communities." Typically, the share of a foreign market held by banks from abroad declined over time, as new domestic institutions arose and substituted for the foreign banks. The copying was part of the impact. Thus, the foreign bank share of Argentine deposits was 39 percent in 1900 but 23 percent in 1914. The percentages declined even further by 1929.

Everywhere they operated, British overseas banks carried with them a reputation for honesty, integrity, and safety. Their modern services were part of the integration of the world economy; the banks were the exemplar, the model. Likewise, European banks abroad provided services not otherwise available.

American banks were latecomers in the process of expanding abroad. But, once US law permitted it, National City Bank took the lead. By 1929 it was truly multinational, with 93 branches in the principal cities in Central and South America, Europe, and Asia. It offered services for major US MNEs, whose principals were on its board of directors (Sosthenes Behn – I.T.T.; Gerald Swope – General Electric; E.A. Deed – National Cash Register; J.P. Grace – W.R. Grace & Co.; and C.H. McCormick – International Harvester). And, for travelers, there was American Express, which supplied banking and travel services; by 1926, it had 47 foreign branches. Thomas Cook did the same for the British traveler.

In addition, other financial intermediaries furnished added connections in the world economy. British and Dutch mortgage companies provided credit on the American frontier and did so through direct investments. Large financial holding companies – some associated with the big German and Swiss banks (and with electrical manufacturing companies) – facilitated the financing for the spread of public utilities on a global scale.

Finally, in considering infrastructure, we need to turn to education – the creation of human capital, of the social norms appropriate to newly industrializing societies, and the introduction of business cultures. Here Geoffrey Jones has made a major contribution in showing how foreign banks in particular developed a corporate culture, which moved abroad with the overseas bank. We can apply his argument on the impact of all the MNE activities. Companies that extended over borders brought with them on-the-job training – but of even greater significance than the specific skills were the "way things were done." Multinational corporations disseminated intangible institutional norms, a framework of new practices. Perhaps we can call it education in innovation, education in management, education in the processes and procedures. In some countries it was education on what a contract meant, respect for private property, what it meant to go to work for a regular working day, and punctuality. The "brand" names of the MNE identified "known" quality. Outsiders' standards (and aspirations) spread through MNEs. There was a learning process circulated through the business abroad. [. . .]

The manufacturing multinational

I have often heard it said that sure there were investments in raw materials, in primary products, but the modern industrial MNE – where the firm starts with manufacturing at home and then extends abroad to manufacture in a variety of countries – is a post-Second World War phenomenon. This is wrong. As noted, the first foreign investments of Standard Oil were in marketing and refining (manufacturing) abroad. But, the skeptic says, sure oil companies were multinational – but not other "industrials." Once again, the skeptic is mistaken.

While industrialization spread in the late nineteenth century and first third of the twentieth century, in 1930 within much of the world agriculture still remained more important than industry. By 1930, the spread of industrialization was such that in fewer than two handfuls of countries did the percentage of gainfully occupied population in manufacturing exceed that in agriculture (only the United Kingdom, the United States, Germany, Belgium, Switzerland, the Netherlands, Czechoslovakia, Austria, and Australia qualify). This was not true in France (36 percent in agriculture, 32 percent in manufacturing), nor in Sweden (36/31), nor in Japan (50/19); in the Soviet Union, 67 percent of the population was in agriculture.

To a large extent, in the nineteenth and early twentieth centuries manufacturing multinationals went first to the countries that were the most advanced in making the transition from agriculture to industry and they contributed to the transition. They went with distinctive products and processes. As far as I can determine the first investment in manufacturing abroad by *a company with manufacturing at home* seems to have been made by the Colt Patent Fire Arms Manufacturing Company, Hartford, Conn., which, four years after its foundation (in 1848), built a London factory, introducing US machinery and US production processes. Samuel Colt (the firm's founder) exported his machinery to England from the United States, because, he wrote, none made in that country "was exact enough for the work necessary to turn out the revolvers." And, Britain was then the world's leading industrial nation. Colt set up his British factory to meet competition from "the destructive effects which would follow the introduction of . . . spurious arms into use in England, where he had no patent." Yet, he found that this branch plant, which opened in 1852, was already by 1853, "a constant drain on [his] resources and energies," so in 1857 he sold the British factory to a group of Englishmen. Coordination and control over distance is by no means an easy matter.

Because there was no continuity in Colt's manufacturing abroad (subsequently, he would license producers on the continent), I do not want to label this the pioneer manufacturing multinational. That title should probably be awarded to J. & P. Coats, the Scottish thread maker, which by the 1830s was selling in the United States (through exports to independent parties) about 60 percent of its Scottish output. In 1839, Andrew Coats (the younger brother of James and Peter) traveled to the United States, where he remained for twenty-one years, building up a sales network and arranging for the marketing of the thread under the Coats name. Coats was not the first company to set up direct representation in the United States, but there seems to have been a discontinuity in the others' subsequent multinational growth. With the Coats firm, the sales network that Andrew Coats put into place could be and was used by J. & P. Coats, when after the American Civil War that firm made its first investments in manufacturing in the United States. In 1869

J. & P. Coats invested in an existing American thread company, the Conant Thread Company, Pawtucket, Rhode Island, which that year began to manufacture Coats thread in America. Even earlier, in 1865, Coats' Paisley, Scotland, competitor, J. & J. Clark, had built a mill for spinning and spool thread manufacturing in Newark, New Jersey. (In 1896 J. & P. Coats would acquire the successor company to J. & J. Clark and in the process its US manufacturing plant.) In 1886, Coats opened a selling branch in Russia and three years later, in 1889, it entered into a joint venture to manufacture thread in Russia. By 1913, Coats had roughly 36 individual investments in Europe (it manufactured thread in Russia, Italy, Belgium, Austria-Hungary, Spain, Germany, Portugal, and Switzerland); in Russia, it had six large manufacturing facilities. It also owned a number of US manufacturing plants. In addition, before the First World War, the Scottish MNE manufactured in Brazil, Mexico, and Japan. The war had its impact . . . [Yet] during the 1920s, Coats maintained most of its vast international business – outside Russia. [. . .]

Such industrial MNEs were not confined to British, US, and German firms. There were French, Swedish, Swiss, Dutch, and Belgian manufacturing multinationals. Industrial MNEs spread a wide range of new producer and consumer products of the industrial world around the globe. Two quotations from my *Emergence of Multinational Enterprise* are indicative of the geographical expanse of MNEs and of their importance in the early twentieth century: In a 1907 letter to an agent in Bangkok, Thailand, H.B. Thayer, Vice President of Western Electric (A.T.&T.'s manufacturing subsidiary), wrote:

> You speak of an anti-American attitude on the part of the [Government] Commission. We have offices and factories making our standard apparatus in Great Britain, Belgium, Germany, France, Russia, Austria, Italy, and Japan so that so far as this matter goes we are international rather than American. If there were time we could arrange to have the order go to any one of those countries that might be preferred.

The second quotation is from a 1901 British publication:

> The most serious aspect of the American industrial invasion lies in the fact that these newcomers have acquired control of almost every new industrial created during the past fifteen years . . . What are the chief new features of London life? They are, I take it, the telephone, the portable camera, the electric street car, the automobile, the typewriter, passenger lifts in houses, and the multiplication of machine tools. In every one of these, save the petroleum automobile, the American maker is supreme; in several he is the monopolist.

And, as I have written, had the same Britisher penned this passage in 1914, he would have to have added that with the Model T, the American maker was also supreme as far as the "petroleum automobile" was concerned.

Ford Motor Company, founded in 1903, exported its sixth car; in its second year of existence it was establishing a manufacturing plant in Canada; by 1914 it was the leading manufacturer in the United Kingdom. In addition to its manufacturing in Canada and England, by 1930 Ford had assembly plants in 18 other countries in Europe, Latin America, Asia, Oceania, and Africa (Belgium, Denmark, France, Germany, Ireland, Italy, Spain, Turkey; Argentina, Brazil, Chile, Mexico, and Uruguay; India, Japan, and Malaya; Australia; and South Africa). In 1931, Frank Southard published a prize winning volume entitled *American Industry in Europe*, which he described as "a study of some aspects of the vast and complex fabric of American enterprise in foreign countries." He wrote only about Europe (including the British Isles) "largely because the author found that area quite large enough when he began going from factory to factory across its many countries." What is evident is that industrialization (and consumerism) spread through manufacturing MNEs. This was not only true in automobiles, but in a whole range of manufacturing goods – products of the post-industrial revolution days – products unknown before the late nineteenth century. [. . .]

PART V

Migrations

INDIVIDUALS AND GROUPS OF PEOPLE have been moving from time immemorial. Diaporas, as Robin Cohen (Professor of Sociology at the University of Warwick) notes in his essay, were a pervasive phenomenon in the ancient Middle East. After 1500, millions of Europeans migrated to the Western Hemisphere to establish settlement colonies, while about fifteen million Africans were forced to cross the Atlantic as slaves. In the nineteenth century, over forty million Indians and Chinese left their homes to relocate in Southeast Asia, in the Pacific, and on the American continent. In the age of imperialism, over five million Europeans lived in Africa, Asia, and the Pacific. After the Second World War, large numbers of Germans were expelled from their homes, as were Palestinian Arabs, Kurds, and other ethnic groups in the Middle East. In the meantime, there were new waves of immigration to Europe, Canada, the United States, and Australia from Third World countries. Today, there are perhaps over 150 million migrants in the world, not including undocumented immigrants or internal migrants.

As both Cohen and Wang Gungwu (Director of the East Asian Institute, National University of Singapore) note, migration is not just an economic phenomenon but is frequently politicized. Immigration restrictions, prejudices toward aliens, wars, and civil wars affect the process of border-crossing. Although globalization is often characterized as the movement of capital, goods, and people across national boundaries, the movement of people usually lags behind that of capital or goods. Nevertheless, migration of people has significantly altered the picture of the world. As Cohen shows, it has encouraged the growth of multiculturalism and "hybridity" in countries receiving large numbers of migrants, while, as Wang suggests, a key phenomenon of the contemporary world has been middle-class "sojourning," temporary residence away from home. Together, such phenomena have contributed to the creation of "diasporic cultures" and in many other ways come to exemplify contemporary globalization.

Chapter 9

Robin Cohen

DIASPORAS, THE NATION-STATE, AND GLOBALIZATION

Diaspora as dispersal

THE TERM *DIASPORA* is found in the Greek translation of the Bible and originates in the words for *dispersion* and *to sow or scatter*. The expression was used to describe the Greek colonization of Asia Minor and the Mediterranean in the Archaic period (800–600 BC). Although there was some displacement of the ancient Greeks to Asia Minor as a result of poverty, overpopulation, and inter-state war, *diaspora* essentially had a positive connotation. Expansion through trade, military conquest, and settlement were the predominant features of the Greek diaspora.

Subsequent definitions and explanations of the term are frequently casual or incomplete, but the use of the word *diaspora* often alluded to Jewish historical experiences. In particular, the idea that diaspora implied forcible dispersion was found in Deuteronomy (28:25), with the addition of a typical thunderous Old Testament warning that a diaspora constituted the punishment for a people who had forsaken righteous paths and abandoned the old ways. The destruction of Jerusalem and razing of the walls of its Temple in 586 BC created the central folk memory of a diasporic experience (enslavement, exile, and displacement). The Jewish leader of the time, Zedekiah, had vacillated for a decade, then impulsively sanctioned a rebellion against the powerful Mesopotamian Empire. The Babylonian king Nebuchadnezzar showed no mercy for his impudence. His soldiers forced Zedekiah to witness the execution of his sons; the Jewish leader was then blinded and dragged in chains to Babylon. Peasants were left behind in Judah to till the soil, but the key military, civic, and religious personnel accompanied Zedekiah to captivity in Babylon. Jews had been compelled to desert their "promised land" and thereafter forever became dispersed. [. . .]

From Robin Cohen, "Diasporas, the Nation-State, and Globalization," in Wang Gungwu, ed., *Global History and Migrations* (Boulder, CO: Westview Press, 1997), pp. 118–21, 123–7, 130–41.

"Babylon" as the site of creativity

Perhaps the obvious starting point to a revisionist view of Babylon is that the benefits of integration into a rich and diverse culture were evident both to many of the
first group of Judeans and to their immediate descendants. A substantial number
adopted Babylonian names and customs; the group as a whole used the Babylonian
calendar and embraced the Aramaic language.

Even for those who wished to stay true to their roots, their enforced residence
in Babylon provided an opportunity to construct and define their historical experience, to invent their tradition. Myth, folk tales, oral history, and legal records were
combined into the embryonic bible, and the earnest discussion groups at the homes
of charismatic figures like Jeremiah and Ezekiel ("the prophets") turned into
rudimentary synagogues.

It was, however, the stirring prophecies of a figure know as the second Isaiah
(not his real name, but subsequent editors of the Bible perpetuated this error) that
galvanized a return movement of the exiles. Isaiah hurled colorful imprecations at
Babylon and the Babylonians:

> [. . .] *wild beasts of the desert shall lie there;*
> *and their houses shall be full of doleful creatures;*
> *and owls shall dwell there,*
> *and satyrs shall dance there.*
> *And the wild beasts of the islands shall cry in their desolate houses,*
> *and dragons in their pleasant palaces;*
> *and her time is near to come,*
> *and her days shall not be prolonged.*
>
> (*Isaiah* 13: 20–2)

While denouncing Babylon, Isaiah hammered home the message that "the remnant
of Israel" had to return to Jerusalem to rebuild the Temple. If they did so redemp-
tion (another great diasporic theme) would surely follow. Return some did, but the
purpose of the journey was neither quite so heroic, nor so spiritually pure, as Isaiah
had suggested. Cyrus, the Persian king who had conquered Babylon, permitted and
even encouraged the return of groups of Judeans as a form of enlightened colonialism. "It suited him to have an enclave of grateful Jews in Palestine, close to the
Egyptian border."

Moreover, the homecoming was far from a triumphant success. The restored
Temple (completed in 515 BC) was a paltry affair, the priests were venal, and
the returnees rubbed raw with the Judeans who had remained. It took a Persian-
supported Babylonian priest, Ezra, to implement the law codified in Babylon
(the Torah). His reforms led to a much greater ethnic particularism and religious fundamentalism. Although previously common, exogamous marriages were
now frowned upon, and the highly prescribed purification rituals (circumcision,
atonement, stringent dietary laws, etc.) also date from Ezra's period.

For the next five centuries, the evolution of Judaism in Palestine was marked
by apocalyptic dreamers, messianic claimants, zealots, revolutionaries, and mystics.
Crude attempts by the Greeks to Hellenize the country (a pig was sacrificed on an

altar to Zeus set up on the Temple in 167 BC), then to Romanize it, only served to fan the flames of resistance and played into the hands of the fundamentalists.

By contrast, the Jewish communities in Alexandria, in Antioch and Damascus, in Asia Minor, and in Babylon became centers of civilization, culture, and learning. The Exilarch (the head of the Babylonian Jews) held a position of honor among Jews and non-Jews alike, Jewish academies of learning flourished, and the center-piece of theological exegesis, the Babylonian Talmud, comprising 2.5 million words, made the religious leaders, the Gaons, the cynosure of Jewish culture until the early eleventh century. Sassanian Persia had provided a cultural mélange of several brands of Christianity, astrology, a Persian literary revival, Zoroastrianism, and Indian and Hellenistic thought. Judaism thrived in this hothouse through engagement, encouragement, competition, and the cut and thrust of religious and intellectual debate.

When the Romans destroyed the second Temple in AD 70, it was Babylon that remained as the nerve- and brain-center for Jewish life and thought. Although the word *Babylon* often connotes captivity and oppression, a rereading of the Babylonian period of exile can thus be shown to demonstrate the development of a new creative energy in challenging, pluralistic context outside the natal homeland. This ancient form of what we would nowadays call "multiculturalism" can be regarded as a precursor of the "hybridity" phenomenon that is celebrated by some contemporary writers in the period of globalization. [. . .]

Other components of the traditional notion of the diaspora

The experience of dispersal and collective suffering constitute the key starting points in the definition of the classic diasporas. But if these factors are necessary, they are also insufficient. Three other dimensions were also characteristic of a traditionally conceived diaspora:

* The relationship between a diaspora and its host societies was generally a troubled one.
* A diaspora evidenced a sense of community that transcends national frontiers.
* A diaspora actively participated in the promotion of a return movement (although all certainly would or could not return) and the constitution or reconstitution of a national homeland. [. . .]

Coethnic communities abroad

The sense of unease or difference that diaspora peoples feel in their country of settlement is paralleled by a tendency to identify instead with coethnic communities in other countries. Bonds of language, religion, culture, and a sense of the common fate impregnate such a transnational relationship and give to it an affective, intimate quality that formal citizenship or even long settlement frequently lack.

Nonetheless, there is often a great deal of tension in the relationship between scattered coethnic communities. A bond of loyalty to the country of refuge/settlement competes with ethnic solidarity, although there frequently is a considerable reluctance by those who have stepped far down Herod's path of assimilation to the majority around them to accept too close a link with a despised or low-status ethnic group abroad, even if it happens to be one's own.

For example, that the image of Africans for many African-Americans was initially largely negative is indicated by the very recency of the adoption of this hyphenated self-description. Previously, Africa signified enslavement, poverty, denigration, exploitation, white superiority, the loss of language, and the loss of self-respect. It is little wonder that the key basis of the appeal of populist leaders like Marcus Garvey was to be the desperate need to escape abasement and to express self-esteem and dignity. Again, Richard Wright, although too sophisticated to sign up himself, was a perceptive observer of the early movements of black consciousness. To him the Garveyites showed:

> A passionate rejection of America, for they sensed with a directness of which only the simple are capable that they had no chance to live a full human life in America . . . the Garveyites had embraced a totally racialist outlook which endowed them with a dignity I had never seen before in Negroes. On the walls of their dingy flats were maps of Africa and India and Japan . . . the faces of colored men and women from all parts of the world . . . I gave no credence to the ideology of Garveyism; it was, rather the emotional dynamics of its adherents that evoked my admiration.

The issue of "loyalty" to a country of settlement being challenged by loyalty to one's ethnicity, expressed here for African-Americans, was posed most acutely for European Jewry in the 1840s. A the beginning of that decade the Sharif Pasha of Syria arrested a Jewish barber on the charge of ritual murder, after the mysterious disappearance of an Italian friar and his servant. Confessions under duress, the arrest of Jewish children, and mob violence followed. Because of the then heated European rivalries in the Middle East, the "Damascus Affair" commanded much attention. The French government got drawn into supporting the charges, the Austrian and British governments denounced them.

For French Jewry, a critical moment of crisis had arrived. Although legally emancipated, with long-held views that their adherence to the Jewish religion was no barrier to full citizenship in France, French Jews were suddenly confronted with an impossible dilemma. To advance French international ambitions, the state that had emancipated them was prepared to countenance an anti-Semitic libel. Finally, the initiative was seized by Adolphe Crémieux, a Jew and a prominent French politician, who cooperated with eminent Jews in Great Britain and Austria (France's enemies!) to secure the release of the prisoners in Damascus.

The outcome was an apparent victory in humanitarian terms, but, as Albert Lindemann shows, it was a Pyrrhic one. Thereafter, French patriots argued that love of their brethren would always be greater than the love of French Jews for France. Jews would always be Jews. Moreover, their increasing prominence in commerce and banking meant that wealthy and powerful Jews could act against the nation's interest. It was but a small step to convince fellow patriots that Jews were part of an omnipotent global conspiracy. Such a widely held perception was later to fuel nineteenth- and twentieth-century anti-Semitism.

Support for a homeland

The final additional aspect of the traditionally conceived diasporas, their promotion of a national homeland, lends some support to the charges of dual loyalty, even if not to the more fanciful notions of an international conspiracy.

In the case of French Jewry, for instance, the Damascus Affair was followed by an equally momentous event, the Dreyfus Affair, when, in 1894, a French Jewish army officer was falsely accused of spying for the Germans. "The affair" led to a profound change of heart in Teodor Herzl, hitherto a Herodian, bourgeois, Viennese journalist, who had been sent to cover the Dreyfus trial and later became the key advocate of Zionism. More in sadness than in anger, he concluded:

> Everywhere we Jews have tried honestly to assimilate into the nations around us, preserving only the religion of our fathers. We have not been permitted to. . . . We are a nation – the enemy has made us one without our desiring it . . . We do have the strength to create a state and, moreover, a model state.

Similar feelings of frustration on the part of New World Africans led to the Ethiopian, Garveyite, and Pan-African movements. Just as "Zion" and "Israel" were imagined entities, the African homeland was an equally problematic and fictive community. African hopes sometimes centered on Ethiopia itself particularly after the crowning of Ras (Prince) Tafari as Emperor Haile Selassie of Ethiopia in November 1930. This led directly to the formation of the Rastafarian movement in Jamaica. But for many New World Africans, "Ethiopia" was more of a concept of "blackness" or "Africanity," only loosely connected with the country of Ethiopia itself.

Other Africans in the Americas looked to Liberia – founded by repatriated post-emancipation American slaves – for guidance and leadership. Regrettably, the often venal Americo-Liberian elite rarely showed themselves worthy of this regard. Another strand of support for an African homeland came from Caribbean intellectuals who were decisive actors in the Pan-African and nationalist movements of the post-1945 period. The influence of George Padmore and C.L.R. James in anglophone Africa has been attested to in many accounts.

In the case of the Armenians, the nationalist movement also developed in the nineteenth century, but the Turks held on fiercely and, as previously discussed, engaged in mass deportations rather than concede to demands for independence. A powerful friend of the Armenians emerged in Joseph Stalin, who, no doubt for his own interests, recognized the Soviet Socialist Republic of Armenia, created in 1920. This provided a homeland of sorts, although the Armenian diaspora in France and the United States felt torn in two ways – between the anticommunist policies of their countries of settlement and their homeland within the Soviet empire, imperfect and incomplete as that undoubtedly was. With the end of the Cold War the prospect dawned for a more open and public identification between the Republic of Armenia (proclaimed in 1990) and the Armenian diaspora, an alliance still complicated, however, by continuing Armenian claims to Turkish Armenia and part of Azerbaijan.

Although the Greek diaspora had been created more by colonization than by forcible dispersal, the subsequent weakness of the natal country also led to nationalist awakening. Before the nineteenth century it would have been stretching credulity to call the Greeks "a nation." Dorians, Ionains, and Aeolians were significant subethnicities in ancient Greece, however the major city-states had virtual autonomy one from another. Modern Greek nationalism was much nurtured by what Benedict Anderson called "the golden age of vernacularizing lexicographers, grammarians, philologists, and litterateurs" and by the growth of Philhellenism in the European universities. Modern Greeks were "debarbarized" by this process and rediscovery and urged to be worthy of the likes of Plato, Socrates, and Pericles. The Greek War of Independence attracted the active support of the Philhellenists: The glamorous poet, Lord Byron, joined the Greek insurgents in 1823 and died in the cause. On the success of the insurgency, those bits of ancient Greece that were prised from the Turks were guaranteed independence by British, Russians, and, later, the French. The expulsion of nearly 2 million Greeks from Turkey and Bulgaria to Greece and Crete over the period 1919–20 also dramatically narrowed the ethnic diversity of the area, especially as considerable numbers of Turks and Bulgarians streamed the other way. [. . .]

The newer claimants to diaspora status

In 1991 the UN recognized 160 states; by the end of the century perhaps another 30 will be added to its membership. However, the number of "nation-peoples" (groups evincing a "peoplehood" though the retention or expression of separate languages, customs, folkways, and religions) is estimated at 2,000, over ten times the anticipated number of recognized nation-states. There is an increasing recognition that such peoples are only imperfectly, and sometimes only violently, held within the confines of the existing nation-states as the multiplicity of secessionist movements, ethnic demands, civil wars, and the fragmentation of the former USSR and several of the eastern European states testify.

Even within settled liberal democracies, the old assumption that immigrants would identify with their adopted country in terms of political loyalty, culture, and language can no longer be taken for granted. To the largely free immigrants of old, are added refugees and exiles (now numbering 17 million worldwide) whose movement was primarily dictated by circumstances in their home countries rather than by a desire to establish a new life. Often received with hostility and resentment by the indigenous populations, there is little bonding in the new setting.

In short, "homeland," that "other place," often buried deep in language, religion, custom, collective historical memory, or folklore, has a continuing claim on the loyalty of many contemporary minority communities. That claim may be strong or weak, boldly or meekly articulated in a given circumstance or historical period, but a member's adherence to natal community rather than a country of settlement is demonstrated by an acceptance that the link with the past is unavoidable and acknowledged to be inescapable. This crucial feature of a transnational identity has produced a rash of externally labeled and self-identified diasporas. I have already alluded to the Lebanese trading and Italian labor diasporas. Other claimants include the Chinese, Indian, Polish, Japanese, Ukrainian, Irish, Palestinian, Sikh, Caribbean, German, British, Portuguese, Turkish, and Kurdish diasporas. No doubt other serious candidates can be added to the list.

Do we, in our contemporary understanding of *diaspora*, wish to let "a thousand flowers bloom," thereby diluting the force of the original concepts, or should there be some clear criteria for membership of this hitherto rather exclusive club? My view is an intermediate one. It seems useful for comparative and analytical purposes to retain some of the defining characteristics of the traditionally conceived diasporas, while simultaneously striving to show openness to the newer aspects arising from the mass movements of population in the nineteenth and twentieth centuries and the crisis of the nation-state as we approach the twenty-first century. [. . .]

A collective trauma

In general terms, it is remarkably difficult to separate out the compelling from the voluntary elements in the motivation to migrate. But when we are talking of a trauma afflicting a group collectively, it is perhaps possible to isolate those events where the suddenness, scale, and intensity of exogenous factors unambiguously compel migration or flight. Being dragged off in manacles (as were the Jews and African captives) or being coerced to leave by force of arms (as were the Armenians) appear to be qualitatively different phenomena from the general pressures of overpopulation, and hunger, poverty, or an unsympathetic political regime.

Of the newly named diasporas, Irish writers emphasize the catastrophic origins of large-scale Irish migration, bitterly recalling both the brutality of English occupation and the ordeal of the famine. James Joyce in *Ulysses* (the title, significantly, is the Latin name for Odysseus) puts these words into the mouth of a Dublin citizen:

> We have our greater Ireland beyond the sea. They were driven out of house and home in the black 1847 [the year of the potato famine] . . . Ay they drove out the peasants in hordes, twenty thousand of them died in the coffin-ships. But those that came to the land of the free remember the land of bondage.

The language used here evokes the biblical Jews and the African slaves, a clear cross-identification with two of the classical diasporas. The Palestinians were also violently displaced by the Israeli Zionists who asserted the right – narrowly recognized in a United Nations vote – to a Jewish state. Some 780,000 Arabs were expelled from the territory controlled by the Israeli army, and a further 120,000 Palestinians were later classified as refugees, because they had lost their homes and livelihoods. [. . .]

A cultural flowering in the diaspora

I have alluded to the early case of the achievement of the Jews in Babylon as one example of this phenomenon. Despite their bitter privations, other groups have also made cultural contributions of global significance. Africans in the diaspora produced prominent musical forms like spirituals, jazz, blues, rock 'n' roll, calypso, and reggae; initiated major innovations in the performing arts; and generated a rich vein of literature and poetry. (The first two Nobel laureates for literature in the 1990s were New World writers of African descent.)

It is perhaps the case (although my view is very impressionistic here) that the Armenian and Greek contributions in the diapsora were somewhat less impressive, as both tended to concentrate on the preservation of their great traditions rather than on making a contribution to popular culture in their counties of settlement. Nonetheless, the interrogation of the old culture with the new provided noteworthy achievements among all groups. The Philhellenism movement allowed the diasporic Greeks to be living bearers of the received virtues of the ancient Greeks – in particular, to their philosophical insights, mathematical genius, and democratic spirit. Literature in the British diaspora (in Australia, South Africa, and the United States) soon rivaled, then outstripped native-grown English literature in its vigor and interest. V.S. Naipaul and Salman Rushdie are just two of the sparkling, creative writers of the Indian diaspora. [. . .]

A troubled relationship with the majority

There is barely a migrant ethnic minority that did not at some stage experience discrimination in the countries of their migration. Whether it be Chinese in Malaya, Poles in Germany, Italians in Switzerland, Japanese in Peru, Irish in England, Palestinians in Kuwait, Caribbean peoples in Europe, Sikhs in Britain, Turks and Roma in Germany, or Kurds in Turkey – all these and many others experienced antagonism, legal or illegal discrimination, and have become the objects of violent hatred by majority populations. However, interethnic tension only becomes part of a diasporic phenomenon when disadvantaged groups look outside (for comfort, comparison, and identification) their immediate context to other coethnic communities elsewhere and to the possibility of return to the "homeland." In other words, the possibilities for the redress of their conditions through local representation, civic action, or political agitation must be limited.

I suggested that marginalization of migrant ethnic groups is a fairly universal phenomenon. The major exceptions to this rule are those diasporas that were either aspiring or real settler colonies. The British in the Dominions and North America, the Portuguese in Brazil, and (for a time) the Spanish in the Americas, the French in Canada, and the Dutch in South Africa were able to establish their own hegemony in language, law, religious observance, property rights, and political institutions, thereby forcing the indigenes on to the defensive. [. . .]

Promoting a return movement

All the traditionally accepted diasporas ultimately were influenced by the lure of nationalism – the creation of an Armenian homeland, Philhellenism, Zionism, and Pan-Africanism – as the only certain means to protect their precarious and isolated existence outside their natal areas. Return movements, nationalist awakenings, and improvement schemes for homelands also were common in later diasporas. Although born in China, Sun Yixian (Sun Yat-sen) developed his political consciousness in Hong Kong and Hawaii. His Society for the Revival of China was a crucial instrument in the promotion of a modern Chinese nationalism. His career is interestingly paralleled by that of Mazzini; again born in Italy, but finding an echo for his republic and nationalist ideals largely in the Italian labor diaspora.

To conclude this section, my comparisons between the accepted diasporas and the newer claimants along eight criteria has yielded significant variations, but sufficient common ground to suggest that it is more than poetic license to describe a number of modern peoples as constituting a "diaspora." It is clear that their diasporic consciousness is often in direct contradiction to the exclusivist claims of the modern nation-state and that this has sometimes created major bifurcations of loyalty, identity, ideology, and consciousness. [. . .]

International migration

In the age of globalization, there are no countries that welcome mass migration. Even where selective migration is welcomed, states have sought to prevent the settlement of unskilled, old, or dependent migrants. This tendency has given new life to an old diasporic practice – that of "sojourning" (a cyclical pattern of migration and return common among Chinese, Mexicans, Italians, and others). As Wang Gungwu has pointed out, many of today's "global" migrants are people of considerable wealth and portable skills, a group different from the unskilled labor migrants of the nineteenth century and the refugees and tightly controlled contract workers of more recent decades:

> New classes of people educated in a whole range of modern skills are now prepared to migrate or re-migrate and respond to the pull of centers of power and wealth and the new opportunities in trade and industry. Even more than the traditional sojourners of Southeast Asia, these people are articulate, politically sensitive and choose their new homes carefully. They study the migrant states, especially their laws on the rights of immigrants and the economic conditions for newcomers. . . . Furthermore many are masters not only in the handling of official and bureaucratic connection but also in the art of informal linkages.

As the same author notes, the Chinese sojourner (*huaqiao*) was regarded with considerable suspicion by nationalists in the emerging postwar states of Southeast Asia, especially after the governments in Beijing and Taipei sought to command these migrants' ultimate loyalty. Like the Indians in East Africa or the Lebanese in West Africa and the Caribbean, the colonial powers, notably the Dutch in Indonesia and the British in Malaya and Singapore, had "noted the usefulness of the Chinese as local experts and middlemen, more useful than other Asian traders who were not as widespread and who did not have their inter-port networks."

Ultimately, the networks established in colonial times were superseded by the emergence of migration opportunities in Canada, the United States, and Australia. Sojourners to the new destinations were helped by the global communications and transport revolutions, the stronger legal protection accorded to minorities in the receiving countries, and by the adaptable tradition of sojourning itself.

Transnational social movements

In his discussion of nationalism, Eric Hobsbawm cites some telling figures charting the increasing shift away from the nation-state as a focus of political action and social engagement. The number of intergovernmental international organizations

grew from 123 in 1951, to 280 in 1972, to 365 in 1984. The number of nongovernmental organizations showed an even more spectacular leap – from 832 in 1951,
to 2,173 in 1972, and 4,615 in 1984. The emergence of three great regional
economic blocs – the European Community, the North American Free Trade Area,
and the Asia-Pacific region – will increasingly involve a network of political,
cultural, and social organizations designed to build affiliations of a more social kind
to the compelling economic logics of these blocs. Finally, global social movements
linking women, the greens, the antinuclear and disarmament movement, human
rights, and charitable organizations, have all been added in the postwar world
to virtually the only transnational social movement in the pre-1945 period – the
international labor movement.

   When the followers of the labor Internationals proclaimed that workers had no
country, they were decisively contradicted by the appeals to patriotism and jingoism
in 1914: the workers merely lining up behind the kings, kaisers, and czars to
slaughter each other. Given the spread of supranational, inter- and nongovernmental
organizations and global social movements, one can hardly imagine a nation-state
being able today to command a similar obedience. (Governments in liberal-
democratic states, Israel excepted, now have to rely on professional soldiers to fight
their wars; the attempt by the United States to use drafted soldiers in Vietnam
having ended in defeat.)

   What has all this to do with diasporas? The point here is a simple one. Like the
worker internationalists of 1914, those who wanted to retain open diasporic links
were pitched against powerful, hegemonizing nation-states who sought to make an
exclusive citizenship a defining focus of allegiance and fidelity. The world is simply
not like that any more; the space for multiple affiliations and associations that has
been opened up outside and beyond the nation-state has also allowed a diasporic
affiliation to become both more open and more acceptable.

Cosmopolitan and hybridized cultures

The final aspect of diasporas in the age of globalization that I want to consider here
is the cultural one. Diasporic communities have always been in a better position to
interrogate the particular with the universal. They are better able to discern what
their own group shares with other groups and where its cultural norms and social
practices threaten majority groups. Such awareness, to echo an earlier remark,
constitutes the major component of sechal, without which survival itself might be
threatened. It is perhaps because of this need to be sensitive to the currents around
one, that diaspora groups are typically over-represented in the arts, the cinema, and
the entertainment industry. Awareness of their precarious situation may also propel
members of diasporas to advance legal and civic causes and to be active in human
rights and social justice issues.

   Although knowledge and sensibilities might have enlarged to the point of
cosmopolitanism (or universal humanism), at the same time traditional cultural
values have often been reasserted. Thus, as the postmodernists have argued, a
perverse feature of globalization at the cultural level is that it has also brought about
the fragmentation and multiplication of identities. This may require, paradoxically,
a return to the local and the familiar. Stuart Hall is perhaps the most insightful
observer of this condition:

> The face-to-face communities that are knowable, that are locatable, one
> can give them a place. One knows what the voices are. One knows what
> the faces are. The re-creation, the reconstruction of imaginary, knowable
> places in the face of the global post-modern which has, as it were,
> destroyed the identities of specific places, absorbed them into the post-
> modern flux of diversity. So one understands the moment when people
> reach for those groundings, as it were, and the reach for those groundings
> is what I call ethnicity.

Although this is a rather idiosyncratic view of ethnicity in general, elsewhere
Hall reminds us that an ethnicity, a cultural identity, is not a "fixed essence." Instead,
it is constructed through a blend of memory, fantasy, narrative, and myth. (Many
anthropologists, of course, were aware of this already: so this insight was not
quite so innovative as postmodernists appear to believe.) But Hall takes this idea
much further trying, in particular, to battle with how a Caribbean identity might
be defined.

This, he suggests, cannot be rendered simply as a transposition of a New World
African identity because the rupture of slavery and the admixture of other peoples
built into a Caribbean identity a sense of hybridity, diversity, and difference.
He poses the question, "What makes African-Caribbean people already people of a
diaspora?" and answers as follows:

> Diaspora does not refer us to those scattered tribes whose identity can
> only be secured in relation to some sacred homeland to which they must
> at all costs return, even if it means pushing other people into the sea. This
> is the old, the imperializing, the hegemonizing form of "ethnicity." We
> have seen the fate of the people of Palestine at the hands of this backward
> conception of diaspora – and the complicity of the West with it. The
> diaspora experience as I intend it here is defined not by essence or purity,
> but by the recognition of a necessary heterogeneity and diversity; by a
> conception of identity which lives with and through, not despite, differ-
> ence; by hybridity. Diaspora identities are those which are constantly pro-
> ducing and reproducing themselves anew, through transformation and
> difference.

Hall's notion of diaspora I shall crudely designate as "postmodern," even though he
distances himself from some aspects of this intellectual movement. It is postmodern
in the sense that he wants to use the notion of diaspora to describe contemporary
identities, while nonetheless lifting the notion from its history – in particular from
its moorings in the catastrophic and territorializing tradition. [. . .]

Conclusion

What I have suggested in this account is that notions of "diaspora" are remarkably
diverse. The original Greek word, which signified expansion and settler colonization, can best be compared to the European (especially British, Portuguese, and
Spanish) settlements of the mercantile and colonial period. But the expression

was "hijacked" to describe a catastrophic dispersal of a people and their subsequent unhappiness (or assumed unhappiness) in their countries of exile. More specialist uses of the expression can also be found in the notions of trade and labor diasporas. [. . .]

Diasporas have also been at some level an alternative form of social organization to the singular identity demanded by the hegemonizing nation-state. Just as prior ethnic identities were not melted in the melting pot, so too did a diasporic consciousness survive in the interstices of the modern nation-state. Just as anti-Semites sigh with apparent resignation at the reappearance of "the eternal Jew" (despite forcible conversion, discrimination, and genocidal onslaughts), it may be that diasporas, seen as forms of social organization, have predated the nation-state, lived within it, and now may, in significant respects, transcend and succeed it.

Finally, although this is as yet unfinished business, we should bear in mind the challenging notions of Hall [. . .] that global diasporas have themselves become the sites for the creation and elaboration of new, original, hybridized cultures. The plasticity and complexity of postmodern identities are such, so these writers suggest, that there is no question of recovering the essence of the original identity. Instead, fragments of a mythologized past are combined with a fractured, multicultural, multisourced present to create a new "ethnicity." This form of local bonding, this "grounding," is necessary precisely because globalization has threatened our structures of meaning and meaningfulness. Diasporas, traditionally conceived, modern, global, and newly affirmed, may provide a vital bridge between the individual and society, between the local and the global. The sense of uprootedness, of disconnection, loss, and estrangement, which hitherto was morally appropriated by the traditionally recognized diasporas, may now signify something of the human condition. Emphasizing the creative, enriching side of "Babylon," the radiance of difference, may provide a new form of universal humanism.

Chapter 10

Wang Gungwu

MIGRATION AND ITS ENEMIES

BOTH UNIVERSAL HISTORY and global history assume the linking of many people over time and space. But the former stresses ideals, common faiths and values crossing national boundaries and even continents; it also points at features that show the oneness of humanity. Global history, on the other hand, arises when the regular linking of physical space becomes possible and significant because of the spread of people and technology. The more recent migrations of large numbers of people who had not been allowed to move freely in the past suggest that another way of looking at the use of physical space may now be more fruitful. Modern transportation and communications, together with modern education, have enabled and even encouraged more people to move from one place to another not just once but again and again, to settle or remigrate, and to do so quickly. Moreover, different kinds of people have begun to move, and the migration of educated people in small groups – as nuclear families and as individuals – has become legitimate and acceptable as a new norm. This, in turn, has contributed to a new emphasis on the autonomy of such groups and the individual rights of their members. Global migration seems to have brought forth a more abstract perception of physical space, changing the emphasis from territorial and historical space to finer distinctions and relationships between public and private space. The part played by migration in this change is an important one that deserves attention. Certainly, migration trends and patterns contribute to the definition of global history.

This [essay] focuses on developments that have been caused by the enemies of migration throughout history. A brief look at three major varieties of migration will establish what is meant by enemies. Large-group migrations of tribes, nations, or whole communities occurred from time to time in the past. They invariably led to conflict and then either to conquest of territory or defeat, slaughter, and possible enslavement of the losers. The new borders that were then erected would discourage, if not end, migrations for a long time. Later, there were enforced migrations

From Wang Gungwu, "Migration and Its Enemies," in Bruce Mazlish and Ralph Buultjens, eds, *Conceptualizing Global History* (Boulder, CO: Westview Press, 1993), pp. 132–5, 137–46.

of smaller groups because of famines, plagues, and other disasters. Some members of these groups became colonists or refugees or offered themselves if not as slaves then as bonded or contract labor of one kind or another. By this time, the obstacles to migration were more specific and less absolute, such as host communities that despised the newcomers and, in modern times, immigration officials and trade unions. Finally, a third variety of migration appeared – featuring "sojourners" who eventually became migrants. These were individuals and families who had not intended to migrate but left their countries to trade, to seek skilled employment, to escape temporarily, or to look for adventure and fresh opportunities for betterment. These people were sometimes called economic refugees, and, by and large, they eventually settled down. Their sojourning was actually a kind of experimental migration: Faced with uncertainty, suspicion, or the possibility of other options, sojourners extended their stays abroad indefinitely until a decision to settle was unavoidable. This type of migration has now reappeared in a new form and is increasingly the strategy of middle-class and educated people who wish to postpone as long as possible the final decision on whether to migrate and settle abroad. Many more people today, especially those with education and skills, have learned to appreciate this form of experimental migration.

Migration history is recognized as an important part of conventional history and has been well studied in terms of local, national, and world history. This is not the place to go over familiar ground. Rather, I would ask how migration history can contribute to our understanding of global history. Clearly, the enemies of migration, like the traditional bureaucratic empires and the modern nation-state, are also obstacles to any attempt to give shape to global history. Conversely, the notion of sojourning in relatively open trading societies was never threatening and therefore seemed to have been acceptable to most governments. Migration patterns based on sojourning were reinforced by safer and faster forms of transport and further encouraged and strengthened by the modern communications technology that is essential for international trade. And there is little doubt today that the great trading nations and their finance and marketing centers contribute much to our understanding of global development. They are the centers of wealth and growth that draw people toward them as sojourners or migrants.

It may be useful to reexamine migration history in the context of the globalization of commerce. Again, the large-scale movements of people in the formative periods of ancient kingdoms, empires, cultures, and civilizations are well known. Prior to the formation of strong centralized states, only natural borders existed, consisting mostly of mountains, deserts, swamps, and river valleys that, sooner or later, some powerful tribe or tribal confederation would cross in mass migrations. The stories of the Aryans who entered India, the Turks who spread to China, Europe, and West Asia, the Arabs who fought their way across North Africa into the Iberian peninsula and traded south into sub-Saharan Africa, and the Teutonic tribes who expanded at the expense of the Celts and the Slavs have all been central to conventional history; indeed, they have made such history exciting and comprehensible. But mass migrations of this kind normally led to settlement and the filling up of empty spaces and therefore to new state formations and defensive structures. These structures were set up against the challenges of further sizable migrations. Thus, migrants involved in large-scale settlement would very naturally have created their own instruments for self-protection and survival. This, in turn, led to the establishment of institutions that themselves became hostile to future migrations. The story of such migrations alone adds little to the idea of global history. The vast spaces they linked together were soon divided from one another: For such mass migrations, linked space was temporary and quickly succeeded by political and military barriers against future links.

The globalization of the modern world has changed that. In the initial stage, following the end of slavery, major migration of cheap contract labor was needed in various parts of the European empires to feed the industrial revolution in Europe. In the Americas, the demand was smaller because the freed slaves and their descendants could still work. And when American capitalists needed fresh industrial labor, they turned to the impoverished parts of Europe itself. In Asia and the Caribbean, however, most of the coolie laborers were Chinese and East Indians. They were shipped overseas to plantations and mines to build roads and railways and clear jungles and bush. They were not skilled enough to be highly regarded or well rewarded, but they were useful and thereby fulfilled one of the principal conditions of migration. Because they were useful to the colonial territories, many stayed on after the end of their contracts and settled down as migrants. Unfortunately for them, they encountered the phenomenon of white superiority that had emerged from the period of imperial power during the nineteenth century and was to last until the end of the Second World War. This had been tolerable in Asia, where the whites were few in number. But in the migrant states of America and Australasia, the Asian migrants could not assimilate as equal citizens, nor were they allowed to enlarge their communities through chain migrations. Many chose to go home instead, while those who stayed were allowed to remain on the periphery of white society as unwelcome sojourners. This was, to be sure, an ambiguous state to be in, but it was the only condition under which they could survive.

The second stage, coming after the end of the Second World War, was an improvement for migration but only marginally so. On the one hand, concepts of racial superiority were on their way out, and greater compassion was found for the victims of war and deprivation, the millions of displaced people and political refugees (especially from Europe) for whom homes had to be found. On the other hand, the modern empires came to an end and were succeeded by scores of new nation-states. Although these new states subscribed to a UN Charter that endorsed great principles dedicated to supporting the poor and the oppressed, assisting migrant labor, and protecting persecuted refugees, the institutions available to implement these principles were still subject to the bureaucratic controls of national bodies. Migration was not a priority, and its enemies, especially those suspicious of what it might do to slow down nation-building efforts, stayed in control. What was remarkable, however, was the change in political conditions that created large numbers of upper- and middle-class refugees all over the world. This was followed by a change in values that permitted these people to become sojourner-migrants. Also unprecedented was the way the modern skilled and educated classes responded to the pull of the centers of power and wealth and the new transnational opportunities in trade and industry. These new types of migrants were articulate and politically sensitive, and they knew how to move in high native circles. They knew the law and their rights, and their successful adaptation to local conditions strengthened their capacity to transform the environment for all migrants. Most of all, as befitting their origins, they were masters in handling official and bureaucratic connections and in the art of informal linkages. They quickly sought to lay the foundations for even greater changes.

The way that varieties of migration evolved and ebbed and flowed through time, I would suggest, is a major feature of global history. Modern sojourning, in particular, has contributed to a better understanding of what global history might mean. The rest of this [essay] will examine the changes in two parts. [. . .]

Why the extended periods of sojourning by the Chinese did not lead to colonization or full-scale migration is relevant to migration history. The *qiao* ("sojourner") or *qiaoju* ("sojourning") phenomenon was a product of Confucian rhetoric, of the exhortations to be filial and loyal to heads of family and the clan-based village so prevalent in southern China. This was a powerful value system that enjoined everyone never to move away from *his* ancestral home (women were carefully excluded from any form of sojourning to ensure that the men returned). Migration was simply not an option; only sojourning on official duty or as a trader was permissible. Any other kind of departure amounted to rejection of the family, and life as an exile from home was punishment indeed in China because no other place would normally receive such people except in bondage. Leaving home was feared, and seeking settlement elsewhere was an unwelcome prospect.

Chinese traders sojourned in Japan, Korea, and Southeast Asia. Most of them returned after a few years overseas, but many stayed on to marry locally and establish second homes abroad. Some had, for all intents and purposes, settled down with their local families. But with advances in transportation during the preceding two centuries, links with their ancestral homes became easier, and regular visits home were possible. Then came the massive migrations of largely unskilled labor during the nineteenth century, not only to Southeast Asia but also the Americas and Australasia. As the Chinese saw it, this was not migration but mere sojourning. But calling the phenomenon sojourning did not prevent migration and settlement. By the twentieth century, Chinese women could also leave their homes to join their husbands abroad, and the conditions for settlement were complete.

Yet the concept of sojourning persisted, even though its meaning had been modified. Now, sojourning was not necessarily temporary but could be for life and could stretch over generations. It also meant that a highly particularistic loyalty toward family and the clan-based village could be the basis of linked space over great distances. This created the conditions for the kind of small-group autonomy (independent of states and governments) that would be strengthened and supported by later advances in communications technology. This kind of linkage has been compared to the kind of autonomous space that enabled Jewish communities in different parts of the world to survive for centuries. But the Chinese idea of sojourning was not expressed in terms of nationality or a single unified and structured religion. Sojourning for the Chinese was predicted on trading relations and physical ties with their ancestral homes. These Chinese sojourners never experienced the intensity of emotional and spiritual power that characterized the relations between Israel and the Jewish Diaspora.

The bulk of the Chinese sojourners went to Southeast Asia, and millions of their descendants are still there. What has changed for them, however, is that new nation-states emerged after the period of Western colonialism. In the context of local nationalism and the powerful pressures of nation-building, those Chinese who have decided to settle have adopted the nationalities of their adopted homes. But Southeast Asian national governments continue to wonder if many of their local Chinese are still unrepentant sojourners. Meanwhile, other local Chinese who have become loyal nationals find the tradition of linked spatial relationships with ancestral homes still invaluable for long-distance trade with China and with other descendants of Chinese elsewhere in the world. One might add that the hundreds of thousands of Chinese who traveled even greater distances – to other parts of Asia and other continents like the Americas, Australasia, Europe, and Africa – had extended their sojourning pattern of spatial relationships everywhere. Also, it is interesting that other East Asians with comparable Confucian familial backgrounds, the Koreans and the Japanese, practiced a diluted form of sojourning but nevertheless achieved, in their own way, the same kind of linked spatial relationships over great distances. Despite the differences among the three major groups of East Asians, it is noteworthy that their behavior patterns and cultural manifestations are often perceived by other ethnic groups as the same, and there is a tendency to group them all together. What is striking, however, is that they are all attuned to the modern communications technology that makes the linking of spatial relationships relatively easy and makes their autonomy as small groups seem unusually well protected, if not invulnerable. [. . .]

The picture of extensive migrations of peoples and culture that made Southeast Asia what it is today is overdrawn and misleading because it neglects indigenous attitudes toward migration. Migration in Southeast Asia was either peripheral to mainstream society (as in the mainland states around the great valleys of the Irrawaddy, Salween, Menam, Mekong, and Red rivers) or integral and vital (as in the coastal and trading ports and kingdoms of the Malay archipelago). In the mainland states, migration communities were rarely significant. But in the archipelago polities of all the centuries before European dominance, overseas trade was an overriding concern. For them, migrant traders in their port cities brought wealth and power. They were therefore welcome for their role in linking these ports with the great ports of other regions, be they Chinese, Indian, Arab, or Persian. The spatial links were essential to the trading relationships. The autonomy of the small groups was a necessary part of those links, and although many of these migrant groups settled down as loyal subjects to the local rulers, they did not have to lose the autonomy that made them the wealth-creating communities they had become. In this context, migration was not associated with absorption or assimilation or integration but with the migrants' usefulness as economic actors across great distances overseas, especially as skilled labor or as commercial agents and advisers. Certainly, superior transport technology (in this case, shipping) had an impact in ways that were impossible for overland trade until the advent of modern railways and highways. Hence, before the nineteenth century, migrants or sojourners who were masters of shipping technology were invaluable, and even those who accompanied them as merchants and skilled hands were welcomed.

The contrast between East and Southeast Asia is clear. People movement was difficult in East Asia: In that region, the enemies of migration were dominant, there were strong local identities in closed societies, there was a centralized bureaucratic state, and foreign trade was not important. This was also true in the mainland Southeast Asian states, which resembled their northern neighbor, China, in many ways. But in the archipelago states of Southeast Asia, there were few enemies of migration before modern times, that is, before the creation of the nation-states that replaced the colonial administrations after the end of the Second World War. Today, the nation-state as an obstacle to the easy movement of peoples (in other words, as an enemy of migration) seems to have come to stay in Southeast Asia. Yet there are extenuating factors that are worth noting in archipelago states that, together with Thailand, have formed the Association of Southeast Asian Nations (ASEAN). While they are all building central bureaucracies and emphasizing strong local identities, they have affirmed the great importance of foreign or international trade and investment and kept their societies relatively open to outside influences. Their history of valuing the long-distance links that were vital to their trading economies and their tolerance of autonomous migrant groups in their midst over the centuries have made them more open to external opportunities. In that way, they have made their contribution to the globalization of history.

The suggestion that the modern nation-state is an enemy of migration needs modification. This institution was created in the modern West, but it had evolved from powerful kingly states, some of them (like the British Isles, Scandinavia, the Netherlands, and Portugal) not unlike the trading port cities and kingdoms of Southeast Asia. Because these nation-states have evolved over time, they are relatively open. There had been no need for painful and melodramatic efforts at nation-building (with the exception of Nazi Germany). Thus, it is not the nation-state itself that is necessarily hostile to migration. Rather, it is the artificial boundaries of some of the Southeast Asian states and the haste with which they were created that made people in these states feel politically insecure and, as a consequence, actively opposed to migration. Yet useful migrant groups in the ASEAN states remain free to participate fully in commercial and industrial enterprises and even play a global role in international finance and trade.

In the nation-states, despite many kinds of newly erected barriers, migrations by individuals, families, and small groups continued as long as they were non-threatening to those who were already settled. Furthermore, it was expected that the migrants would eventually be absorbed into the native populations. And until modern times, this was inevitable if only because the means of transport allowing the migrants to return to their original homes were limited and difficult. Perhaps the only exception to the norm of assimilation involved some groups of Jews, whose struggle to survive as a distinct people was a truly exceptional story that would later play a part in global history.

Before I turn to that topic, it would be useful to focus on the paradoxes of migration history in the two major North Atlantic regions: Europe and North America. Like many other aspects of modernization and globalization, the key ideas and institutions underlying the paradoxes originated in these regions.

Europe, fragmented throughout its history, may be compared to Southeast Asia, but it has been culturally homogenous in ways that Southeast Asia has never been. Except for brief interludes when Muslim forces led by the Arabs and the Turks dominated the Mediterranean and southeastern Europe respectively (and an even briefer period when Mongol armies rode in from the east), the European heritage has been Christian. With a common religion, small group migrations before modern times from one part of Europe to another were never a problem, and they were rarely mentioned in the history books. Much of conventional history has been convened with dynastic, civil, and sectarian religious wars, defenses against the power of Islam, and the political and constitutional evolution from monarchies to democracies; with qualitative changes in the feudal and capitalist economies of the region; with overseas expansion since the sixteenth century; and with the scientific and technological revolution that is still with us. The dynamics of such historical developments, including the increasingly major migrations across the Atlantic from the 1500s onward, led to worldwide modernization and obviously are part of global history. But insofar as those developments also produced the conditions leading to plethora of nation-states around the world – one manifestation of the enemies of migration – they have also produced paradoxes that need to be explained.

The roots of the paradoxes may be found in the unique separation of church and state that evolved gradually in most of the western and central regions of the Christian world. That eventual separation produced parallel legal concepts, if not systems, that protected subjects from their rulers, individual citizens from the authorities, minorities from majorities, and even migrants from the natives. These radical changes were indeed slow to come about whether under monarchic rule or in republican nation-states. For a long time, even when the legal provisions were agreed upon, they were often poorly administered or not followed. And when they were too slow in coming about, the subjects or citizenry who felt disadvantaged, dispossessed, and oppressed and those who knew they were discriminated against voted with their feet and migrated to new lands, especially those opened up for settlement in North America.

Of course, not all migration from Europe to the Americas was of this kind. More common were poor and landless migrants in search of land and new opportunities. Others were recruited for jobs not available at home. There were also better-off people, sojourners of a type, who could afford to try to seek their fortunes in the New World. For example, many of the soldiers and officials who set up the administrative and legal structures, the adventurers who probed the frontiers and opened up the wilderness, and the traders who linked the newly settled places with the centers of civilization in the Old World had not intended to migrate but eventually either did so themselves or made it possible for their families or descendants to do so. But unlike the usual migrants in search of land and work, there were also those who wanted to be free and equal – more specifically, free to worship in their own faith and be equal before God and the law. Theirs were far-reaching goals that proved difficult to achieve. But the ideals that were transplanted to the migrant-established new nation-state known as the United States of America found the soil congenial. And the leaders there established new and higher standards of rights and duties in order to protect those who came after them. These standards, in turn, greatly influenced several other migrant states that also drew their populations from Europe.

Thus, in the course of the past two centuries, the Old World states and societies of Europe spawned a number of migrant states in the Americas and Australasia. Thankfully, these new states have sustained the peoples' desire to start afresh in the New World and have not reproduced all the narrow-minded traditions and practices of the Old World. On the contrary, they have translated most of the Old World's arbitrary migration controls into channels of regular and continuous migration. Such a transformation was by no means straightforward: Indeed, the convoluted story of the different migration stages – freedom-seeking colonization, convict transportation, markets for slave labor, refuge for the poor and the persecuted, down to the selective "brain-draining" immigration of recent years – makes fascinating reading.

By the beginning of the twentieth century, these developments had become part of the larger picture of globalization.

More specifically, four factors have assisted the transformation in the migrant states that have challenged the enemies of migration. These factors have, in turn, influenced migration policies of the old nation-states of Europe and, to a lesser extent, even of some of the new nation-states elsewhere. The four are the Holocaust experience in Central Europe and its ramifications; the new categories of political refugees; the communications revolution; and the evolving concept of universal human rights. I will briefly outline the reasons for their powerful influence on patterns of migration.

The story of the Jewish Diaspora, an unfinished migration history, stands alone. As a chain of anti-Semitic pogroms and a symbol of unrelenting religious persecution, it also surpasses the experience of all other migrant groups. How that extraordinary heritage of an unassimilated migrant minority led to the Holocaust perpetuated by Nazi Germany belongs to the history of the explosive power of nationalism and the new nation-state. Had the Germans succeeded in establishing the Third Reich in Europe, their racial policies would have led to the end of migration as we know it in that part of the world. The only exceptions would have been the returning migrants of the same nation and culture, for example, the Sudeten and Volga Germans and the German settlers in the Americas. Beyond that, Hitler's solution was to expand Germany to encompass all people of the same "race." Ultimately, however, the horror of the Holocaust challenged some earlier claims to European civilization. The Second World War led to the creation of the state of Israel, which embodied the idea of a historic homeland that migrating Jews could return to or identify with. That is still a mixed blessing, encompassing, on the one hand, the ideals of the rights of minorities and, on the other, also representing the narrow interests of a nation-state. But the overall effect of the tragic events of the Holocaust is still a positive one. [. . .]

The second new factor concerns a subtype of migratory peoples, the refugees who had never sought to migrate but were forced to leave their homes because of religious and political persecution or because of their racial or ethnic origins. The flood of refugees driven from one territory to another is not a new phenomenon. The idea of the exodus or the exile (of the Jews from Egypt or from Babylon) has come down to us from ancient history, and there have been many other equally dramatic examples of enforced migration through the centuries, most of them related to religious or racial persecution. But it was not until the late nineteenth century that national borders became barriers to refugees. And, following the large-scale displacement of people in Europe during and after the First World War, Western governments were forced to take the problem seriously and acknowledge the need for joint international efforts to deal with it. Organizations within the League of Nations and then, after the Second World War, the United Nations were created to take care of the millions of refugees created by wars both large and small.

The problem became global when more and more refugees had to be shipped thousands of miles in every direction. The idea of refugeeism itself, especially in terms of political refugees persecuted for holding dissident views, had to be further refined and related to the wider question of migration. In particular, refugees had to be clearly distinguished from different kinds of involuntary migrants in a world ever more divided between very rich and very poor countries. As more people feel compelled to leave their homes in search of a livelihood and to escape not only from war and chaos but also from dire poverty, death by disease, and starvation, the claims to refugee status – seeking freedom from want – have grown rapidly and globally. And, as with the early migrations of pilgrims and religious minorities to North America, the new categories of migrants now include those seeking freedom and protection from political persecution. This recent development, which blurs distinctions, adds a political dimension to the concept of linked global space. It enables migrants of like political faiths and goals to globalize their ideals and have their values physically linked through networks independent of the nation-states and their narrowly defined migration targets. It has given new meaning to small groups, families, and individuals scattered about the world. And it has joined them together, through their political beliefs, within the realm of global history.

The third factor, the communications revolution that made fine technical networks of spatial relationships possible, also sprang from Europe and North America. But today these networks now reach every corner of the globe. All they need are people to use and service them, and migrants, especially better educated ones, are well positioned to take full advantage of the power and range of these networks. The rapid rate of scientific discovery in the field of transport and communications and the speed at which these discoveries have been translated into practical applications have been sources of wonderment for decades. This is even more true of the ability of every country, city, and territory in the world to respond quickly and acquire the skills to use these applications effectively.

The technological links now established between distant places have strengthened the spatial relationships created by past and present migrations. If the links are also open and accessible, they further reinforce the idea of ethnic minority rights, as well as the multicultural conditions that several migrant states have consciously supported. And not least of all, such links and conditions may ultimately encourage the globalization of the special form of migration found in East and Southeast Asia, known by the Chinese as sojourning – being temporarily away from home for generations. The new communications links would enable many migrants or migrant communities to live, behave, think, and feel as if they had never really left home. The influence such developments would have on cultural renewal, exchange, and intercrossing is considerable. But, more immediately, the challenge they pose to older ideas like settlement and assimilation would have to be met, not by violence and force, it is hoped, but with patience and imagination. Certainly, if the phenomenon has come to stay, much rethinking in the context of global history will be needed.

The fourth factor is connected to the three already outlined. The concept of universal human rights has become less abstract because of the shock of the Holocaust, the plight of political refugees, and the widespread access to speedy communications. Although human rights appear superficially comparable with other, more traditional, ideas about fellowship, compassionate humanity, and equality before God and are therefore generally appealing to the common man or woman, the concept is different in nature and goes much further than the earlier ideas. Human rights must be traced to the same tradition of church–state separation that was there at the beginning of modernization in western Europe. Hence, there is a strong connection with the law that protects one's rights and with individuals who wish to guard the right to be true to their own consciences. The concept of human rights has already found application in the right to migrate, whether as free labor or as refugees, and no doubt it will be further refined to defend the rights of migrants to preserve their cultural values and their private relationships with their ancestral homes. There is still a large gap in understanding between peoples and also in the institutional structures needed to implement such rights. Moreover, there are political barriers, both national and international, that may inhibit the rapid promotion of the idea of human rights for decades to come. But the first step has been taken in the attempt to globalize the right of an individual to his or her own private spatial relationships with whomever he or she likes in the world. That migrants might choose to use this right to intensify their relations with their original homes would be understandable. It also seems clear that this could minimize the difference between these migrants and sojourners. The decision, then, for migrants to redefine themselves as sojourner-migrants would not be a difficult one to make. It is not too early to recognize this step as a part of global history.

Many remarkable developments have followed the globalization of issues and problems in modern history. There is the fact that the enemies of migration are being challenged, if not undermined. And there is the paradox that the attempts to control migration have actually led to greater protection of migrant and refugee rights. In turn, closer study of migration issues should throw much light on global history.

PART VI

Consumerism

THE RISE OF THE "CONSUMER SOCIETY" is an important aspect of the global age. For most countries, whether predominantly agricultural or heavily industrialized, production was the key economic activity. The transition from a producer society to a consumer society has been a rather recent phenomenon, although there have always been activities catering to the consumption of goods that are produced: salesmanship, marketing, advertisement, and the like. These activities have become much more intensive and, significantly, global as consumerism has spread all over the world. As Saskia Sassen (Professor of Sociology at the University of Chicago) notes, global cities have developed as centers of finance, services, and consumption.

Consumption is not just an economic activity, however. It has a psychological as well as a political dimension. As Bruce Mazlish points out, consumption becomes a "self-consuming force" as people try to vie with one another to demonstrate their higher standard of living, and of taste, in what they consume. To the extent that in many societies the housewife determines what is purchased, consumerization may tend to enhance the role and status of women. Since what to purchase and consume is almost always a question of choice, consumption may be linked to freedom, and ultimately to democratization.

Chapter 11

Saskia Sassen

THE GLOBAL CITY:
NEW YORK, LONDON, TOKYO

FOR CENTURIES, THE WORLD ECONOMY shaped the life of cities. [. . .] Beginning in the 1960s, the organization of economic activity entered a period of pronounced transformation. The changes were expressed in the altered structure of the world economy, and also assumed forms specific to particular places. Certain of these changes are by now familiar: the dismantling of once powerful industrial centers in the United States, the United Kingdom, and more recently in Japan; the accelerated industrialization of several Third World countries; the rapid internationalization of the financial industry into a worldwide network of transaction. Each of these changes altered the relation of cities to the international economy.

In the decades after World War II, there was an international regime based on United States dominance in the world economy and the rules for global trade contained in the 1945 Bretton Woods agreement. By the early 1970s, the conditions supporting that regime were disintegrating. The breakdown created a void into which stepped, perhaps in a last burst of national dominance, the large US transnational industrial firms and banks. In this period of transition, the management of the international economic order was to an inordinate extent run from the headquarters of these firms. By the early 1980s, however, the large US transnational banks faced the massive Third World debt crisis, and US industrial firms experienced sharp market share losses from foreign competition. Yet the international economy did not simply break into fragments. The geography and composition of the global economy changed so as to produce a complex duality: a spatially dispersed, yet globally integrated organization of economic activity.

The point of departure for the present study is that the combination of spatial dispersal and global integration has created a new strategic role for major cities. Beyond their long history as centers for international trade and banking, these cities now function in four new ways: first, as highly concentrated command points in the organization of the world economy; second, as key locations for finance and for specialized service firms, which have replaced manufacturing as the leading economic

From Saskia Sassen, *The Global City*, 2nd edition (Princeton University Press, 2001), pp. 3–13.

sectors; third, as sites of production, including the production of innovations, in these leading industries; and fourth, as markets for the products and innovations produced. These changes in the functioning of cities have had a massive impact upon both international economic activity and urban form: Cities concentrate control over vast resources, while finance and specialized service industries have restructured the urban social and economic order. Thus a new type of city has appeared. It is the global city. Leading examples now are New York, London, and Tokyo. [. . .]

As I shall show, these three cities have undergone massive and *parallel* changes in their economic base, spatial organization, and social structure. But this parallel development is a puzzle. How could cities with as diverse a history, culture, and economy as New York, London, and Tokyo experience similar transformations concentrated in so brief a period of time? Not examined at length in my study, but important to its theoretical framework, is how transformations in cities ranging from Paris to Frankfurt to Hong Kong and Sao Paulo have responded to the same dynamic. To understand the puzzle of parallel change in diverse cities requires not simply a point-by-point comparison of New York, London, and Tokyo, but a situating of these cities in a set of global processes. In order to understand why major cities with different histories and cultures have undergone parallel economic and social changes, we need to examine transformations in the world economy. Yet the term *global city* may be reductive and misleading if it suggests that cities are mere outcomes of a global economic machine. They are specific places whose spaces, internal dynamics, and social structure matter; indeed, we may be able to understand the global order only by analyzing why key structures of the world economy are *necessarily* situated in cities.

How does the position of these cities in the world economy today differ from that which they have historically held as centers of banking and trade? When Max Weber analyzed the medieval cities woven together in the Hanseatic League, he conceived their trade as the exchange of surplus production; it was his view that a medieval city could withdraw from external trade and continue to support itself, albeit on a reduced scale. The modern molecule of global cities is nothing like the trade among self-sufficient places in the Hanseatic League, as Weber understood it. The first thesis advanced in this [study] is that the territorial dispersal of current economic activity creates a need for expanded central control and management. In other words, while in principle the territorial decentralization of economic activity in recent years could have been accompanied by a corresponding decentralization in ownership and hence in the appropriation of profits, there has been little movement in that direction. Though large firms have increased their subcontracting to smaller firms, and many national firms in the newly industrializing countries have grown rapidly, this form of growth is ultimately part of a chain. Even industrial homeworkers in remote rural areas are now part of that chain. The transnational corporations continue to control much of the end product and to reap the profits associated with selling in the world market. The internationalization and expansion of the financial industry has brought growth to a large number of smaller financial markets, a growth which has fed the expansion of the global industry. But top-level control and management of the industry have become concentrated in a few leading financial centers, notably New York, London, and Tokyo. These account for a disproportionate share of all financial transactions and one that has grown rapidly since the early 1980s. The fundamental dynamic posited here is that the more globalized the economy becomes, the higher the agglomeration of central functions in a relatively few sites, that is, the global cities.

The extremely high densities evident in the business districts of these cities are one spatial expression of this logic. The widely accepted notion that density and agglomeration will become obsolete because global telecommunications advances allow for maximum population and resource dispersal is poorly conceived. It is, I argue, precisely because of the territorial dispersal facilitated by telecommunication that agglomeration of certain centralizing activities has sharply increased. This is not a mere continuation of old patterns of agglomeration; there is a new logic for concentration. In Weberian terms, there is a new system of "coordination," one which focuses on the development of specific geographic control sites in the international economic order.

A second major theme of this [study] concerns the impact of this type of economic growth on the economic order within these cities. It is necessary to go beyond the Weberian notion of coordination and Bell's notion of the postindustrial society to understand this new urban order. Bell, like Weber, assumes that the further society evolves from the nineteenth-century industrial capitalism, the more the apex of the social order is involved in pure managerial process, with the content of what is to be managed becoming of secondary importance. Global cities are, however, not only nodal points for the coordination of processes; they are also particular sites of production. They are sites for (1) the production of specialized services needed by complex organizations for running a spatially dispersed network of factories, offices, and service outlets; and (2) the production of financial innovations and the making of markets, both central to the internationalization and expansion of the financial industry. To understand the structure of a global city, we have to understand it as a place where certain kinds of work can get done, which is to say that we have to get beyond the dichotomy between manufacturing and services. The "things" a global city makes are services and financial goods.

It is true that high-level business services, from accounting to economic consulting, are not usually analyzed as a production process. Such services are usually seen as a type of output derived from high-level technical knowledge. I shall challenge this view. Moreover, using new scholarship on producer services, I shall examine the extent to which a key trait of global cities is that they are the most *advanced* production sites for creating these services.

A second way this analysis goes beyond the existing literature on cities concerns the financial industry. I shall explore how the character of a global city is shaped by the emerging organization of the financial industry. The accelerated production of innovations and the new importance of a large number of relatively small financial institutions led to a renewed or expanded role for the marketplace in the financial industry in the decade of the 1980s. The marketplace has assumed new strategic and routine economic functions, in comparison to the prior phase, when the large transnational banks dominated the national and international financial market. Insofar as financial "products" can be used internationally, the market has reappeared in a new form in the global economy. New York, London, and Tokyo play roles as production sites for financial innovations and centralized marketplaces for these "products."

A key dynamic running through these various activities and organizing my analysis of the place of global cities in the world economy is their capability for producing global control. By focusing on the production of services and financial innovations, I am seeking to displace the focus of attention from the familiar issues of the power of large corporations over governments and economies, or supra-corporate concentration of power through interlocking directorates or organizations, such as the IMF. I want to focus on an aspect that has received less attention, which could be referred to as the *practice* of global control: the work of producing and reproducing the organization and management of a global production system and a global marketplace for finance. My focus is not on power, but on production: the production of those inputs that constitute the capability for global control and the infrastructure of jobs involved in this production.

The power of large corporations is insufficient to explain the capability for global control. Obviously, governments also face an increasingly complex environment in which highly sophisticated machineries of centralized management and control are necessary. Moreover, the high level of specialization and the growing demand for these specialized inputs have created the conditions for a freestanding industry. Now small firms can buy components of global capability, such as management consulting or international legal advice. And so can firms and governments anywhere in the world. While the large corporation is undoubtedly a key agent inducing the development of this capability and is a prime beneficiary, it is not the sole user.

Equally misleading would be an exclusive focus on transnational banks. Up to the end of the 1982 Third World debt crisis, the large transnational banks dominated the financial markets in terms of both volume and the nature of firm transactions. After 1982, this dominance was increasingly challenged by other financial institutions and the innovations they produced. This led to a transformation in the lending components of the financial industry, a proliferation of financial institutions, and the rapid internationalization of financial markets rather than just a few banks. The incorporation of a multiplicity of markets all over the world into a global system fed the growth of the industry after the 1982 debt crisis, while also creating new forms of concentration in a few leading financial centers. Hence, in the case of the financial industry, a focus on the large transnational banks would exclude precisely those sectors of the industry where much of the new growth and production of innovations has occurred; it would leave out an examination of the wide range of activities, firms, and markets that constitute the financial industry in the 1980s.

Thus, there are a number of reasons to focus a study on marketplaces and production sites rather than on the large corporations and banks. Most scholarship on the internationalization of the economy has already focused on the large corporations and transnational banks. To continue to focus on the corporations and banks would mean to limit attention to their formal power, rather than examining the wide array of economic activities, many outside the corporation, needed to produce and reproduce that power. And, in the case of finance, a focus on the large transnational banks would leave out precisely that institutional sector of the industry where the key components of the new growth have been invented and put into circulation. [. . .]

A third major theme explored in this [study] concerns the consequences of these developments for the national urban system in each of these countries and for the relationship of the global city to its nation-state. While a few major cities are the sites of production for the new global control capability, a large number of other major cities have lost their role as leading export centers for industrial manufacturing, as a result of the decentralization of this form of production. Cities such as Detroit, Liverpool, Manchester, and now increasingly Nagoya and Osaka have been affected by the decentralization of their key industries at the domestic and international levels. According to the first hypothesis presented above, this same process has contributed to the growth of service industries that produce the specialized inputs to run global production processes and global markets for inputs and outputs. These industries – international legal and accounting services, management consulting, financial services – are heavily concentrated in cities such as New York, London, and Tokyo. We need to know how this growth alters the relations between the global cities and what were once the leading industrial centers in their nations. Does globalization bring about a triangulation so that New York, for example, now plays a role in the fortunes of Detroit that it did not play when that city was home to one of the leading industries, auto manufacturing? Or, in the case of Japan, we need to ask, for example, if there is a connection between the increasing shift of production out of Toyota City (Nagoya) to offshore locations (Thailand, South Korea, and the United States) and the development for the first time of a new headquarters for Toyota in Tokyo.

Similarly, there is a question about the relation between such major cities as Chicago, Osaka, and Manchester, once leading industrial centers in the world, and global markets generally. Both Chicago and Osaka were and continue to be important financial centers on the basis of their manufacturing industries. We would want to know if they have lost ground, relatively, in these functions as a result of their decline in the global industrial market, or instead have undergone parallel transformation toward strengthening of service functions. Chicago, for example, was at the heart of a massive agroindustrial complex, a vast regional economy. How has the decline of that regional economic system affected Chicago?

In all these questions, it is a matter of understanding what growth embedded in the international system of producer services and finance has entailed for different levels in the national urban hierarchy. The broader trends – decentralization of plants, offices, and service outlets, along with the expansion of central functions as a consequence of the need to manage such decentralized organization of firms – may well have created conditions contributing to the growth of regional subcenters, minor versions of what New York, London, and Tokyo do on a global and national scale. The extent to which the developments posited for New York, London, and Tokyo are also replicated, perhaps in less accentuated form in smaller cities, at lower levels of the urban hierarchy, is an open, but important question.

The new international forms of economic activity raise a problem about the relationship between nation-states and global cities. [. . .] I posit the possibility of a systematic discontinuity between what used to be thought of as national growth and the forms of growth evident in global cities in the 1980s. These cities constitute a system rather than merely competing with each other. What contributes to growth in the network of global cities may well not contribute to growth in nations. For instance, is there a systemic relation between, on the one hand, the growth in global cities and, on the other hand, the deficits of national governments and the decline of major industrial centers in each of these countries?

The fourth and final theme in the [study] concerns the impact of these new forms of and conditions for growth on the social order of the global city. There is a vast body of literature on the impact of a dynamic, high growth manufacturing sector in the highly developed countries, which shows that it raised wages, reduced inequality, and contributed to the formation of a middle class. Much less is known about the sociology of a service economy. Daniel Bell's *The Coming of Post-Industrial Society* posits that such an economy will result in growth in the number of highly educated workers and a more rational relation of workers to issues of social equity. One could argue that any city representing a post-industrial economy would surely be like the leading sectors of New York, London, and increasingly Tokyo.

I will examine to what extent the new structure of economic activity has brought about changes in the organization of work, reflected in a shift in the job supply and polarization in the income distribution and occupational distribution of workers. Major growth industries show a greater incidence of jobs at the high- and low-paying ends of the scale than do the older industries now in decline. Almost half the jobs in the producer services are lower-income jobs, and half are in the two highest earnings classes. In contrast, a large share of manufacturing workers were in the middle-earnings jobs during the postwar period of high growth in these industries in the United States and United Kingdom.

Two other developments in global cities have also contributed to economic polarization. One is the vast supply of low-wage jobs required by high-income gentrification in both its residential and commercial settings. The increase in the numbers of expensive restaurants, luxury housing, luxury hotels, gourmet shops, boutiques, French hand laundries, and special cleaners that ornament the new urban landscape illustrates this trend. Furthermore, there is a continuing need for low-wage industrial services, even in such sectors as finance and specialized services. A second development that has reached significant proportions is what I call the downgrading of the manufacturing sector, a process in which the share of unionized shops declines and wages deteriorate while sweatshops and industrial homework proliferate. This process includes the downgrading of jobs within existing industries and the job supply patterns of some of the new industries, notably electronics assembly. It is worth noting that the growth of a downgraded manufacturing sector has been strongest in cities such as New York and London.

The expansion of low-wage jobs as a function of *growth* trends implies a re-organization of the capital–labor relation. To see this, it is important to distinguish the characteristics of jobs from their sectoral location, since highly dynamic, technologically advanced growth sectors may well contain low-wage dead-end jobs. Furthermore, the distinction between sectoral characteristics and sectoral growth patterns is crucial: Backward sectors, such as downgraded manufacturing or low-wage service occupations, can be part of major growth trends in a highly developed economy. It is often assumed that backward sectors express decline trends. Similarly, there is a tendency to assume that advanced sectors, such as finance, have mostly good, white-collar jobs. In fact, they contain a good number of low-paying jobs, from cleaner to stock clerk.

These, then, are the major themes and implications of my study.

As a further word of introduction I must sketch the reasons why producer services and finance have grown so rapidly since the 1970s and why they are so highly concentrated in cities such as New York, London, and Tokyo. The familiar explanation is that the decade of the 1980s was but a part of a larger economic trend, the shift to services. And the simple explanation of their high concentration in major cities is that this is because of the need for face-to-face communication in the services community. While correct, these clichés are incomplete.

We need to understand first how modern technology has not ended nineteenth-century forms of work; rather, technology has shifted a number of activities that were once part of manufacturing into the domain of services. The transfer of skills from workers to machines once epitomized by the assembly line has a present-day version in the transfer of a variety of activities from the shop floor into computers, with their attendant technical and professional personnel. Also, functional specialization within early factories finds a contemporary counterpart in today's pronounced fragmentation of the work process spatially and organizationally. This has been called the "global assembly line," the production and assembly of goods from factories and depots throughout the world, wherever labor costs and economies of scale make an international division of labor cost-effective. It is, however, this very "global assembly line" that creates the need for increased centralization and complexity of management, control, and planning. The development of the modern corporation and its massive participation in world markets and foreign countries has made planning, internal administration, product development, and research increasingly important and complex. Diversification of product lines, mergers, and transnationalization of economic activities all require highly specialized skills in top-level management. These have also "increased the dependence of the corporation on producer services, which in turn has fostered growth and development of higher levels of expertise among producer service firms." What were once support resources for major corporations have become crucial inputs in corporate decision-making. A firm with a multiplicity of geographically dispersed manufacturing plans contributes to the development of new types of planning in production and distribution surrounding the firm.

The growth of international banks and the more recent diversification of the financial industry have also expanded the demand for highly specialized service inputs. In the 1960s and 1970s, there was considerable geographic dispersal in the banking industry, with many regional centers and offshore locations mostly involved in fairly traditional banking. The diversification and internationalization of finance over the last decade resulted in a strong trend toward concentrating the "management" of the global industry and the production of financial innovations in a more limited number of major locations. This dynamic is not unlike that of multisite manufacturing or service firms.

Major trends toward the development of multisite manufacturing, service, and banking have created an expanded demand for a wide range of specialized service activities to manage and control global networks of factories, service outlets, and branch offices. While to some extent these activities can be carried out in house, a large share of them cannot. High levels of specialization, the possibility of externalizing the production of some of these services, and the growing demand by large and small firms and by governments are all conditions that have both resulted from and made possible the development of a market for freestanding service firms that produce components for what I refer to as global control capability.

The growth of advanced services for firms, here referred to as producer services, along with their particular characteristics of production, helps to explain the centralization of management and servicing functions that has fueled the economic boom of the early and mid-1980s in New York, London, and Tokyo. The face-to-face explanation needs to be refined in several ways. Advanced services are mostly producer services; unlike other types of services, they are not dependent on proximity to the consumers served. Rather, such specialized firms benefit from and need to locate close to other firms who produce key inputs or whose proximity makes possible joint production of certain service offerings. The accounting firm can service its clients at a distance but the nature of this service depends on proximity to other specialists, from lawyers to programmers. Major corporate transactions today typically require simultaneous participation of several specialized firms providing legal, accounting, financial, public relations, management consulting, and other such services. Moreover, concentration arises out of the needs and expectations of the high-income workers employed in these firms. They are attracted to the amenities and lifestyles that large urban centers can offer and are likely to live in central areas rather than in suburbs.

The importance of this concentration of economic activity in New York, London, and Tokyo is heightened by the fact that advanced services and finance were the fastest-growing sectors in the economies of their countries in the 1980s. It is a common mistake to attribute high growth to the service sector as a whole. In fact, other major services, such as public and consumer services, have leveled off since the middle or late 1960s in the United States and since the 1970s in the United Kingdom and Japan. In other words, the concentration of advanced services and finance in major urban centers represents a disproportionate share of the nationwide growth in employment and GNP in all these countries.

The combination of high levels of speculation and a multiplicity of small firms as core elements of the financial and producer services complex raises a question about the durability of this model of growth. At what point do the larger banks assume once again a more central role in the financial industry? And at what point do competition and the advantages of scale lead to mergers and acquisitions of small firms? Finally, and perhaps most important, at what point do the sources of profits generated by this form of economic growth become exhausted?

Over the last ten years, major economic growth trends have produced spatial and social arrangements considerably divergent from the configuration that characterized the preceding decades. The economic sectors, localities, and occupations that account for a large share of economic growth today differ from those central to the immediate post-World War II period. Most commonly, this process has been interpreted as the decline of old and the emergence of new industries, typically seen as two somewhat unconnected events necessary for the renewal of all economy. I shall challenge this disconnecting view, which means asserting that new growth rests, to a significant extent, on deep structural processes of decline. The question of the long-term durability of the global city that I have just posed turns on not seeing decline and growth as distinct. The "high-flying" 1980s might emerge as a passing phenomenon, even as manufacturing of the old sort continues to decline.

This systemic connection, I will argue, plays itself out in several economic arenas. I propose to examine this through several working hypotheses. They are the following: First, the geographic dispersal of manufacturing, which contributed to the decline of old industrial centers, created a demand for expanded central management and planning and the necessary specialized services, key components of growth in global cities. The move of large corporations into consumer services and the growing complexity of governmental activity further fed the demand for specialized services and expanded central management and planning, though they did not necessarily feed the decline of certain localities, as in the case of the dispersal of manufacturing. Second, the growth of the financial industry, and especially of key sectors of that industry, benefited from policies and conditions often harmful to other industrial sectors, notably manufacturing. The overall effect again was to feed growth of specialized services located in major cities and to undermine the economic base of other types of localities. Third, the conditions and patterns subsumed under the first two working hypotheses suggest a transformation in the economic relationships among global cities, the nation-states where they are located, and the world economy. Prior to the current phase, there was high correspondence between major growth sectors and overall national growth. Today we see increased asymmetry: The conditions promoting growth in global cities contain as significant components the decline of other areas of the United States, the United Kingdom, and Japan and the accumulation of government debt and corporate debt. Fourth, the new conditions of growth have contributed to elements of a new class alignment in global cities. The occupational structure of major growth industries characterized by the locational concentration of major growth sectors in global cities in combination with the polarized occupational structure of these sectors has created and contributed to growth of a high-income stratum and a low-income stratum of workers. It has done so directly through the organization of work and occupational structure of major growth sectors. And it has done so indirectly through the jobs needed to service the new high-income workers, both at work and at home, as well as the needs of the expanded low-wage work force.

Chapter 12

Bruce Mazlish

CONSUMERISM IN THE CONTEXT
OF THE GLOBAL ECUMENE

CONSUMERISM IS A PRIME FORCE in the creation of a global society, and, as many see it, may be a prime cause of the destruction of the globe and the societies that inhabit it; thus, it may become, in the deepest sense, a self-consuming force. Consumerism is a fairly recent term to describe the ethos and practice of some modern societies, since about the eighteenth century. Globalism, in its current usage, is of even more recent vintage, and its shape even less known. The complicated interplay of these two terms is what this paper is about.

My focus will be on two aspects of the topic. I will deal with the first under the heading, "the global and the local." How global is global consumerism? Are all parts of the globe being swept into what we are labeling as globalism, and to what extent? If globalism is prevailing, how, concretely, are accommodations being made to and by the local? For example, can multinational corporations impose a uniform brand on diverse populations, or must their products be tailored to prevailing conditions?

The second aspect to be dealt with here concerns a different set of questions. Is consumerism a "good thing?" Must it inevitably sweep the globe, or can some societies choose a separate path? Ought the developed countries themselves to moderate their consumerism? And, an even more daunting question: Can a "stable society" (by which I mean a stable consumerist society) even be realistically envisioned?

Each question interlocks with all the others; and each set of questions – my two aspects of the topic – with the other. In a short paper such as this I can only hope to raise the questions as such, touch on a few features of their possible answers, supply some notion as to the concrete data involved, and suggest the outlines of a more extended inquiry. [. . .]

Consumerism is generally seen as based on the possession by humans of inexhaustible desires. Adam Smith made famous the idea of a "propensity to barter," i.e. to trade for things desired. Hegel, who read Smith carefully, recognized the

---

From Bruce Mazlish, "Consumerism in the Context of the Global Ecumene," unpublished paper, 2001.

sublime infinity of the human "system of needs" and wrote of the "insatiable" desire of consumers. So viewed, of course, as a universal, eternal drive of humans, questions immediately arise: Why has desire of the kind being discussed manifested itself convincingly only in certain societies, why in Western Europe has it taken on a mainly mercantile appearance, and how has it expanded in this form so as to dominate modern, global society?

Such questions are the stuff of many books and articles. Here I want only to note that what we are calling consumerism arose in the institutional context of the nation-state. Smith's title, after all, was *The Wealth of Nations*. Wealth, that is, the creation of what Smith called "objects of comfort," became the mark of civilization. The ability to satisfy the desire for material wealth distinguished "civilized and thriving nations" from "savage" ones. The justification for the oppressive, destructive, and exploitive features of advanced society, all recognized by Smith, was as follows: first, the accommodation of the average member of the nation was equal if not superior to that of an "African king, the absolute master of the lives and liberties of ten thousand naked savages"; and second, a state of advanced civilization justified a nation in considering itself as superior to others lacking such distinction.

While nations have continued to proliferate since Smith's time, the locus of consumerism, and thus presumably civilization, has shifted increasingly from the national to the global arena. It is global wealth that becomes the subject of our discourse, and the condition of our existence. Yet, nations continue to exist; and we still measure GNP in their terms. It is between the nation and the globe that we must place our subject, in the form of globalism and localism (with localism, however, *not* being merely synonymous with the nation).

One approach to this tension is to think in terms of a North/South divide. In such a scheme, the North represents global developments, and the South is the "local" landscape on which Northern hegemony is to be imposed. While there is some truth to this division, it is far too simplistic. It also misrepresents the facts, as a moment's reflection on Japan and *South* Korea reminds me.

It will be more profitable for us simply to look at some of the data in regard to consumption patterns first, and then to draw possible conclusions. Let us briefly make a few observations about a few representative nations, with an eye to the global/local relation.

The US is clearly a consuming nation par excellence. The litany of figures is all too familiar. With 5 percent of the world's population, it consumes 30 percent of its resources. It uses annually 25 percent of the world's fossil fuel, employing for each American an amount of energy equivalent to that used by 14 Chinese, 38 Indians, or 531 Ethiopians. Where 8 percent of all humans own a car, 89 percent of American households own 1 or more cars. [. . .]

One could go on and on in this vein. I will refrain, and content myself with drawing two points from such data. The first is that it must be matched with the destruction wrought in the name of consumption: the wetlands, forests, and prairies lost, and the toxins, polluted waters, and smog-laden air created, to name only a few. The second is that, while most Americans appear to recognize that they greatly overconsume, they show little inclination to change their habits: in a recent poll people were asked, "Don't you think Americans overconsume?", to which 77 percent replied, "Yeah, I think Americans overconsume"; the follow-up question,

"Do you think we should change that?" elicited the response, "No, it's one of the great things about being American."

It is this ethos of consumerism that is being globalized. The US, of course, is hardly the only nation responsible. For example, the average German uses roughly 35 times more resources, we are told, and produces 30 times as much waste as the average third-worlder. Even supposedly depressed Great Britain demonstrates the increase in consumption: Real disposable income grew 46 percent between 1971 and 1992, allowing for 96 percent of households to have color TV, 88 percent a washing machine (compared to 66 percent in 1972), and most to own microwaves (62 percent), an item that didn't exist in the early 1970s.

Ah, one might say, these are those Northern countries so cavalierly dismissed earlier. Let me then cite Japan. Without tossing out comparable data about TVs and microwaves, a glance at the material and pictures in the book, *Material World: A Global Family Portrait*, shows that, even given its high rate of saving and presumed lack of consumption, a Japanese household looks about as cluttered as its American counterpart. (Hardly a surprise when we note that Japan's per capita income is $26,824 (US) versus the American $22,356.)

Even as we drop rapidly down the scale of consuming nations, we see similar incipient patterns. As we are now informed, in India surveys point out that "the consumer class is much larger than earlier suggested; that the biggest consumption boom is taking place in rural areas; and that even low-income households at or about the poverty line are significant purchasers of manufactured goods" (for example, they buy 18 percent of sales of lipstick, 33 percent of nail polish, 58 percent of detergent soap, as well as 48 percent of tea, and 31 percent of toothpaste). Even farther "South," we are told that "fans, refrigerators, televisions, stereos, even air-conditioners, VCRs, computers and fax machines: these once unattainable luxuries have become increasingly familiar in Ghanaian homes and offices."

Of course, one must be a bit suspicious of all such figures and assertions, but they do indicate a direction: toward increased consumption in all nations around the entire globe, North and South. First-hand observation in such countries generally confirms this finding.

Of all the nations becoming consumerist, and also exporting its products to be consumed in other nations, China stands out most dramatically. It has the biggest potential in both directions. I shall use it to illustrate the challenges faced by trans-national corporations and to analyze with some specificity the interplay of global and local features of consumer culture and economy.

It is well known that the sleeping giant has awakened. In the last decade and a half, China's GNP has grown by almost 9 percent a year: among another results, the number living in absolute poverty has dropped from 200–270 million to about 100 million; and the familiar increase in appliances – from 6 washing machines in 1981 for each 100 households to 80 in 1991, etc. – can be quickly sing-sung. As anyone who repeats the visit I paid a few years ago will observe, the bustle and buzzing of consumer life can be found in innumerable Chinese cities.

Yet, such sights and figures can be misleading, pointing more to potential than to present consumption patterns that come close to matching the more developed countries. It is estimated that there are only about 100 million in China earning over $1,000 a year – according to *The Economist* "the point at which consumer spending takes off." Thus, it is the huge size of the population that accounts for its importance in consumption, which is engaged in by a small minority (though it is estimated to grow to 300 million by the end of the century). As *The Economist* concludes,

> China's consumer market will one day be enormous, but for most of its 1.2 billion people the purchase of electronic goods, stylish clothes or even ice cream remains a distant dream. For these people, mostly the 80% of the population who live in the countryside, the 6m folk who live in Guangzhou are a fabulously wealthy but tiny minority.

Distribution channels are chaotic, marketing must cope with regional peculiarities. As global firms converge on China, they must deal with the local at every turn. Thus, Avon, the cosmetics group, has recruited 40,000 women to sell its products direct to their friends; often these ladies have to cycle miles to pick up their orders from local depots. Proctor & Gamble and Unilever have entered into joint ventures to market their soap products, using local brands, and seeking for the first time to advertise them; only later will they attempt to add international brands.

The multinationals are clearly pushing in the direction of global brand names, having become converted completely to the idea of globalism with whatever concessions to the local are necessary (and the multinationals themselves have discovered the virtues of small batch production, innumerable styles – Seiko has 3,000 watch styles! – and quick changeover of models, all to satisfy non-homogenous "local" tastes). Typical is a brochure from Colgate-Palmolive. As the chairman's greeting informs us, "From China to Poland and India to Venezuela, millions of people around the world use Colgate-Palmolive products . . . A key element of Colgate's continuing consumer products success is the company's global reach and geographic diversity." His proud boast is that Colgate toothpaste is the "number one consumer choice in the world." In this case, the global brand has been victorious.

Having plucked material from hither and yon, a few conclusions are now in order. The first is that the global and the local are inextricably intertwined. Nevertheless, as a result of a combination of satellite TV and media (whose details I have not even touched on here); multinational joint ventures, and of ubiquitous advertising and promotion, globalism is spreading and becoming increasingly significant in the lives of all peoples and nations.

The next is that as a key factor in this increased globalism we have found increased consumerism. It is, in fact, the spread of consumerism that looms so visibly in our growing sense of globalism. For example, only when a majority of Chinese have entered into a global market will we be able to say that their country has become both a society characterized by what I have defined as consumerism, and one that is possibly taking on a global nature.

Our final conclusion is, in fact, the beginning of a new inquiry, in two parts. First, is the global, based on consumption, on the point of overriding the nation, class, ethnic, and other forms of "local" identity? (To anticipate, I think not; all these identities will co-exist, globally and locally, and the study of how they do so will be the core of much future research.) Second, is consumerism, in its global dress, necessarily the path all nations must take, thus provoking the destructive tendencies alluded to earlier, in which consumerism consumes itself?

For a few tentative views on this last question, we must turn to a consideration of what I shall call "values."

The value and necessity of consumerism

At the end of the eighteenth century the right to consume was declared to be a human right. The American and French were democratic revolutions, and, at least in principle, democratized desire and its satisfactions. A law passed on 8 Brumaire an II (October 29, 1783), decreed that freedom of dress was a basic human right, thus symbolizing the great change: Consumption, in this case of clothes, was open to all and could not and should not be restricted by "sumptuary" laws. The pursuit of happiness was to be defined in terms of goods, freely available to all who had money to buy them. With "careers open to talent," and "Captains of industry" permitted free acquisition, we are well under way toward key requirements of the consumer society.

It is extremely important to remember that consumer society in its early history constituted a liberating, democratic movement. The insatiable desires of such a society only become truly worrisome when they push aside all other values, as they have in societies characterized by consumerism (which I have differentiated from consumer society by the dominance of the ethos of consumption), and unthinkingly enter into the "tragedy of the commons," i.e. the creating of unacceptable environmental and other pressures.

Only now, in fact, do we fully realize the dark side of consumerism, as a result of globalism itself. This does *not* mean that there were not protests and oppositions to consumer society earlier; one need only think of figures such as Jefferson and Carlyle. It simply means that what may have seemed utopian or Luddite then takes on a realistic and even scientific tone today. In thinking about the inevitability of continued consumerism – its spread globally – and the possibility of its curtailment even where it now predominates, we can gain by earlier reflections.

In the eighteenth century, before it launched fully on its consumerist path, the United States presumably had a choice. Jefferson is the prototypic figure who argued in favor of the former colonies remaining a land of agrarian virtues, standing aloof from the production/consumption revolution sweeping over its former ruler, England. In his well-known version, he framed the question in terms of America abjuring manufactures at home, with their attendant festering cities, and thus avoiding the corruptions of wealth. As he remarked, "It is the manners and spirit of a people which preserve a republic in vigor. A degeneracy in these is a canker which soon eats to the heart of its laws and constitution." (Query XIX of *Notes on Virginia*.)

In fact, the seeds of "corruption" were already in the soil tilled by the early Pilgrim and Puritan settlers. For example, as studies of Plymouth Colony show, growth of population placed pressure on dividable land in the towns, turning many inhabitants from agriculture to various trades. Many others, of course, left for the frontier. William Bradford understood clearly what was happening:

> Some were still for staying together in this place, alleging men might here live *if they would be content with their condition* [italics mine], and that it was not for want or necessity so much that they removed as for the enriching of themselves.

Land was becoming a commodity like any other, and with the introduction of paper money in 1702, coupled with inflation, speculation soared. Money, then trade, then investments in incipient manufactures followed, preparing the way for

Jefferson-like forebodings. As we know, his warnings did not suffice. Though the Revolution of 1776 temporarily produced an anti-consumer movement – symbolized by the famous Boston Tea Party – it soon gave way to the commercial and industrial development of the US, culminating in today's society of consumerism.

I instance this history in order to suggest that, in principle, even the US might have taken a different road. We must continue our inquiry now along two directions: The first reprises the question, whether in an epoch of globalism any country can stand outside the development to consumerism, while the second takes up the question whether advanced consumerist countries can curtail their consumption, involving thereby a transformation of values. In regard to this second question, I shall raise the subject of "stable society."

Three case studies of societies that are on a spectrum in regard to globalism and consumerism may shed light on our inquiry. The first concerns the Kapayo Indians of Brazil. They are the most "primitive" and "uncivilized" people of our sample, living in the southern fringe of the Amazon forest. At first, they sought to block development projects, such as dams and gold mines, incidentally making themselves heroes of the environment movement. Gradually, however, some of their leaders "sold" out. These few, Portuguese-speaking and thus able to transact business with the powers-that-be, subsequently bought town houses in regional Brazilian cities, acquired cars and trucks, and generally succumbed to "the lure of wealth and a high-consumption style."

The drama is still being played out, and it is not clear whether the Kapayo can defend themselves against the global forces invading their forests, and work out some sort of modus vivendi with the consumerist pressures. The historical record of similar cases does not make one optimistic; what is different in this case is that globalism itself has made the rest of the world highly conscious of the environmental threat not only to the Kapayo but to themselves. Ironically, then, the Kapayo have strong allies in preserving their existing ways among those who, by introducing consumerism, otherwise wish to destroy their "backward" culture.

Our next case concerns Haiti. Do we hear a modern-day Jefferson in Jean-Claude Martineau, a minister in the Aristide government? It is necessary to quote him at some length, in order to get the full force of his vision. As he remarked in an interview:

> We are not talking about a modern republic in which the country will be rich. We don't need that. It seems to me, the world has gone the wrong way by thinking that personal fortune is the solution. Personal fortune is going to be only for the minority, no matter how rich the country is. What we want to do in Haiti, what I would like to see, is a country in which everybody would have the necessities of life. We don't need a swimming pool and two cars in every house: we have the Caribbean Sea, and we will use that. We have a small island, and we can walk around the small island . . . In Haiti, we have so many cars because of the imported dream that we have. Port-au-Prince has traffic jams that you wouldn't see in major US cities.

Haiti is a tiny country. Perhaps it can be left out of the global/consumer takeover, if there are enough Jean-Claude Martineaus in the public arena. India, in contrast, is an enormous country, with a huge population. We have already noted this drift to consumerism in a global economy. Yet, there are voices seeking to steer the country in another direction. V. Kurien, chairman of the National Dairy Development Board, is described by Jean-Jacques Salomon as the man who "made it possible for India to become the world's second largest producer of milk and most likely to overtake the United States around the turn of the century"; as Salomon continues, he is also the man who "challenged the complacency towards the pressures of globalization and market forces." In Kurien's own words,

> I am an old-fashioned person and I was brought up to believe that when we obtained freedom our independent India was to be a humane society, one guided by noble principles. Markets are not noble . . . No civilized society entrusts its destiny to the market.

Obviously, we have here a definition of civilization quite different from its equation with the level of consumerism. On this account, India is not opting out of the global market, but choosing simply to tailor it to its own measures. Again, whether it will be more successful than the Kapayo or Haiti remains to be seen. Each of the three, it should be noted, is seeking its own "local" response to a similar set of pressures inherent in the forces of globalism and consumerism.

The advanced or developed nations, so called, face the same pressures, but in a different context. In their cases, they are already mounted on the tiger's back; and the question is how to get off or what happens if they are unable to dismount. I shall suggest two lines of inquiry: Is a stable society possible? And what value changes are necessary to bring such a society about?

The fact is that most societies before the coming of modernity were stable societies, in the sense of not changing and expanding rapidly in their economic and social spheres. The threat to stability generally came in the form of military conquest. Consumerism, and mass consumerism, was hardly a driving force. In early modern Europe, mercantilist thought assumed a fixed amount of production and goods; the aim was to get a larger share of a given pie.

It is only in the eighteenth century that economic expansion becomes a sustained thrust, even though still precarious. Thus, Adam Smith speaks of a progressive state, while noting the dangers, as he sees it, of a "stationary state." Many of his contemporaries, however, still held to the ideal of a stable or stationary state, and viewed China as its epitome. Smith's own admired predecessor, Quesnay, praised China's despotism as ensuring enlightened stability. On another front, American Indians, before the coming of the white man, were admired as having a "stable" society, in tune with nature.

Nature, in this view, was non-competitive. It is a pre-Darwinian view, and no longer sustainable. As it turns out, the expansive nature of capitalism is more in tune with Darwin's competitive ecological system. In this "new world," stability is hard to come by. A consumer society, and then consumerism, seems to fit more readily with both capitalist practice and Darwinian theory.

Can a stable society, i.e. a form of society that maintains consumption growth but at a modern level, be reached in the advanced countries enjoying a high level of consumption? Or is this merely a utopian idea? An entire conference would be needed to clarify and analyze this subject.

What level of population would allow for a stable society, and how would one achieve that level? How would one deal with work and employment in a relatively non-expanding economy (one need only think of the problems presently involved in so-called defense conversion)? Does such a stable society have to be global in nature, or can it be achieved in one country? If the latter, how does the country deal with immigration problems? In short, if consumerism is to be checked, what are the social–economic consequences that must be faced?

It would appear that capitalism, by its nature, is an inherently unstable and expanding system, working against a stable society. Even to contemplate a transition to the latter requires a transformation of values, and this is my second suggested line of inquiry. What might be involved in such a transformation, while remaining within the general framework of capitalism? (Or would the latter have to be abandoned, and what would *that* mean?)

One must recall again a world before consumerism. In fact, as we have suggested, it required a transformation of values around the eighteenth century to allow consumer society to emerge. It was a slow transformation, but triumphed, presenting us with our present dilemma in which we must change or moderate values once again.

In the advanced countries, and, as we have seen, now spreading globally, the dominant ethos constantly presses us in the direction of unlimited consumerism. Advertising pushes the message everywhere and at all times. In 1994, in America alone, marketers spent over $150 billion to persuade people to buy their products, a sum amounting to over $500 annually for every man, woman, and child in the country. It has supplanted public education with its advocacy of private expenditure. It has crossed the boundaries of entertainment, and one can no longer tell the difference between the two forms of expression. [. . .]

An unending?

It is time for a conclusion, but, of course, there is none. I have touched on consumerism in a global ecumene, seeking to open up inquiries along the fault lines of the global and the local, and asking how one might get off the tiger. Globalism is undoubtedly growing, and consumerism seems an unending and deadly factor in that growth, as well a consequence of it.

Yet, there are grounds for optimism in the long run (if we are not all dead). As I noted at the beginning of this paper, there are other factors along with consumerism that power globalism. Such factors, operating synergistically, are slowly creating a consciousness concerning the consequences of unlimited material desire, an identity that transcends the narrowly national, and institutions that permit intervention on a worldwide scale, as well as other effects that could contribute to an amelioration of the consumerism that otherwise might consume us all, globally.

I should like to "end," therefore, with a paradox. It is simply that the factor of consumerism, which so powerfully promotes globalism, will itself be moderated by the globalism that it helps bring into existence and extension. The poison, in short, can contain its own antidote.

PART VII

The natural environment

ENVIRONMENTALISM, or the movement to protect the natural environment, has had a long history. Both preservationists (those who are primarily interested in preserving the natural habitat as they are) and conservationists (those who seek to make the best use of natural resources without doing damage to the environment) have been active in North America and Europe for over a century. However, it was only in the last decades of the twentieth century that the movement became global and international. Awareness of environmental degradation (polluted air, soil, and water) and of the threat to the ecological system (deforestation, disappearance of endangered species) spread to other parts of the world, and international conferences began to be convened in order to devise effective means of coping with the crisis. Thus environmentalism became a key phenomenon of the global age.

The two essays that follow provide useful information on this phenomenon. The first, by Margaret Keck (Professor of Political Science at the Johns Hopkins University) and Kathryn Sikkink (Professor of Political Science at the University of Minnesota), presents case studies of various activities to stop deforestation in South America, while the second, by Lynton Caldwell (Professor Emeritus of Political Science at Indiana University), describes efforts made by the United Nations since the landmark Stockholm conference of 1972 to deal with environmental issues through international agreement. Both point to complex political and social issues that arise at the local level when outsiders bring their expertise and enthusiasm to alter existing patterns of life.

As environmentalism gained momentum, there were often clashes between the perspectives of the more advanced industrialized nations that were now eager to slow down the pace of economic growth so as to protect the environment, and of the less developed countries, the so-called Third World, that were committed to economic growth and resented interference with that undertaking. The potential polarity between environmentalism and development threatened to undermine international cooperation, but the United Nations and other organizations sought to solve the impasse by developing the idea of "sustainable development," the notion that the Third World would be assisted in its programs of economic development within limits so as not to damage the environment, which would be detrimental to continued economic growth. Thus we see that many themes of recent global history – internationalism, non-governmental organizations, economic development, environmentalism – are intimately connected.

Chapter 13

Margaret E. Keck and Kathryn Sikkink

ENVIRONMENTAL ACTIVISM

IN THE 1980S AWARENESS OF GLOBAL ISSUES stimulated by ozone and climate change negotiations gave a new urgency to older concerns like tropical deforestation. By the end of the decade many northerners saw defor-estation as the epitome of Third World environmental problems. In the United States, rainforest campaigners focused on the Brazilian Amazon; deforestation in Southeast Asia, proceeding at equal or greater speed, mobilized publics in Europe and Japan more than it did in the United States.

The term "tropical deforestation" only became part of the environmentalist's daily vocabulary in the early 1970s. Before that, concern with tropical forest loss fell under the rubric of habitat protection. The 1968 Latin American Conference on Conservation of Renewable Natural Resources had no session on forests, and there is no entry for forests, deforestation, or tropical forest in the index for the volume of the *IUCN Bulletin,* which covers 1967–71. The problem had yet to be named.

The IUCN [International Union for Conservation of Nature and Natural Resources] took up the tropical forest issue for the first time in 1972, in response to the Brazilian government's decision to accelerate colonization and development projects in the Amazon. UNESCO picked up on the problem as the first project of its Program on Man and the Biosphere. A letter to Brazil's president Emilio Garrastazú Médici, jointly signed by IUCN president Harold J. Coolidge and WWF president Prince Bernhard of the Netherlands, pointed out "the need for careful consideration of the environmental problems involved in Amazonian development." Not surprisingly, the Brazilian government was not pleased.

Concern grew rapidly. At the urging of the NGOs, in 1973 a number of UN agencies and the Organization of American States cosponsored international meetings of scientists, government representatives, and representatives of international agen-cies to discuss guidelines for economic development of Latin American and Southeast Asian tropical forest areas. By 1974, the IUCN and the WWF considered tropical rainforests "the most important nature conservation programme of the decade."

From Margaret E. Keck and Kathryn Sikkink, *Activists Beyond Borders. Advocacy Networks in International Politics* (Ithaca and London: Cornell University Press, 1998), pp. 133–47.

Scientists and conservationists also pushed the rainforest issue in the United States, and President Carter called tropical forest loss a crucial global issue. In 1977, an Environmental and Natural Resources sector was added to the US Foreign Assistance Act, and the Agency for International Development (USAID) began to sponsor projects aimed at natural resource management. Congress held hearings on tropical deforestation in 1980, and the United States put pressure on the UN General Assembly and UNEP to take action. Those initiatives quickly foundered under President Reagan, and several of the most important tropical forest countries (including Brazil, Zaire, Colombia, Venezuela, and Burma) refused to participate in UNEP meetings on the subject.

The network of scientists and conservationists that initially worked on the tropical forest issues fits very nicely into [Peter] Haas's definition of an epistemic community. Either by becoming part of the policy process or by working through NGOs or international organizations, its members hoped to persuade people of goodwill to adopt rational guidelines for tropical forest use. Tropical forest experts held meetings, shared information, and discussed strategies and action plans. But the epistemic community was relatively small; a handful of people carried the issue alone.

Frustrated with the meager results of their efforts, several organizations initiated studies and negotiations in the early 1980s to seek new ways of intensifying and broadening their influence. As conservationists' focus shifted from preservation to sustainable development, they needed a better understanding of how human populations – including indigenous peoples – interacted with forests. Around the same time, the newly formed World Resources Institute worked with the UNDP, FAO, and the World Bank on a proposed tropical forestry action plan, FAO designated 1985 as the International Year of the Forest, and WWF launched a highly successful fund-raising campaign around tropical forests.

In sum, the first decade of the activity around tropical forests created networks of scientists and policymakers who produced and exchanged a great deal of information, placed the issue on the agendas of a variety of international organizations, and expanded the issue from one concerned primarily with trees and soils to one that at least recognized the problems of indigenous peoples. The 1980 IUCN/WWF/UNEP World Conservation Strategy recognized the need to integrate discussions of development and environment, and IUCN's network of scientists and policymakers tried to stimulate governments to engage in rational resource planning. There was not yet an attempt to gain leverage over recalcitrant actors in the system.

The multilateral development bank campaign

As conservation organizations diversified their approaches, a new group of actors appeared on the scene, determined to extend to the international arena the kinds of advocacy tactics that had served them well in environmental campaigns in the United States. In 1983 a small group of individuals in Washington, DC, began to form a network of activists and organizations to target multilateral bank lending in developing countries.

The NGO campaign around multilateral bank lending differed from traditional environmentalist campaigns by focusing not on a particular substantive issue, but rather on a set of political relationships within which activists believed they could obtain leverage. They chose the multilateral banks for their potential impact on the incorporation of environmental concerns into development policy in the Third World.

This campaign was clearly a case where strategy moved from the domestic to the international arena. The stress on leverage followed two decades of environmental litigation in the United States, where lawyers from environmental NGOs successfully used the National Environmental Policy Act (NEPA) and other measures to extend the range of environmental protection in a variety of areas, including the international activities of US agencies. By the late 1970s these lawyers had begun to concentrate more on influencing administrative and regulatory processes. Several key multilateral bank campaign activists were lawyers – Bruce Rich of the National Resources Defense Council (NRDC) and later the Environmental Defense Fund (EDF), Barbara Bramble of the National Wildlife Federation, and David Wirth of the NRDC. Stephan Schwartzman, an anthropologist who joined the group in 1984 after returning from his dissertation fieldwork in the Brazilian Amazon, contributed a strong concern with traditional peoples.

While the activists in Washington, DC, were developing their strategies, *The Ecologist* in Britain weighted in with a January 1985 special double issue on the World Bank. Introduced by an "Open Letter to Mr Clausen, President of the World Bank," the issue included a contribution from Bruce Rich on multilateral development banks, as well as case studies that included Brazil's Polonoroeste project. Subsequently, *The Ecologist* would be at the forefront of a radical critique of the bank's policies and was particularly active in promoting campaigns around World Bank projects in Asia. Although our focus here is on the institutional strategies of the Washington-based campaign, *The Ecologist* played an important working role, beyond its importance for disseminating information about bank projects and campaigns.

The multilateral bank campaign was not intentionally organized around tropical deforestation. Activists involved in it would eventually try to influence bank policies in a variety of areas (energy, water, resettlement) and in specific projects. The activist critique of the environmental impact of bank projects focused at least as much on their human impact as on their effect on wildlife or natural resources. In the 1986 campaign pamphlet *Bankrolling Disasters*, Schwartzman described the Polonoroeste project in Brazil, the Indonesian Transmigration project (involving resettlement from Java to less populated parts of the archipelago), the Narmada Dam project in India, and a cattle ranching project in Botswana – all of which involved migration or resettlement issues along with environmental destruction. This evolution lends weight to the argument that cases involving physical harm or loss of livelihood are particularly susceptible to transnational advocacy campaigning; it is not obvious that for a campaign designed to promote environmental preservation this should be so.

Donor influence helped consolidate the multilateral development bank campaign. In 1987 the Charles Stewart Mott Foundation asked the Sierra Club, the Environmental Defense Fund, the Environmental Policy Institute (later Friends of the Earth), the National Wildlife Federation, and the Natural Resources Defense Council to design a five-year plan for the campaign, on the basis of which the

Foundation awarded $1.8 million between 1988 and 1992 to advocacy NGOs. Other foundations joined the effort, but the Mott Foundation's initiative was a strong incentive to strategic activity.

The campaign's goal was to change the behavior of multilateral banks (especially the World Bank), making their projects at least less destructive to the environment and at best positively beneficial. This aim would require effecting changes in the banks' project cycles, personnel, internal organization, and permeability – that is, access to information, and breadth of consultation with those affected by the banks' activities. To bring home the need for such changes, the campaigners began with a substantive critique of particular projects.

Deforestation in the Brazilian Amazon

One of the first cases for the campaigners was the World Bank's loan to Brazil's Polonoroeste program, an effort to rationalize seemingly out-of-control colonization in the Brazilian northwest. The timing – the project began in 1981 – placed it just on the cusp of Brazil's democratization process; the first free gubernatorial elections took place in 1982, and Brazil's first civilian president since the 1964 military coup took office in 1985. Democratization stimulated political and social organization and greater circulation of information. Although Rondônia, the area where the Polonoroeste project was mainly to be implemented, lagged behind the rest of Brazil on all of these counts, the overall loosening of political controls affected this region as well. By 1985 many Amazonian areas previously classified as national security zones came under civilian control. Unfortunately the military's withdrawal from its customary role as guardian of order in the Amazon allowed levels of violence, particularly in land conflicts, to rise.

Colonization in the northwestern territory (as of 1981, a state) of Rondônia took off during the 1970s, pulled by the concentration of landholdings in the south and northeast. Rondônia's population increased from 111,064 in 1970 to 904,298 in 1985. The World Bank agreed to finance part of the Polonoroeste development program, but with misgivings. The loan was intended to pave the main highway through the state and implant social infrastructure in colonization areas; the bank insisted as well on components insuring protection of ecological and indigenous areas. Although bank officials knew that such programs might intensify settlement and further aggravate deforestation, they reasoned that if the Brazilian government carried out its plans without bank participation the prospects would be worse.

The most vocal early critics of the loan were anthropologists who saw the destabilizing impact deforestation was having on Amerindian populations and did not expect the Brazilian government to respect the bank's demand for demarcation of indigenous areas. Indigenous rights organizations like Cultural Survival, Survival International, and the Anthropological Resource Center in Cambridge, Massachusetts, were among the first to sound the alarm. Anthropologist David Price, hired by the World Bank to report on the situation of the Nambiquara Indians in the project area, went public with criticism of the project after feeling that his dire predictions were being ignored by bank staff.

The Polonoroeste network and the bank

Social networks of foreign and Brazilian anthropologists were crucial for the early stages of the external critique of Polonoroeste. When Steve Schwartzman returned to the United States from fieldwork among the Krenakore Indians in Xingu National Park, he quickly began to participate in campaign activities in the name of Survival International. Information on Polonoroeste came from the Ecumenical Center for Documentation and Information (CEDI) in Brazil, where anthropologist Carlos Alberto Ricardo headed up an indigenous rights project, from several anthropologists who had been consultants on the project, from the filmmaker Adrian Cowell, and from a few other journalists and academics. It did not, at this stage, come from organizations on the ground in Rondônia.

In the United States, campaigners lobbied key congressional appropriations committees and the Treasury Department in an attempt to influence positions taken by the US executive directors of the multilateral banks. This strategy proved unexpectedly successful. In May 1983, campaign organizers testified before congressional committees on the lack of environmental impact assessments for multilateral development bank projects, and in June produced dramatic testimony from David Price accusing the bank of watering down his negative assessment of Polonoroeste's indigenous components. By 1984, the Polonoroeste case had become a focus of congressional inquiry.

Between 1983 and 1986 the US Congress held seventeen hearings related to MDBs and the environment. Wisconsin senator Robert Kasten, chair of the Foreign Operations Subcommittee of the Senate Appropriations Committee, became a very important ally; his desire to increase US influence at the World Bank fit very nicely with the environmentalists' agenda. Congressional committee chairs had direct leverage over the bank through their power of appropriation; in addition, they got the Treasury Department involved in its capacity as the liaison with the US executive director for the bank.

The World Bank is vulnerable to US pressure because of its system of weighted voting, by which the United States, the United Kingdom, Germany, Japan, and France have 40 percent of the voting shares; these countries also provide the lion's share of money for the International Development Agency (IDA), the bank's soft loan facility. Beginning in the late 1970s, negotiations over IDA replenishment became increasingly complicated, and the bank did not want to see yet another roadblock established in this process.

In December 1984, and again in 1986, the US Congress adopted a set of recommendations suggested by NGOs to strengthen the bank's environmental performance. In 1985, largely as a result of the MDB campaign, the World Bank temporarily suspended disbursements for Polonoroeste on the grounds that the Brazilian government was violating loan conditions on protecting natural and indigenous areas; this was the first loan suspension on such grounds. In 1985, the Senate Appropriations Committee attached a strongly worded environmental report to the foreign aid appropriation bill asking US executive directors of multilateral development banks to promote a series of reforms in project design and implementation. The World Bank's decision to create a top-level environmental department in 1987 was designed to stem the rising tide of criticism. In his speech at the World Resources Institute announcing the changes, bank president Barber Conable referred to Polonoroeste as something the new department was designed to prevent from happening.

The impact of local organizing

At this stage of the campaign Brazilian NGOs and individuals served mainly as informants. This changed in the second half of the 1980s, for two reasons: first, the connection some Washington activists forged with rubber tapper organizers from Acre, Brazil had a deep influence on their subsequent activity; and second, other instances of transnational environmental networking, in which Third World (especially Asian) activists played a more central role, highlighted the importance of local protagonists. Information on multilateral bank activities became more widely available, also, and opportunities for organizations to share their experiences and discuss strategy increased. The most visible opportunity was the annual NGO meeting held parallel to the annual meeting of the World Bank and the International Monetary Fund (IMF) beginning in 1986.

For the initial group of multilateral bank campaigners, contact established in 1985 with the Acre rubber tappers was a watershed event. Francisco "Chico" Mendes was the leader of a group of rubber tappers (gatherers of natural latex from rubber trees) who had been fighting since 1975 to guarantee land use rights and improve the living standards of forest peoples. They were central to rural union organizing in the state of Acre, and had close relationships with other social movements in the area during Brazil's transition to democracy. Anthropologists working in Brazilian NGOs met with Steve Schwartzman in Washington in 1985, and recognized a potential synergy between the multilateral bank campaign and the rubber tappers' struggle; subsequently Schwartzman attended the founding meeting of the National Council of Rubber Tappers in Brasilia.

The relationship that developed between the bank campaigners and the rubber tappers was mutually beneficial. It took the teeth out of accusations that rainforest destruction was simply a concern of privileged northerners. Over time it helped activists from distant political and social universes to understand better their different perspectives on the same problems, and to build elements of a common understanding. For the rubber tappers, who had struggled for a decade against the encroachment of cattle ranchers on forest they had traditionally used, contact with the bank campaigners gave them access to international opinion- and decision-making arenas that they could not have gained on their own. When they joined forces to influence a proposed road project in Acre for which Brazil sought Inter-American Development Bank funding, a struggle for land rights waged by rural unions became simultaneously a struggle to preserve the standing forest.

In December 1988 Chico Mendes was murdered by hired guns of irate landowners. But he had made his point abroad. Invited by the bank campaigners to Washington and Miami to meet with members of the US Congress and with multilateral bank officials, he had helped make the rubber tappers' proposal to create "extractive reserves" in the Amazon one of the few concrete illustrations of the "sustainable development" idea. By linking environmental destruction to a concrete picture of how local populations lived in the forest, environmentalists were able to make the tropical forest issue real to an international public.

The murder of Chico Mendes had enormous symbolic impact – so much so that it made page one of the *New York Times*. It embodied at the same time an issue – deforestation in the Amazon – and a set of complex social relationships in which the roles of rubber tapper, cattle rancher, the justice system, Brazilian government programs, multilateral development banks, and North American and European taxpayers all became transparent. The rubber tapper case thus reinforced an approach to tropical deforestation that focused on social relations. This approach is very different from one that sees forest loss as a set of technical or scientific issues to be resolved by experts, or from one that looks at it primarily in terms of trees and wildlife.

The relationship with the Acre rubber tappers had important ramifications for transnational networking on the environment. It showed that testimony from those most directly affected by bank projects was often a more powerful organizing tool than information produced by outside experts. Calls for participation in the early stages of project design by those likely to be affected by a bank-funded project became a constant of activist critiques. Notably, the Third World social movements whose participation the campaigners advocated focused overwhelmingly on the human dimension of environmental change.

The negotiation of different goals in the context of network activity is one of the most interesting dimensions of this story; this is a process by which the principled basis of the networks comes to include the recognition of differences as well as claims on behalf of a universal good. By the late 1980s the preferred language of the campaign had become a language of "partnership" in which genuine links between organizations of those suffering harm and those speaking for them were crucial to a campaign's legitimacy. Building partnerships, however, is fraught with difficulties.

Distinct visions of the tropical forest problem produce very different proposals for its solution. The development of a commitment to the communities affected by bank projects often placed advocates at loggerheads with borrowing country governments, as well as the bank. If on one hand this put environmentalists in a position long familiar to human rights and indigenous advocates, it also potentially politicized their commitment beyond what many in their organizations were prepared to support. Advocates who traveled between Washington and the Amazon especially had to negotiate a fine line between the lobbying and pressure strategies they employed at home and the requirements of grassroots support in the areas affected by bank projects.

From Polonoroeste to Planafloro

In 1986 technical personnel in the Rondônia state government began to work with World Bank staff on a successor project to Polonoroeste. Based on a zoning plan, this new project, called the Planafloro, was intended to prevent further ecological damage by helping to intensify agricultural activity in settled areas, and institutionalize varying degrees of environmental protection for the remainder of the state. In 1990, in the midst of the approval process, the Environmental Defense Fund led the bank campaign network in a series of objections that relevant local groups had not been consulted on the project.

In response to the bank's claims that such consultations had taken place, Washington environmentalists requested information from their contacts in Rondônia. Brazilian groups reported that rubber tappers, rural workers, and indigenous organizations knew little or nothing about the project, but had requested information and expressed interest in discussing it. Brazilian and foreign NGO representatives simultaneously raised the issue with the newly appointed environmental secretary, José Lutzenberger, who asked the bank to suspend consideration of the project until consultations could take place. This forced the bank's hand, and the project was taken off the agenda of the executive directors. There were other objections to the loan too; the Ministry of the Economy installed in 1990 wanted to cut foreign borrowing, and doubted the Rondônia state government's ability to repay.

In 1990–1 rubber tappers, indigenous peoples, and rural unionists held a series of meetings, partially funded by the National Wildlife Federation, to discuss the Planafloro project. The meetings helped stimulate the self-organization of the first two groups; rubber tapper and indigenous organizations were weak in Rondônia, and advisory NGOs and competing national indigenous organizations were contending among themselves to organize them.

Incentives for local groups to become organized were high. With foreign attention focused on the Amazon and the approach of the 1992 "Earth Summit" in Rio de Janeiro, money and media attention were available as never before. Conflicts among NGOs in the region were smoothed over, and in 1991 the Rondônia NGO Forum was created. This forum became the formal NGO interlocutor from Rondônia for the Planafloro project and another large environmental project, the Amazon Project sponsored by the Group of Seven (G-7). With NGO agreement, the Planafloro returned to the World Bank's docket in 1991. The bank pressed the Rondônia state government to accept as part of the project's governance structure a deliberative council that gave NGOs voting parity with state secretariats to decide on the project's operating plans, and seats in the planning commissions.

Although this was one of the biggest procedural victories of the campaign, it did not immediately produce results. The organizations in the forum did not have enough local clout to make their positions effective, and the state government did not intend for them to gain such clout. Nonetheless, local groups gained access to information and greater capacity to monitor government actions. They could then assess government claims in the light of direct experience and demand that the bank be held accountable. Although the Rondônia activists did try to use hearings in the Brazilian Congress and lawsuits in Brazilian courts to stop violations of the zoning plan, ultimately their best strategy remained one that put the onus of restraining the Brazilian government onto the World Bank. This is a case where a boomerang strategy resulted from the political weakness of actors rather than from complete blockage of access, as in the human rights cases; transnational networking helped to amplify local demands by resituating them in different arenas with more potential allies.

In June 1994, only a year after the loan's disbursements had begun, the NGO forum resigned from the deliberative council, reporting multiple violations of the loan agreement. A bank mission brokered a short-lived agreement between the NGOs and the state government, but in November 1994, the forum decided to collaborate with Friends of the Earth (and eventually Oxfam as well) in bringing a formal claim that the Planafloro was violating the bank's own policies before the newly established World Bank Inspection Panel. Friends of the Earth, with funding from the Dutch agency NOVIB to finance research, presented the claim to the bank on June 14, 1995.

Although it was ultimately rejected, simply filing the claim produced a flurry of activity. The Rondônia state government and the Brazilian federal government signed a long-delayed agreement committing the Federal Land Institute to respect the state's zoning plan, and reserves whose demarcation had been unaccountably delayed were suddenly demarcated. Bank personnel finally took a serious look at the project's shortcomings, and proposed revisions that they hoped might overcome previous gridlock.

The organizing of the network

In defining the network, we need to distinguish between that part of it that follows any particular project closely and the multilateral bank campaign network generally. Within the latter there is a division of labor, and different individuals and groups act as leads on particular areas of expertise. It is possible to list actual network participants at any point in the campaign. For example, a reasonable measure of the members of the United States–Canada bank campaign network could be gleaned from the list of participants at a 1991 strategy meeting, called in conjunction with the Mott Foundation, to discuss the bank campaign's next steps.

The Planafloro network reactivated connections forged in the campaigns around Polonoroeste and the Acre rubber tappers. EDF's Steve Schwartzman played a leading role in coordinating the Washington side of the multilateral bank campaign's activities on Brazil, and activities from Friends of the Earth and the World Wildlife Fund (WWF) were important on the European side. With the approach of the 1992 "Earth Summit" in Rio de Janeiro, several other European and international NGOs became more active: Italy's FOE affiliate began to develop an Amazon program by working with Brazilian NGOs on the G-7 Amazon project, and Greenpeace, newly installed in Brazil, began a series of occupations of illegal timbering operations. The WWF also established a Brazilian branch after UNCED. Both Greenpeace and WWF developed close relationships with indigenous rights NGOs. Establishment of Brazilian branches of international NGOs diversified local NGOs' access to information and allies. Oxfam-UK, which had been active in the Amazon region in the early to mid-1980s, became so again.

Personal connections were crucial. Schwartzman had gotten to know individuals in Rondônia who worked with rubber tappers, via the National Council of Rubber Tappers. In a conversation with a social worker and rubber tapper organizer from Rondônia at a meeting of the national council, he discovered that the bank's claims about having consulted local NGOs on the Planafloro were suspect. Berkeley graduate student Brent Millikan, who had previously spent several years doing masters research in Rondônia during the Polonoroeste period, was back doing doctoral research beginning in the late 1980s; a member of the San Francisco-based Rainforest Action Network, Millikan knew the bank campaigners, had considerable experience in the state, and had close relations with scholars of the region. Wim Groenvelt, the Dutch expatriate head of the Institute for Pre-History, Anthropology, and Ecology (IPHAE), had close links with European and Brazilian forestry groups. Several organizations that became involved in the Rondônia NGO forum were themselves parts of other networks: the Indigenous Missionary Council (CIMI) was a pastoral activity of the Brazilian Catholic Church; the state rural union confederation was affiliated with the national labor confederation (CUT).

The quality of the local nodes of the advocacy network was more important in the Planafloro campaign than with Polonoroeste. "Local participation" became an important part of such campaigns in the 1990s, made so by the publicity given to the Acre rubber tappers and several other campaigns where vigorous grassroots protest was a crucial element, such as the Narmada Dam campaign in India. On the Polonoroeste project foreign NGOs had spoken freely in place of the Brazilians on whose behalf they claimed to act, but with the Planafloro project accountability issues were raised more often.

In the early 1990s EDF and Oxfam, recognizing the need for a more solid Brazilian domestic base for the multilateral development bank campaign, sponsored a meeting in Brasilia in March 1993 for Brazilian environmental and indigenous NGOs, to form a Brazilian campaign network. In principle, this national network was to make multilateral bank-related activities more sensitive to national political dynamics. Although slow to get off the ground, by mid-1996 the Brazilian network had a strong national coordination and regular information exchange.

Network strategies

[. . .] Unable effectively to influence the activities of the state government and of federal agencies acting in Rondônia at the state level, local groups applied pressure either at the national or international levels. In the United States, activists lobbied Congress and the Treasury Department. In addition, inclusion of NGOs in the Planafloro's governance structure legitimized their intervention to an unprecedented degree. However, Brazilian NGO strategies were complicated by the pervasive crisis of governance and economy that Brazil was experiencing for most of the period. The Planafloro was only one, and far from the most egregious, of the abuses of public authority that competed for attention.

Such abuses were all the more striking given the Brazilian administration's adroit use of "green" public relations. Soon after Fernando Collor's election to the presidency in 1989, he stunned environmentalists by appointing internationally known ecologist José Lutzenberger secretary of the environment. Asked by a *New York Times* reporter for his impression, Steve Schwartzman called the appointment "stupefyingly positive." Hopes that the advocacy network had penetrated to the heart of the environmental decision-making apparatus proved elusive, however. Collor's environmentalism was more show than substance, and Lutzenberger was a colorful but ineffective minister. Nonetheless, governmental machinery did become more accessible. The Brazilian Environment and Renewable Resources Institute (IBAMA), through its traditional peoples program, began to support rubber tapper and indigenous organizing.

The Planafloro strategy was primarily an accountability strategy, attempting to leverage environmental, land, and indigenous rights policy by asking the World Bank to hold Brazilian government institutions to the commitments they had made. Although initially reluctant to exert major pressure on Brazil, bank personnel became increasingly resentful at taking the heat themselves for failures on the Brazilian side, and began to monitor the project more closely. Eventually, weakly organized local movements and NGOs in Rondônia gained experience.

The multilateral bank campaign has clearly had an impact on World Bank procedures, as with most institutional change, external pressures reinforced internal reformers. The 1987 World Bank reorganization created a central environmental department and environmental units within each of the bank's four regional offices.

By 1990 some sixty new positions had been created. Over the next few years the World Bank's role in environmental issues grew. After 1990 it helped elaborate the G-7's Amazon project, and later assumed management of the Global Environmental Facility, a funding mechanism for national projects in the areas of climate change, ozone depletion, and biodiversity. The bank's 1992 reorganization added a central vice presidency for environmentally sustainable development (within which is also located the Social Policy and Resettlement Division). Further reform followed upon network agitation over the Sardar Sarovar Dam project on the Narmada River in India. In that case the World Bank convoked an independent commission to report on the project's status. After the Commission's June 1992 report and an NGO campaign around the tenth replenishment of IDA monies in 1993, the bank created a semi-independent inspection panel and instituted a new information policy, both in response to NGO demands. The inspection panel was "empowered to investigate complaints from people directly affected by Bank projects regarding violations of World Bank policy, procedures, and loan agreements." The information policy essentially declassified a wide range of World Bank documents, making them available for public scrutiny.

Chapter 14

Lynton Keith Caldwell

INTERNATIONAL ENVIRONMENTAL POLICY

Strategies for global environmental protection

THE RECORD OF BOTH organized and individual efforts to safeguard the biosphere and the quality of the human environment has been impressive, and the commitment of governments within the last two decades to protection of the biosphere is without precedent. While specific international agreements had addressed particular environmental problems prior to both the Biosphere Conference of 1968 and the United Nations Conference on the Human Environment of 1972, no worldwide concerted or comprehensive approach toward international responsibility for the safeguarding of the biosphere had occurred. Today, however, an extensive and complex network of intergovernmental, nongovernmental, and scientific organizations addresses a broad range of international environmental problems. The twenty years between the Stockholm Conference in 1972 and the UN Conference on Environment and Development at Rio de Janeiro in 1992 culminated in a most extensive and detailed statement of international goals and national responsibilities – Agenda 21 – a "roadmap" for international policy and action into the twenty-first century. Treaties and other international agreements have been negotiated to such an extent that environmental protection is now recognized as a significant aspect of international law.

What outcome may we anticipate from these worldwide efforts in defense of earth? Popular attitudes toward environmental protection are ambivalent. In technologically and scientifically advanced countries, opinion polls show strong public support in principle for environmental protection. On specific issues and in competition with other priorities public support is often much less certain. People in large numbers seem to prefer positive, reassuring assessments of environmental trends to objective reports based on factual and holistic evidence. Critics of environmentalism welcomed Gregg Easterbrook's *A Moment on Earth* (1995), which they regarded as refuting the so-called "doom and gloom" warnings of future environmental disaster.

From Lynton Keith Caldwell, *International Environmental Policy: From the Twentieth to the Twenty-First Century*, 3rd edition (Durham and London: Duke University Press, 1996), pp. 323–35.

But the scientific community of the world did not agree, as witness *The World Scientists Warning to Humanity* (1995).

So recent is this comprehensive international effort that it would be unrealistic to expect more than a beginning to have been made. While tangible accomplishments have been reported [. . .], it must be conceded that, as of the mid-1990s, the principal results of international cooperation were investigations of the causes of environmental problems and identification of needs for action. Action programs have been initiated, but most of the action has yet to be undertaken. The unprecedented environmental efforts of the last quarter of the twentieth century are no match for the magnitude of the problems.

An international structure for environmental policy is now in place, and some experience with intergovernmental cooperative environmental programs has been acquired. But governments have found it easier to sign declarations and to collaborate in joint scientific investigations such as the International Geophysical Year, the International Indian Ocean Expedition, and the Global Atmospheric Research Programme than to fulfill environmental agreements through regulatory measures of their own, or through conformity to international policies or standards. International environmental cooperation even in scientific endeavors has not been an easy achievement.

One cannot be sure that these hard-won beginnings will succeed. As the implementation of a particular treaty moves toward the point of action, those problems and practices that made the action necessary are confronted. At this point environmentally concerned people and their governments face a task as difficult as humans ever face – the changing of human behavior. It is not yet clear that a sufficient number of people will become sufficiently convinced that their well-being depends upon the preservation of the integrity of the biosphere to cause their governments to act and to act together. And whether such consensus may be achieved in time to prevent serious impoverishment of the biosphere and severe diminution of environmental quality cannot be foreseen. Destructive and irreversible environmental effects such as significant change in the composition of the earth's atmosphere could occur before people and nations are prepared to transcend the barriers that limit their cooperation in mutual self-interest.

The uncertain human dimension

The question of mankind's ability to protect the biosphere is a multiple question of understandings, values, priorities, and their behavioral consequences – not primarily one of technical possibilities. Technology may be a powerful instrument of environmental protection and improvement, but its uses may also be destructive. Where technologies are incompatible with environmental protection (e.g. certain persistent pesticides), restraint in their use is the rational though often impolitic alternative. Looking only at technical possibilities employed with informed discretion, the prospects appear good; and viewed alone, technological advancement might justify an optimistic assessment of mankind's ability to manage the biosphere. But technologies are not employed in isolation from other things; their effects transcend their immediate applications. As their power and applicability increase, it is increasingly important to know how and where they may be safely used. Much of what people need to know about the biosphere and about themselves in order to be responsible custodians probably remains to be learned. Scientific understanding of the environment and of human behavior as it affects the earth is growing – and with adequate investment might advance more rapidly. The need for more rapid advancement is evident from the record of the environmental impact of science-based technology: Know-how has outrun the guidance afforded by fundamental knowledge.

Conceding the shortfalls between aim and achievement among international agencies and national governments, experience in the organization and technical aspects of environmental protection and management has been increasing. Environmental sensitivity is beginning to characterize public policies in many countries, and public opinion surveys in several major industrial nations consistently show widespread and growing commitment in principle to environmental protection. Social demand for environmental protection, like technological innovation, threatens to outrun the scientific knowledge needed for soundly based environmental development policies.

The principal hazards to positive prospects for environmental policy are social. Political instability, ignorance, avarice, rapid population growth, disorder, and violence are deterrents to all aspects of environmental protection. The contention that the environment must wait until social justice is achieved could well lead to the failure of both objectives. Inertia in dealing effectively with the basic social problems of the world's peoples – poverty, overpopulation, environmental degradation, and violation of human rights, among many others – could also weaken the basis for international cooperation necessary for environmental protection. The social theories which underlie the policies of contemporary political systems have shown little success in coping with the enormous problems of social condition and behavior that threaten the integrity of most nations of the world today. Hence the pessimistic probability that real progress toward responsible international custody of the biosphere may be slowed, halted, or even reversed by international and intranational social–political conflict.

The depth of informed environmental concern among the world's peoples and governments, however real, is difficult to ascertain. Environmental awareness, although spreading nearly everywhere, is still concentrated in a few advanced countries. The declared intention of the Stockholm Conference and of UNEP to combine socioeconomic reform and environmental protection received more tangible operational expression in the Rio Conference and Agenda 21. Still, peoples and governments almost everywhere have been harassed by problems of economic and political instability, ethnic and sectarian violence, crime and corruption that distract them from the fundamental problem of achieving a sustainable relationship with the earth.

The enormously increased impact of humankind upon the physical and living systems of the earth makes ever more important an understanding of human behavior. The role of humans in changing the face of the earth has been described at length and in detail. But implicit in much of this literature is an assumption that if people understood the harmful consequences of environmental mismanagement, their behaviors would change. However, the ways in which people relate to their environments and to other living species appear to be influenced by their entire cultural matrix. If this is true, and if the tendencies of modern cultures have caused the continuing attrition and destruction of the biosphere, then fundamental cultural change will be required if the many efforts now focused in various aspects of environmental and biospheric protection are to succeed. There may be psycho-genetic factors that affect human environmental behavior (i.e. territoriality and urge to dominate), but as yet we know too little to speculate upon this possibility.

The human dimension of environmental protection is the complex range of attitudes and behaviors, embedded in culture, that account for the ways in which humanity impacts the environment. Foreknowledge of environmental consequences is only one of many (and often stronger) considerations influencing human behavior. Immediate advantages, personal and social, have often outweighed long-range considerations. For as long as it pays for people to destroy living systems unnecessarily, to deplete nonrenewable resources, and to degrade the quality of the biosphere, they may be expected to do so except as influenced by social or political restraints. To attempt to protect the environment against the preferences of people for its exploitation would entail certain costs and uncertain effectiveness. More effective and less costly would be a pervasive popular attitude of respect for the environment and regard for its self-renewal that would reduce the need for regulatory or coercive protection. If the future of world cooperation depends upon the fulfillment of unrealizable goals and purposes, the prospects for international protection of the biosphere are dubious. But it is possible that the peoples of the world have learned more about working together than might be inferred from the literature of international relations or the rhetoric of nationalism and class warfare. The evolution of international environmental policy described [here] makes this possibility plausible.

For informed persons who hope for a better world, the prospect is discouraging, but there remains the outside possibility of a sufficient reversal of destructive trends to redirect the world toward a more sustainable future. To realize this possibility, it will probably be necessary to clear away some of the misconception and wishful premises that have led modern industrial society to its present predicament.

World change in retrospect

To describe an international order as changing is to imply that it is moving from a circumstance that *was* to a circumstance that is *becoming*. The condition of all human societies has been transitional, but the duration of specific conditions, along with rates of change, have varied greatly over historical time. For a variety of reasons – ecological, economic, technological, and psychological – it seems clear that the present time is a period of massive, swift, fundamental change. But it is change with cross-currents and contradictions.

What may be called the old international order developed during the last five hundred years. It began with the expansion overseas of the principal European nations following their formation at the end of the fifteenth and the beginning of the sixteenth centuries. The political consequences of this expansion were the conquest and settlement of the American continent and Australia, the partition and colonization of Africa, and the European domination of large parts of Africa.

By the beginning of the twentieth century this European-dominated international order had reached its maximum extent, and beginning in 1914 with World War I the order began an uneven but continuous political decline throughout the balance of the century. Reasons for the decline of this international order are directly related to the consequences of its expansion, to the consequences of the changes that it wrought – ecological, cultural, ideological, demographic, and technological – throughout the world.

During the five centuries following 1492, European-initiated science and technology transformed the earth. This enormous extension of European economic power and technology was aided by the Industrial Revolution. Industrialization enjoyed an immense bonus from the exploitation of forests, soils, minerals, and fossil fuels that were accessible to development and seemingly undiminished by human use. By the twentieth century much of the cream had been skimmed off the earth's resource base, but demands upon resources and the environment had grown. Although in monetary terms the costs of most resources continued to decline until the latter third of the century, the increased uses to which these resources were put, together with demands upon them by growing numbers of people everywhere, created economic environments of impending scarcity rather than of abundance. In the long run, environmental degradation and impoverishment will be followed by economic impoverishment. Short-term affluence may result from excessive exploitation of the material resource base. But technology alone cannot sustain an economy if erosion of the natural resource base deprives it of the material required for meeting human needs. The argument that resources may be created and substitute materials may be found may be true, in a limited, technical way. But the ultimate end of economic activity is not merely survival; it is rather the improved quality of life. Economic affluence might yield little satisfaction in an environmentally impoverished world.

A major and lasting effect of the old international order of European political dominance was massive acculturation: Traditional ways of life were changed almost everywhere. The process was often tragic. The movement of Europeans to the Americas, the Pacific islands, southern Africa, and northern Asia resulted in the degradation or extinction of numerous traditional cultures and civilizations. African Negro slavery and Asian contract labor accompanied European colonization and led to the transplantation of African and Asian populations and cultures to tropical and subtropical America. At the end of the European colonial period, reverse colonization brought large numbers of Asian and African peoples as migrant workers, refugees, or students into the former colonizing nations of Europe and to the United States and Canada. Distinctive national and cultural traits and values were visibly disintegrating in the industrialized or so-called First World during the last third of the twentieth century. The ethnic and economic bases that had supported nationalism as a political ideology for five centuries were eroding in the nations that had heretofore been the great powers. But in many of the Third World and former colonized states, nationalistic feeling was intense. Perspectives on international cooperation have differed among the old international and environmental policy.

A second important effect of the old international order was development of a complex network of economic interconnections and interdependencies. Interpretations of the significance of interdependence vary widely: Some have read into it social and political implications that find little support in the actual behavior of nations. There is a large contemporary literature devoted to the celebration of interdependence among peoples and nations. International interdependence has been described in a generalized and quasi-ethical sense as both necessary and desirable, yet much of this literature tends toward economic rationalization or moral exhortation. It often confuses interdependency with interconnectedness, suggesting by inference that interrelationships among nations imply unavoidable interdependencies. Quasi-interdependencies that are voluntary, and could be terminated readily, are too often not differentiated from dependencies of fundamental and lasting character. There sometimes appears to be an assumption that legal quality should be considered wholly apart from economic equality in matters of international interdependence. One need only compare the economic strength of the great continental powers with that of small island states to see the implausibility of this assumption. Nations, often for economic reasons, are not equally able to fulfill international obligations. Interdependent nations are not necessarily economic or political equals.

Viewed globally, interconnectedness is a characteristic of the modern world and is one of the changes brought about over the centuries by the old international order. This network of relationships is continued by multinational corporations, which, of course, had antecedents in the Dutch and English trading companies of the seventeenth, eighteenth, and nineteenth centuries. But examined at closer range, it appears that interconnectedness involving interdependency becomes, in the case of certain nations, outright dependency with relatively little reciprocity. Thus, to picture international relations in the modern world as a matrix of mutual and reciprocal interdependencies is to fabricate an idealized representation of the present order that may obstruct consideration of its real problems.

Bilateral and multilateral interdependencies among particular nations exist chiefly among those most highly developed as, for example, between the United States and Japan; explicitly among Canada, the United States, and Mexico under the North American Free Trade Agreement; or among the countries of the European Union. If, however, one examines relationships between developed and less developed nations, reciprocal dependencies are less easily generalized. For those nations whose economies are heavily dependent upon the production of raw materials from natural resources, there is dependency upon consumers in the developed world. But the developed countries often have options with respect to where they obtain their raw materials. The nature of resource flows and their effects upon environmental policy will be considered presently. It is sufficient here to observe that the dependencies that have been created by modern economics and technology do not necessarily bring a competitive world together in a relationships of mutual self-interest.

Thus, present-day efforts to preserve and protect the biosphere take place among multiple contingencies in which perceived national interests and the factors determining the survival of peoples are interpreted in radically different ways. The difficulty in dealing with so large and complex a subject as international environmental policy is increased by lack of common understanding regarding the fundamental causes of people's discontents. Not only have people seldom developed a common perception of the forces and trends with which they are contending, but there has also been a lack of agreement upon the fundamental meanings of words and concepts. And so before dealing specifically with some of the more important environment-related concepts of the changing international order, it is necessary to understand how differing understandings regarding the meaning of words and concepts complicate the ability of nations to cooperate in shaping mutually acceptable policies.

Conceptual obstacles to international order

Differences of opinion and debate over the political economy of the environment are complicated by disagreement, often unperceived, over the meaning and implications of fundamental terms. Vagueness and ambiguity in word meaning lead to confusion over concepts, which exacerbates political and ideological differences to the point that they may be, or appear to be, irreconcilable. Following are some examples of conceptual confusion that have proved to be obstructive of environmental policy and international cooperation.

Ecology and economics may appear to be opposed, which they may be, in the sense that opposite sides of a coin are – they are different aspects of the same thing. Energy, for example, is drawn from resources in the planetary environment and then returned as residual particulates, radioactivity, gases, water vapor, and heat. The applications of energy impact upon the environment through agriculture, mining, manufacturing, construction, transportation, and other activities. It therefore follows that public policies for energy, natural resources, the environment, the economy, and health cannot realistically be separated.

Nor can they be separated from policies concerning so-called growth and development. The qualifier "so-called" is attached to these terms because their use, while widespread and often official, is ambiguous until clarified by agreed understanding or by practical example. Politicians, economists, and planners act mainly as if the meaning of growth and development is so well understood that no explanation is needed. Unfortunately what everyone *knows* is often what anybody really *understands*. And if one asks the meaning of these terms, the reply is usually a synonym, not an explanation. Qualified definitions may sometimes be more explicit – or at least their implications may be deduced from the context of their usage.

Thus "economic growth" implies in the vernacular a rising standard of living, more economic activity, and a larger gross national product – but with the particular style or quality of life seldom specified. The assumption that economic growth always correlates with more food, clothing, shelter, health, education, and security is contrary to the experience of many people in countries where economic growth has been substantial. It may be argued that in poor, less developed countries, people in the aggregate are better off than they would have been without "growth"; some people at least appear to be better off. This argument, however, is questionable when one considers the extent of rural poverty and urban squalor in the Third World (the same argument is hardly less questionable in the First World). Even with commitments to planning for human betterment assisted by United Nations agencies, development banks, and bilateral programs, economic growth has fallen far short of its alleged results. And because of the way in which it has been promoted, and its benefits distributed, such growth may have increased social disorder, material and psychological deprivation, and political discontent.

The term "development" is equally misleading. It is literally no more than a synonym for a certain kind of growth and progress. Some conventional definitions of development equate it with terms hardly less ambiguous – for example, with modernization, democratization, or (less commonly today) industrialization. Taken literally, growth and development are *processes*; they are terms without content, implying nothing per se about the substance of goals or outcomes. Yet there must be some content in a term about which hundreds of articles, books, and official reports have been written, and in the name of which governments and international agencies have employed experts, administered programs, and expanded funds.

Assuming that the terms "growth" and "development" do represent real concerns that many people believe to be (or should be) the major focus of relations among nations today, these concerns are not well served by the language used to identify them. "Growth" and "development" are terms that everyone ostensibly understands but no one can define to general satisfaction in simple unequivocal language. To discover what these terms mean to those who use them one must look to practice – to what is done in the name of growth and development. Clarification of the development concept and reconciliation of ecological and economic values has been sought through the qualifying concept of "sustainable development." [. . .] As previously noted, "sustainability" tells us nothing about what the development process will sustain and at what level of environmental quality. Still, the term has won widespread acceptance and to this extent lowers a barrier to international environmental cooperation.

Beyond these ambiguous concepts the jurisprudential doctrine of "national sovereignty" is a politically resistant barrier to international environmental cooperation (as it is also in the other areas of policy). Rhetorical assertions of national sovereignty continue to be heard, but the imperatives of geophysical hazards to all nations are pushing their governments toward modification of their asserted freedom to act as they please in relations to their natural resources, industrial practices, and the environment. A rhetorical strategy to evade the sovereignty roadblock is the concept of "merged sovereignty," which in fact occurs when nations seek to realize their own national objectives through treaties with other nations having interests in common.

Salient features of the international environmental movement have been openness, diversity, complexity, dynamism, and purposiveness. No other international movement – world peace included – engages so large a number of individual participants, so many and such diverse forms of cooperative effort, so broad a range of human skills and interests, and such complex relationships among governmental and nongovernmental organizations. For persons not accustomed to organizational complexity, the matrix of interactive relationships that shape international environmental policy could indeed be incomprehensible. It defies description in detail. [. . .]

Although some aspects of the environmental movement are aesthetic or atavistic, its greater and more compelling function has been an intermediary role between the environmental findings of the sciences and the policies and actions of governments and intergovernmental organizations. Credible forecasts from the sciences in matters such as global climate change, ozone layer depletion, acid precipitation, toxics in food chains, effects of deforestation and loss of biodiversity – among many other issues – have provided the substance for environmental policies and a geopolitics of the planet Earth.

Implications for the sciences are far-reaching. Every science, from agronomy to zoology, is somehow drawn into environmental investigation; and beyond the continuing mandatory agency missions of a specialized and narrow focus, interactive interdisciplinary approaches are developing, notably through the large-scale environmental investigations. [. . .] The outcomes of these investigations frequently contain important implications for the non-science disciplines and the humanistic and the science-based professions.

The foundations of sound environmental policy require a substratum of understanding of the earth's atmosphere, hydrosphere, biogeochemical cycles, ecological interrelationships, and basic human needs and behaviors. But these fields of investigation are collectively insufficient to provide a holistic approach to environmental policymaking. In order to build their findings into public and international policies, an even wider range of disciplines must be involved: law, medicine, economics, ethics, aesthetics, engineering, and the design arts, among many others. An integrated interdisciplinary use of scientific and technical knowledge is required to assist the formulation of policy. There are, of course, precedents for the collaboration of science and policy, but what is different today is the greatly increased scope of the relationships and their international character. This increasing recourse to science for guidance in policymaking remains in addition to policies predetermined in the absence of full knowledge of their impacts, costs, and benefits, as in the issue of global climate change. Indeed, the criteria for judgment in science and politics are very different. Science draws conclusions on weight of evidence or probabilities. It seldom expresses its conclusions in absolutes. Politics, in contrast, often alleges self-evident truths and unequivocal conclusions based on opinion.

Science may not be counted upon to transcend introverted nationalism, but it does have that capability. Scientific knowledge is not immune to political manipulation, but there are remedies for the resultant misrepresentation. The growth of science in the less-developed countries is gradually enabling their leaders to assess national capabilities more realistically and to participate with greater confidence in international cooperative efforts. This growing scientific component of international environmental cooperation is a factor that can help to offset political antagonisms. The extent that representatives of governments can agree upon the implications of demonstrable facts, they may to that extent also agree to cooperation in the policies implied, even though they continue their disagreements on other matters.

Science in principle is a system of thought and action open to all who can fulfill its requirements of preparation, accuracy, and candor. Throughout a large part of the world, and even under ostensibly despotic regimens, science and scientists may have a measure of freedom from political control that enhances their ability to collaborate in international environmental research and planning. Scientific associations are prominent among the many nongovernmental organizations (NGOs) that play important roles in international environmental affairs. The NGOs, moreover, are not wholly dependent upon governments for their information or agendas, and the relative autonomy of science thus reinforces the relative independence of environmental NGOs from political and ideological divisions.

The importance of NGOs in international environmental policymaking can hardly be overemphasized. NGOs have been influential, both within and among nations, and they have been the instigators of numerous treaties and international cooperative arrangements. Because NGOs form extra-governmental networks among as well as within nations, they are less constrained by the characteristic inhibitions of diplomatic protocol and bureaucratic procedure. In both the forming and execution of international policy they may act more rapidly and directly, and with less risk to national sensitiveness, than can the official intergovernmental agencies. [. . .]

With environmental policy increasingly built into the normal bureaucratic structures and agendas of governments and intergovernmental agencies, one cannot safely predict the future role of NGOs in international environmental politics. The role of the multinational corporation as a special class of NGO is ambiguous. Its position in international environmental politics is widely believed to be neutral or negative. But multinationals are increasingly drawn into environmental policy-making, and their influence has been felt in the Law of the Sea Conferences, in UNEP's Regional Seas Programme, in the deliberations of IMO, in debates on orbiting satellite communication, in energy and natural resources policies, and in government policies for the transportation and management of hazardous materials. Support of international environmental protective measures might well be consistent with long-term corporate interests. But it is uncertain whether many of these firms presently see it in that context. Meanwhile, the International Chamber of Commerce has established an International Environmental Bureau, headquartered in Geneva, which has been actively involved in a broad range of environmental issues in which industrial research and development are needed. In addition, the New York City-based World Environment Center is a clearinghouse for environmental information published largely by business firms. Annually it awards a Gold Medal for International Corporate Environmental Achievement pursuant to its mission "to contribute to sustainable development by strengthening the management of industry-related health and safety practices worldwide." At the time of the Rio Conference a Business Council on Sustainable Development was formed under the leadership of Swiss industrialist Stephan Schmieheiny and published a case book of thirty-eight studies of business initiatives under the title *Changing Course: A Global Business Perspective on Development and Environment* (MIT Press, 1992). Corporate enterprise today needs reliable environmental information, a need documented in 1984 for the US Council on Environmental Quality by Russell E. Train, president of the World Wide Fund for Nations (WWF).

The most significant augury for the future importance of NGOs in world environmental affairs has been their widespread increase in numbers and members during the post-Stockholm decade. In 1980 the Environment Liaison Center (ELC) in Nairobi reported that of the more than one thousand NGOs represented "half are from less developed countries." More significantly the ELC reported in 1982 at the tenth anniversary of the Stockholm Conference that "there are 2,230 non-governmental environmental organizations in developing countries of which 60 percent were formed in the last ten years, and 13,000 in developed countries of which 30 percent have formed in the last ten years." Of particular political significance is the fact that the NGOs could provide a constituency for the official agencies for environmental protection now established in most countries and could function as receptors and disseminators of the concepts embodied in the World Conservation Strategy. The number of environmental NGOs continues to grow. The 1987 Annual Report of the executive director of UNEP stated that ELC "coordinates a network of over 6,000 NGOs dedicated to the protection and improvement of the environment." The *BNA International Environment Daily* (June 8, 1992) estimated that two thousand NGOs were in some respects represented at the 1992 UN Conference in Rio.

In summation, a dynamic, composite, and flexible structure, partly official, partly unofficial, has emerged during the two decades following Stockholm. This interactive structure has formed and grown so rapidly that many experts in international affairs are unaware of its extent or significance. Its purpose – international environmental protection – is novel in substance and scope, while including elements that existed before environment became a focus of public policy. Obstacles to its effective functioning lie in inappropriate human responses to impending environmental disasters, and in the antagonistic postures of nations divided within and against one another. Hope for international cooperation toward safeguarding the human environment and the biosphere lies in the demonstrated capacity of human beings, and their governments, to transcend their differences where mutual interests and mutual survival should be evident.

PART VIII

Human rights

H UMAN RIGHTS GRAPHICALLY symbolize recent global history. Although the notion of human rights goes back at least to the Enlightenment in eighteenth-century Europe and North America, it spread to other parts of the world only toward the end of the nineteenth century. In the twentieth century, the idea gained momentum and came to provide ideological underpinnings for civil rights, women's rights, colonial liberation, and other movements throughout the globe. As these movements spread and virtually engulfed the world, it became an integral part of the phenomenon of globalization.

In this section, Jack Donnelly (Professor of International Relations at the University of Denver) and Louis Menand III (Senior Lecturer in Political Science at Massachusetts Institute of Technology) trace the historical evolution of human rights, showing how human rights have steadily become an international issue and defined not just domestic movements but also activities by international organizations, notably the United Nations. The two essays present by and large positive assessments of the internationalization of human rights, but they also point to difficulties in implementing the principle. The sovereign state is often concerned more with security than with human rights, and it can resist interference from international organizations in the name of human rights. Some insist that the allegedly universal principle of human rights actually is a product of Western civilization and may be at variance with value systems upheld elsewhere. These issues have continued to be raised, itself an indication that the subject of human rights is inseparable from global history.

Chapter 15

Jack Donnelly

HUMAN RIGHTS AS AN ISSUE
IN WORLD POLITICS

BEFORE WORLD WAR II, human rights were rarely discussed in inter-national politics. Most states violated human rights systematically. Racial discrimination pervaded the United States. The Soviet Union was a totalitarian secret-police state. Britain, France, the Netherlands, Portugal, Belgium, the United States, and Spain maintained colonial empires in Africa, Asia, and the Caribbean. And the political history of most Central and South American countries was largely a succession of military dictatorships and civilian oligarchies.

Such phenomena troubled many people. They were not, however, considered a legitimate subject for international action. Rather, human rights were viewed as an internal (domestic) political matter, an internationally protected exercise of the sovereign prerogatives of states. Even genocidal massacres, such as Russian pogroms against the Jews or the Turkish slaughter of Armenians, drew little more than polite statements of disapproval. Less egregious violations were typically not even considered a fit subject for diplomatic conversation. [. . .]

[International] relations have for the past three centuries been organized around the principle of sovereignty. States, the principal actors in international relations, are seen as *sovereign*, that is, subject to no higher political authority. The duty correl-ative to the right of *sovereignty* is *nonintervention*, the obligation not to interfere in matters that are essentially within the domestic jurisdiction of sovereign states. Human rights, which typically involve a state's treatment of its own citizens in its own territory, were traditionally seen as just such a matter of domestic jurisdic-tion. One purpose of this [essay] is to chronicle a fundamental change in this dominant international understanding of the range of state sovereignty over the past fifty years.

In the nineteenth and early twentieth centuries, the European Great Powers and the United States did occasionally intervene in the Ottoman and Chinese empires to rescue nationals caught in situations of civil strife and to establish or protect special rights and privileges for Europeans and Americans. Rarely, though, did they intervene to protect foreign nationals from their own government. In fact,

From Jack Donnelly, *International Human Rights*, 2nd edition (Westview Press, 1998), pp. 3–17.

human rights were seldom even a topic of diplomatic discussion. Likewise, the "humanitarian law" of war, expressed in documents such as the 1907 Hague Conventions, limited only what a state could do to *foreign* nationals, not its own nationals (or people over whom it exercised colonial rule).

The principal exception was the campaign against slavery. The major powers recognized an obligation to abolish the slave trade at the Congress of Vienna in 1815. A comprehensive treaty to abolish the slave trade was (finally) concluded in 1890s. But a treaty to abolish slavery, as opposed to international trade in slaves, was not drafted until 1926. After World War I, the International Labor Organization (ILO) dealt with some workers' rights issues, and the League of Nations had limited powers to protect ethnic minorities in selected areas. With these marginal exceptions, however, human rights were not an accepted subject of international relations prior to World War II. In assessing current international human rights activity, we must keep in mind this starting point.

The emergence of international human rights norms

A problem often becomes the subject of international action only after a dramatic event crystallizes awareness. For example, the discovery of the Antarctic ozone hole contributed significantly to the recent upsurge of international environmental action. The catalyst that made human rights an issue in world politics was the Holocaust, the systematic murder of millions of innocent civilians by Germany during World War II.

The human rights response of the victorious Allies was shameful. Before the war, little was done to aid Jews trying to flee Germany and the surrounding countries. In fact, some who escaped were denied refuge by Allied governments, including the United States. During the war, no effort was made to impede the functioning of the death camps. For example, the Allies did not even target the railway lines that brought hundreds of thousands to the slaughter at Auschwitz. The world watched – or, rather, turned a blind eye to – the genocidal massacre of 6 million Jews and half a million Gypsies, and the deaths of thousands of Communists, Social Democrats, homosexuals, church activists, and just ordinary decent people who refused complicity in the new politics and technology of barbarism.

Only as the war came to an end were Allied leaders and citizens, previously preoccupied with military victory, willing to begin to confront this horror. But in international relations, they were forced to face the Holocaust armed only with their moral sensibilities. As we have seen, international law and diplomacy before the war had not addressed human rights.

The first step in filling this void came with the Nuremberg War Crimes Trials (1945–6), at which leading Nazis were prosecuted under the novel charge of crimes against humanity. Human rights really emerged as a standard subject of international relations, though, in the United Nations (UN). The Covenant of the League of Nations did not mention human rights. The Preamble of the Charter of the United Nations, by contrast, includes a determination "to reaffirm faith in fundamental human rights." Article 1 lists "encouraging respect for human rights and for fundamental freedoms for all" as one of the organization's principal purposes. And the United Nations moved quickly to elaborate international human rights standards.

On December 9, 1948, the Convention on the Prevention and Punishment of the Crime of Genocide was opened for signature.

On the following day, the UN General Assembly (GA) unanimously adopted the *Universal Declaration of Human Rights*, which even today provides the most authoritative statement of international human rights norms. [. . .]

From cold war to covenants

Following the adoption of the Universal Declaration, human rights continued to be discussed at the United Nations. The momentum of the immediate postwar years, however, was not sustained. The rise of the *cold war*, the ideological and geopolitical struggle between the United States and the Soviet Union, brought this initial progress to a halt.

After the descent of the Iron Curtain in Central and Eastern Europe in 1948 and the final Communist victory in China in 1949, human rights increasingly became just another arena of superpower struggle. For example, in the late 1950s the Commission of Human Rights, under Western (US) control, extensively discussed freedom of information (a right that the Soviets systematically violated) but ignored all economic and social rights, as well as most other particular civil and political rights. Conversely, the Soviets tried to focus attention on racial discrimination and unemployment in the capitalist West. Although each side pointed to real abuses, charges of human rights violations were largely tactical maneuvers in a broader political and ideological struggle.

Furthermore, both superpowers regularly revealed a flagrant disregard for human rights. For example, in Guatemala in 1954 the United States overthrew the freely elected government of Jacobo Arbenz Guzmán, in part because of its redistributive policies that aimed to better implement economic and social rights. This ushered in thirty years of military rule that culminated in the systematic massacre of tens of thousands of Guatemalans in the early 1980s. Elsewhere as well, the United States not only tolerated gross and systematic violations of human rights in "friendly" (anticommunist) countries but often warmly embraced the responsible regimes. Likewise, the Soviets forcibly insisted upon one-party totalitarian dictatorships in their sphere of influence. For example, Soviet tanks rolled into Hungary in 1956 to put an end to liberal political reforms and (re)impose totalitarian dictatorship.

The impact of the cold war is also evident in the derailing of work on further elaborations of international human rights standards. Because the Universal Declaration of Human Rights is a resolution of the UN General Assembly, not a treaty, it is not per se legally binding. [. . .]

Its drafters intended to follow the declaration with a covenant (treaty) that would give human rights binding force in international law. Although largely complete by 1953, the covenant was tabled for more than a decade, in large measure because of ideological rivalry over the status of economic and social rights.

Progress again began to be made in the early 1960s, in part as a result of the one line of effective UN human rights activity in the 1950s, namely, decolonization. In 1945, when the United Nations was founded, most of Africa and Asia were under Western colonial rule. The process of decolonization that began in 1947 with the independence of Indonesia and India accelerated dramatically in Africa in the late 1950s and 1960s. UN membership doubled in barely a decade, and, by the mid-1960s, Afro-Asian states formed the largest voting bloc in the UN.

These countries, which had suffered under colonial domination, had a special interest in human rights. They found a sympathetic hearing from some Western European and Latin American countries. The UN thus began to reemphasize human rights. In 1965, the International Convention on the Elimination of All Forms of Racial Discrimination was opened for signature and ratification. And in December 1966, the *International Human Rights Covenants* were finally completed. (In deference to the lingering cold war, the single treaty envisioned in 1948 was broken into two, the International Covenant on Economic, Social, and Cultural Rights and the International Covenant on Civil and Political Rights.)

The Covenants, together with the Universal Declaration, represent an authoritarian statement of international human rights norms, standards of behavior to which all states should aspire. These three documents, which are referred to collectively as the *International Bill of Human Rights*, present a summary statement of the minimum social and political guarantees recognized by the international community as necessary for a life of dignity in the contemporary world. [. . .]

The very comprehensiveness of the Covenants, however, meant that further major progress in international action on behalf of human rights would lie primarily in implementing (or monitoring the implementation of) these standards – an area in which the United Nations had been, and still is, far less successful.

The 1970s: from standard setting to monitoring

The existence of international norms does not in itself give the United Nations the authority to inquire into how states implement (or do not implement) them. Through the Universal Declaration and the Covenants, states have agreed to follow international human rights standards. But they did not authorize the UN to investigate their compliance with these standards.

This began to change in the late 1960s. In 1967, the Economic and Social Council Resolution 1235 authorized the Commission on Human Rights to discuss human rights violations in particular countries. In 1968, a Special Committee of Investigation was created to consider human rights in the territories occupied by Israel after the 1967 war. In the same year, the UN Security Council imposed a mandatory blockade on the white minority regime in Southern Rhodesia. The 1965 racial discrimination convention, which requires parties to file periodic reports on implementation, came into force in 1969. And in 1970, Economic and Social Council Resolution 1503 authorized the Commission on Human Rights to conduct confidential investigations of complaints that suggested "a consistent pattern of gross and reliably attested violations of human rights and fundamental freedoms."

Each of these efforts was limited or partial. The procedures authorized by Resolution 1503 have had little demonstrable, concrete impact. The implementation provisions of the racial discrimination convention are extremely weak [. . .]. The initiative in Southern Africa and the Occupied Territories reflected the special political concerns of the newly dominant Afro-Asian bloc. Optimists could argue that these developments provided precedents for stronger action. Their significance, though, was largely symbolic: The UN was at last beginning to move, however tentatively, from merely setting standards to examining how those standards were implemented by states.

The severe structural constraints on the UN need to be emphasized. The United Nations is an intergovernmental organization, established by a treaty (the UN Charter) among sovereign states. Its members are sovereign states. Delegates to the United Nations represent states, not the international community, let alone individuals whose rights are violated. Like other intergovernmental organizations, the UN has only those powers that states – which are also the principal violators of human rights – give it. Thus, perhaps more surprising than the limits on its human rights monitoring powers is the fact that the UN actually acquired even these limited powers. Although of little comfort to victims, a balanced assessment of the human rights achievements of the UN and other intergovernmental organizations cannot ignore the central fact of state sovereignty and the restrictions it imposes.

Modest monitoring progress continued in the 1970s. In response to the 1973 military coup in Chile [. . .], the UN created an Ad Hoc Working Group on the Situation of Human Rights in Chile. In 1976, the International Human Rights Covenants entered into force; that is, following the ratification of thirty-five states, the Covenants became binding legal obligations for those states. This led to the creation of the Human Rights Committee (HRC), charged with monitoring implementation of the International Covenant on Civil and Political Rights.

The 1970s also saw human rights explicitly introduced into the bilateral foreign policies of individual countries, beginning in the United States. In 1973, Congress recommended linking US foreign aid to the human rights practices of recipient countries. In 1975, this linkage was made mandatory: US foreign aid policy was required to take into account (although not necessarily be determined by) the human rights practices of recipient countries. Such legislation was both nationally and internationally unprecedented. When Jimmy Carter became president in 1977, the executive branch also became generally supportive of pursuing human rights in foreign policy. Although practice still regularly fell short of rhetoric, these American initiatives helped to open space for new ways of thinking about and acting on international human rights concerns. [. . .]

The 1970s also saw substantial growth in the number and activities of human rights *nongovernmental organizations* (NGOs), private associations that engage in political activity. Such groups act as advocates for victims of human rights violations by publicizing violations and lobbying to alter the practices of states and international organizations.

Best known is Amnesty International (AI), which was founded in 1961, received the Nobel Peace Price in 1977, and has an international membership of more than 1 million people. AI's best-known activity is letter writing on behalf of individual prisoners of conscience, incarcerated for their beliefs or nonviolent political activities. In its first thirty years, it investigated the cases of over forty-two thousand individual prisoners. Amnesty International also publishes an annual report, special reports on individual countries, and occasional reports on torture and other general issues of concern. In addition, its representatives testify before national legislatures and intergovernmental organizations and publicize human rights issues through public statements and appearances in the media.

The private status of NGOs allows them to operate free of the political control of states. And unlike even states with active international human rights policies, human rights NGOs do not have to take into account other foreign policy objectives. Therefore, they are often better able to press human rights concerns.

NGOs, however, must rely on the power of publicity and persuasion. They lack the resources of even weak states. States remain free to be unpersuaded. And many states have used their powers of coercion against the members of human rights NGOs, turning them into new victims.

Nonetheless, human rights NGOs have played an important role in legitimating international concern with human rights. NGO lobbying helped to assure that human rights language was included in the United Nations Charter. Since then, NGOs have become regular, active, and occasionally influential participants in the human rights work of the UN. For example, national and international campaigns by Amnesty International played an important role in UN initiatives on torture in the 1970s and 1980s.

NGOs have also helped to incorporate concern for human rights into the foreign policies of individual states. For instance, Amnesty's Dutch section contributed to the drafting of the 1970 White Paper that made human rights a formal part of the foreign policy of the Netherlands. In the United States, AI has been especially active on Capitol Hill, lobbying, testifying, and providing information and support to sympathetic members of Congress and their staff. In Australia, there is even an Amnesty International group in the Parliament. And national human rights NGOs, such as the American Civil Liberties Union in the United States, have been involved in the domestic politics of numerous states.

The 1980s: further growth and institutionalization

Multilateral, bilateral, and nongovernmental human rights activity continued to increase, more or less steadily, through the 1980s. Norms continued to be developed. In December 1979, the Convention on the Elimination of Discrimination Against Women was opened for signature and ratification. This wide-ranging treaty, addressing systematic discrimination against one-half of the population of the globe, in every country of the world, was the first major human rights treaty to emerge from the UN since the Covenants in 1966. Drafting of the Convention Against Torture and Other Cruel, Inhuman, or Degrading Treatment or Punishment was completed in 1984. The General Assembly adopted a Declaration on the Right to Development in 1986. The decade came to a close with a Convention on the Rights of the Child in November 1989.

In the area of monitoring, the Human Rights Committee began to review periodic reports submitted under the International Covenant on Civil and Political Rights. The Committee on Economic, Social, and Cultural Rights was created in 1986 to improve reporting and monitoring in this important area. The Commission on Human Rights undertook "thematic" initiatives on disappearances, torture, and summary or arbitrary executions. Furthermore, a larger and more diverse group of countries came under commission scrutiny.

The process of incorporating human rights into bilateral foreign policy also accelerated in the 1980s. For example, the Netherlands and Norway have had particularly prominent international human rights policies [. . .]. Both the Council of Europe and the European Community (EC) introduced human rights concerns into their external relations [. . .]. A few Third World countries, such as Costa Rica, have also emphasized human rights in their foreign policies.

Perhaps more surprising was the persistence of the issue of human rights in US foreign policy. Ronald Reagan campaigned for the presidency in 1980 against Carter's human rights policy. His revival of the cold war against the Soviet "evil empire" led many people to fear (or hope) that human rights would again be forced to the sidelines. And US international human rights policy did become less even-handed and more controversial in the 1980s. Nonetheless, when George Bush took office in 1989, human rights had a secure (although hardly uncontroversial) and well-institutionalized place in US foreign policy. The Bureau of Human Rights and Humanitarian Affairs was increasingly seen as an integral part of the State Department rather than as an unwanted intrusion. Regular, continuing action on behalf of international human rights had bipartisan support in Congress.

The 1980s also saw a dramatic decline in the fortunes of repressive dictator-ships. Throughout Latin America, military regimes that had appeared unshakable in the 1970s crumbled in the 1980s. By 1990, elected government held office in every continental country in the Western Hemisphere (although the democratic creden-tials of some, such as Paraguay, remained extremely suspect). In addition, there were peaceful transfers of power after elections in several countries in 1989, including Argentina, Brazil, El Salvador, and Uruguay.

In Asia, the personalist dictatorship of Ferdinand Marcos was overthrown in the Philippines in 1986. South Korea's military dictatorship was replaced by an elected government in 1988. Taiwan ended four decades of imposed single-party rule. In Pakistan, Benazir Bhutto was elected president in December 1988, ending a dozen years of military rule. Asia, however, also presented the most dramatic human rights setback of the decade – the June 1989 massacre in Beijing's Tiananmen Square. [. . .]

The changes with the greatest international impact, however, occurred in Central and Eastern Europe. Soviet-imposed regimes in East Germany and Czecho-slovakia crumbled in fall 1989 in the face of peaceful mass protests. In Hungary and Poland, when liberalization had begun earlier in the decade, Communist Party dicta-torships also peacefully withdrew from power. Even Romania and Bulgaria ousted their old Communist governments (although their new governments include numerous former Communists with tenuous democratic credentials). In the USSR, where glasnost (openness) and perestroika (restructuring) had created the inter-national political space for these changes, the Communist Party fell from power after the abortive military coup of August 1991, and the Soviet Union was dissolved four months later.

The 1990s: continuity and change in the post-cold war era

With the collapse of the Soviet empire, the cold war international order crumbled. Although this has certainly altered the context for international human rights, the "new world order" proclaimed by President George Bush has proved not entirely new and often rather disorderly. A region-by-region review shows mostly gradual, but generally positive, change.

In Latin America and Central and Eastern Europe, the progress of the 1980s has largely been maintained. In many cases, such as El Salvador and Hungary, liberalization has substantially deepened. In a few countries, such as the Czech Republic and perhaps Argentina, something close to full democratization seems to have been achieved. In most of the former Soviet republics, however, the commitment to and understanding of both democracy and human rights of the countries' elected leaders (and most of their opponents) is hardly inspiring. In several Latin American countries as well, such as Guatemala and Paraguay and to a lesser extent Mexico and El Salvador, elected governments provide a sort of liberalized, semi-authoritarian rule.

In Sub-Saharan Africa, where one-party and no-party states remained the norm throughout the 1980s, political liberalization has been widespread. Although progress has been less consistent (and usually less deep) than in much of Latin America, relatively open multiparty elections are becoming common. In March 1991, Benin's Nicephore Soglo became the first candidate in the history of mainland Africa to defeat an incumbent president in a democratic election. Even more dramatic was the November 1991 defeat of Kenneth Kaunda, Zambia's president for the first twenty-five years of its independence. And the end of apartheid in South Africa was a dramatic change indeed.

But Nigeria, Africa's most populous country, remains under military rule. Zaire has just emerged from four decades of suffering under the personalist dictatorship of Mobuto Sese Seko. In Mauritania, policies of forced relocation and state-sponsored ethnic violence and repression continue, as does genocide in Rwanda and Burundi and a brutal civil war in Liberia. Furthermore, most African countries still systematically infringe on a number of internationally recognized civil and political rights, and most are experiencing a second decade of stagnation or decline in the enjoyment of economic, social, and cultural rights.

In Asia, the picture remains mixed but improved. South Korea and Taiwan have made significant progress toward establishing democratic, rights-protective regimes. Cambodia, with a substantial assist from the United Nations, has cast off Vietnamese occupation and freely elected a government that, although politically precarious, is by far the most liberal it has seen in decades. Tentative and partial but real liberalization has occurred in Vietnam. And India, for all its problems, remains the world's largest multiparty electoral democracy.

China, however, despite its substantial economic opening and reform, remains a highly repressive, Stalinist party state. Burma continues to push aside its internal democracy movement and international pressures for liberalization. Pakistan and, even more so, Afghanistan are racked by ethnic and religious violence. North Korea continues to be arguably the world's most closed and politically backward state. And some, especially in Singapore, Malaysia, China, and Indonesia, have begun to argue that international human rights standards do not apply in their entirety in Asia.

The mixed pictures in Africa and Asia are, sadly, far more encouraging than those in the Middle East. Hafiz al-Assad's brutal dictatorial rule continues in Syria, as does Saddam Hussein's in Iraq. Libya remains subject to Muammar Qaddafi's personalist dictatorship. Religious intolerance and the suppression of all dissent remain the norm in Iran. The Gulf States remain as closed and undemocratic as ever. Increasingly violent Islamic fundamentalist movements have led to growing repression in Egypt and military dictatorship and shockingly brutal civil war in

Algeria. In Yemen, earlier progress has largely been reversed. The new Palestinian entity, run by Yasir Arafat's Palestinian Liberation Organization (PLO), has shown little more concern for human rights than the former Israeli occupiers. In Saudi Arabia, very modest reforms to increase input into the decision-making process were instituted in 1992, in the aftermath of the Gulf War, but they do not even extend to the toleration of independent human rights NGOs: In April 1993, the founders of the Committee for the Defense of Legitimate Rights were removed from their jobs and jailed. Modest liberalization of the monarchies of Jordan and Morocco, including unusually free elections in 1993, are about the only examples of substantial progress in the region.

A similar pattern of solidifying past gains coupled with modest progress in selected areas is apparent at the international level. Perhaps most striking was the decisive rebuff of arguments by China and other countries at the World Human Rights Conference in Vienna in 1993 against the full implementation of internationally recognized human rights in the short and medium term. And the very decision to hold the world conference indicates the growing force of the idea of international human rights. Such events, particularly when coupled with the changes in national practices already noted, signify a deepening penetration of the international consensus on human rights norms, which was often shallow in the 1970s and 1980s.

This deepening penetration of international norms can be seen in the United States as well. Although probably the most vocal proponent of international human rights in the 1970s and 1980s, the United States steadfastly refused to be bound by international human rights treaties in its own practice. In 1992, however, the Senate finally ratified the International Covenant on Civil and Political Rights (but not the International Covenant on Economic, Social, and Cultural Rights). And in 1994, the United States also became a party to the conventions on torture and women's rights.

Multilateral institutions continue to function at least as well as they did in the past. At the United Nations, there has even been a noticeable decline in political partisanship. And the creation, at the end of 1993, of a high commissioner for human rights has the potential to increase both the scope and depth of multilateral monitoring (although the high commissioner's activities to date have been modest).

In bilateral relations, human rights continue to become a more deeply entrenched and less controversial foreign policy concern. In contrast to the 1970s and early 1980s, when debate often focused on whether human rights should be an active foreign policy concern, today the question is usually which rights to emphasize in which particular cases. Furthermore, nongovernmental human rights organizations and advocates have become a significant part of the political landscape in a growing number of countries in the Third World and former Soviet bloc.

International human rights today are not only more frequently discussed in a wider range of countries, but they are treated as an ordinary part of international relations. States that are targets of international human rights pressure continue to appeal to sovereignty. But almost all other states have rebuffed claims, made perhaps most strenuously by China, that human rights practices are not a legitimate concern of foreign states and international organizations.

More dramatic changes in the international politics of human rights have come in response to a series of post-cold war political and humanitarian crises. After repelling the Iraqi invasion of Kuwait, the United Nations set up security zones in northern Iraq to protect Iraqi Kurds against their own government. In the face of the complete breakdown of centralized political authority in Somalia, the United Nations launched a massive, militarized humanitarian relief mission that saved hundreds of thousands of Somalis from starvation and civil war. The United States, the Organization of American States (OAS), and the United Nations mobilized substantial political pressure, instituted economic sanctions, and successfully threatened armed force to remove military rule in Haiti.

Perhaps the most dramatic progress has been in international responses to genocide. During the cold war era, genocide and politicide, in places such as Burundi, East Pakistan (Bangladesh), Cambodia, and Uganda, were met by verbal expressions of concern but little concrete action (except by neighboring states – India, Vietnam, and Tanzania – with a strong selfish interest in intervening). But the international tribunals for the former Yugoslavia and Rwanda, created in 1991 and 1994, have revived the Nuremberg precedent. And the General Assembly's decision at the end of 1995 to create an international criminal tribunal suggests a deeper normative transformation.

Of no less importance has been the post-cold war penetration of human rights into other areas of international concern, most notably multilateral peacekeeping. Until the late 1980s, peacekeeping operations were scrupulously organized and operated to avoid direct reference to human rights. This reflected the politicized nature of UN human rights discussions and the desire of most states to avoid creating precedents for UN field action on behalf of human rights. In recent years, however, the link between human rights and international peace and security, which has been a central part of United Nations rhetoric since the drafting of the Charter, has finally become part of UN practice.

UN peacekeeping operations in Namibia, El Salvador, Cambodia, Somalia, Northern Iraq, Mozambique, Bosnia, Croatia, and Guatemala have had explicit human rights responsibilities, and the operations in Haiti and Rwanda had primarily human rights mandates. The task of these peacekeeping forces have included monitoring the activities of the police and security forces, verifying the discharge of human rights undertakings in agreements ending civil wars, supervising elections, encouraging authorities to adopt and comply with international human rights treaties, and providing human rights education. In El Salvador, Haiti, Guatemala, and Rwanda, peacekeepers have even had explicit mandates to investigate human rights violations.

Bosnia [. . .] and Rwanda are the two clearest cases of the convergence of human rights, humanitarian, and peacekeeping concerns and activities. The UN sent peacekeepers to Rwanda in fall 1993 and touched off the resumption of the civil war that led to the massacre of over half a million civilians and forced 2 to 3 million people to flee their homes. Both were tragically belated efforts, and the first mission in particular was denied the resources necessary to succeed as the crisis worsened. Nonetheless, these were operations that would have been inconceivable during the cold war. And in Bosnia, although international interventions have been criticized as too little, too late, the humanitarian efforts on behalf of Sarajevo and other protected enclaves were substantial and sustained, despite the costs and dangers. Furthermore, extensive UN, US, and European diplomatic and political efforts produced the Dayton Agreements of November 1995, which have stopped the fighting and established a (precarious) political foundation for the country.

Such events – especially in the context of the already noted continuing national political progress, international normative deepening, and the maturing of human rights as an international issue – have been taken by many to suggest a qualitative transformation of the international politics of human rights in the 1990s. But whatever we conclude about the character of changes in the post-cold war politics of human rights, not only do human rights have a firm place in international relations, in sharp contrast to just a half century ago, but their place is more prominent than at any other time in modern history.

Chapter 16

Louis Menand III

HUMAN RIGHTS AS GLOBAL IMPERATIVE

To THOSE WHO HAVE accepted Enlightenment teaching, it may seem incredible that any rational person would not readily accept as self-evident truths individual freedom and equality regardless of sex, race, or religious belief. To others, it may seem incredible that any person would willingly inject some notion of individualism into a belief system and thereby disrupt the sense of community essential to that system. It is this tension between an essentially secular worldview and more proscribed belief systems that sets the stage for the extension of human rights doctrines. Add to this the autocratic bullies in some nations who will let nothing stand in the way of their bullydom, and the tension becomes more acute. Whither, then, human rights?

In the last years of the twentieth century, there has been an explosion of interest in and a declaration of faith in international standards of human rights. In 1992, the twelve-member European Community (EC) agreed to grant diplomatic recognition to each of the emerging states resulting from the breakup of Yugoslavia, provided that these new units each agreed to institute democracy and guarantee respect for human rights. A similar position was taken in late 1991 by the EC, the United States, and other democracies vis-à-vis the republics created by the dissolution of the Soviet Union. The king of Saudi Arabia proclaimed a change in his autocratic form of governance in early 1992 by making provision for citizen consultative councils, and he suggested that some measures for human rights be instituted. The US Congress attempted to establish a human rights standard in that nation's trade relations with China (although the president ultimately vetoed the measure). And in early 1992, the minority white population of South Africa voted overwhelmingly to move toward a new constitutional system granting full electoral and other participation to the black majority, thereby moving closer to an end to apartheid. In addition, there was a growth in the number of plebiscites calling for ethnic autonomy in Russian Armenia and a continuing search for independence for Quebec. In short, plebiscites, elections, and human rights standards were all a significant part

From Louis Menand III, "Human Rights as Global Imperative," in Bruce Mazlish and Ralph Buultjens, eds, *Conceptualizing Global History* (Boulder, CO: Westview Press, 1993), pp. 173–7, 181–2, 194–202.

of world politics in the early 1990s. Writing in 1991, political scientist Samuel Huntington noted that "between 1974 and 1990 more than 30 countries in Southern and Central Latin America, East Asia, and Eastern Europe shifted from authoritarian to democratic systems of government."

All of this comes as the human rights emphasis in world politics by the United Nations continued. Since 1948, eight conventions on human rights have been adopted by decisive votes in the General Assembly. And yet, a series of contrary moves in several areas occurred at the same time. In Algeria, a military junta annulled a national election because voters showed overpowering support for Islamic fundamentalists. In Myanmar, a military junta not only annulled a national election but also put under house arrest the newly elected leader, Daw Aung San Suu Kyi, who was subsequently awarded the Nobel Peace Prize for her efforts toward establishing a democratic regime for her country. Meanwhile, the troubled peoples of Africa were still seeking stability between autocracy and democracy in lands populated for centuries by proud tribal groups for whom clan relations are paramount. And much of the Middle East remained governed by autocracies with no regard for human rights – Syria, Saudi Arabia, Kuwait, Iraq, Iran. In short, establishing a human rights standard for the world's population remained a tenuous proposition.

In this period, private international agencies such as Amnesty International continued to document, nation by nation, severe human rights infractions: torture, terrorism, brutal treatment of prisoners, and less violent but equally firm suppression of individual rights. Index on Censorship publicized infractions of speech, press, and assembly rights around the world. Individual rights organizations like Human Rights Watch continued to note human rights abuses in South and Central America, Africa, and elsewhere. And the United States Department of State, under congressional mandate, again published its annual review of human rights issues, by nation, as part of the effort to determine whether the United States should grant aid to specific nations. Terrorism has been stopped in Argentina and Chile but not in Haiti, and only in 1992 did a semblance of domestic peace return to El Salvador. In 1992, Peru abrogated its democratic institutions. Repression and street-fighting erupted in Thailand once again, and universities on the West Bank in Israel/Jordan had been closed for over four years as of 1992.

In the midst of these events, the United Nations Committee on Human Rights and the Center for Human Rights in Geneva are increasingly active in monitoring such rights around the globe and considering cases of individual abuses brought to their attention by citizens in countries that are party to the International Political Rights of the Economic and Social Council Convention of 1966. The UN Human Rights Commission is now in its fifth decade, and it has been repeatedly noted that the issue of human rights has been embraced as an important concept by almost all the nations of the world and that, at least on paper, a standard is acknowledged. Writing in 1983, John Ruggie, Professor of International Relations at Columbia University, said:

> Virtually every state in the world accepts the concept of human rights, and most grant that human rights are an appropriate area of international concern. A substantial number of states have accepted the United Nations Conventions on Economic, Social and Political Rights, all members of

the Council of Europe have ratified the European Convention for the Protection of Human Rights and Fundamental Freedoms, and seventeen states in the Western Hemisphere adhere to the American Convention on Human Rights. In addition, numerous other international human rights instruments are in place. What do all of these developments signify?

It is precisely this question that I will address in the pages that follow. [. . .]

The proximate cause for the development of human rights concerns can be traced to World War II and the conditions that gave rise to it and followed in its wake. The growth of military power in the Axis nations was accomplished domestically by a suppression of parliamentary pluralism in Italy and Germany; by the elimination of freedoms of speech, press, and religion; and, in Germany, by a declaration of war on German and, subsequently, all European Jews.

When the war started, the Western democracies' response to fascism was couched in the language of civil liberties so important to their pluralist societies. The "four freedoms" of Franklin Roosevelt (freedom of speech, freedom of worship, freedom from want, and freedom from fear) became an important standard for the Allied governments in prosecuting the war (including the Soviet Union, itself a totalitarian state). In January 1942, the Allied nations organized themselves as the United Nations and called for "complete victory" and, among other things, the preservation of human rights. This group's concerns included the nature and shape of the world organization formed to help keep the peace and the commitment it would make to guarantee certain human rights as international standards to forestall the recurrence of totalitarian governments in the aggressor nations and elsewhere in the world.

Finally, in 1945, the fifty-five-member group calling itself the United Nations completed a charter for a permanent UN, with each nation pledging, in Articles 55 and 56 of the new charter, to promote human rights. The document provided for an economic and social council, which would include human rights in its purview (Chapter X, Article 62.2). Thus, for the first time in international organizational life, the concept of human rights was advanced. Despite the growth of democracy in Western Europe and the Asian subcontinent, it is remarkable that the concept of an international standard of human rights had not emerged until then. But it was not the Gulag in the Soviet Union, the dictatorships in South America, or the arbitrary rule of French, Dutch, or British imperial commands that caused the emergence of human rights. Rather, it was Fascist totalitarianism and the tragedy of World War II that illuminated the need for standards of individual rights. And oddly enough it was the world imperial powers – France, the Netherlands, and the United Kingdom – that joined the United States, Canada, Australia, and the Scandinavian countries to secure the adoption of the UN charter and launch the subsequent drive for human rights. It is pointless to speculate on whether human rights on an international scale would have emerged had there been no war, but it is true that, unlike the development of the hapless League of Nations, the creation of the United Nations after the war was the single most important factor in setting the world agenda for human rights. [. . .]

No sooner had the United Nations begun its organizational life than the Economic and Social Council created the Commission on Human Rights. Its central task was to devise from political history a statement of human rights that would be applicable globally. And as the world knows, the General Assembly adopted the Declaration on Human Rights in 1948, not as a prospective treaty but as a statement made by the forty-eight nations that voted for it. (No one voted against the declaration, and eight nations abstained.) The declaration has two undivided parts. The first twenty-one clauses concern what are called political and civil rights; the later clauses address so-called social rights. The early clauses begin with a statement that all human beings are free and equal in dignity and rights (Article 1). Articles 2 through 21 enumerate rights regarding speech, press, due process, religious beliefs, migration, marriage, property, assembly, and periodic franchise. It is this set of political/legal rights that I refer to when using the term *human rights* in this chapter. Articles 22 through 29 of the declaration address social and economic rights, such as the right to a job, to social security, to a decent standard of living, and so forth. [. . .]

As I have noted, there has been significant growth of democracy and the rule of law since 1945. The three Axis powers – Germany, Italy, and Japan – were forced to forswear totalitarianism, and each adopted a strong democratic system of government patterned after the Anglo-American, Scandinavian, and Western European models. Now, over forty-five years later, the notions of democratic pluralism, human rights, and the rule of law form the basic fabric of these countries. And it is because of this extraordinary development – over a period of forty years, not six centuries – that democracy and law are now proclaimed in much of the world as the accepted standards for political systems.

A significant development in human rights law can be seen in the European Conventions on Human Rights and Fundamental Freedoms and the European Court of Human Rights created by that convention. The signatories now comprise twenty-one nations, which have agreed to accept the jurisdiction of the court's human rights judgments in their domestic law. The convention, adopted in 1952 and entered into force in 1961, made a significant change in the concept of standing in international law by endowing the individual citizens of a member nation the "right" to have a legal judgment made by the European Court in a dispute with his or her own government. The individual must exhaust national remedies before approaching the court in Strasbourg. But if the court, applying the list of rights contained in the 1952 convention, finds for the individual, then each member nation has agreed to accept that judgment. This is a magnum jump in the evolution of international law, and by 1992, after some 400 or 500 cases, it was clear that the system works. A similar court, sitting in Luxembourg, was established under the twelve-nation European Community. It considers economic, labor, finance, and market issues that concern the EC, headquartered in Brussels.

Without being too chauvinistic, it is possible to say that Western European democracies and the rule of law under which they are now functioning are the outgrowth of the early Anglo-American experience. The task of political science has always been to attempt to understand power and the institutions that try to control the exercise of power. Terms of office, periodic franchise, pluralist politics, and due process under law are among the most important of these. In every society, throughout history, political and religious power have almost always been sought by those who gravitate toward forms of control for whatever reasons. And the individuals in any society are affected by the ways in which those powers are exercised, all too often without having any voice in controlling power themselves. Mystery, magic, and authority formed the basis of community in Sumeria, Egypt, India, China, and Babylonia. Not even in the brief experience of the Greeks in the fourth and third centuries BC and, somewhat later, of the Romans under the law of *jus gentium* has there been "freedom" in the sense in which it is used in the late twentieth century, and certainly no agreed upon mechanism has existed for controlling political and other forms of power. It is the late twentieth-century experience of the English-speaking nations and of Western Europe that motivates the current insistence on democracy and human rights for the emerging nations of Eastern Europe. It also stimulates the continuing activities of the Human Rights Center of the United Nations and the Inter-American Treaty statements about human rights, and it plays a central role in congressional concerns about the foreign policy of the United States. In short, it is only now at the end of the twentieth century, that democracy, human rights, and the rule of law seem to dominate public discourse. [. . .]

A major variable to the full exercise of human rights is a nation's sense of security, most frequently meaning what is called national security but also trade security and, increasingly, resource security. In defense of interest and borders, governments implement policies designed to limit or prohibit migrations of individuals and groups of citizens. For example, while there was free movement across national boundaries in Europe prior to 1914, the introduction of passports on a large scale put a stop to such movement. But that was a small matter when compared to the prohibition of migration of hundreds of thousands of Jews wishing to flee the Soviet Union after World War II. And legislation in the United States – keeper of the flame with its Bill of Rights – prohibited the immigration, even for short visits, of people who had an affiliation with Communist groups; in essence, this was a limitation on political speech for those denied visas and for those in the United States who wanted to talk to such people.

The existence of a so-called national security issue is recognized even in treaties written to expand human rights. The European Convention on Human Rights noted in Article 10, paragraph 2, that the charter's freedoms "may be subject to such formalities, conditions, restrictions, or penalties as are prescribed by law and are necessary in a democratic society, in the interests of *national security*." In the 1966 International Covenant on Civil and Political Rights, adopted by the General Assembly and ratified in 1992 by ninety-two nations, Article 12 stipulated that "the above-mentioned rights shall not be subject to any restrictions except those which are provided by law, and necessary to protect *national security*." (In both quotations, the emphases are mine.)

The national security standard is, of course, nation-specific, whereas human rights are thought to be global-specific. The instances when and where a nation involves national security are many and varied. What these provisions imply is that the undersigned nation subscribes to an international human rights standard – except for reasons sufficient to itself. In the name of national security, it may decline to follow that standard. It should not be a surprise, although it is undoubtedly regrettable, that this should be so in a world of nation-states. For those who search for a more serene global standard, the national security rationale does not ring true.

In addition to these caveats in international treatises, there are ever-present national intelligence agencies whose concerns run from high technology spying to gathering information about people exercising some aspect of supposedly protected freedoms. In sixteenth-century England, for example, Queen Elizabeth's officials had a most remarkable espionage network targeting Catholics in a Protestant society. This was only one of the many "intelligence" functions carried out in secret and reporting to the highest authorities. Looking for heretics from officially sanctioned ideology is very old hat, indeed. One hesitates to mention the Holy Catholic Church inquisitions in Europe in the Middle Ages for fear of sounding trite. More recent organizations include the Okhrana in Czarist Russia, the Mossad and Shin Bet in Israel, the Savak in Iran, the KMT in Taiwan, and the FBI and CIA in the United States. The existence of such intelligence agencies has historically chilled, if not prohibited, free speech and the free exercise of religion, and in modern democratic societies, they have often created a chilling environment in which citizens have been loath to fully exercise their guaranteed rights. In fundamentalist societies, as in China or in much of Islam, the same sorts of institutions exist to guarantee loyalty to the power structure. Thus, the intelligence agency is the instrument most frequently created and turned to in efforts to protect "national security." In a democracy, the control of such agencies in the interest of freedom becomes one of the most important of tasks. In non-democratic nations where there is not a spirit of openness, the opportunity to control the "thought police" is that much more difficult to realize.

The search for "national security" through such instruments creates a system of secrecy in government that is distinctly antithetical to democratic government and to citizens' effort to acquire the knowledge needed for forming a political view. Without information, the citizens' right to free expression becomes devalued. In the United States, James Madison, the father of the US Constitution and the principal author of the Bill of Rights, aptly remarked that:

> a popular government without popular information, or the means of acquiring it, is but a Prologue to a Farce or a Tragedy; or perhaps both. Knowledge will forever govern ignorance. And a people who mean to be their own governors, must arm themselves with the power which knowledge gives.

The triad of national security, secrecy, and intelligence, when invoked by any government, can nullify expressive freedoms. It is this triad that can and does stand in the way of the full exercise of human rights. Indeed, I believe that the first obstacle to a healthy rights tradition is the obsession of those in power for *control*. This obsession is independent of governmental systems. It is defeated, however, when the practice of democratic politics and adherence to law prove too strong for the strongman, for the "democrat" who wants to rule by plebiscite, or for the bully who would destroy democracy and the law for personal satisfaction and for power and control.

At the same time, in many nations a university or university system has evolved that, by the very nature of education, embodies many attributes so essential for democracy – high literacy; a search for truths in the natural and social sciences; an acknowledgment of complexity; a willingness to investigate, to weigh evidence, and to test hypotheses; and a strong sense of history. When these universities have had a semblance of freedom, they have frequently provided the student shock troops to work for and to fight (often literally) for democracy and rights. Beijing University was the source of the democracy movement so brutally crushed in 1989. University students in Thailand have frequently had to take to the streets, as have students in Korea and as students in the United States and many other countries certainly did over the conflict in Vietnam. Why but for fear of what the university might project did Israel close the colleges in the occupied West Bank? The free university is a blessing in any nation, particularly as a countervailing center of power against injustice; the purpose of the university is education and not the accumulation of power or political agency, but the essential attributes of the university are the very reasons its students and faculty act as a conscience for the society.

Three centers – the Western democratic states (mainly those in Western Europe), the English-speaking community, and Japan – have now assumed responsibility for furthering democracy and human rights in the world. They have made clear their determination to stand by their national and community policies and insist on measures of democratic representation and law-based rights for themselves and in their dealings with other nations. Individual national policies vary, however, sometimes insisting on national rights in favor of dealings with other nations and sometimes muting the insistence on human rights in favor of some other objective – as exemplified by the US trade policy toward China and the West's pusillanimous dealings with much of the Arab world for, among other things, oil. Ultimately, individual national policies may come and go, and the natural supply of oil will vanish, but world citizens and their pursuit of rights will continue, just as the individual existed for many millennia before world trade, rigid ideologies, oil, or other modern factors came into being. Nonetheless, it is to the examples and policies of the Western democracies that nascent human rights groups turn for guidance and assistance.

A second source of support is the multitude of nongovernmental rights groups around the world, aided and abetted by the private rights groups in the United States and Western Europe. Human Rights Watch in New York City is one of the most significant, with its regional watch groups. Such groups have many tools at their disposal, including fact-finding, publicity, litigation when the legal system permits, and direct involvement with government policymakers. To the extent that their research and formulations of rights positions are credible, such organizations have access to government and business leaders. They write, they speak, they organize arts and film festivals to benefit rights causes, and they make themselves visible. They cannot sail into a nuclear test zone as Greenpeace can, but their fleet, though not waterborne, is powerful and composed of policies, facts, and peaceful agitation.

A strong network of rights groups has emerged around the globe, attracting academics, lawyers, physicians, business people, and citizens of all kinds. Many of these individuals are active in their domestic parliaments or universities, and they serve as nongovernmental observers to the varied regional and UN activities centered on human rights. The 1993 United Nations Conference on Human Rights will demonstrate the numbers and resources of these groups.

The third and definitely not the least of the centers for human rights advocacy is the United Nations itself. From the outset in 1946, the UN has been considered the world's spokesgroup for human rights, particularly since the General Assembly adopted the Universal Declaration in 1948. The Human Rights Commission has, over the past forty-six years, continued monitoring human rights and, in recent years, has grown ever more active. At the forty-seventh session of the commission in early 1991, 43 member nations attended as did more than 130 nongovernmental "consulting" associations, ranging from Planetary Citizens, International Federation of Newspaper Publishers, Friends of the Earth International, Disabled Peoples International, World Muslim Congress, Amnesty International, and many world religious groups.

The agendas for meetings like that are long and varied, covering the general furtherance of human rights as well as specific topics; "the right to development," the "human rights and dignity of migrant workers," and "rights of the child" were among the twenty-seven issues considered at the 1991 UN sessions. This range of issues and the many groups attending the session further attest to the role the United Nations plays as the world's forum. Among the decisions made at that meeting were recommendations for a study on human rights and the environment and a decision to send the commission's special rapporteur as an observer to the preparatory meetings of the 1992 Brazil United Nations Conference on Environment and Development.

The commission and the individual organizations that serve as consultants to it have long since begun to take a global view by urging that rights and human dignity, as envisaged in the universal declaration, are now very much tied to the world's environment. Their insistence on the need to protect individuals, their communities, and the fragile ecology suggest the obvious – that humanity is part of a natural community and thrives or suffers along with it. In 1948, the year the universal declaration was promulgated, Fairfield Osborn published *Our Plundered Planet*, and read together, these two works depict a central portion of the globe's agenda at the end of the century.

The Third Committee of the General Assembly has assumed responsibility for the United Nations Human Rights Committee, which concerns itself with the record of activities in light of the 1966 International Covenant on Civil and Political Rights. As of 1991, ninety-two nations had ratified the covenant, making it possible for their citizens to request a hearing on instances of alleged human rights abuse before the Human Rights Committee. (Of all the Western democracies, only the United States had failed to ratify the covenant by 1991; finally, in late spring 1992, it did so, some fifteen years after President Jimmy Carter had submitted the covenant to the US Senate.) In its 1991 report, the Human Rights Committee noted,

> Referring to certain positive developments of the previous year and to the fact that the importance of human rights was receiving greater international recognition, the Under-Secretary-General stressed that, nevertheless, the underlying reality of the era continued to be marked by massive and widespread violations of human rights. The challenge to the international community to promote and ensure respect for human rights was in fact greater than ever. The Center for Human Rights was seeking, with in the means at its disposal, to respond to that continuing challenge as energetically as possible. The General Assembly's decision in 1988 to launch World Public Information Campaign on Human Rights had greatly enhanced the practical possibilities in the month and years ahead for collaborating with various United Nations bodies, Member States, and non-governmental organizations in an effort to reach out to

the hundreds of millions of human beings who needed information about fundamental human rights.

At that meeting, recommendations to the Preparatory Committee for the 1993 World Conference on Human Rights were adopted. Among the recommendations for strengthening UN and world concern for human rights was a suggestion that the group create a high commissioner for human rights, an international court of human rights, and a human rights institute. Any or all of these would be significant steps forward, particularly a court if it is fashioned after the European Court of Human Rights, which has, in essence, compulsory jurisdiction in cases brought before it.

Complementing the commission and the Committee on Human Rights is the United Nations Development Program (UNDP). The 1992 Human Development Report, issued in March of 1992, was both a sobering and a hopeful document. The UNDP has developed two indices to bring some measure of comparative analysis to human development. The Human Development Index in 1992 examined "the links between human development and the environment – between human development and global markets." In its first Human Development Report in 1990, the UNDP defined human development as "a process of enlarging people's choices." The report placed the responsibility for enlarging choices squarely on the individual state, describing this as the "real challenge at the national level. Each country, developing or under trial, must set its own goals and design its own strategy."

To complement the Human Development Index, the UNDP has now created the Political Freedom and Human Development Index. The 1992 report noted that "democracy and freedom rely . . . on much more than the ballot box." In urging world consideration of developmental growth and political freedom: "personal security, rule of law, freedom of expression, political participation, and equality of opportunity." (It should come as no surprise that these six points are a 1990s counterpart to Franklin Roosevelt's four freedoms proclaimed just fifty years earlier.) The report insisted that

> the personal freedom index is a reflection of people's lives. The sum-total is human freedom. People know when they are tortured, when they are without a political voice, when they are unable to express views and preferences, when they are discriminated against and when they fear that, if detained, they may be without defense. They know what and how much they have lost.

The report also noted that

> there are no development institutions managing the new integrated global economy – much less doing so democratically in the interests of the world's people. Democracy may be sweeping through individual nation-states, but it has yet to assume a global economic dimension.

The report stated that "visionary blueprints must at least be prepared."

All three of the 1991–2 reports (Human Rights Commission, Committee on Human Rights, and the Human Development Report) strongly reflect a growing consensus that development, environment, the world economy, and the planet's ecology are intertwined and indivisible. They remain divisible as long as individual governments over time fail to recognize the limitations of the earth's carrying capacity, as well as the limits of sovereign power. The Rio Conference of 1992 clearly demonstrated an awareness of the interconnectedness of these issues. It underscored democracy and freedom of political expression and itself demonstrated ways by which citizens around the globe can participate fully in helping address each and all of the interlocked issues.

The globe's peoples, living in a natural environment shared by all, have created a system of livelihood and governance that is still fractured but that is so clearly an indivisible unit. One is now reminded of the title of Barry Commoner's path-breaking ecological study of 1971, *The Closing Circle*. Everything correlates.

There are, in my judgment, four issues that will impede movement toward a broader pluralist democracy and respect for human rights globally: unchecked population growth; ethnic, religious, and nationalist xenophobia; the world's fragile ecology; and the baleful results of unrestrained trade in armaments and the heedless industrialism that makes such trade possible. Each of these issues separately and together can present us with terrible choices about our cultures and life-styles. International competition for resources alone can have a severe adverse impact on food availability and on attempts at population control. And, should there be a significant shift in the ecological balance of the earth and this atmosphere, there may be a further mad scramble by nations to secure and protect scarce resources. There is mounting evidence that this is already happening in concerns about the ozone layer, the depletion of fish stocks and rain forests, and solid waste management. The list of horrible scenarios is endless, but the reality of these scenarios is real: Just see the agenda of the Earth Summit for Brazil in June 1992. [. . .]

The "luxury" of having a human rights standard is to be expected in advanced industrial democracies of the world because of current economic stability, flourishing agriculture, and reasonably stable populations. But in the non-industrialized world, the situation is more often reversed. Poverty in India, hunger in the Saheel, population pressures in China, and war, terrorism, and vast hunger in Somalia all speak of continuing difficulties. The so-called North–South dichotomy is a real one – part economic, part ideological, part ecological. The 1992 Human Development Report noted that "developing countries enter the market as unequal partners and leave with unequal rewards." Furthermore, "In 1960, the richest 20% of the world's population had incomes 30 times greater than the poorest 20%." By 1990, the richest 20% were getting 60 times more. And this comparison is based on the distribution between rich and poor countries, the richest 20% of the world's *people* get at least 150 times more than the poorest 20%. It is crucial to acknowledge these issues while at the same time attempting to move the global system toward a greater human rights standard.

Do human rights have a future globally? The evidence presented here suggests that with sufficient political pressure and an outcry about every known situation – torture, terror, suppression of religious expression, restriction on migration, genocide, and other violations of the several extant human rights protocols – individual nations can be muscled into some agreement. But this will take enormous and continuing political activity and steadfastness on the part of the present world's democracies. The funding of private international rights organizations is a major task, and those concerned nations will have to stand by the NGOs and help expand the existing machinery for human rights concerns. Moreover, each nation will have to fully fund its stipulated contributions to UN activities – supporting the Center for Human Rights, ratifying and implementing treaties, adhering to a human rights standard for a nation's diplomacy and trade policies, and issuing a clear, positive statement of adherence to human rights. In any case, it will be a long leap from a *politics* of human rights to a *law* of human rights. The European convention is, thus far, unique in this process. A similar inter-American effort has never taken hold, and there is no similar effort in Asia or Africa. In the long run, a functioning law of human rights must be governed by a law-based polity. In the short run, over many decades, a vigorous international rights movement must be funded to continue to alleviate human rights abuses and to help more nations move toward recognition of the need for a human rights law. After all, this is what democratic politics is all about.

In his closing address at the Nuremberg trials of the Nazi leaders in 1946, Chief Counsel Robert H. Jackson said, "If you were to say of these men that they are not guilty, it would be as true to say that there has been no war, there are no slain, there has been no crime." Similarly, to say that humankind cannot move toward respect for the freedom and dignity of each person is to say that democracy cannot be realized – that those global citizens not enjoying protection of their inalienable rights face arbitrary autocracy forever, and that, for them, that is the way the world will end – with a whimper.

PART IX

Non-governmental organizations

A S WE SAW IN THE PRECEDING SECTION, human rights have
been promoted not only by states and international organizations but also by
non-governmental organizations. These organizations are part of what are often
called "non-state actors," entities that are not part of the state apparatus, although
few of them are entirely autonomous and/or totally free of state regulation. We have
already looked at one type of non-state actor: multinational enterprises. In this
section, we focus on non-governmental organizations, sometimes called non-profit
organizations. They are groups of individuals that exist outside the government and
exist for not-for-profit activities such as philanthropy, educational exchange, and
foreign assistance.

Akira Iriye's essay notes that the development of globalization has been intimately linked to the growth of international organizations, especially of the
non-governmental variety. Indeed, they grew so numerous and, in some instances,
powerful that some began to voice concern that they could become unmanageable.
They were not, after all, elective bodies accountable for their action to an electorate. How would non-governmental organizations share ideas and influence with
states, and with multinational enterprises? The answer to such a question would in
large part determine the shape of the world to come.

S. Frederick Starr (Chairman of the Central Asia/Caucasus Institute at the
School of Advanced International Studies of the Johns Hopkins University) examines that question in the context of the evolution of the Soviet Union and other East
European countries. The steady growth of civil society in these countries during the
Cold War, even under communist dictatorships, hinged upon the creation and growth
of non-governmental organizations. In the post-Cold War era, democratization of
the formerly communist states was inseparable from the activities of these organizations, both domestic and transnational. Civil society development and the
state–society relationship throughout the world have been, and will continue to be,
important themes of global history.

Chapter 17

Akira Iriye

THE ROLE OF INTERNATIONAL ORGANIZATIONS

AT THE END OF THE TWENTIETH CENTURY and the beginning of the twenty-first, few phenomena attracted more attention, and at the same time aroused more controversy, than globalization. The twentieth century, Ralf Dahrendorf wrote in 1998, "has been largely . . . determined by divisions which led to wars, hot and cold, but which also provided sources of identity." All that had changed. Globalization had come to "dominate people's lives, hopes, and fears," and people everywhere had "to think globally to respond to an increasingly global reality."

In the rapid advancement in information technology, the development of a global financial market, or the spread of the English language and other manifestations of American popular culture, human affairs were unmistakably globalizing or becoming globalized. At the same time, debate ensued as to the direction and desirability of the phenomenon. Was the world going to continue the process of globalization, or would the pace eventually slow down or even be replaced by other developments? Would the people and countries of the world be better or worse off when they were more globalized? What tasks should individual states and such traditional institutions as families, local governments, churches, and schools perform in the age of globalization? Such questioning suggested the fascination with the possible role of globalization in defining future history. Just as earlier generations speculated on the implications of industrialization for nations and individuals, now there was much interest in the impact globalization would have upon the shape of the world to come.

[. . .] [A]n increasing number of scholarly books and articles with titles that included the word "global" or "globalization" began to appear in the 1990s, especially during the second half of the decade, suggesting that the term that mass media were widely using was also gaining intellectual respectability. By then, globalization had generally come to mean not just technological innovations and economic forces linking different parts of the world, but something even more extensive; as James H. Mittelman wrote in 1997, "globalization is a coalescence of varied

From Akira Iriye, *Global Community: The Role of International Organizations in the Making of the Contemporary World* (University of California Press, 2002), pp. 195–209.

transnational processes and domestic structures, allowing the economy, politics, culture, and ideology of one country to penetrate another." Political scientists, sociologists, anthropologists, and economists debated whether such a seemingly inexorable process should be left to develop with its own momentum, or if it could somehow be controlled or steered in a desirable direction. In the latter case, should the state be the key to the future direction of globalization, or would some other agency emerge to take its place? If globalization became too "predatory," to use Richard Falk's word, what institutions could tame such a tendency? Such debate would undoubtedly continue and be joined by intellectuals in all parts of the world; this itself would be an aspect of globalization. As yet few historians were involved in the debate, perhaps because they had not yet come to reconceptualize history in the framework of globalization.

[. . .] [The historical significance of globalization may be well understood if we note] the growth of international organizations. This phenomenon has not been systematically examined in the literature on globalization, but there seems little doubt that international organizations have served to turn the world's attention to global issues – humanitarian relief, development, human rights, the environment, cross-national understanding – when geopolitics and military strategy have divided nations against one another. Awareness of transnational problems – in other words, global consciousness – is not the same thing as globalization. One could develop a sense of transnational interconnectedness and at the same time question aspects of globalization, such as environmental hazards resulting from foreign investment in developing countries or the use of child and female labor in degrading circumstances by manufacturers interested in competitive advantages. The 1999 meeting in Seattle of the World Trade Organization, an intergovernmental organization, drew world attention because many non-governmental organizations staged demonstrations to protest against what they took to be the trade organization's connivance at the destruction of the natural environment and the employment of "slave labor" as it sought further to deregulate international trade. A Washington meeting in the spring of 2000 of the International Monetary Fund drew a similar protest from various private associations and groups. These incidents gave the impression that non-governmental organizations were opposed to globalization, whereas intergovernmental organizations were pushing for it, but that was missing the point. Both were becoming active participants in the worldwide debate on the nature and the possible future direction of globalization and were thus very much part of the emerging global community. Besides, the protesting organizations were all making use of the Internet, a crucial means for spreading information and coalescing individuals and groups for specific objectives.

Most supporters and opponents of globalization alike assumed that there had to be some universal, global standards, in financial, accounting, environmental, human rights, and other matters. Standardization in some of these areas would be extremely difficult to achieve, but the idea itself would be very much part of the phenomenon of globalization. The debate in Seattle or Washington was not so much about globalization as about the specific fields (labor, environmental protection) in which global standards should be applied. To deny the very idea of universal standards was, of course, possible, but the majority of the protesters in Seattle or Washington were not doing so; they accepted the notion of transnational interconnectedness. They were keenly aware of the global issues, and their activities revealed not so much forces opposed to globalization as those that recognized the transnational nature of contemporary issues. Even those opposed to globalization in the business sphere considered themselves members of a global community, committed to supporting "poor people in representing their own interests in global decision making," as a statement by the American Friends Service Committee pointed out. In this sense, the organizations that staged demonstrations in Seattle and Washington were no different from the large number of international organizations that had, over the decades, constructed transnational networks.

And those organizations were more active than ever before. Underneath the headline-grabbing incidents in these cities, various types of non-governmental organizations were quietly carrying on their tasks, suggesting that their growth had not been affected, nor had their activities been discouraged, by occasional incidents and disturbances. It was symbolic that the Seattle demonstrations coincided with the awarding of the Nobel Peace Prize to Doctors Without Borders for its humanitarian activities. Accepting the prize, the organization's director, James Orbinski, stated, "We don't know for sure whether words save lives, but we know for sure that silence kills." Two years later, in December 2001, representatives of Doctors Without Borders joined those of the International Committee of the Red Cross, Amnesty International, the Office of the United Nations High Commissioner for Refugees, the American Friends Service Committee, the International Campaign to Ban Landmines, International Physicians for the prevention of Nuclear War, and other organizations in a ceremony held in Oslo to commemorate the hundredth anniversary of the Nobel Prizes. These organizations were all recipients of the Nobel Peace Prize, and by participating in the ceremony [. . .], they were demonstrating that international organizations had played just as significant roles as states and statesmen in promoting peace throughout the twentieth century.

In August 2001, Moral Rearmament, a non-governmental organization established in 1938 by Protestant clergymen in the United States, changed its name to Initiatives of Change. The idea, according to its new director, Cornelio Sommaruga, who had served as president of the International Committee of the Red Cross for eighteen years, was to work for "globalization of responsibility." Ethical and spiritual values, which Moral Rearmament had emphasized over the years, would form the basis of the organization's new initiatives. The transformation of an organization that at the height of the Cold War had been closely identified with the free world into a broader global movement – only one-fourth of its twenty thousand members was now Protestant – was symbolic of the changing international circumstances at the beginning of the new century. Likewise, in December 1999, as President Kim Dae Jung of South Korea, whose personal and political life had been deeply involved in the vicissitudes of the Cold War, welcomed a gathering of representatives of non-governmental organizations from over one hundred countries who assembled in Seoul, he told them that in the coming century democratic government, the market, and civil society would constitute the three pillars of national and international development. In all these three, non-governmental organizations play crucial roles. At this meeting, some members of Chinese, Korean, and Japanese organizations conferred among themselves and decided to launch a regional forum of non-governmental organizations to which delegates from North Korea and Taiwan would also be invited. Korean and Japanese non-governmental organizations, in the meantime, were collaborating in such diverse fields as humanitarian relief of North Korea, environmental protection, access to information, joint inquiry into the past, and assistance to Korean victims of atomic bombings.

These were typical examples. Throughout the world, non-governmental organizations were continuing to expand in the number and scope of their activities. On one hand, many small, local organizations were being built. Their agendas were often parochial, such as planning for a park, proposing regulations to restrict automobile traffic, or building a community center. Others were national in scope, such as the Community Technology Center Network, established in the United States to teach how to use Internet-accessed information to those too poor to afford computers. Regardless of scope, however, most such organizations were invariably establishing ties with one another, not just within a country but across nations. When, for instance, in 1995 a faculty member at Peking University opened a small office, renting an inexpensive room at a local inn, to serve the needs of women suffering from domestic violence, job discrimination, and other problems, it quickly established itself as one of the first non-governmental organizations in China concerned with women's issues. When President Bill Clinton made an official visit to China in June 1998, his wife included the organization in her itinerary. Non-governmental organizations from South Korea, Thailand, and India contacted the Beijing office so as to form an Asian network. Women's groups in Europe and North America also came in touch with it through its Internet home pages. That this and many other private associations were created in China in the wake of the 1995 Beijing conference on women suggests the cumulative effect of such events. Whereas few Chinese had ever heard of non-governmental organizations, by the end of the 1990s over two hundred thousand of them were said to have come into being.

Examples can be multiplied. Non-governmental organizations had grown to such an extent that Lester Salamon, one of the leading scholars of the subject, was calling it a "revolution," comparable in its impact on world affairs to the emergence of the nation-state in the nineteenth century. His research group conducted a survey of nonprofit organizations in twenty-two countries (thirteen from Europe, five from Latin America, and Japan, Australia, Israel, and the United States) in the late 1990s and found that altogether they employed nineteen million individuals, or 4.9 percent of their combined workforce. In some countries the ratio was much higher: In the Netherlands, 12.4 percent of workers were employed by nonprofit organizations, and in the United States 7.8 percent. All these organizations, according to Salamon, produced goods and services amounting to $1.1 trillion, a figure that exceeded the gross domestic products of most countries, including Russia, Brazil, or Spain. Although his "nonprofit organizations" may not be wholly interchangeable with the non-governmental organizations [. . .], it is clear that no matter what they are called and whatever their definition, something unprecedented was taking place. Moreover, while Salamon's study included national as well as international nonprofit organizations, the distinction between the two was often blurred, as some of the previous examples suggest. Here was a phenomenon that demanded attention, a development that had to be incorporated into any discussion of national and international affairs at the turn of the new century.

A century earlier, some astute observers were noting a new trend in the world that, they were convinced, would profoundly alter human life. Some called it "internationalism," others "international life." Many had no precise word to describe what they saw. J.A. Hobson referred to the "great world forces" that were creating "bonds of interests which band us together irrespective of the natural limits of the country to which we belong and in which we were born." H.G. Wells predicted the emergence of "a new kind of people" as a result of these forces who would come to constitute a "floating population . . ., developing, no doubt, customs and habits of its own, a morality of its own, a philosophy of its own." These observers were certain that the new phenomenon, which would in time be called "globalization," would fundamentally alter the nature of both national and international affairs.

From the perspective of 2001, it is, of course, possible to argue that these prophets a hundred years ago were to be proven wrong, that the forces of globalization, or whatever the term they preferred to use, did not really transform how nations behaved, either domestically or toward one another. After all, imperialism, or control by one state over another, was a powerful force at that time and would remain so for several more decades. Part of the phenomenon of globalization was undoubtedly attributable to imperialism, involving the breaking down of national and ethnic boundaries and the penetration of "uncivilized" parts of the world by forces of "civilization." To say that globalization was imperialism by another name, however, would be to ignore that forces of globalization continued to strengthen themselves, while empires came and went – and they were conspicuous by their rarity at the end of the twentieth century. Anti-imperialism as much as imperialism proved to be a key theme of the century, and the former, if anything, was a more global phenomenon than the latter. To be sure, many of the postcolonial states were to be just as concerned with their self-interests as had the colonial powers, and the state, new or old, still remained the key unit of human association in most parts of the world.

Conceptually, therefore, one could write a history of twentieth-century international affairs as a story of interstate interactions without introducing extraneous themes like globalization. [. . .] However, [. . .] to do so would be a gross oversimplification [for,] underneath the geopolitical realities defined by sovereign states, the century witnessed a steady growth of another reality, the global (and globalizing) activities by international organizations. Hobson, Wells, and others may have too hastily concluded that the geopolitical realities would soon be transformed by newer forces of globalization. These realities continued to shape international relations at one level, but these thinkers were justified in believing that cross-national movements of men, their ideas, and their organizations would sooner or later come to revolutionize the way in which people and nations dealt with one another. They would feel vindicated if they came back to life today and saw the activities by thousands of transnational organizations.

Will the alleged "revolution" in today's world, evidenced in the growth of international organizations, be shown to have been an exaggeration, if not a misperception, a century hence? Will those organizations, no matter how numerous and how extensive, remain largely confined to their own spheres of activity and have little impact on the nature of national and international affairs? Or will they come to alter fundamentally how states deal with their own people and with other states? Instead of these two extreme possibilities, will a situation develop in which states and nonstate actors come to cooperate more closely than in the past and in that process define yet another world order?

Any response to those questions must remain tentative and speculative. But even before speculation is attempted, it is important to pay attention to many issues that have arisen because of the very growth of international organizations, especially of the non-governmental variety. For one thing, such a variety of organizations has emerged that different, often clashing, orientations and agendas among them have become virtually inevitable. Even in the earlier years, divergent objectives were sometimes pursued by organizations allegedly sharing a common goal, such as the conservation of nature or the promotion of women's rights. Among intergovernmental organizations, the United Nations' Economic and Social Council has often been at odds with its other agencies such as the Human Rights Commission or the International Labor Organization. With a rapid increase in international organizations, it is not unimaginable that anarchy instead of order might come to characterize their relationships with one another, just as it has characterized interstate relations. An example of this took place in April 1999 when the Armed Forces Communications and Electronics Association, a non-governmental organization founded in the United States in 1946 to sponsor exhibitions and conferences all over the world on military communications, electronics, and intelligence systems, ran into opposition to its plans for holding a European fair in Brno, the Czech Republic. A founder of Doctors Without Borders in Belgium vehemently sought to stop the event on antimilitaristic grounds. Even among humanitarian agencies, there is not always agreement as to how they should aid victims of earthquakes or volcanic eruptions, and sometimes they could work at cross-purposes. For instance, the non-governmental organizations that sent rescue missions to Colombia when it was devastated by an earthquake in January 1999 followed their respective agendas and failed to coordinate their activities, with the result that there was no systematic distribution of food and medical goods sent from overseas.

To cope with such problems, many individuals and groups have agreed that it would be necessary to establish a minimum of guidelines or common standards to govern the conduct of non-governmental organizations. Already in 1994, the International Red Cross, Oxfam, and other agencies came together to draft basic principles to guide humanitarian activities, and the document was accepted by over 150 non-governmental organizations from forty-three countries. Then in late 1998, the United Nations as well as other intergovernmental organizations and non-governmental groups adopted a list of "minimum standards" for such matters as nourishment, water quality, and toilet facilities in areas where relief work was to be carried out. These guidelines amount to international protocols, akin to treaties and agreements among states, and provide some order amid the seeming disorder created by the establishment of so many international organizations.

Would it be possible to draft similar standards for international organizations engaged in other than humanitarian work? In the area of environmental protection, international standards have already been promulgated in such matters as the preservation of the whale, the prohibition of trade in ivory, and restrictions on the emission of carbon dioxide. The relative success at arriving at international environmental standards owes itself to a great extent to cooperation among intergovernmental organizations, non-governmental organizations, and national governments. On the other hand, establishing global standards in human rights would be more difficult. Although such standards exist on paper, thanks to the work of the United Nations Human Rights Commission and many non-governmental organizations, activities by these organizations have frequently been uncoordinated. When human rights concern political affairs, domestic and international organizations have been able to work together quite well in such matters as the observation of a local election, but applying uniform standards to the treatment accorded women or political inmates has been more difficult. Nevertheless, the growth of civil society throughout the world may make it possible to apply certain standards of democratization and human rights to all countries. The establishment in 2000 of the International Court of Criminal Justice is a good case in point. It is seen as a custodian of human rights everywhere in the world, a reflection of shared consciences that transcend national boundaries.

Some such institutional framework for coping with transnational issues has become more urgent than ever because of the increasing number of migrant workers, expatriates, and others who are not confined to a given territorial state, as well as the growth of transnational issues that need the attention of the electorate of more than one country. As David Held has observed, because "[national] boundaries have traditionally demarcated the basis on which individuals were included and excluded from participation in decisions affecting their lives," the questions of representation, legitimacy, and democratic governance might have to be recast in a globalizing world. In this connection, the fact that some government officials and thinkers in Europe have developed an idea of "European citizenship" is interesting and may possibly be a harbinger of things to come. A conception of citizenship that transcends national units is congruent with such other notions as "hybridization" and "syncretism" that have begun to appear in the literature. They all challenge traditional definitions of space, territory, and nationality and raise the question of just what it is that binds people together, what it is that constructs a human community. Although no consensus yet exists as to who would be included in, and who excluded from, European citizenship, the vision seems to indicate the awareness that transnational society is here to stay, even if it is still vaguely understood.

With regard to the work of international organizational activities in the field of developmental assistance, some serious problems have also arisen. Here, the issue of interorganizational coordination has been bound up with the very important question of accountability. [. . .] International relief organizations faced [difficulties] in administering their aid because of complex local political problems and divergent perspectives between such organizations and the United Nations as well as some of the nations providing peacekeeping forces. Economic assistance programs were even more complicated because they were designed as long-term projects. The more numerous such programs became, the more varied grew their approaches, and, above all, the question of how to keep track of their activities inevitably arose. Were they using their funds wisely? To whom were they reporting? Who was keeping records? Were those records available for inspection by governmental officials and private groups?

These problems have always existed, but in the recent years they have come to command much public and scholarly attention because of the very fact that aid projects have literally come to cover the entire globe. (The number of developmental non-governmental organizations registered with the Organization of Economic Cooperation and Development had neared three thousand by the early 1990s, and their total spending approximated $6 billion.) In a widely read article published in *The Economist* in January 2000, the writer chided some non-governmental aid workers for bringing in "western living standards, personnel and purchasing power which can transform local markets and generate great local resentment." The discrepancy between "expatriate staff" and "impoverished local officials trying to do the same work" was a source of "deep antipathy." Already in 1988, a scholar was warning that "the corruption of NGOs will be the political game in the years ahead." Scholarly specialists have been raising serious questions about the conduct of aid workers and the organizations they represented. As just one example, in a book entitled *Non-Governmental Organisations – Performance and Accountability* (1995), one of the first serious attempts at examining the issue of accountability, the editors noted, "Performing effectively and accounting transparently are essential components of responsible practice, on which the legitimacy of development intervention ultimately depends." And yet most of the case studies contained in this volume pointed out that there had been no standardized system for measuring accountability of non-governmental organizations. In some instances pertinent data were missing, while in others data were there, but the organizations were reluctant to divulge them for fear of political or ideological intermeddling with their affairs. Because donor agencies, whether governmental or non-governmental, would want the receiving organizations to account for the funds they received, financial accountability was often a condition of such grants. But the staff involved in developmental programs found bookkeeping time-consuming and thought their time could better be spent in more constructive ways. For all organizations, a writer noted, "*who* defines accountability, *for whom* and *why*, are questions" that required careful analysis.

The question of accountability has grown in seriousness in the recent years because of the tendency on the part of a large number of development-oriented organizations to receive funding from public agencies. Michael Edwards and David Hulme note that already in the mid-1990s, non-governmental organizations "which are *not* dependent on official aid for the majority of their budgets are now the exception rather than the rule." In such a situation, it is not surprising that governments would insist on budgetary oversight of aid programs. But that in turn raises the question of the proper relationship between governmental and non-governmental organizations. The latter, according to *The Economist*, had become "the most important constituency for the activities of development aid agencies." The symbiotic relationship between the state and nonstate actors inevitably leads to the question of the latter's autonomy. Are they becoming an arm of the state, doing for the latter more informally and cheaply what it wants to be accomplished? With so much funding coming from public sources, accompanied with the need for more strict accountability for how the money is used, would non-governmental organizations be able to remain "non-government"? Could their staff, who are not accountable to the electorate, be counted on to serve the public interest? Conversely, to the extent that private organizations work in collaboration with government bureaucracies, how would the latter be required to share policy deliberations with them or give them access to official information, however confidential? Should non-governmental organizations be allowed to have an input into official decision making?

Similar questions may be raised regarding the relationship between non-governmental organizations and business enterprises. Both are nonstate actors, but they have traditionally been distinguished because only the latter are profit-seeking. The relationship between the two has more often than not been adversarial. According to a survey of 140 international non-governmental organizations, 41 percent of them expressed such an attitude toward multinational corporations, and 47 percent said they had had little to do with them. Some, such as Greenpeace, have organized a worldwide boycott of certain firms suspected of causing damage to the natural environment, while others, such as Transparency International – established in 1992 to respond to the worldwide "corruption eruption" – have periodically published reports on cases of bribery involved in local negotiations for establishing plants. The Seattle demonstrations in December 1999 against multinational businesses were but the tip of the iceberg; global networks connected by the Internet spread information on corporate practices that appear to violate the principles for which the non-governmental organizations stand.

The situation, however, may be changing, just like the relationship between state and nonstate actors. The line between business enterprises and non-governmental organizations is becoming blurred as some business organizations sponsor humanitarian work abroad while individuals with extensive experiences with relief, aid, or environmental activities are hired by manufacturing or marketing firms. Moreover, some multinational corporations have begun soliciting the views of non-governmental organizations on the impact of their business activities on local environmental and labor conditions. These instances suggest that some sort of collaborative relationship may develop between profit-seeking and nonprofit organizations. In the past, regulation of businesses was largely in the hands of the state, whether national or local. This may be changing as non-governmental organizations are steadily gaining in visibility and self-confidence. In particular, international non-governmental organizations, as well as intergovernmental organizations, may develop a new definition of their relationship with multinational corporations. If that happens, it will mean that even the notions of profit and nonprofit may change. For that matter, the distinction between state and nonstate actors, state and society, public and private, may also undergo reformulation. A realization may emerge that all organizations – the state, business enterprises, international organizations, and non-governmental associations – will form what Kofi Annan, secretary general of the United Nations, has called a "strategic partnership" in the service of all people as the world becomes ever more globalized.

That is a grand vision, far grander than the image of global community that has been proposed by any international organization. Whereas most ideas of international society, global community, and "planet earth" have supposed an interdependence of nations and peoples, none has yet developed a view of the world's organizations that interact with one another and promote the common welfare of humankind. That would be too much to expect at this stage of global history. The global community that international organizations have been seeking for decades will be a good beginning. That community has tended to develop with its own momentum, on a separate level of existence from the international system defined by sovereign states or from the business world. If these separate communities were to come closer together, then there would truly emerge a human community that would consist of various complementing organizations sharing the same concerns and seeking to solve them through cooperative endeavors. Whether such a situation will ever arrive is far from clear, but to the extent that it is now possible even to speculate on such a possibility, credit should be given to international organizations, especially non-governmental organizations, for having led the way.

Chapter 18

S. Frederick Starr

THE THIRD SECTOR IN THE SECOND WORLD

Sovereignty and the first and second sectors

THE REVOLUTIONS OF 1989 brought stunning changes to Central and Eastern Europe. Communist parties collapsed or reconstituted themselves into socialist parties. Elective parliamentary bodies gained independence from communist tutelage and asserted new powers of control over governments. Free elections brought to the fore new parties and political groupings within those parliamentary bodies. Various historic states absorbed into the Soviet Union asserted their autonomy, if not full independence, and a newly legalized private sector began to create the independent financial base that could support those policies advocating pluralism in all areas.

The pace of these changes varied radically, with Poland maintaining its early lead, Czechoslovakia and Hungary moving forward swiftly, and Rumania, Bulgaria, and the Soviet Union lagging behind. Whatever the tempos of change, all the countries moved toward a common goal: the establishment of limited government where totalitarian rule had prevailed, and the creation of private, or at least independent, market-driven firms where governmental industrial ministries had formerly held sway. Thus, the revolutions of 1989 led affected countries in the direction of creating limited "first sectors" and expanded "second sectors" out of the ruins of the unrestrained party-state.

The process as a whole greatly enhanced the sovereignty of the new governments, both because it led to a genuinely democratic basis for legitimacy and because it transformed governments into institutions protecting the rights of citizens rather than restricting them. The new governments deliberately reached into the past to establish continuity with their precommunist heritage. By doing so, they underscored that communism had been imposed from outside, while the new order emerged from the popular will and national history.

From S. Frederick Starr, "The Third Sector in the Second World," *World Development*, January 1991, pp. 65–71.

Even as they enhanced their nations' sovereignty in some areas, the new governments limited it in others. Leaders who emerged from the revolutions of 1989 quickly distanced themselves from the Soviet Union, but just as quickly began campaigning to affiliate their countries with the European Economic Community, the Scandinavian Free Trade Zone, and the major international monetary organizations. Calls for confederation in the Danube basin and in the Baltic region were raised within the new governments, while the Baltic republics of the Soviet Union actually established formal ties with one another even while still part of the Soviet Union as a whole. Leaders of the private industrial second sectors also showed themselves ready to limit their absolute independence by seeking international investments and co-ownership by multinational firms. Newly legalized political parties also demonstrated that they did not equate independence with political autarky by working hard to affiliate themselves with like-minded international political movements. The rapid replacement of the East German "New Forum" and other recently formed indigenous movements with Christian Democratic and Social Democratic parties fully integrated with West German counterparts was but the most conspicuous example of this phenomenon. As far away as Latvia and Estonia, Christian and Social Democratic groups strained to forge links with West European parties and their international organizations. Green parties, too, were founded in every country, some working within mainstream parties as factions and others functioning fully independently.

These constraints on absolute sovereignty were real, but placed few practical limits on action by governments or corporations in the emancipated lands. Far more important in terms of practical constraints was the growing specialization practiced by each sector. Governments drastically reduced their sphere of action, withdrawing from many of their old commitments in the areas of culture and the management of information, and taking various steps to reduce their engagement in social welfare. Industry, freed from ministerial tutelage, focused on meeting normal standards of profitability in market economies. As they did so, leaders of the second sector, too, sought to withdraw from other areas they deemed peripheral, including public welfare and cultural matters.

Who, then, will see to the needs not addressed by the first and second sectors, e.g. by neither governments nor markets? Who will address the most local social concerns, as well as the most global ones? What institutions will be sufficiently adaptable to deal with new groups and interests as they arise, and will command the financial resources necessary to be effective?

To varying degrees, pluralistic systems elsewhere in the advanced industrial world meet these needs through a third sector consisting of non-governmental organizations (NGOs) of various types, including both church-related and secular voluntary associations, and foundations. Such entities gain importance as both the ideal of state-centered organization and the financial possibility of its realization wane. These third sector organizations are neither governmental nor private; they are not driven by voters or by the market, nor are they dominated by families or clans as are many NGOs in developing countries. They provide a relatively efficient means of focusing resources on issues of importance at local, national, and international levels. They constitute useful outlets for civic energies that might otherwise go unchanneled and lead only to alienation. Finally, by addressing the myriad civic needs which cannot or should not be addressed by government or business, they enable both the first and second sectors to function more efficiently.

What are the prospects for the emergence of such a third sector in the newly emancipated states of Central Europe, Eastern Europe, and the Soviet Union? If they are good, the new governments and market-oriented economies stand to benefit immensely. If these prospects are poor, the new regimes will face a tide of unmet social, cultural, and even spiritual needs, and the possibility of alienation among the citizenry upon whose good will their legitimacy and success depends. The question is of critical importance.

The totalitarian background

Whether a vital and independent third sector will emerge in the former Second World depends on many factors, among them being legal provisions established by the new governments, the ability of such organizations to capture whatever favorable local traditions survived the last four decades, and the state of the economies. In every country, however, the outcome will also be significantly affected by the Marxist-Leninist system that prevailed for two generations. This system, which established the complete control of the Communist Party over economic and organizational life, politics, and even values, has rightly been called "totalitarian" by Vaclav Havel and others. Under it, the monopolistic party swallowed all three sectors of social organization under discussion here.

The systems imposed on Central Europe by the Soviet Union after 1945 all had two essential features in common: the immense strengthening of vertical organizational structures and communication links, and the destruction of all horizontal structures and links that could not be subjected to control by the vertical elements. Lower-level and local entities of all sorts became merely smaller replicas of central institutions. Information flowed mainly from the top down, as did commands. Private and voluntary entities, being independent of (and hence potentially subversive to) this structure, were abolished, as were independent organizations that might have mediated between the party-state and individual citizens. During the perestroika or reconstruction of 1945–53, all societies in the region were reorganized to fit this Soviet model. "Bourgeois" or "civil" societies disappeared together throughout Central Europe, as they had in Russia after 1917.

Tens of thousands of independent associations and foundations dealing with religion, welfare, education, labor, trade, and cultural matters were closed, their functions either abolished, transferred to ministerial control, or placed in the hands of government-controlled "societal" organizations which were nominally independent but in reality financed and wholly controlled by the party-state.

How should this historical legacy be interpreted? Is it more important that all the countries of Central and Eastern Europe were reorganized to fit this template, or that all of them, prior to the Soviet takeover, had been evolving toward civil societies complete with independent sectors? Obviously, both facts are important. However, we have been far too quick to ignore or under-value whatever impulses toward self-organization, voluntarism, and civic initiative persisted in these societies prior to communism. Instead, we have dwelt only on the brute fact that statism and totalitarianism triumphed. Many would go so far as to assert that democratic and civil institutions had utterly failed and collapsed and that communism therefore filled a vacuum. Curiously, however, some of the same observers who duly note that communism was not imposed easily or immediately fail to ask why the task proved so difficult. It has not occurred to many that the very bloodiness of all wars which the communist regimes waged against civil society in the various countries attested to the extent to which civil society had in fact taken root in those lands.

The effort by communist regimes to stamp out civil society and third sector activity took place within the memory of tens of millions of people still living in Central and Eastern Europe. Even in Russia, where this struggle was waged between 1917 and 1932, the memory of functioning NGOs is passed down by living grandparents to people in their twenties and thirties. Of course, third sector organizations today cannot draw on the citizenry's direct experience in this area. But it is wrong to claim either that all such inclinations were stamped out or that the memory of them has utterly faded.

The revolutions of 1989: controlled reform, collapse, or mass movements?

Even before the revolutionary year of 1989 ended there were various explanations of what had happened in circulation. In gauging the future prospects of a third sector in Central and Eastern Europe, three of these explanations are particularly important, since each of them points toward a different path ahead.

The first view placed Mikhail Gorbachev squarely at the center of events, and is therefore Russocentric. It holds that change was brought about from above, and that Gorbachev's initiatives were the *sine qua non* of transformation everywhere. It accepts Gorbachev's own view that stagnation prevailed everywhere until his own accession to power. Thanks to his unique political skills, Gorbachev has been able to call forth forces supportive of his program and then channel them like rivers into the mill races he had prepared for them. His example in the Soviet Union, it is argued, emboldened Central Europeans to follow suit.

Whatever validity this conception holds for the Soviet Union, it is only tangentially relevant to other countries in the region. No Gorbachevs arose through the system elsewhere, and the revolutions in fact brought to the fore an unlikely assemblage of leaders, among them a playwright, a former violinist, and a conservatory pianist. Even for the Soviet Union, this conception must be qualified, for it presents the oversimplified picture of change coming to a passive society through the agency of an activist state. Gorbachev's notably slow start as a reformer lends credence to the opposite view, namely, that it was the threat of an activated society that sparked change in the inert government.

The second line of argument stresses the universal collapse of Marxism-Leninism and the regimes founded in its name. Beginning with the economies and spreading then to the other institutions of society, decay gradually set in after the early 1970s. That Poland led the way was due to the fact that the early demise of the economy there affected social life early and deeply. Gorbachev's progressive radicalization correlates with the collapse of the Soviet economy. Even relatively prosperous Hungarians were radicalized by the experience of deepening decay as their government struggled under soaring debt.

If the first explanation grossly overstates the causal role of one man, this version understates the role of thousands to a like degree. It greatly understates the initiative of the Solidarity movement in Poland, the many organizations working through the Evangelical Church in the German Democratic Republic, the role of Charter 77 and Catholic organizations in Czechoslovakia, and the part played by the host of ecological and cultural activist organizations in Hungary and elsewhere. In short, it denies to self-organized forces in these societies the role that they actually played in mobilizing the populations.

According to the third argument – the one upon which this paper is based – it is increasingly clear that the old regimes collapsed both economically and politically, and that the roots of this collapse must be sought in the 1970s and earlier. It is evident, also, that the deft leadership of a Gorbachev or a Jaruzelski was able partially to control the tempo of events so as to moderate the shock and reduce dislocation. But whatever prodded them to action, it was above all the mobilized and organized citizenry throughout the region which brought down the communist regimes, whether by sudden coup as in Czechoslovakia and East Germany, violent outbursts as in Rumania, by the ballot box as in Hungary and (as appears imminent at this writing) the Soviet Union and some provinces of Yugoslavia, or by combination of attrition and the ballot box as in Poland and Bulgaria.

Until each revolution is more closely analyzed, this hypothesis cannot be proven beyond doubt. The general notion of collapsing party-states being taken over by self-organized and active citizenries has the advantage of giving due weight to the extraordinary proliferation of non-governmental organizations everywhere in recent years, their widespread politicization immediately before the 1989 upheavals, their immediate recognition by the new regimes, and their consolidation under favorable laws instituted by the new rulers.

Connections: the new organizational networks

All revolutions carried out under the inspiration of France in 1789 cast the individual citizen as both end and means. The revolutions of 1989 also reaffirmed the sanctity of the individual under law. However, these revolutions were also directed against the extreme atomization of individuals imposed by the Marxist-Leninist order. Thus, the legal recognition and acceptance of voluntary associations in all spheres figured prominently among the objectives of the post-totalitarian revolutionaries. This is not surprising, since so many of the leaders of the new governments had formed their political ideas and gained practical experience while working in the proliferating NGOs.

Given their importance, it is surprising how late the proliferating NGOs of Central Europe came to international attention. To be sure, the establishment of Charter 77 in Czechoslovakia and of the Solidarity movement in Poland in 1980 were noted with interest. But since the spreading network of small-scale NGOs that supported these nationwide and politicized efforts was largely ignored until the mid-1980s, the social and intellectual base of public mobilization was underestimated.

Poland provides a good example of the urge for self-mobilization. Even in the 1970s, an informal Flying University provided lectures and seminars in faculty members' apartments. In 1982 this was supplemented with a self-organized Independent Education Team, which served as a kind of anonymous lecture bureau for prestigious speakers unacceptable to the state. An independent National

Education Council was also founded that year. By 1983 the Flying University was sponsoring research, particularly in the social sciences. In that year an independent Social Committee on Learning was established to provide modest survival grants to unemployed doctoral candidates.

Other fields of endeavor followed a similar pattern. When independent news sheets like *Robotnik* were suppressed in the early 1980s, "spoken newspapers" provided information to small gatherings of interested listeners. By 1982, former members of the official Association of Polish Journalists banded together to create an independent professional organization in that field, even as the old, coopted one continued. The government banned a new Association of Polish Plastic Artists in 1983 but it continued to function, even as a new government-sponsored artists' union came into being.

No profession was immune to the urge toward self-organization. A Social Commission on Health arose as an alternative to the government's inefficient health ministry. Lawyers and technocrats in various fields banded together in a similar fashion, their organizations constituting a network of NGOs outside the state.

Communications represented a particularly lively field of independent activity. By 1985 four independent periodicals had published over 150 issues each, 20 having released over 100 issues. Scarcely had the communist government instituted its coup against Solidarity in late 1981 than an independent publishing house, *Krag*, was established in Warsaw. Books, records (through the Polish Jazz Society), and sound tapes (from independent operators like *Nowa-kaseta*) deluged the Polish public with information and performances in every area. The Committee for Independent Culture served as an informal umbrella for such NGOs, linking them with each other and with both Solidarity and the Catholic Church. Similar umbrella groups were constituted to enhance communication among environmentalists, peace activists, and the like.

It is doubtful that any other society in the region equaled Poland for the enthusiasm with which it set about the task of self-organization. However, even if the Polish public set records by its fervor, its activity was not qualitatively different from what was going on in Czechoslovakia, Hungary, the German Democratic Republic, the Soviet Union, and eventually even Bulgaria. Careful study will be needed to determine the extent to which the Poles inspired and provided models for other nations in the region. In each country the mix among various types of NGOs reflected local conditions.

None of these new entities, it should be stressed, enjoyed a legal right to exist, since this was excluded by law in all the communist countries in question. Thus, when the Soviet press by 1988 began claiming that some 40,000 clubs and associations had been established in that country, it was acknowledging the existence of 40,000 illegal NGOs.

Nearly all the new groups and associations can be assigned to one of seven general categories: (1) Protestant and Catholic religious groups in all fields, (2) specialized groups advocating historic preservation, (3) groups fostering popular culture, (4) groups promoting ecological concerns, (5) trade unions, (6) groups promoting economic and social development, and (7) trade associations. This is not the place to review in detail each of these categories. However, a few general notes are in order.

Not only did Christian Churches provide a convenient cover for non-governmental organizing, but spiritual commitment seems to have sparked millions of people in the region to action. The Evangelical Churches of East Germany, Catholics in Poland and Czechoslovakia, Calvinists and other Protestants in western Rumania, Uniates in the western Ukraine, and the Orthodox elsewhere in the Ukraine and in Russia all played a part. Sometimes these concerns merged with those of ecology and historic preservation. Efforts to preserve historic buildings provided some of the first models for public self-organization in both Moscow and Leningrad.

The passion for Western popular culture crystallized an extraordinary amount of non-governmental activity in all countries. Particularly notable were the Polish Jazz Society and the so-called Jazz Section in Czechoslovakia, both of which demonstrated astonishing boldness and organizational agility, inspiring tens of thousands of enthusiasts in other areas of activity to follow suit in their own fields of interest.

Both of these jazz societies managed to get themselves registered with the United Nations as branches of an "International Jazz Federation." This entity may have existed largely on paper, but its official recognition by the UN long stymied the efforts of communist authorities in the two countries to suppress the jazz societies.

No issue proved to be a more potent stimulus to public action than the degradation of nature. The ecological movement by 1990 had moved to the forefront of all causes, and had given rise to literally hundreds of organizations in every country from Czechoslovakia to Bulgaria and Soviet Central Asia. Some, like the Virumaa Foundation in Estonia, were focused on a single industry; others focused on a single city or district; still others, such as the Ukrainian and Czech Green movements prior to their establishment as political parties, were national in scope; yet others, such as the International Union for the Conservation of Nature or the International Fund for Developmental Alternatives, were transnational.

Since most non-governmental economic energies have been channeled into the twilight "second economies," relatively few economic development projects have been organized as legal and visible NGOs. The American Trust for the Development of Polish Agriculture would be an exception, but the initiative for its creation came as much from outside Poland's borders as from within.

The single greatest NGO of the postwar period and the only one to assume national power in Central Europe is Poland's Solidarity. Until recently, however, it was without progeny. But the collapse of communist governments soon transformed most of the old official unions into independent entities, some of them with great political aspirations. Even in the various republics of the Soviet Union, independent labor movements emerged with great vitality by 1989, in which year the coal miners' union successfully forced the government to capitulate on virtually all its demands. The first two months of 1990 saw a greater level of independent strike activity in the Soviet Union than all of 1989.

Trade associations, the final type of NGO to be considered, are fated to be the last category to emerge, since they presuppose the existence of legal private or "cooperative" enterprises. However, by early 1990 such associations were functioning in every country except Rumania and Bulgaria, usually at the national level, but also at more localized levels as well.

Where do these proliferating NGOs get their money? Most exist solely on gifts by individual members. A large number, however, receive grants from public institutions and agencies. Many others, ranging from the Polish Jazz Society to the

Ecological Fund in Sverdlovsk, engage in entrepreneurial activities of various sorts and earn considerable money thereby. Most function entirely with volunteer staffs, although increasing numbers are hiring full-time employees.

A few of the most fortunate NGOs receive international funding. The Biocultural Association of Hungary receives hard currency from the Rockefeller Brothers Fund to train its staff for membership development. The Green Libraries in Poland also receive US aid, as does the independent environmental foundation, Panos Budapest, and several others. The Autonomy Foundation in Hungary was chartered in 1990 to support the development of voluntary associations and community groups, with over half of its resources coming from abroad.

Foundation support from the United States and, to a lesser degree, West Germany, is by no means the largest source of international funds for Central and East European NGOs. They have also received money from West European political parties and their foundations (Friedrich Ebert, etc.) and from the few multinational corporations that have invested in the region's economies. The Soviet Foundation for Social Initiatives has received generous subvention from individual Western donors as well. Finally, mention should be made of gifts from US nationals who have returned with their Social Security funds to retire in their lands of origin. In some countries, notably Poland, they figure as significant patrons for NGOs.

Reliable data on the flow of hard currency into Central and East European NGOs are lacking. However, such funds appear to be concentrated mainly in Poland and Hungary, with Czechoslovakia a distant third. Assuming that international support provides only a minor part of the budget of the new NGOs in formerly communist countries, is it insignificant? Almost certainly not. Such support brings contact with people abroad who may offer expertise relevant to the new NGOs. Even if NGOs remain modest as channels for bringing hard currency to bear on local social problems, they are already proving to be useful conduits for expertise. Western-sponsored conferences for NGOs in Budapest, Moscow, Krakow, and Prague bring Soviet and Central European activists in the third sector in touch with counterparts from abroad, and thus add legitimacy to the fledgling efforts in the region.

Evaluating the new NGOs

What is the scale of the entire voluntary and NGO sector in Central Europe and the Soviet Union? The number of institutions changes constantly, but it is probable that there are somewhere between 30,000 and 70,000 such groups operating at any one time. Some embrace thousands of members, others only a dozen. Assuming even the upper estimate, the total number of people directly and actively involved in NGOs remains a very small part of the total population. However, remembering that some of the areas in which they function are new, and that the number of activists must be multiplied by the large number of people affected by NGO activity, it is clear that the third sector has the potential to be a major social force. Already it is filling the void left by the collapse of governments in Central Europe. It is at once a safety valve for social energies and a flexible means of productively chan-neling cash accumulated in the large currency overhangs in the region. In ecology and in certain areas of welfare served mainly by church organizations, the third sector is already making a unique contribution. It is able to represent interests that might not otherwise have a voice in society, and to use that representational function to shape the agenda of public issues in each country. It has contributed directly to the formation of independent political parties, and, working both directly and indirectly, has brought influence to bear on the allocation of resources nationally.

How far will the third sector develop in Central Europe and the Soviet Union? Based on the record to date, the likelihood is that it will continue to expand and flower. Its flexibility, its ability to act when government and industry cannot, and its attractiveness to the energetic and civic-minded – all these factors augur well for the future. The breakdown and uncertain transition of both the first and second sectors all but guarantee that citizen initiative and NGOs will have an important part to play in the coming period.

In no other countries have voluntary associations proliferated more rapidly or gained more solid public acceptance than in Central Europe and the Soviet Union in recent years. From Sakhalin Island in the Soviet Far East, where a citizens' initiative reversed a government decision to construct a hydroelectric dam, to Budejovice in western Czechoslovakia, where citizens participated in the grassroots effort that brought down the communist government, self-organization has proven an effective tool for expressing citizens' interest. This, along with the reappearance of voluntarism in such traditional areas as church-based help to the poor, the Sunday-school movement, and counseling for the hospitalized, has assured the movement a powerful momentum, at least for the short term.

What factors are most likely to impede the further development of the third sector in the former Second World? However powerful the positive forces, there exist at least five powerful elements that could thwart the further expansion of voluntarism and NGOs. Each warrants discussion.

First, the third sector must gain a solid legal base in all of the formerly communist lands. The civil rights of NGOs must be defined in law and there must exist courts that are capable of adjudicating infractions of those rights. This has not been achieved anywhere, with the partial exception of Poland, where the legislative first steps have been accomplished. Work on such statutes is proceeding in Czechoslovakia (with the help of the US Charter 77 group) and Hungary. Draft laws have been prepared in the Soviet Union but have not yet been enacted. Meanwhile, such organizations as the International Foundation for the Salvation of Humanity continue to base their operations merely on Politburo decrees rather than on a more substantial legal charter.

Second, even if adequate laws, courts, and judicial machinery are put in place, relations with the state can remain a problem. On the one hand, grave harassment of NGOs will continue as long as their legal protections can be infringed by administrative decrees from the myriad of state agencies. On the other hand, central and local governments will have to draw back from their overweening tutelage of society, or there will be no sphere in which the new organizations can function unimpeded. General statements about dismantling the totalitarian system will not suffice. A nontotalitarian system based on thoroughgoing socialism will still pit the government against the NGOs.

The third impediment to the further development of the third sector is the absence of a base of private property sufficient to sustain NGOs. If private individuals and groups cannot amass significant amounts of expendable wealth, NGOs will continue to depend entirely on small, pass-through gifts, modest entrepreneurial activities unprotected by law, gifts from tax-supported agencies, or subventions from abroad. These are not adequate to sustain a vital third sector.

It may be too much to hope that gifts to future NGOs in Central Europe and the Soviet Union would be tax deductible, as in the United States. However, even if that were to occur, such institutions would need access to capital markets so that their resources could be invested and the return dedicated to fulfilling their mission. Stated differently, the creation of a viable third sector will depend upon the existence of a strong and fully institutionalized second sector of private enterprise that sees itself as a partner rather than a rival of the service-oriented voluntary associations.

A fourth potential impediment to the flowering of NGOs is the inadequate development of managerial skills and habits of independence in society at large. The absence of such habits and expertise will cripple the voluntary sector, even if it is otherwise protected by adequate laws and undergirded by private economic activity. Whether or not such capabilities existed prior to the establishment of communist regimes in the era, they have been stifled for half a century. Their development now will depend on the extent to which they are nurtured by all the principal institutions of society, from schools through communications media to public agencies. For NGOs to succeed, in other words, the culture of the society as a whole must support them as a kind of informal school for independent initiatives.

Finally, it is doubtful that this situation can exist under any political system other than a democracy. The expansion of modern communications and travel can give citizens of nondemocratic societies direct contact with democracy; such contact was a powerful stimulus to the revolutions of 1989 in the first place. However, such second-hand exposure to democracy will never engender the attitudes of sustained civic initiative necessary for NGOs to endure. The existence of a democratic regime is thus probably the *sine qua non* to the creation of a vital and independent third sector.

PART X

Internationalism

H OW DO NATIONS BEHAVE in the global age? The foregoing essays, as well as many others in this book, suggest that the economic, social, and cultural forces of globalization have significantly altered the nature of the sovereign state. The state now has increasingly had to cope with forces and issues that are transnational in nature and require multinational responses. At the same time, however, in external relations, traditional patterns of international affairs may have survived, indeed may have been reinforced, because of globalization. Due to technological innovations, nations have been in greater proximity with each other than ever before; their weapons have become steadily more destructive; and it has been much easier than in the past to mobilize and manipulate national opinion to arouse nationalistic sentiments. All these factors have played important roles in the devastating wars of the twentieth century that resulted altogether in the death of over one hundred million people.

Against that background, it is important to note that, precisely because globalization has tended to make international conflict so destructive, efforts have been made to develop a more peaceful and stable world order. After all, if globalization creates closer networks of people and groups across national boundaries, can it not be expected to foster forces for the establishment of a world of interdependence in which war becomes less frequent and international cooperation more routine?

In this section, two essays examine internationalism, or efforts to foster cooperation, not conflict, among nations. Akira Iriye gives a historical introduction to the subject, pointing out that significant beginnings were made to strengthen forces of internationalism at the beginning of the twentieth century. Ulf Hannerz (Professor of Anthropology at the University of Stockholm) makes a useful distinction between the nation and the state and argues that, while interstate affairs may not have been significantly altered by globalization, nations have changed in the direction of diversity and hybridity. That will surely have significant implications for international relations.

Chapter 19

Akira Iriye

INTERNATIONALISM

BECAUSE MOST STUDIES of international relations focus on national interests, national strategies, national rivalries, nationalistic emotions, and the like, it seems justifiable to trace the evolution of ideas and movements that have sought to develop alternative definitions of world affairs. Among the most potent of these definitions have been an number of internationalist schemes – reformulations of foreign and domestic policies in such a way as to overcome excessive parochialism, with its suspicion and hatred of "the other," and to establish a more interdependent, cooperative, and mutually tolerant international community.

Such visions of international community may be termed *internationalism* to oppose them to forces of nationalism. The latter have been by far the more influential and pervasive "realities" for more than three centuries, but internationalism has also gained strength, if not consistently then at least as an expression of hope on the part of an increasing number of people everywhere. To the extent that a nation is an "imaginary community," as Benedict Anderson has argued, the international community must also be "imagined." (Some writers find the term "imagining" too tame and use "inventing" instead: as, for instance, Declan Kiberd does in *Inventing Ireland*.) All the same, the internationalist imagination has exerted a significant influence in modern world history. [. . .]

The polarity of nationalism and internationalism was particularly marked in the decades preceding World War I, when war and peace appeared to hang in a balance and when many internationalist proposals were put forward as alternatives to nationalistic rivalries. In the 1860s, Henry Thomas Buckle had written that, whereas "the actions of men respecting war" had changed over time, their "moral knowledge respecting it" had not. Nevertheless, he was confident that wars were "becoming less frequent." At least until the Crimean War, he noted, "we had remained at peace for nearly forty years: a circumstance unparalleled not only in our own country, but also in the annals of every other country which has been important enough to play a leading part in the affairs of the world." Half a century later, most observers

From Akira Iriye, *Cultural Internationalism and World Order* (Johns Hopkins University Press, 1997), pp. 15–29.

agreed that "moral knowledge" concerning war derived overwhelmingly from modern nationalism. As a Serbian journalist told Trotsky in 1912, "what is at stake here really is our right to live and to develop. The people cannot but know and feel that without war there is for them no way out of the blind alley Serbia is in. The people want war." Contrast this with Jean-Jacques Rousseau's well-known dictum that war "is a relation . . . between State and State, and individuals are enemies . . . as soldiers; not as members of their country, but as its defenders."

During the heyday of Victorian liberalism, such a distinction could be accepted. Immanuel Kant's view that war was characteristic of arbitrary government and that peace was characteristic of a constitutional republic gained influence, as did the Manchester liberals' supposition that the commercial classes desired peace across national frontiers. Increasingly, however, such optimism had to confront the realities of aroused nationalisms. The Rousseauian distinction between state and nation was challenged by Lord Acton as early as the 1860s, when he noted that nationality was a force of growing importance in Europe, destabilizing interstate affairs and enhancing the chances for war. Acton traced this new development to the French Revolution, which had produced the first modern wars in the sense of wars fought by the masses imbued with nationalism. The idea that ordinary people could unite in the name of their nationality and organize their own country was abhorrent to Acton, but he readily admitted that this was the trend throughout Europe. He saw this modern nationalism as a force against international order.

Clearly, Acton rather than Buckle was the more accurate prophet of the world to come. Nationalism would prove to be the most decisive force in international affairs to such an extent that it came to be equated with military power and with war. As the world was seen to consist of sovereign national entities, whose number appeared destined to grow, the chances for armed conflict could easily be considered to be increasing. As Michael Howard has noted, in prewar Europe nationalism was "almost invariably characterized by militarism." This militarism, he writes, was reinforced by an educational system whose aim "was to produce generations physically fit for and psychologically attuned to war."

All this is clear and points to the daunting task undertaken by those who sought to do something to mitigate forces of nationalism so as to produce a less warlike international environment. Because nationalism was recognized as the key to international tensions, its opposite, internationalism, had to be strengthened if the trend were to be checked. The parallel development of nationalism and internationalism thus makes a fascinating chapter in the story leading up to World War I. Just as nationalism and war were imagined to be interchangeable, internationalists assumed peace was possible only if the forces of internationalism could be strengthened.

Internationalism, of course, existed long before the nineteenth century. The idea of international community developed in parallel with the growth of the nation-state in modern Europe. It is useful to recall that the emergence of secular sovereign states in the seventeenth century, out of the universalism defined by the Christian Church, created a new universalism in the form of international law. There could be no international law without nations, but at the same time it was assumed that the existence of independent states necessitated the definition of a larger community, *magna civitas*, of which the states were members. They would be governed by certain rules and precepts of the community, and these would take precedence over the laws of individual states. Thus, international law was built upon internationalist assumptions. As developed initially by such jurists as Hugo Grotius and Christian Wolff, there was a congruence between the laws of nations and the laws of nature. Both were universalistic in character and could be comprehended by rational faculties. It is true that international law was more often than not honored in the breach, and after the eighteenth-century writers came to distinguish the behavior of nations from natural laws and ethical precepts. Moreover, the concept of international law came to lose its universalistic connotations after the eighteenth century and became interchangeable with the European community of nations. Europe, wrote Emerick de Vattel in 1758, was "a sort of republic, whose members – each independent, but all bound together by a common interest – unite for the maintenance of order and the preservation of liberty."

Internationalism in Europe, then, had developed both as a universalistic doctrine, inspired by the concept of natural law, and as a particularistic conception, privileging the European states among nations and empires. By the nineteenth century, international law, having survived numerous wars among European (and North American) states, came to be equated with norms and procedures governing the conduct of "civilized" nations. Among "civilized" nations, it was widely held in Europe and North America, it should be possible to codify laws defining the acceptable behavior of governments and individuals, in war as well as in peace. As Henry Wheaton, American diplomat and jurist, wrote in his influential *Elements of International Law*, first published in 1836, "civilized nations" adhered to certain rules of conduct that they deduced "from the nature of the society existing among independent nations." Those states and peoples that did not accept the laws were by definition "uncivilized"; by the same token, "uncivilized" countries would become "civilized" only by adhering to the existing international law. The Ottoman Empire was admitted to the "civilized" community of nations when it signed treaties with the Western powers in the aftermath of the Crimean War, as were China, Japan, Siam, and Korea, which established formal diplomatic relations with these powers throughout the course of the nineteenth century. Even so, these non-Western countries were not exactly equal members of the "civilized" community of nations: "unequal" treaties continued to function between these two sets of nations.

What is important in our discussion, however, is the fact that even as Turkey, China, Japan, and other countries struggled to become modern states, they were drawn into the system of laws that had been established by Western nations. In other words, these non-Western countries had to embrace both nationalism (imagining themselves to be modern nation-states) and internationalism (imagining themselves as members of the world community) as they sought to transform themselves. It is interesting to note that several non-Western countries, including Persia, Siam, China, and Japan, were represented at the Hague conference of 1899, convened to modify and strengthen international law.

That conference was a landmark in that it established the first international court of arbitration. Such an undertaking was grounded on the assumption that it was possible for modern nations to cooperate with one another in the international sphere and to agree among themselves to solve their disputes through arbitration, not war. That disputes could be peacefully arbitrated was, of course, an optimistic presupposition that proved premature, but the optimism was a necessary antidote to the prevailing nationalism of the age, by which the great powers were trying to strengthen themselves further through armament. Even as they did so, they were willing to enter into various arbitration agreements. Many of these were signed after the turn of the country, indicating the awareness that, just as nationalism was interchangeable with war, internationalism was an essential condition for the avoidance of war.

How to strengthen forces for internationalism at a time when nationalism appeared to be growing stronger by the day? International law and arbitration was one answer, but internationalists did not stop there. They proposed additional programs and movements. Some offered radical solutions, extending the logic of the nationalism–internationalism polarity by calling for severe restrictions on the rights of sovereign nations and for the organizing of an international regime with authority to maintain the peace. In 1895, Urbain Gohier, who was beginning his long and controversial career as a Paris journalist, published his essay "On War," which argued that wars were advocated by (because they benefited them) dynasties, governments, politicians, large financial organs, capitalists, arms manufacturers, and the military. These entities would go to war in the name of *patrie* and honor, but these were mere words to hide their self-interests. "Our patriotism should consist in working for the well-being of our citizens, not in killing them in order to bring about [their rulers'] well-being." Militarism would bring ruin to the people, and war would cause oppression and servitude in the country. "War is the extreme expression of violence and injustice," and the French nation had established a militaristic regime "for having loved war too much." War created the pretext for "maximum government," whereas justice and well-being required "minimum government." But given the growing power of the state, war could be prevented only if common people, representing "human conscience," rose against war-making leaders. War would cease when would-be war makers recognized that their own lives depended on the support of ordinary people.

Ultimately, however, no amount of domestic reform would suffice unless efforts were made to strengthen the forces for internationalism. Gohier argued that since war was an expression of nationalism, peace would prevail only when nationalism was moderated, if not replaced, by internationalism. And this could be done through coalescing various peoples in a joint effort at international organization. Although he was vague as to details, Gohier was convinced that possibilities existed for developing a world government, embracing at least the civilized peoples, and pointed to the example of the United States. After five months of touring the country, he published a book entitled *The People of the Twentieth Century in the United States* (1903); the American people would dominate the world in the new century, he declared, because of their abundant natural resources, political institutions, republican instincts, and audacious practices of extreme liberty. Europeans would do well to realize that people's liberty in all forms and their initiatives in all degrees were the two factors that made for wealth and civil peace. What struck Gohier above all was that the United States, despite its appearance of "nationalism, particularism, and jingoism," was actually a "splendid example of internationalism." This was because Americans were heirs to all that Europe had produced, without, however, having transported Europe's nationalistic rivalries. "This fusion of European races in America justifies all the doctrines of internationalists who are denounced by mendacious governments and attacked by stupid savants. The American nation is the living realization of the dream of internationalism." Why would the same people, who would be engaged in a fratricide if they fought in the United States,

still go to war on the European continent? "We want peace and a close unity between Europeans in Europe and Europeans in the United States. This is the first
article of internationalism." Gohier was mindful of the Philippines and warned that
if imperialism should turn the United States into a militaristic nation, it would be
a disaster for the whole of mankind. Fundamentally, however, he remained hopeful
that the more internationalist side of the United States would prevail and lead the
world to peace. It would point the way to organizing the nations of the world better
for mutual cooperation and peace.

Gustave Hervé, another French writer, established an even more explicit
connection between peace and internationalism. In a 1910 book entitled *Internationalism*, he argued that modern states such as France and Germany were
temporary and inferior forms of human association that were steadily being undermined by forces of internationalism; namely, the movement of people, goods, and
capital across national frontiers. Internationalism, he asserted, "is nothing but an
instinctive or reflective aspiration of the modern world for political forms superior
to the actual states" so that the whole of humanity could live as in one country
covering the entire earth – *la grande patrie universelle*. This was an inevitable historical evolution, starting with the Protestants helping one another across national
boundaries and the French Revolution's universalistic doctrines. Like Gohier, Hervé
gave credit to the United States, which, he wrote, had established the idea of
humanity as one family of which all members shared the same rights.

In the second half of the nineteenth century, Hervé maintained, the development of modern science and technology had made "historically determined political
frontiers appear anachronistic." There had developed an internationalism of capital
and labor, neither of which knew political boundaries. As capital and labor continued
to cross frontiers, the distinction between domestic and foreign goods and populations would diminish, and international regulations would be promulgated to govern
their behavior. Capitalists and workers, thus internationalized, would try to avoid
disastrous economic competition as well as "the most disastrous of all competitions,
war." Although at that moment the chances of war or peace appeared evenly
balanced, the latter would be the ultimate winner, especially since the world's
working class wanted it. "The nineteenth century was a century of nationalism,"
Hervé asserted, "but the twentieth century will be a century of internationalism.
. . . There will eventually be a United States of Europe and America, perhaps a
United States of the world." The book concluded with a ringing declaration:

> Future generations will marvel that at the beginning of the twentieth
> century, barbarism had divided the world into small compartments filled
> with bayonets and canons, that they would destroy one another at the
> order of their masters, and that those who dared to speak of the end of
> this barbarism were considered fools and public misfits.

Hervé's conviction that capital and labor were tending toward internationalization echoed widespread ideas in the second half of the nineteenth century and the
first years of the twentieth that economics was prevailing over politics. Against the
all too apparent tendency of modern nation-states to arm themselves in preparation
for war against one another, many assumed that the best way to combat this trend
was through encouraging economic activities across national boundaries. If carried

out unfettered, such activity would inevitably weaken the forces of nationalism. This idea, that economic transactions would strengthen interdependence and peaceful relations among nations, may be termed *economic internationalism*, in contrast to *legal internationalism*. The latter stressed legal agreements and institutions for the sustenance of an international community, whereas the former saw the answer to modern national antagonisms in international commerce and worldwide economic development.

The origins of modern economic internationalism go back to the eighteenth century, when Enlightenment thinkers and officials began challenging the theories and practices of mercantilism and argued that increased commercial transactions benefited all nations. Some went further and conceptualized a vision of international relations in which there was an inherent connection between trade and cross-national understanding, and between cross-national understanding and world peace. As Joseph Priestley wrote,

> by commerce we enlarge our acquaintance with the terraqueous globe and its inhabitants, which tends greatly to expand the mind, and to cure us of many hurtful prejudices, which we unavoidably contract in a confined situation at home. . . . [No] person can take the sweets of commerce, which absolutely depends upon a free and undisturbed inter-course of different and remote nations, but must grow fond of peace in which alone the advantages he enjoys can be had.

Such a conception of economic internationalism was given additional theoretical underpinnings in the nineteenth century, as world trade expanded in the wake of the Congress of Vienna and brought peoples and their products closer together. Perhaps the best-known writer in this regard was the sociologist Herbert Spencer, whose 1876 *Principles of Sociology* was enormously influential. In this volume, Spencer sought to trace the evolution of human societies, from the isolated primitive communities to organizations dominated by the military in order to ensure collective survival and territorial expansion, and to modern industrial nations whose primary function was to undertake economic development. In these latter, "civilized," societies, human activities not directly linked to military affairs and therefore pursued by private individuals and groups were constantly being enlarged. As a result, interconnections among nations in a similar stage of development would grow, which ultimately would bring them closer to the ideal of universal peace.

Already in such thinking one notes an interest in social and cultural, not just economic, aspects of international relations. For what Priestley, Spencer, and others were presenting was a vision of an international community in which nations and peoples gained a more mature understanding of one another than had been possible when commerce was combined with military conquest and seen in terms of sovereign states' struggles for power. Distant parts of the world were being brought closer together through modern shipping, trade, and marketing organizations, and it seemed possible to expect the growth of mutual knowledge, and, as a result, a greater sense of shared concerns and interests across national boundaries. This additional element in internationalist thought may be termed *cultural internationalism*; that is, the idea that internationalism may best be fostered through cross-national cultural communication, understanding, and cooperation. A more peaceful world order could develop not just through the drafting of legal documents, the establishment of international courts, or engagement in unrestricted commerce, but through the efforts of individuals and organizations across national boundaries to promote better understanding and to cooperate in collaborative enterprises. Such ideas significantly enriched, even transformed, modern internationalism. Any conception of world order or international community would now have to contain all elements: legal, economic, and cultural.

This last element, the cultural, emerged as a major characteristic of twentieth-century internationalism. It is an important phenomenon. [. . .]

It was not surprising that cultural internationalism emerged in the last decades of the nineteenth and the first decades of the twentieth centuries, as if to challenge the growing tides of nationalism and militarism. In confronting the realities of armed rivalries and geopolitical calculations that were then dominating international rela-tions, internationalists felt the need for cross-national efforts to keep alive the vision of an interdependent world community. The new internationalism in the age of the new imperialism thus inevitably called for cooperative undertakings among nations to promote a sense of global interdependence. More specifically, officials and intel-lectual leaders in various counties became strongly interested in establishing international organizations for carrying out joint cultural projects. H.L.S. Lyons notes in his pioneering study *Internationalism in Europe* (1963) that more than four hundred international organizations had been established prior to World War I, ranging from the Red Cross to associations of scientists and doctors, all dedicated to the proposition that such organizations would promote interdependence and peace. For instance, in 1885 an International Institute of Statistics was founded to standardize national statistical information. Two years later, an international bureau was established to collect and publish tariffs of many countries. These instances were in effect attempts at internationalizing national data, an idea that was also behind such other examples as the Universal Postal Union and an international agreement on standards of weights and measures. Lyons shows that the bulk of these organ-izations came into being after the 1870s — an indication that they were responses to the growing nationalism and militarization of the age.

It is true that the majority of these institutions were functional, in the sense of having been created in order to serve specific purposes such as establishing inter-national postal rates or collecting customs information. Some may argue that those devices merely facilitated the execution of national policies and that whatever cultural internationalist ideas these institutions may have implied were of secondary importance. Nevertheless, such modest beginnings in the functional sphere provided evidence that, even as the nations of the world were turning themselves into military powers, it was possible to achieve cross-national cooperation and establish inter-national structures. These agencies could, and did, stimulate and encourage cultural internationalist thought.

Chapter 20

Ulf Hannerz

THE WITHERING AWAY
OF THE NATION?

IN THE CONCLUDING PAGES of *Nations and Nationalism since 1780*, [Eric] Hobsbawm asks whether the world history of the late twentieth and early twenty-first century will be written, as that of the nineteenth century could be, in terms of "nation-building." He does not think so:

> It will see "nation-states" and "nations" or ethnic/linguistic groups primarily as retreating before, resisting, adapting to, being absorbed or dislocated by, the new supranational restructuring of the globe. Nations and nationalism will be present in this history, but in subordinate, and often rather minor roles. . . . After all, the very fact that historians are at least beginning to make some progress in the study and analysis of nations and nationalism suggest that, as so often, the phenomenon is past its peak. The owl of Minerva which brings wisdom, said Hegel, flies out at dusk. It is a good sign it is now circulating round nations and nationalism.

The owl of Minerva (here perhaps looking rather more like a vulture) might well be the historians' favorite bird, insofar as it can be relied on to lend its wings to their claims to superior understanding. And if we try to inquire into present or even future states of affairs, and more especially into what might be grounds for the retreat or decline of national ideas, we would seem to have both Hegel and Hobsbawm advising us against the undertaking. Nonetheless, what I want to do here is to consider some of the circumstances which could contribute, to one degree or other, and among some people but not necessarily all, to a weakening of the nation as imagined community and sources of identity. I will proceed largely by arguing with or against some of the more prominent recent commentators on nations, national culture, and nationalism, letting their voices be heard as well; and also some other voices, in accord or discord, which may enrich our own imagination.

Before proceeding any further, however, I should probably say something about the title I have chosen. I distinguish between the nation and the state. In recent

From Ulf Hannerz, "The Withering Away of the Nation? An Afterword," in *Ethnos* vol. 58 (1993), pp. 377–90.

times we have indeed seen what might look a little like a withering away of states, in some places in the Second and Third Worlds; but when I use the notion "withering away of the nation," I do not assume that such a process would necessarily entail a withering of the states as well. It may be, as Benedict Anderson argues in *Imagined Communities* (1983), that "nation-ness is the most universally legitimate value in the political life of our time," but states or whatever other agents use this value for purposes of legitimation can conceivably find ways of continuing without nationhood, and might find other ways of establishing their worth (if they in fact concern themselves with legitimacy). Moreover, and very significantly, there is that question mark at the end of the title. I do not promise that it will be gone by the time I am through.

There are two kinds of issues I will be concerned with in what follows. One, on which I will say more, involves variations in personal experiences of the national and the transnational, and their relationship to time. The other concerns the relationship between symbolic modes, media technologies, and cultural boundaries; on this I will comment more briefly.

The nation and cultural resonance

Hobsbawm, we just saw, had his doubts about the continued strength of nations in the era of globalization and transnational structures. We can juxtapose him with another of the more diligent writers on national phenomena in recent times, Anthony D. Smith, who looks with great skepticism at the power of contemporary transnational culture to impress itself upon people's more deeply held, enduring perspectives and sentiments. This transnational culture, Smith argues, consists of a number of discrete elements:

> effectively advertised mass commodities, a patchwork of folk or ethnic styles and motifs stripped of their context, some general ideological discourses concerned with "human rights and values" and a standardized quantitative and scientific language of communication and appraisal, all under pinned by the new information and telecommunications systems and their computerized technologies.

It is "eclectic," "fundamentally artificial," and "indifferent to place and time," Smith goes on; its pastiche is "capricious and ironical," and its "effects are carefully calculated." It "lacks any emotional commitment to what is signified," and "is more interested in means and in reformulating dilemmas of value into the technical problems with purely technological solutions." And then Smith reaches the big question: Can such a culture "put down roots among the populations of the world?"

By the time Smith gets to the question, one might note, the metaphors have been fairly well stacked against an affirmative reply. Transnational culture has been declared "fluid and shapeless," carries "surface decoration," is "shallow," and has a "veneer of streamlined modernism"; we are also "deluged with a torrent of standardized mass commodities." Confronted with so much evidence of both superficiality and quite violent fluidity, and then asked if something like this can "put down roots," you would have to be an idiot to answer "yes" – or perhaps someone just a little provoked by rhetorical overkill.

If Smith is less than impressed with the depth and coherence of the transnational culture of the late twentieth century, he is the more so with national culture, and national identity. The idea of the nation is ubiquitous, itself globalized, as well as pervasive:

> Though there are some situations in which is felt to be more important than others, it may also be said to pervade the life of individuals and communities in most spheres of activity. In the cultural sphere national identity is revealed in a whole range of assumptions and myths, values and memories, as well as in language, law, institutions, and ceremonies. Socially, the national bond provides the most inclusive community, the generally accepted boundary within which social intercourse normally takes place, and the limit for distinguishing the "outsider." The nation may also be seen as the basic unit of moral economy, in terms both of territory and of resources and skills.

Such pervasiveness, and not least the durability of such pervasiveness, sets the context for Smith's argument concerning the continued viability of nations as imagined communities. The action has a perceived collective past, and much as scholars (including, of course, Hobsbawm), with an ironical glint in the eye, have taken to celebrating the recent and ongoing manufacture of traditions, Smith believes such innovations would get nowhere unless they offered a sufficiently close fit with existing ideas and emotions. This collective past, this "ethnohistory," together with its promise of a future, he proposes, offer people above all three deep satisfactions. There is an answer to the problem of personal oblivion; your destiny is with the nation's future generations. There is also the sense of a national restoration of dignity. If there was a glorious past, there must be a glorious future, and a personal share in that coming renewal. Thirdly, the nation offers the possibility of fraternity. Those living are of one large family. Yet this is made clear, of course, through shared symbolic references to the past, to the ancestors held in common. [. . .]

Varieties of transnational experience

Let us consider some recurrent varieties of personal experience today; experiences which touch on issues of time, space, loyalty, and identity and which relate somehow uneasily to national boundaries.

Increasingly in the current era, Robert Reich has argued in *The Work of Nations*, work in advanced societies falls into three main categories; those he calls routine production services, in-person services, and symbolic analytic services. The first of these entail the endlessly repetitive tasks of a great many blue-collar as well as white-collar workers. The major difference between these and the in-person services is that the latter must be provided, if not face to face with customers, at least in their immediate environment; in-person services include the jobs of retail sales people, waiters and waitresses, janitors, secretaries, hairdressers, taxi drivers, and security guards. The third category is that with which Reich is most directly concerned; the symbolic analytic services, including for example research scientists, consultants, corporate headhunters, publishers and writers, musicians, television and film producers [. . .] "even university professors."

What the symbolic analysts have in common, Reich suggests, is the non-standardized manipulation of symbols – data, words, oral and visual representations. They are problem-identifiers, problem-solvers, strategic brokers; highly skilled people whose continuously cumulative, varied experience is an asset which makes them relatively autonomous *vis-à-vis* particular places and organizations.

The symbolic analysts, in the contemporary picture which Reich draws, are linked to global webs of enterprise. They are no longer particularly dependent on the economic performance of other categories of people in their national contexts, such as people in routine production services. And in the American case, which is Reich's major concern, he finds that the "symbolic analysts have been seceding from the rest of the nation." It has been a secession taking place gradually and without fanfare. The symbolic analysts may pledge allegiance to the flag with as much sincerity as ever, yet "the new global sources of their economic well-being have subtly altered how they understand their economic roles and responsibilities in society."

Among the tribes of symbolic analysts we seem to get the closeup view of the nation retreating, as suggested by Hobsbawm. They build their own monuments – the convention centers, the research parks, the international airports – and withdraw into their own private habitats, enclaves with security guards if need be. If they are less concerned with local routine production services, which are liable to be replaced more cheaply somewhere else in the world, they may on the other hand be more interested in the quality of the in-person services.

The tendency toward a withdrawal of the symbolic analysts is not only American, although Reich sees some variations of degree in different places. It is not a tendency which pleases him. Symbolic analysts, he believes, are not likely to exchange an old commitment to the nation for the new global citizenship, with an even more extended sense of social responsibility. There are no strong attachments and loyalties here, but more likely a sense of resignation. "Even if the symbolic analyst is sensitive to the problems that plague the world, these dilemmas may seem so intractable and overpowering in their global dimension that any attempt to remedy them appears futile." What Reich argues for, then, is a revitalized commitment to the nation, more especially a shared investment in the productivity and competitiveness of all its citizens, within the framework of the globalized economy.

When Reich's book was published, he was a Harvard political economist. Since then, he has become Secretary of Labor in the Clinton Administration, and thus he is perhaps now in a position to do something about all this. Yet it is hardly obvious how such a renewed political will, including the symbolic analysts in the alliance, is to come about. In any case, if we consider Reich's ethnography of recent trends rather than his enlightened nationalist call to action, we see that the symbolic analysts, in all the internal diversity, would appear to have distanced themselves from much of what Smith, as quoted above, sees as characteristic of the nation. The latter hardly "provides the most inclusive community, the generally accepted boundary within which social intercourse normally takes place," it is questionably "the basic unit of moral economy." The possibility of fraternity does not seem to be embraced. Yet there is no doubt room for some symbolic ambiguity even among symbolic analysts – national allegiance may be proclaimed even when not really practiced, and to the problem of personal oblivion, for example, a better answer may still be waiting to be found.

Again, the ideal type symbolic analyst according to Reich is fairly autonomous in relations to organizations as well as places. This would seem to be not quite the kind of person, then, that another commentator on the contemporary restructuring of the world, Kenichi Ohmae, has in mind. Ohmae, author of *The Borderless World* and several other books, and a frequent contributor to *Wall Street Journal* as well as *Harvard Business Review*, is an international management consultant – "guru" is a term that comes to mind – concerned in particular with the workings of corporations in the global market place. What he has to say about the internal life of a corporation reaching the highest stage of globalism also reflects interestingly, I think, on our assumptions about the national. The global corporation, in Ohmae's view, must loosen its ties to any particular country, "get rid of the headquarters mentality," "create a system of values shared by company managers around the global to replace the glue a nation-based orientation once provided." It needs an "amoebalike network organization." This organization depends on a shared unofficial culture which cannot be learned by reading the same manual or going to the same brief training program. It can only grow over time, Ohmae argues, as people develop a broad range of common references and experiences. They must meet face to face over the years, they must stay at each other's homes, their families must know each other; and at the same time formal structures – training programs, career planning, job rotation, evaluation systems – must also be the same wherever the corporation first finds you, and wherever it then places you. Only thus is the highest stage of corporate globalism reached:

> The customers you care about are the people who love your products everywhere in the world. Your mission is to provide them with exceptional value. When you think of your colleagues, you think of people who share that mission. Country of origin does not matter. Location of headquarters does not matter. The products for which you are responsible and the company you serve have become denationalized.

> You really have to believe, deep down, that people may work "in" different national environments but are not "of" them. What they are "of" is the global corporation.

Ohmae admits that few if any corporations have quite reached this far, although "the signs of movement in this direction are numerous and unmistakable." It is interesting, in any case, that here the vision seems to go beyond that of Robert Reich, who sees among the symbolic analysts mostly an attenuation of national ties. Here the corporation apparently becomes an alternative, a transnational source of solidarity and collective identity, a basic unit of moral economy in Smith's terms again, while the nation at the same time becomes defined as little more than an environment, a local market (and, moreover, not the only one). In the shared life and personal ties of the corporation, it is implied, cultural resonance can again be found. The corporation may even have a history, a mythology of the past, and celebrate it. More certainly, it will offer some vision for the future.

Ohmae's transnational organization man and Reich's symbolic analyst are two recognizable social types of the present, fairly closely related. But listen now to another voice, the reggae fan Jo-Jo, as recorded by Simon Jones (and quoted by Dick Hebdige) in Birmingham's multi-ethnic Balsall Heath neighborhood:

> there's no such thing as "England" any more . . . welcome to India brothers! This is the Caribbean! . . . Nigeria! . . . There is no England, man. That is what is coming. Balsall Heath is the centre of the melting pot, 'cos all I ever see when I go out is half-Arab, half-Pakistani, half-Jamaican, half-Scottish, half-Irish. I know 'cos I am (half Scottish/half Irish) . . . Who am I? Tell me who do I belong to? They criticize me, the good old England. Alright, where do I belong? You know I was brought up with blacks, Pakistanis, Africans, Asians, everything, you name it . . . who do I belong to? I'm just a broad person.

Jo-Jo, I take it, is a young man of the streets, not a self-conscious and well-read intellectual. Nonetheless, his point of view reminds me strikingly of some formulations in Salman Rushdie's collection of essays, *Imaginary Homelands*. (I assume that the resemblance between this title and that of Benedict Anderson's book is coincidental.) Commenting on his best-known novel and the controversy to which it gave rise, Rushdie notes that the characters at the center of the book are people struggling with problems of ghettoization and hybridization, of reconciling the old and the new:

> *The Satanic Verses* celebrates hybridity, impurity, intermingling, the transformation that comes out of new and unexpected combinations of human beings, cultures, ideas, politics, movies, songs. It rejoices in mongrelization and fears the absolutism of the Pure. Melange, hotchpotch, a bit of this and a bit of that is *how newness enters the world*. It is the great possibility that mass migration gives the world, and I have tried to embrace it.

It seems to me that Jo-Jo and Rushdie are on to the same thing. But Rushdie, of course, gets both more reflective and more elaborate, and so we may record a little more of his comments. Here and elsewhere, in commenting on his own writing, Rushdie sees it as drawing on the migrant condition. Before writing the earlier novel *Midnight's Children*, he had spent months trying to recall as much as he could of his childhood Bombay. He was thrilled to see how much had in fact been stored somewhere in his memory, and yet it was precisely the partial nature of his recollections that made them so evocative to him:

> The shards of memory acquired greater status, greater resonance, because they were remains; fragmentation made trivial things seem like symbols, and the mundane acquired numinous qualities . . . It may be argued that the past is a country from which we have all emigrated, that its loss is part of our common humanity. Which seems to me self-evidently true; but it suggests that the writer who is out-of-country and even out-of-language may experience this loss in an intensified form. It is made more concrete for him by the physical fact of discontinuity, of his present being in a difficult place from his past, of his being "elsewhere."

This may enable him to speak properly and concretely on a subject of universal significance and appeal.

The migrant looks here to a past which is spatially as well as temporally distant; it may be reflected in his present in different ways. For the Mauritian in Paris or the Belizean in Los Angeles, we have seen, it may intensify the sense of nationhood and national identity, rooted back home. Rushdie, it appears, is also concerned with a more general human experience of migration and uprootedness. Yet he sees the possibility of a continuous reconstruction of the past of his adopted country as well. Others have become British before him – the Huguenots, the Irish, the Jews; Swift, Conrad, Marx. "America, a nation of immigrants, has created great literature out of the phenomenon of cultural transplantation," Rushdie concludes, and suggests that the example can be followed elsewhere.

Indeed it seems that much of the most gripping in recent fiction and autobiography thematizes what Rushdie calls "hybridity, impurity, intermingling." If the great literature also becomes national literature may be another matter. It is one thing for the United States, more accustomed to defining itself as a nation of newcomers, to find its identity in a master narrative of migration and melting pot (yet even here we see the current problems of multiculturalism and the canon). In Britain, the dominance of other ideas of historical roots would seem much more difficult to challenge successfully. As Jo-Jo of Balsall Heath has it, "they criticize me, the good old England."

In any case, my general point is this. From Reich to Rushdie, by way of Ohmae and Jo-Jo, we seem to see that there are now various kinds of people for whom the nation works less well, or at least less unambiguously, as a source of cultural resonance. In the instance of the symbolic analyst, and perhaps for some variety of others, it may even turn out to be less a richly imagined community than what Morris Janowitz, in an entirely different context, referred to as a "community of limited liability" – one has a largely transactional relationship to it, and one withdraws if it fails to serve one's needs. So the big question would be, what can your nation do for you that a good credit card cannot do?

If the nation as an idea is culturally impoverished here, we cannot be quite certain whether it is replaced by anything else. Reich has little to say on this point. Ohmae, on the other hand, suggests that the global corporation should turn itself into something like a nation. Perhaps we disapprove of this, seeing it only as the business consultant's utopia, a manipulated product of corporate managerial ideology (but then some measure of manipulation has certainly gone into the building of other nations as well). With Jo-Jo and Rushdie, however, it seems undeniable that much of the most deeply felt, highly resonant, personal experience is at odds with ordinary notions of the national. It may be that this experience, and the shared understandings which grow out of it, are "eclectic," as Smith has it in his portrayal of transnational culture, but it does not appear either "fundamentally artificial," "indifferent to place and time," or "carefully calculated." To say that it "lacks any emotional commitment" is hardly correct. Admittedly, we are looking here at something other than the commercial, bureaucratic, or technical transnationalism, of large-scale, impersonal organizational characteristics, which Smith has in mind. The argument, however, is that transnationalism and globalization nowadays have more varied characteristics, and that sometimes, for some people (a growing number), they include precisely the kinds of sites where cultural resonance is generated.

It used to be, more often, that people's more real communities, those made up of people known personally to one another, primarily through enduring face-to-face relationships, were continued within the boundaries of those entities which could be made into nations and imagined communities. There was no great obstacle to a symbolic transformation of the concrete experience of the former into the imagery of the latter; hence, for example, "peasants into Frenchmen." Now a great many real relationships to people and places may cross boundaries. Intimate circles and small networks can be involved here; the transnational is not always immense in scale. These relationships are sensed not to fit perfectly with established ideas of the nation, and in this way the latter becomes probably less pervasive, and even compromised. The feeling of deep historical rootedness may be replaced by an equally intense experience of discontinuity and rupture, as in the case of the transcontinental migrant; the fraternity of the present, as in Balsall Heath and innumerable places like it, is in opposition to the sedimented differences of history.

We should not take for granted, either, that such personal experiences come in only a few varieties. It seems, rather, that in the present phase of globalization, one characteristic is the proliferation of kinds of ties that can be transnational; ties to kin, friends, colleagues, business associates, and others. In all that variety, such ties may entail a kind and a degree of tuning out, a weakened personal involvement with the nation and national culture, a shift from the disposition to take it for granted; possibly a critical distance to it. In such ways, the nation may have become more hollow than it was.

On the other hand, in all their diversity, these outside linkages tend not to coalesce into any single conspicuous alternative to the nation. The people involved are not all "cosmopolitans" in the same sense; most of them are probably not cosmopolitans in any strict sense at all. It is also in the nature of things that we are not always sure who is affected by these linkages. Some may be of a more dramatic and conspicuous kind, others apparently mundane and hardly noticeable to anyone not in the know, not intimately familiar with the other's network and biography. Globalization of this kind, diffused within social life, is opaque. The deep personal experiences of an individual, and their distribution within his transnational habit of meaning, can be in large part a private matter.

What we may find at the present time, then [. . .] is a situation where to some people, no doubt a great many, the idea of the nation is still largely in place, where it has been perhaps for some centuries. In some ways, here and there, it may even be strengthened. It still encompasses virtually all their social traffic, and offers the framework for thinking about past and future. Yet interspersed among those most committed, encapsulated nationals, in patterns not always equally transparent, are a growing number of people of more varying experiences and connections. Some of them may wish to redefine the nation; place the emphasis, for example, more on the future and less on that past of which they happen not to have been a part. Of such desires, and their clash with established definitions, cultural debates may be made. Others again are in the nation but not of it. They may be the real cosmopolitans, or they are people whose nations are actually elsewhere, objects of exile or diaspora nostalgia (and perhaps of other debates), perhaps projects for the future. Or they may indeed owe a stronger allegiance to some other kind of imagined occupational community – to a youth style. There may be divided commitments, ambiguities, and conflicting resonance as well. It may work at the personal level and at the situational. All this need not come to a withering away of the nation, but would seem to make it an entity rather different from the one that possibly used to be.

Cultural technologies, symbolic modes, national boundaries

My other set of concerns relates in a way to Smith's identification of transnational culture with media technology, and more directly to Benedict Anderson's view of the impact of print on the growth of the imagined community. To put it differently, I want to consider the historical importance of language in defining cultural boundaries more generally.

"The search was on," Anderson writes, "for a new way of linking fraternity, power, and time meaningfully together. Nothing perhaps more precipitated this search, nor made it more fruitful, than print-capitalism, which made it possible for rapidly growing numbers of people to think about themselves, and to relate themselves to others, in profoundly new ways." Widespread literacy and easily accessible reading materials, books as well as newspapers, in one's own language made it possible to recognize that there were people like oneself, in large numbers, beyond the local face-to-face community. It is true that there were a great many more spoken dialects than written languages, and that writing and print thus raised the status of some of the former above the others. They also drew boundaries more sharply than dialects would often do. Yet they ensured that people would think of culture and its boundaries in terms of language and linguistic distinctions, and that the fraternity of the nation would be defined in terms of the users – perhaps writers/readers, rather than speakers – of one language.

It is one quite obvious aspect of this that as globalization entails multilingualism, or at least bilingualism, personal identification with one language may change character, together with the identification with the one imagined community attached to it. Kenichi Ohmae exemplifies this:

> Quite literally, global firms must share a common language, English, in addition to all the languages spoken locally. I know of two German companies that have recently changed their official language of business from German to English for just this reason. Talent must be accessible throughout the world . . . mother-country identity must give way to corporate identity.

The fact that in one's ongoing life one is not always using the same language can stand as one very tangible sign of the fact that this life is not all carried on within the national framework. Speaking (or writing, or reading) one's "mother tongue" is no longer taken for granted in all contexts; if this increases one's identification with it, as one becomes aware of how naturally it flows compared to one's not altogether painless efforts to use the languages, or if one's intellectual distance to it grows as certain things seem to be better said in the other languages, is a question with no single simple answer. Meanwhile, it also seems possible to take Anderson's line of argument a step further. As English becomes the dominant language in the world, used by an increasing number of people in a large number of contexts, at a reasonably high level of skill, does it not offer possibilities for a variety of imagined communities, including even the global community itself?

Another issue perhaps relating to language, print, and their part in defining the nation is perhaps less obvious, but still seems worth raising. Writing and print as cultural technology long defined the most inclusive community within which people could be communicatively in touch, could effectively make themselves intelligible to one another. This gave language as a symbolic mode a head start over other symbolic modes – music, gesture, and others, as well as their combinations – which for centuries had no equally efficient technologies, and which tended therefore to be confined to more local circumstances, and to face-to-face relationships. As the world has left the Gutenberg era, however, can we in somewhat McLuhanesque terms ask what are the implications of the wider range of cultural technologies for our understandings of imagined communities, and for the way we think about cultural units?

On the one hand, it may quite credibly be argued that among the symbolic modes at the disposal of humanity, language is in any case the most important, due to its unique richness and flexibility. On the other hand, we know what barriers of incomprehension it imposes, the barriers which have also assisted in creating nations. When the technology is available to carry expressions in other symbolic modes over great distances, will the communities of intelligibility sort themselves differently? We have some sense of the labor involved in learning a foreign language – either through informal interactions over a long period, or through intensive lessons. How are competences of interpretation, appreciation, and production in other symbolic modes built up – is anything more or less immediately accessible, what is involved in acquiring skills for comprehending what is initially alien, what are our chances of forming alternative imagined communities?

I am reminded here of Dan Sperber's suggestion of an "epidemiology of representations." Depending on the nature of our cognitive capacities, and on the interplay between mental representations and the public representations available to the senses, Sperber argues, some representations are more contagious than others, spreading efficiently and often swiftly through human populations. These are the ones which become "more cultural," in the sense of establishing themselves more widely and more enduringly in society. As I read Sperber, he is more interested in human cognitive capacities "in the raw," as it were, and their variously effective handling of different representations. But it seems to me that we could also consider how differently cultivated competences for symbolic modes relate to the flow of cultural norms throughout the world. Could there be affinities which allow a Swede, for example, to appreciate what a Nigerian or an Indonesian does as he sings or dances, even if what he says as he speaks sounds only like gibberish? Perhaps we have to draw different boundaries of intelligibility for each symbolic mode; if that is the case, the notion of the boundaries of "a culture," as a self-evident package deal, becomes apparent. And the idea of the nation as a cultural community cannot avoid being touched.

Conclusion: not withering, perhaps, but changing

I have tried to identify some ways in which the conditions of the present, and in particular processes of globalization, may affect nations and the ways in which, as citizens or as scholars, we may think about them (or, alternatively, not think about them). Stating things briefly, even with a handful of examples, one tends to generalize. As far as the nation is concerned, it is undoubtedly true, as [Orvar] Löfgren has noted, that it seems often to be constructed with the same tool kit of ideas and symbols, recurring in different places. Yet the tools of identity and imagination may not always be equally available to all nation builders, nor are the contexts of assembling, disassembling, or reconstructing all the same. At the very same time as globalization may lead us to rethink the notion of the nation in one array of instances, and perhaps look for signs of organizational or symbolic decay, in other cases nations and nationalism appear to be on an upswing. When it is dusk in one place, and Minerva's owl flies, dawn may arrive somewhere else. One would need to consider the circumstances in each instance.

The particular sources of relative weakening of nations I have suggested here are surely most in evidence in those areas of Western Europe and North America which have been most centrally involved in what Hobsbawm described as "the new supranational restructuring." If the nation is not really withering here, it would seem that it is changing. It is not, however, being replaced by any single "transnational culture." "It is not enough to imagine the global community; new and wider forms of political association and different types of cultural community will first have to emerge," Anthony D. Smith argues, apparently in a polemic against those commentators whom he sees as too inclined toward vocabularies of invention, construction, and imagination; "it is likely to be a piecemeal movement, disjointed and largely unplanned." With the latter I agree. But I think it is a process of the piecemeal, the disjointed, and the frequently unplanned (but sometimes planned), on variously large and small scale, which we can already observe.

PART XI

Global culture

HAS A GLOBAL CULTURE EMERGED? To the extent that globalization has a cultural aspect, has the spread of globalization resulted in cultural changes all over the world to such an extent that there is indeed something akin to global culture? How do we know? What are its specific manifestations?

Traditionally, culture has been territorially defined: ancient Greek culture, Chinese culture, American culture, and so on. Can culture be "de-territorialized" in the process of globalization? What happens to local, territorially specific cultures in the process? To take a specific example, global culture is often viewed as the spread of American culture to other lands. American consumer culture has penetrated all regions of the earth, often obliterating indigenous products and significantly altering traditional ways of life. Nevertheless, local cultures have not gone away; they may have incorporated American cultural influences, but they have not lost their identities. Thus the relationship between global and local cultures presents a fascinating question through which to study global history.

In the two essays that follow, these questions are given careful examination. John Joyce (Professor of Music at Tulane University) cites many examples to support his contention that "a global society through the world of music" may already have emerged. Ulf Hannerz, whose essay on nationalism and internationalism we have already encountered, pays particular attention to the "periphery" and analyzes the ways in which remote communities deal with forces of cultural homogenization, ranging from submission to resistance and to "creolization." No matter what perspective emerges, it is clear that the encountering between cultures, some of which are more global than others, defines one fundamental aspect of the contemporary world.

Chapter 21

John Joyce

THE GLOBALIZATION OF MUSIC

T HE INTRODUCTION OF WESTERN MUSIC to other parts of
the globe is, in itself, hardly recent: In most post-Columbian colonized regions,
it goes back several hundred years – as early as the first half of the sixteenth century
with the incursion of the Spanish conquistadors and their attendant missionaries into
Mesoamerica and the Andes. What is unique to the past hundred years is the vastly
more intensive imposition of Western music abroad. This is a genuinely contemporary phenomenon, beginning about a century ago but accelerating and expanding
dramatically after World War II. How has this phenomenon taken shape?

To begin with the present, a record review, entitled "Global Rachmaninoff",
crossed my desk. It is a glowing report of S.V. Rachmaninoff's Second Symphony,
performed with a Japanese conductor leading a Welsh orchestra. The conductor in
question was trained at a Tokyo conservatory and did master classes in Sweden with
an Estonian conductor and, later, with another Japanese conductor in Boston.
According to the reviewer, the BBC Welsh Symphony Orchestra, a little-known
provincial group, has been welded by Mr. Otaka into an absolutely first-rate
ensemble. The term *global* has been used increasingly of late to characterize just this
kind of phenomenon in the field of European concert music. A century ago, such
a juxtaposition of geographically disparate music and musicians would have been
unimaginable, and, even as recently as the 1950s, it was more than a little unusual.

Until the past generation, the world of European art music was almost entirely
Western, that is, bifurcated between Europe and the Americas, especially the
United States. By the turn of the [twentieth] century, the United States possessed
a half dozen symphony orchestras as good as the best of Europe. A majority of the
personnel of these orchestras were Europeans, as were all of the conductors,
without exception. The same was true of the major American opera companies in
this period, and, following this tradition, it was de rigueur for American composers
to hone their craft by finishing their studies in Europe.

From John Joyce, "The Globalization of Music," in Bruce Mazlish and Ralph Buultjens, eds,
Conceptualizing Global History (Boulder, CO: Westview Press, 1993), pp. 205–12, 214–19, 224.

By mid-century, with the maturing of American conservatories, the balance shifted. Well over half of the instrumentalists in US symphony and opera orchestras were American born and trained, a new generation of American conductors were taking the helm of the top US orchestras, and American opera singers were increasingly being imported by major European opera houses. The status of American composers, too, had risen, to the point that by the 1960s, their compositions were becoming part of the fixed repertory of European orchestras.

The entry into this close-knit and highly specialized field of music by non-Western musicians was entirely unexpected by most Western concert and opera audiences. Beginning in the 1960s and rapidly accelerating since then, instrumentalists and singers from a remarkable range of non-Western nations joined European and American orchestras and opera companies; many of them were thoroughly trained at Western music schools in their own countries, and others came to the West to perfect their craft. A new generation of non-Western piano and violin virtuosos, opera stars, and conductors have moved into the forefront of what is now a globally international concert scene, jetting not only between European and American cities but to the growing number of non-Western capitals boasting Western orchestras and concert halls. A casual survey of classical recordings of the past ten years offers eloquent testimony to this global development: Japanese conductors leading orchestras in Boston, Berlin, and Melbourne; Israeli conductors in Frankfurt and Arnhem; Hindi conductors in Toronto; an African-American conductor in Helsinki; a Korean conductor in Gothenburg and Paris; a Mexican Amerindian conductor in Dallas; Korean and Japanese violinists recording major violin concertos with orchestras in London, Berlin, Leningrad, New York, and Montreal; and a Japanese pianist, trained in Tokyo and Vienna, recording the complete sonatas and concertos of Mozart. To this I can add recent "live" performances: of Palestrina masses by a Polynesian choir in Samoa; a Japanese baritone performing Schubert's song-cycle, "Die Winterreise," on five successive nights to packed theaters in Tokyo; one of Tokyo's six major symphony orchestras playing Strauss waltzes with sobbing Viennese "glides" and luftpausen after upbeats, another doing the cycle of nine Beethoven symphonies, and a third devoting a concert to the works of the American composers Aaron Copland, George Gershwin, and Charles Ives. Perhaps most remarkably, given the radically dissimilar singing methods of the two source cultures, there is the quite recent entry of designers of Asian-Pacific provenance into the bel-canto style of European opera. There are video recordings of a young Japanese coloratura soprano executing, with great virtuosity, the role of the Queen of the Night in *The Magic Flute*; a Chinese lyric soprano singing the role of Mimi in *La Bohème*; a Maori dramatic soprano performing, with an appropriately opulent vocal tone, the role of the Marschallin in *Der Rosenkavalier*. Nor has there been a dearth of non-Western composers working in contemporary Western idioms. Japanese and Korean as well as Greek and Turkish composers have mastered, with effortless facility, such abstract, nationally "neutral" styles as atonality, serialism, and various forms of electronic music.

In this closing decade of the twentieth century, the remarkable embracing of Western classical music by culturally alien societies proceeds apace and would, indeed, appear to be a primary example of the process of globalization in the field of music. And yet, while its striking development is certainly an important aspect of cultural interaction in music, it must be regarded in the first instance as a further expansion of the history of Western music – a unilateral and, therefore, a more superficial manifestation of musical globalization. [. . .]

By the end of the nineteenth century, a watershed had been reached in Western musical influence. A wide repertory of church hymns and Western band music had been absorbed by those far-flung colonial choirs and wind ensembles. The universal adoption of these polished Western musical forms served as conspicuous emblems of their collective ability to adapt themselves to the "higher" accomplishments of Western culture. Here lay the foundation of their future mastering of Europe's highest genres of art music. In virtually every more or less colonized region, from Japan, Korea, and China to Egypt, Lebanon, Madagascar, and sub-Saharan Africa, church choirs evolved into schools for choral singing and voice training, and military bands turned into instrumental academies. By the 1920s, many of these were consolidated into Western-style music conservatories, and an infrastructure for a burgeoning of Western concert music was in place.

But this whole development, as I have already suggested, is only part of a more intricate pattern of musical interchange between the Western and non-Western worlds that has unfolded in the present century. The slavish mimicry of an invading culture's forms, no matter how accomplished, is regarded by modern cultural anthropologists as a superficial facet of intercultural influence precisely because it is formally imposed. These scholars, whose field of research is itself a part of the intensive interchange of world cultures today, have come to recognize that, given sufficient contact between two cultures, a more informal and open interchange takes place. The host culture's response becomes more active; emulation leads to variation, adoption to adaption. Bruno Nettl was thinking primarily of this more fertile stage of musical response when he declared the "intensive imposition" of Western music abroad to be "the most significant phenomenon in the global history of music . . . of the last hundred years." "What is of concern to us here," he stated, "is the way in which the world's musical traditions have responded to the invitation . . . it is the variety of responses and of ways in which [they] have managed to maintain themselves in the face of the onslaught."

Here, then, is a second view of musical globalization, a perhaps more advanced stage in that cultural reaction from beyond a strictly Eurocentric sphere of influence. If the acceleration of Western colonialism that began a century ago actively fostered the adoption of Western music, it also opened the door for the adaptation of that music. Nettl stated it well: "As European and American nations began the business of colonizing more extensively even than before [the 1800s], Western technology clearly gained the upper hand, and there developed a musical system [the European] obviously symbolic of this superiority, but also adaptable to other musics." This was a crucial moment in the evolution of world music. What had been an age-old business – the meeting and commingling of different musical cultures – that occurred infrequently and sporadically since it was dependent upon the migration of human groups was now, on the threshold of the twentieth century, poised to become a common event on a worldwide scale. And Nettl here identified the factor that, beyond all others, is fundamental to the globalization of music: technology.

To better understand the particulars of this adaptive "stage" of musical globalization and, indeed, to place the complex developments of twentieth-century world music in a comprehensible perspective, it would be well to examine the relationship between technology and music, particularly since the beginning of the industrial revolution. In the narrower sense, the technology of music refers to its handicrafts, chiefly the making of musical instruments but also the writing of musical scores. Both of these activities have become increasingly mechanized, beginning with mechanically printed musical scores in the sixteenth century and the factory production of instruments in the nineteenth century.

Since the industrial revolution and particularly in the past hundred years, technology has been increasingly linked to music as an ever more efficient means of dissemination. In all previous centuries, music circulated by means of travel – the transporting of instruments, of scores, or of the musicians themselves. Because travel before the nineteenth century was limited to "natural" methods of locomotion, such as horse-drawn vehicles and wind-driven vessels, it was an arduous and time-consuming endeavor. Distances between places were a major obstacle to communication and severely curtailed the spread of a given music from one region to another. In the Middle Ages, the compositions of even the greatest composers, each of which might exist in two or three manuscript copies, were known in only a few court circles, monasteries, and cathedral towns. As late as the eighteenth century, the works of Johann Sebastian Bach were virtually unknown outside Saxony, his immediate region of Germany. The nonliterate folk musics of the rural regions of Europe were utterly isolated from one another, as were the major music cultures in separate parts of the world. As I have shown, the meeting of such musics occurred through the uncommon and fitful processes of migration or exploration.

The achievements most central to nineteenth-century invention were those that significantly enhanced long-distance communication and, therefore, the dissemination of music. In the first half of the century – Carlyle's "mechanical age" – this took the form of two vital developments in rapid transportation, both made possible by James Watt's steam engine: steamships (in regular use from 1824) and railroads (in regular use from 1830). These twin land and sea media rapidly transformed the face of long-distance travel. By mid-century, a network of railroads interlocked Europe; by 1870, the Atlantic and Pacific coasts of the United States were linked by a transcontinental railroad line; and by 1891, the trans-Siberian railroad made it possible to travel by train through the entire Eurasian continent, from Lisbon to Vladivostok.

The steamship radically shortened transoceanic travel in these same years, beginning with the transatlantic crossing of the steam-powered American schooner *Savannah* in 1819. In 1838, Great Britain inaugurated a regular steamship service across the Atlantic, and by the 1850s steam travel to Asia was offered by Great Britain, France, and the Netherlands. In 1869, the opening of the Suez Canal cut the length of Asian voyages virtually in half.

With the girding of the earth in rapid, mechanized transportation, distance ceased to be an insurmountable obstacle to communication; international exchange at every level became commonplace. The establishment of world fairs and international time zones in the second half of the century symbolized this new global integration. Their effect on the dissemination of music can be exemplified by a single event in 1889.

In that year, the composer Claude Debussy attended the Grand World Exposition in Paris, where he first heard the exotic music of Southeast Asia. He was particularly struck by the shimmering sounds of the Javanese gamelan, an Indonesian orchestra composed of tuned metallic and wooden percussion instruments. The music was, in all respects, utterly different from any European music. Its complex interplay of bell-like timbres, pentatonic scales, and hypnotically repetitious rhythms were to affect Debussy's emerging compositional style more radically than the most progressive trends in European art music of the time. His mature style, a wholly original synthesis of European and Asian techniques, was to form one of the primary bridges to twentieth-century music.

The significance of this event, beyond the fact that it was the first direct encounter between a European composer and East Asian music, is that it could not have happened even a single generation earlier. The appearance of the Javanese musicians at the 1889 Paris exposition was only possible because a shortened steamship route to Asia, through the Suez Canal, had been completed just twenty years before. The era of international music tours had begun.

If the obstacle of distance was effectively reduced by advances in mechanized travel, it was virtually erased by the radically new technology of the second half of the century – telecommunications. Based upon the transmission and reception of electromagnetic waves between two remote parties, this was a true quantum leap in communications technology. It redefined the basis of technology itself, from the invention and building of mechanical apparatus to the discovery and control of electrical phenomenon – a scientific process that runs from the development of telegraphy in the 1830s to the most sophisticated electronic automation today.

The first two telecommunication media, the telegraph and the telephone, firmly established the viability of electrical communication, but because they were vehicles of verbal information, they had no direct effect on the diffusion of music. The third medium, however, transformed it. This was the discovery and refinement of wireless communication at the end of the nineteenth century. The wireless transcended the unidirectional transmission of electrical signals through the closed medium of a cable or wire, by transmitting them omni-directionally through the open medium of air. This rendered telecommunications universal by "broadcasting" signals to anyone with the proper receiving equipment. Wireless broadcasting was initially applied to the transmission of simple Morse code signals (called wireless telegraphy, refined in 1901). But its true potential was tapped when broadcasting was equipped with a newly developed vacuum tube capable of "modulating" the flexible sound patterns of speech (or music) onto the transmitted signal and amplifying them at the receiver end. This permitted the direct transmission of speech (or music) that came to be called "radio" broadcasting. Thus, to the universality of the medium (wireless telecommunication) was added the public utility of the message (information and entertainment), a combination that was to make radio one of the seminal mass communications media of the twentieth century. Statistics are eloquent: The first commercial radio station (KDKA in Pittsburgh) broadcast to 15,000 receivers in 1920; by 1927, there were 700 stations in the United States alone, broadcasting to nearly 8 million receivers.

As radio broadcasting began in earnest in the 1920s, it was powerfully reinforced by still another seminal nineteenth-century technology reaching commercial maturity at the same time: the phonograph. This was the mechanism to artificially reproduce sound, discovered and invented by Thomas Edison in 1877. Though he conceived it as a means of recording telephone conversation and other human speech, its commercial potential quickly proved to lie in the reproduction of music.

By 1900, a number of fledgling recording companies such as Victor and Columbia were competing with the Edison Talking Phonograph company to produce recordings of famous performers, most of them classical artists such as the opera singer Enrico Caruso and the piano virtuoso Ignaz Paderewski. It was thought – naively – that this kind of music was the proper subject for recording because of its prestige and greater historical value. But this notion was forever erased by the spectacular sales of popular dance records, including the first jazz recordings in 1917. From 1920 until the present, popular records have been the profit-earning items that subsidize classical records.

It was at this juncture that the paths of radio and phonograph crossed. The year 1921 saw the release of inexpensive home models of both radios and phonographs. They quickly became fixtures in the American home and complemented each other nicely: Radio found in records a perfect medium for entertainment broadcasting, and listeners brought popular records heard on the radio. The two media came together in another important way, as well: In 1925, the electrical elements of the radio (vacuum tube amplification, microphone, electromagnetic speakers, and electric power source) were applied to the phonograph and vastly improved its sound quality.

The phonograph record was a completely new element in musical life, eventually reaching and changing every aspect of it. Audiences, performers, music historians and critics, music educators, even composers – all were touched in some way by this invention. Sound recording, the first means of capturing a musical performance in a permanent and portable form, revolutionized the dissemination of music by sales of the records themselves and by the broadcasting of them over radio and television and on film sound tracks. As noted earlier, before this century, the exposure of all listeners and musicians to "live" music was sporadic and severely limited. If one lived in Vienna in Beethoven's day, one could hear his music only when a live performance took place, which was only moderately frequent. If one lived in Philadelphia at that time, opportunities to hear his music – and Philadelphia lacked a symphony orchestra in those days – were far less frequent, perhaps only an occasional evening of his chamber music. And if one lived in an American frontier town like Louisville, Kentucky, opportunities were virtually nonexistent – unless one had that rare commodity at this early date, a piano.

The comparison with the situation today is startling. In the twentieth century, we have an unprecedented awareness and knowledge of an incredible range of music, gained, in large part, by hearing this music on recordings. Just a century ago, orchestra conductors had to struggle from place to place to hear a performance of a Beethoven symphony – or to conduct a performance themselves. Today, anyone with a record player or tape recorder can listen to all nine symphonies in a single day. In a single afternoon, a listener can hear the music of Stephen Foster, J.S. Bach, Felix Mendelssohn, George Gershwin, the Rolling Stones, and Igor Stravinsky or a Javanese gamelan, a Navajo harvest dance, a Hindu raga, a Japanese koto ensemble, a mariachi band, and a Cajun band. In short, the sound recording has been a unique tool for exploring, with the greatest efficiency, both the history and geography of music. [. . .]

To modern ethnomusicologists, those entering the field after about 1960, this early emphasis on non-Western musics as fixed systems rather than dynamic processes seems myopic: Perhaps it was the inevitable myopia of an incipient field of research with too few samples for analysis, but it was also the myopia of historically oriented Western scholars attempting to come up with modern, ephemeral musics. Whatever the causes, today's ethnomusicologists have the improved perspective of nearly a half century of dramatically accelerated interchange between the Western and non-Western worlds, beginning after World War II. They have had a broader experience of Western music, including jazz, folk music, and the various strands of popular music. They have also lived in an environment in which the sounds of non-Western music are readily available (through radio, recordings, and so forth) and no longer a shock. And many of them have experienced direct contact with non-Western peoples through military occupation in World War II, Korea, and Vietnam, through organizations such as the Peace Corps, and, as jet travel increased accessibility, as tourists. The striking feature of "exotic" peoples and their cultures is no longer their fixed isolation but the ways in which rapid change has taken place and the problems of coping with Western values and technology.

These younger ethnomusicologists were thus predisposed to observe the mutability of non-Western musics and to take an active interest in the effects of adaptive change on a given musical system. Toward this end, they developed or borrowed a number of flexible concepts to explain and describe kinds and degrees of change. Basic to all of these is the concept of centrality, the notion that in any musical idiom, certain features are more central than others and function as hallmarks. They can be recognized by their pervasiveness in a musical repertory and how they symbolize the style of that repertory, both to its own society and to outsiders. Separating central and non-central features of a music is important to a study of adaption since the adapting musician, rather than adopting a new music outright, selects certain traits and not others; on the other hand, he or she may choose to preserve at all costs certain traits of his or her own music in the process. The concept of centrality enables scholars to define Western music, despite its great variety, as a unitary concept. However different the styles of classical, "Broadway," folk, jazz, or rock, they all share certain central features, easily recognizable to musicians of other cultures. In addition to the obvious elements of Western music – harmony, even-tempered scales, metrical rhythm, notation – defined by their predecessors, modern ethnomusicologists extend the concept of centrality to aspects of musical process or behavior in Western music: the predilection for ensemble performance, especially large orchestras; the importance placed on planning, with the norm being the carefully composed piece, meticulously rehearsed; the idea of presenting music as an end in itself, at a public concert; and the emphasis on doing what is difficult and showing it off.

Basic, too, is the concept of acculturation, which refers to the process of adaption itself. It is defined, variously, as the modification of a primitive culture by contact with an advanced culture or the process of intercultural borrowing between diverse peoples resulting in new and blended patterns, dictionary descriptions that perhaps reflect the changing biases of scholars toward the concept of cultural change. Degrees of acculturation are loosely measured by the complementary concepts of Westernization and modernization. Westernization is the substitution of central features of Western music for their non-Western analogues, often with the sacrifice of essential facets of the adapting musical tradition. Modernization is less drastic: the incidental movement of a music system or its components in the direction of Western music without, however, requiring major changes in those aspects of the non-Western tradition that are central and essential. Bearing on the process of acculturation is the basic idea of syncretism, that is, the confluence of similar or compatible culture traits to create new, mixed forms. This concept requires the recognition that certain cultures or musical forms are compatible, perhaps by having similar centralities.

The classic application of this concept to music is in the confrontation of African and Western musics in the New World, as opposed to the confrontation of Amerindian and Western musics. It is accepted by ethnomusicologists that African and Western musics have such compatibility (a major-sounding scale, use of harmonized thirds, underlying steady beat, and so on), while Amerindian and Western musics strikingly lack any compatibility. Hence, there is a rich variety of Afro-European musical blends in Afro-American musical styles and a singular dearth of any such blendings in Amerindian musics, even today.

The number of case studies bearing directly on the adaptive interaction between non-Western and Western music, though still small, is beginning to grow rapidly, and the conceptual framework of ethnomusicology since about 1950 has been changing to accommodate the new directions suggested by these studies. To describe the process of adaption on an individual case basis would easily require an entire volume. For the purposes of this chapter, a few generalizations by region regarding the degree of adaption found in each will suffice.

To start with a richly documented area, it can be said that significant accultur-ative musical blends are the norm in sub-Saharan Africa. As mentioned, there is a fairly strong degree of syncretism between the two base cultures, Europe and Africa. Reinforcing this is the fact that African music was brought to America in the centuries of slavery and had already blended with European styles. The modern examples of blended African music have cross-fertilized with the Afro-American music of the United States and the Caribbean, resulting in such popular musics as highlife, Congo jazz, and juju, all marked by simplified Western harmony, emphasis on brass instruments, Latin American-style drum rhythms, and the use of string bass and guitar. All these musics have audible style influences from reggae, Mexican tropical, rhythm and blues, and samba.

In the Middle East, it is quite different. Various degrees of Westernization and modernization have occurred but only with difficulty. As Bruno Nettl indicated, the source musics – European and Muslim – are so fundamentally different, not only in sound ideas but also in the whole conception of the use of music, that the host music seems to be attempting to resolve the basic conflict. There are cases of outright adoption of Western classical music (with many pianos and violins) and the formation of large ensembles of Muslim string instruments in the manner of the Western orchestra, and a fad has developed for playing local instruments in Western-style concerts, with a strong emphasis on Western-style virtuosity. But in general, the basic Muslim functions of musical performance, never done for the pure pleasure of listening, have remained strongly intact. In sum, throughout the Middle East, there is a fitful mixture of Westernized and modernized tendencies.

The subcontinent of India has shown a remarkable resistance to a radical absorption of Western music. Where in Iran, for example, there are traditions of European classical recitals and concerts (on violin, piano, or guitar) as well as various nightclubs where a generic Western dance music is played, in India, the powerful institution of the country's own "classical" raga performances, rooted in a quasi-religious format and function, is still the central musical tradition. In fact, such Western instruments as the violin and the guitar have been totally absorbed into these performances; some younger Indian violinists and guitarists have even hotly contested the suggestion that their instruments are from Europe!

Regarding Southeast Asia, I will quote Nettl's succinct characterization:

> Southeast Asia may be the one [culture area] coming closest to practicing virtual rejection of the impinging music; and perhaps, along with Java and Bali, it comes closest to having a full-blown musical system in a modern urban context built almost entirely on a repertory of non-Western sound.

Finally, the situation in Northeast Asia is completely different. In Japan and Korea, Western music of all sorts has had a strong impact. In urban areas, Western classical music and all kinds of Western popular music and jazz have been so extensively and effectively cloned that these cities can almost be regarded as annexes of Western cities. Interestingly, the various forms of traditional musics in both nations have been perfectly preserved as "shrines" to their histories. Japan and Korea have been almost totally Westernized. [. . .]

But the processes of Westernization and modernization reflected therein are presently being superseded by more powerful Westernizing tendencies in global music, namely, urbanization and its close corollary, industrialization. These concepts and the processes they describe are hardly new. Cities have existed in non-Western societies for centuries, and urbanization is not, in itself, an effect of Western culture. But the kind of rapid urbanization that has taken place in the latter half of the twentieth century is associated with the development of Western technology, Western-style nation-states, and large-scale immigration. Industrialization, on the other hand, is a distinctly Western development, but it began as early as the late Renaissance and developed to an initial peak in the century of the Industrial Revolution.

What is new is the extraordinary escalation of urbanization and industrialization in the past few decades into worldwide cultural forces. Recent urban growth, especially in Third World countries, has been phenomenal – an estimated 70 percent of the world's people now live in cities. Many of these cities are newly established urban centers in underdeveloped nations; others are older cities that have expanded into large, multicultural units.

Industrialization, for its part, has been virtually redefined by Western space-age technology and has been the trigger and central shaping force of the rapid urbanization of the globe. Jet travel has bound these cities into an integral worldwide urban network, and the ever-expanding advancements in electronic communications (radio, television, videocassette, cinema, satellite, and computer) have imposed on them all a single, Western-based social structure and a common set of Westernized living patterns. What has developed and developed swiftly from this is a new form of society: an international urban culture that operates on its own scale and follows its own trends, beyond the boundaries of the nation-state. Its significance to the process of globalization is, surely, central, if not yet entirely foreseen. Its significance to the future of global music is, on the other hand, already clear, namely a phenomenally rapid expansion – through the new transnational urban infrastructure – of Western popular music around the globe.

This was surely an inevitable, if abrupt, event, given the urban nature of popular music and its intimate ties to electronic technology. In its characteristic twentieth-century form, popular music first coalesced in America in the 1920s, in conjunction with the twin emergence of commercial radio and the phonograph. From the beginning and throughout its history, this music has been commercially directed toward the large urban and suburban audience. Toward this end, popular music has exploited electronics not only as a means of efficient dissemination but increasingly as a part of its sound production and, hence, its communicative impact. By the 1960s, with the coming of American rock music and its mass youth audience, popular music had become almost purely a technological entity, using electronics as a means of amplification, of sound manipulation and distortion, and of developing new instruments, such as the electric violin and trumpet, the electronic piano, and the computerized sound synthesizer. It was at this stage and in this form that popular music began its dramatic expansion around the world.

The internationalization of Western popular music is an event of far greater potential significance than the nearly simultaneous internationalization of Western classical music. Despite a continuing "official" resistance in many nations to the former phenomenon and a continuing "official" encouragement of the latter, it is popular music that has proven the more hardy survivor in foreign soil and begun to develop an international life of its own. With the possible exceptions of Korea and Japan, Western classical music has made no more impact on the larger populace than it has in Europe and America.

This is, of course, partly attributable to the simpler nature of popular music – shorter in duration, simpler melodies, fewer chords, and, always, a pronounced and constant beat. Beyond this, there is the commercial dimension of all popular music. Reflecting its origins in America, popular music was, from the start, bought, adapted, and marketed by business enterprises dedicated to detecting and serving the tastes of an independent consumer public. As such, it has been an open, democratic music that was, in the apt phrase of S. Frederick Starr, "truly popular and, equally important, in no way beholden to the state for its creation and maintenance." It is this capacity to thrive and develop outside the control of "official" approval or disapproval that accounts, as much as any factor, for its spectacular ability to travel.

For whatever reasons, the rise of a worldwide popular music linked to the West and to the United States in particular is a phenomenon that bids fair to produce the first music of genuinely global range. [. . .]

Thus, as we approach the year 2000, we may already have entered a global society through the world of music. Certainly, it has become clear that, in a world of total mass communication, music, that most fluid of human languages, has assumed an entirely new significance. It has become a form of energy in its own right that is capable, whatever its style or verbal message, of unifying people, regardless of race, region, or language. Just how this new potential will be played out in the coming years only time will tell.

Chapter 22

Ulf Hannerz

SCENARIOS FOR PERIPHERAL CULTURES

THE TWENTIETH CENTURY has been a unique period in world cultural history. Humankind has finally bid farewell to that world which could with some credibility be seen as a cultural mosaic, of separate pieces with hard, well-defined edges. Because of the great increase in the traffic in culture, the large-scale transfer of meaning systems and symbolic forms, the world is increasingly becoming one not only in political and economic terms, as in the climactic period of colonialism, but in terms of its cultural construction as well; a global ecumene of persistent cultural interaction and exchange. This, however, is no egalitarian global village. What we see now is quite firmly structured as an asymmetry of center and periphery. With regard to cultural flow, the periphery, out there in a distant territory, is more the taker than the giver of meaning and meaningful form. Much as we feel called upon to make note of any examples of counterflow, it is difficult to avoid the conclusion that at least as things stand now, the relationship is lopsided.

We do not assume that this is the end point of these globalizing developments. The shaping of world culture is an ongoing process, toward future and still uncertain states. But perhaps one conceivable outcome has come to dominate the imagery of the cultural future, as a master scenario against which every alternative scenario has to be measured. Let us call it a scenario of global homogenization of culture. The murderous threat of cultural imperialism is here rhetorically depicted as involving the high-tech culture of the metropolis, with powerful organizational backing, facing a defenseless, small-scale folk culture. But "cultural imperialism," it also becomes clear, has more to do with market than with empire. The alleged prime mover behind the pan-human replication of uniformity is late Western capitalism, luring forever more communities into dependency on the fringes of an expanding worldwide consumer society. Homogenization results mainly from the center-to-periphery flow of commoditized culture. Consequently, the coming homogenous world culture according to this view will by and large be a version of

From Ulf Hannerz, "Scenarios for Peripheral Cultures," in Anthony D. King, ed., *Culture, Globalization and the World-System: Contemporary Conditions for the Representation of Identity* (Department of Art and Art History, State University of New York at Binghamton, 1991), pp. 107–11, 121–8.

contemporary Western culture, and the loss of local culture would show itself most distinctively at the periphery.

This master scenario has several things going for it. A quick look at the world today affords it a certain intrinsic plausibility; it may seem like a mere continuation of present trends. It has, of course, the great advantage of simplicity. And it is dramatic. There is the sense of fatefulness, the prediction of the irreversible loss of large parts of the combined heritage of humanity. As much of the diversity of its behavioral repertoire is wiped out, *Homo sapiens* becomes more like other species – in large part making its own environment, in contrast with them, but at the same time adapting to it in a single, however complex, way.

There is also another scenario for global cultural process, although more subterranean; thus not so often coming out to complete openly with the global homogenization scenario. We may call it the peripheral corruption scenario, for what it portrays as a recurrent sequence is one where the center offers its high ideals and its best knowledge, given some institutional form, and where the periphery first adopts them and then soon corrupts them. The scenario shows elected heads of state becoming presidents for life, then bizarre, merciless emperors. It shows Westminster and Oxbridge models being swallowed by the bush. The center, in the end, cannot win; not at the periphery.

Biases

The peripheral corruption scenario is there for the people of the center to draw on when they are pessimistic about their own role in improving the world, and doubtful and/or cynical about the periphery. It is deeply ethnocentric, in that it posits a very uneven distribution of virtue, and in that it denies the validity and worth of any transformations at the periphery of what was originally drawn from the center. There is little question of cultural difference here, but rather of a difference between culture and no-culture, between civilization and savagery.

The global homogenization scenario may have a greater intellectual appeal than its shadowy competitor, but I think a brief exercise in the sociology of knowledge may suggest that this is because many of us share some sources of bias which contribute to making it plausible.

First of all, this scenario, too, may draw on a certain kind of ethnocentrism. The global homogenization scenario focuses on things that we, as observers and commentators from the center, are very familiar with: our fast foods, our soft drinks, our sitcoms. The idea that they are or will be everywhere, and enduringly powerful everywhere, makes our culture even more important and worth arguing about, and relieves us of the real strains of having to engage with other living, complicated, puzzling cultures. Grieving for the vanishing Other is after all in some ways easier than confronting it live and kicking.

Furthermore, the homogenization scenario is directly tied to a line of domestic cultural critique. There are surely those who see the worldwide spread of their culture as a cause for celebration, but for many of us it would be something to regret. And those at the center who have taken the greatest, reasonably consistent interest in the circumstances of life at the periphery, for some decades at least now, have usually been those who are also critically inclined toward many of the effects of the market economy back home. The homogenization scenario, then, allows the export, and globalization, of cultural critique; or alternatively formulated, bringing in fuel from the periphery for local debates at the center.

Finally, one may have some doubts about the sense of time in the homogenization scenario. If indeed there is often an idea that peripheral cultures come defenseless, unprepared, to the encounter with metropolitan culture, that they are insufficiently organized and are taken by surprise, then this notion would frequently entail a measure of ignorance of the continuous historical development of center–periphery contacts. It may well be that the First World has been present in the consciousness of many Third World people a great deal longer than the Third World has been on the minds of most First World people. The notion of the sudden engagement between the cultures of center and periphery may thus in large part be an imaginative by-product of the late awakening to global realities of many of us inhabitants of the center.

Perhaps all of us began long ago to nourish doubts about the two scenarios I have identified, and would be ready on demand to improvise a critique of each. Yet some of their continued viability as constructs in the mind of the general public may depend on a lack of available alternatives, alternatives which would also offer ways of thinking and talking about what may happen at the periphery in a world of increasingly connected culture. As any such scenario that we would find reasonably satisfactory would probably have to be more complicated than these two, and thus more demanding of our and everybody else's patience, it might automatically be at some rhetorical disadvantage. Yet if it can both identify the weaknesses of the competitors and use whatever grain of truth may be in them, it might do better in long-term credibility.

As an anthropologist, I may have other biases than those which seem to be built into the global homogenization and peripheral corruption scenarios. Anthropologists are perhaps forever rooting for diversity; some would suggest we have a vested interest in it. In any case, I see the scrutiny of such scenarios, and attempts to formulate alternatives to them, as an important task for a macroanthropology of contemporary culture – not the only task, but not a very special one set aside in its own intellectual corner either. What is required is rather an overall conceptualization of contemporary culture which incorporates a sense of the pervasiveness of globalization. I also think that this is a task which one may well try and deal with in relatively general terms. Anthropologists, again, may have some predilection for variability and for the particular, exceptional, and unique, but I do not think it serves us well to respond to the scenario of global homogenization, or that of peripheral corruption, only as ethnographers with a myriad of stories. If we want an alternative to them, it had better be at a level of generality where the points of difference can be readily recognized.

Yet I would hardly be an anthropologist if there were not some concrete ethnography lurking behind my abstractions, and I should say that it is a more general familiarity with, as well as specific research experiences in, West African urban life that have done most to provoke my interest in the center–periphery relationships of world culture and to shape my gut reactions to the scenarios I have pointed to. [. . .]

Prospects: saturation and maturation

Let me approach now the question of longer-term trends of cultural process at the periphery. The interactions between the several frameworks of cultural process depend on their respective contents and modes of organization as well as their relative strengths, which may change over time. The movement framework, about which I have said least here, obviously waxes and wanes. The state, especially apart from what it does in the field of education, is quite variably strong. It may speak in a very loud voice in its celebration of national ideology, or it may be barely audible. With regard to what I described before as policies of cultural welfare, one has to be especially aware that peripheral states are often what Gunnar Myrdal some twenty years ago described as "soft states," with very limited capacity for policy implementation. This tends to be obvious enough in the area of cultural policy.

Clearly the performance of the state in managing cultural flow depends in some significant part on material conditions. The soft state is often an impoverished state which may ill afford to maintain a powerful cultural apparatus. The factor of material bases is no less important within the market framework – when culture is commoditized, it has to be materially compensated for.

This simple but fundamental fact seems often to be treated in a rather cavalier manner within the global homogenization scenario. One would have to take a range of possibilities into account here. If the involvement of the periphery with the international division of labor is not to its advantage, at any one time or over time, this would rather suggest that the periphery through its involvement with the world system becomes a poorer market for a transnational flow of cultural commodities; with the possible exception of what we have labeled "cultural dumping," which may involve low, affordable prices, but otherwise often unattractive goods. Conversely, of course, if some part of the periphery becomes nouveau riche, it may be flooded with the cultural commodities of the center. In recent times, again, the economies of some parts of the periphery, including Nigeria, have been on a rollercoaster ride, and it is not altogether obvious what are the longer term implications of such shifts in the cultural market. One question is certainly at what points local entrepreneurs will become more active in import substitution, and in what form.

There are noteworthy uncertainties here, then, which we have to bear in mind even as we try to think of what may be trends of cumulative change. This much granted, I propose that it may be useful to identify two tendencies in the longer-term reconstruction of peripheral cultures within the global ecumene. One might think of each (although as will be noted later, I prefer not to) as a distinctive scenario and the peripheral corruption scenarios respectively.

I will call one the saturation tendency, and the other the maturation tendency. The maturation tendency is that which may be seen as a version of the global homogenization scenario, with some more detailed interest in historical sequence. It would suggest that as the transnational cultural influences, of whatever sort but in large part certainly market organized, and operating in a continuously open structure, unendingly bound on the sensibilities of the people of the periphery, peripheral culture will step by step assimilate more and more of the important meanings and forms, becoming gradually indistinguishable from the center. At any one time, what is considered local culture is a little more penetrated by transnational forms than what went before it as local culture, although at any one time, until the end point is reached, the contrast between local and transnational may still be drawn, and still be regarded as significant. The cultural differences celebrated and recommended for safeguarding now may only be a pale reflection of what once existed, and sooner or later they will be gone as well.

What is suggested here is that the center, through the frameworks of cultural process within which the transnational flow passes most readily, and among which the market framework is certainly conspicuous, cumulatively colonizes the minds of the periphery, with a corresponding institutionalization of its forms, getting the periphery so "hooked" that soon enough there is no real opportunity for choice. The mere fact that these forms originate in the center makes them even more attractive, a peculiar but undeniable aspect of commodity esthetics in the periphery. This colonization is understood to proceed through relentless cultural bombardment, through the redundancy of its seductive messages. As the market framework interpenetrates with that of forms of life, the latter becomes reconstructed around their dependence on what was initially alien, using it for their practical adaptations, seeing themselves wholly or at least partially through it.

It would appear, however, that one can turn this sort of argument at least some of the way around. The form of life framework, as I have said, also has a redundancy of its own, built up through its ever recurrent daily activities, perhaps at least as strong as, or stronger than, any redundancy that the market framework can ever achieve. It may involve interpersonal relationships, resulting configurations of self and other, characteristic uses of symbolic modes. There is perhaps a core here to which the market framework cannot reach, not even in the longer term, a core of culture which is not itself easily commoditized and to which the commodities of the market are not altogether relevant.

The inherent cultural power of the form of life framework could perhaps also be such that it colonizes the market framework, rather than vice versa. This is more in line with what I see as the maturation tendency; a notion which has its affinities with the peripheral corruption scenario, although probably with other evaluative overtones. The periphery, it is understood here, takes its time reshaping metropolitan culture to its own specifications. It is in phase one, so to speak, that the metropolitan forms in the periphery are most marked by their purity; but on closer scrutiny they turn out to stand there fairly ineffective, perhaps vulnerable, in their relative isolation. In a phase two, and in innumerable phases thereafter, as they are made to interact with whatever else exists in their new setting, there may be a mutual influence, but the metropolitan forms are somehow no longer so easily recognizable – they become hybridized. In these later phases, the terms of the cultural market for one thing are in a reasonable measure set from within the peripheral forms of life, as these have come to be constituted, highly variable of course in the degree to which they are themselves culturally defined in the terms drawn from the center.

Obviously what I have already said about the creativity of popular culture in much of the Third World, and not least in West Africa, fits in here. Local cultural entrepreneurs have gradually mastered the alien cultural forms which reach them through the transnational commodity flow and in other ways, taking them apart, tampering and tinkering with them in such a way that the resulting new forms are more responsive to, and at the same time in part outgrowths of, local everyday life.

In this connection I should return to the doubts I expressed before about the sense of time, or perhaps lacking sense of time, in the scenario of global homogenization. The onslaught of transnational influences, as often described or hinted at, seems just a bit too sudden. In West Africa, such influences have been filtering into the coastal societies for centuries already, although in earlier periods on a smaller scale and by modest means. There has been time to absorb the foreign influences, and to modify the modifications in turn and to fit shifting cultural forms to developing social structures, to situations and emerging audiences. This, then, is the local scene which is already in place to meet the transnational culture industries of the twentieth century. It is not a scene where the peripheral culture is utterly defenseless, but rather one where locally evolving alternatives to imports are available, and where there are people at hand to keep performing innovative acts of cultural brokerage.

The periphery in creolization

I should begin to pull things together. It is probably evident that I place some emphasis on the theme of maturation, and that I continue to resist the idea of saturation, at least in its unqualified form, which is that of global homogenization. In fact, in that form, it has suspiciously much in common with that 1940s or 1950s imagery of mass culture within the metropole which showed a faceless, undifferentiated crowd drowning in a flood of mediocre but mass-produced cultural commodities. Since then, metropolitan scholarship at home has mostly moved away from the imagery, toward much more subtle conceptions of the differentiation of publics, and the contextualized reception of culture industry products. Exporting the older, rather worn-out and compromised notion to the periphery, consequently, looks suspiciously like another case of cultural dumping.

It is no doubt a trifle unfortunate that there seems to be no single scenario to put in the place of that of global homogenization, with similarly strong – but more credible – claims to predictive power. But then prediction is not something the human sciences have been very good at, and, in the case of the global ordering of culture, what I have said may at least contribute to some understanding of why this is so. The diversity of interlocking principles for the organization of cultural process involves too many uncertainties to allow us to say much that is very definite with regard to the aggregate outcome.

A few points about how things seem to be going may at least sensitize to some issues in studying culture in the world, now and in the future. The center–periphery structure is one undeniable fact. When studying culture, we now have to think about the flow between places as well as that within them. Each society at the periphery, each Third World society, has its own cultural distinctiveness, but it is not as absolute as it has been (which was never quite absolute). Increasingly, distinctiveness is a matter of degree, as it has long been within that North Atlantic ecumene made up of a number of societies of the center and the semi-periphery; let us say between the United States, Germany, Sweden, and Portugal. Interactions of many sorts have been going on in this ecumene over a very long time and the cultural affinities are obvious, yet nobody would deny that there are differences as well. Increasingly, however, we find the cultural differences within societies, rather than between them. If you look within some society for what is most uniquely distinctive, you will perhaps look among peasants rather than bank mangers, in the country rather than in the city, among the old rather than the young. And obviously the reason is that through the operation of the varied frameworks for cultural process, and the interaction between them, some meanings and meaningful forms become much more localized, much more tied to space, than others. Using the word "societies" in the plural as we often do in a loose manner, conflating its meaning with that of "states," which refers to undeniably territorial phenomena, we are misled toward very partial understanding of contemporary cultural process as some of its frameworks are not contained within particular states.

If there is any term which has many of the right associations by which to describe the ongoing, historically cumulative cultural interrelatedness between center and periphery, it is, I think, "creolization," a borrowing from particular social and cultural histories by way of a more generalized linguistics. I will not dwell on the potential of a creolization scenario for peripheral cultures very long here, and it may be that what I take from a rather volatile field of linguistic thought is little more than a rough metaphor. Yet it has a number of components which are appropriate enough. I like it because it suggests that cultures, like languages, can be intrinsically of mixed origin, rather than historically pure and homogeneous. It clashes conspicuously, that is to say, with received assumptions about culture coming out of nineteenth-century European nationalism. And the similarities between "creole" and "create" are not fortuitous. We have a sharper sense than usual that Creole cultures result as people actively engage in making their own syntheses. With regard to the entire cultural inventory of humanity, creolization may involve losing some, but certainly gaining some, too. There is also in the creolization scenario the notion of a more or less open continuum, a gradation of living syntheses which can be seen to match the cultural distance between center and periphery. And just as it is understood to involve a political economy of language, so the creolization continuum can be seen in its organization of diversity to entail a political economy of culture.

Furthermore, there is the dimension of time. Looking backward, the creolist point of view recognizes history. Creole cultures are not instant products of the present but have had some time to develop and draw themselves together to at least some degree of coherence; generations have already been born into them, but have also kept working on them. Looking forward, the creolization scenario is open-ended. This is perhaps an intellectual copout, but, again, probably an inevitable one. It suggests that the saturation and maturation tendencies are not necessarily alternatives, but can appear in real life interwoven with one another. When the peripheral culture absorbs the influx of meanings and symbolic forms from the center and transforms them to make them in some considerable degree their own, they may at the same time so increase the cultural affinities between the center and the periphery that the passage of more cultural imports is facilitated. What the end state of this will be is impossible to say, but it is possible that there is none.

Along the creolizing continuum, then, I see the various frameworks for cultural process exercising their continuous influence. Forms of life, variously place-bound, take their positions on it, and help tie it together as the people involved also observe each other; the people in the small town idolizing the jet set, perhaps, and the jet set mythologizing the peasants. They may open themselves to varying degrees to the transnational culture flow of the market, or allow middlemen to occupy the cultural space between the center and whatever is their place on the periphery.

Or they may do both, since the two need not be mutually exclusive. Now and then a movement from the metropolis perhaps comes traveling along the continuum. At other times, what the metropolis offers may clash instead with a movement generated at the periphery. And finally, a word about the state. We have seen that the state is both a large-scale importer of culture from the center and a guardian of either more or less authentic traditions from the periphery. But in between, frequently, there is nothing, or not very much. Perhaps it is inevitable that the state, for the sake of its own legitimacy, is a promoter of uncreolized authenticity. Yet it is also possible that this is a rather quixotic struggle, a production of culture of dubious merit in the view of large parts of the citizenry whose minds are elsewhere. It may be a perverse proposal, but it could be that to play its part in cultural welfare, to cooperate with that citizenry in shaping intellectual and esthetic instruments which help people see where they are and who they are today, and decide where they want to go, the state has to be more self-consciously, but not self-deprecatingly, a participant in a mixed cultural economy, a creole state.

PART XII

The globalization of disease

G LOBALIZATION FACILITATES trans-national and trans-regional
transmission of disease. This is one of the negative aspects of the global era.
Because people migrate with greater ease than ever before, they can carry potentially harmful diseases with them to all parts of the globe. The SARS crisis of 2003,
in which the virus spread from Hong Kong to the rest of the world, causing the death
of thousands, showed how liable all humans were unless effective means were undertaken. But, short of shutting down borders and restricting the movement of people,
it is extremely difficult to guard against such an outbreak of communicative illness.
Nevertheless, just as SARS spread instantaneously to various parts of the globe,
there was awareness that only through systematic international efforts the crisis
could be mitigated. And on the whole the World Health Organization and other
bodies cooperated with local governments to prevent the situation from further
deterioration.

While SARS appeared to have been contained, however, the threat of another
disease, AIDS, never abated. Starting in the 1970s, it has claimed the lives of millions of people, especially in Southeast Asia and Africa. Indeed, it is estimated that
in recent years several thousand people in Africa have died every day of AIDS. This
catastrophe is also very much an aspect of the global age, as are the determined
efforts by the United Nations and other agencies to mobilize international resources
to combat it.

The following excerpts, taken from recent writings by Erica Barks-Ruggles
(former Director of African Affairs on the National Security Council) and Mary E.
Wilson (Associate Professor of Medicine at the Harvard University School of Public
Health) reflect contemporary awareness of the threat to health that is an aspect of
the increasingly interdependent world.

Chapter 23

Erica Barks-Ruggles

THE GLOBALIZATION OF DISEASE

IN A BOLD SPEECH IN EARLY JUNE marking the 20th anniversary of the first report of HIV/AIDS, United Nations Secretary General Kofi Annan called on the private sector as well as donor governments to contribute to a $7–10 billion global trust fund to combat HIV/AIDS, malaria, and tuberculosis. His call for action to the business community was based on a sensible dose of "enlightened self-interest."

Annan warned that AIDS leaches profits out of economies and businesses and raises new barriers to development and economic growth. He cautioned that the widening gaps between wealthy and poor, which AIDS and other diseases are expanding, could accelerate the growing backlash against globalization. While global markets have created unprecedented economic opportunities and growth, the benefits have not been equally distributed, and the risks – especially the health risks – of an increasingly interlinked and interdependent world have not been thoroughly considered.

As trade, travel, and food sources become more global, humans, animals, and plants are being exposed to myriad new and ever more resilient diseases. Increasingly antibiotics fail to subdue multi-drug-resistant forms of diseases, such as tuberculosis, that they once nearly eliminated. Although there is no agreement on what is causing this trend – theories include climate changes, manipulation of plants and animals, genetic engineering, increased mobility of humans and food sources, and terrorism – the fact remains that disease threats are increasing. Officials in the United States and the international community need to begin containing the threat that diseases and pests pose in an increasingly globalized world, by putting into place reliable, cooperative, and responsive systems to anticipate, prevent, detect, and react to outbreaks – both those caused inadvertently and those caused by terrorist attack.

From Erica Barks-Ruggles, "The Globalization of Disease: When Congo Sneezes, Does California Get a Cold?" *Brookings Review*, vol. 19, no. 4 (Fall 2001), pp. 30–3.

Old and new disease risks

In December 1999 the National Intelligence Council released an unprecedented unclassified assessment of the threat that new and reemerging diseases pose to the United States and other countries. The report highlighted a few key facts. First, infectious diseases are a leading cause of death worldwide, accounting for one-quarter to one-third of all deaths globally in 1998. Second, 20 diseases that had been in decline reemerged or spread geographically between 1973 and 1999, including new multiple-drug-resistant strains of tuberculosis, malaria, and cholera. And third, 29 previously unknown diseases were identified in the same period, including HIV/AIDS, Ebola, and hepatitis C. There are no cures for many of these diseases.

The United States, despite its sophisticated medical care and infrastructure, has not been immune to this trend. Between 1980 and 1999, deaths due to infectious diseases doubled. Multiple-drug-resistant forms of TB and staphylococcus alone kill more than 14,000 Americans annually. HIV/AIDS is experiencing a resurgence, especially among minorities and women. In 1999, new HIV infections rose from 40,000 annually to 46,000, according to the Institute of Medicine. However, only 70 percent of Americans infected with HIV know their sero-status, and many who do know are failing to protect and educate themselves. Unprotected sex in some high-risk gay communities has risen to 50 percent, and a survey released by the Centers for Disease Control (CDC) in December 2000 found that 40 percent of the 5,600 Americans questioned believed that AIDS could be transmitted by sharing a glass with or being coughed on by an infected person. Though some lessons have been learned from the struggle against HIV/AIDS, the US health care system is ill equipped to deal with large-scale outbreaks of new or rare diseases. As evidenced by the outbreak of West Nile virus in New York in August 1999, an unknown and relatively weak virus can easily gain a foothold and quickly spread. Although only 82 people had been infected by the end of 2000 and only 8 had died, more than 4,000 birds and 59 horses had tested positive or died from the virus. Even though the CDC alone spent nearly $10 million in 1999 and 2000 to contain West Nile virus, it spread from 3 states in 1999 to 12 states and the District of Columbia by the end of 2000, and its spread continues.

Crops and animals at risk

The risks posed by new and reemerging diseases are not limited to humans. Crop and livestock diseases can exact steep health and economic costs. As seen during recent disease outbreaks in Europe, global trade's transfer of products, animals, and people around the world can speed the spread of infection. The British government anticipates paying around £1 billion to farmers in compensation for culling animals potentially exposed to foot-and-mouth disease. With large parts of the countryside closed to both foot and vehicle traffic, losses to Britain's tourism industry are expected to top £5 billion. More than 4.5 million animals in Britain have been slaughtered, and others have been killed in France, the Netherlands, and other European countries where the disease spread. Likewise, in Britain, bovine spongiform encephalopathy (BSE or "mad cow" disease) killed nearly 200,000 cattle. Nearly 5 million more were preemptively slaughtered. As of last November, 90 people had died from variant Creutzfeldt-Jakob Disease (vCJD), a malady linked to eating animals infected with

BSE. By December, the cost of BSE in the United Kingdom alone was estimated by the British government to exceed £1.5 billion.

The United States is the world's largest food producer and exporter. Agricultural products contributed more than $97.2 billion to the US economy in 1997, and the Agriculture Department estimates that farm exports alone contributed more than $49 billion to the US economy in 1999. The potential for harm to the nation's agricultural industry from alien pests and diseases is enormous.

Lethal tourists and cargo?

According to the Agriculture Department, the number of passengers traveling to the United States increased from 27 million in 1984 to 66 million in 1996. More than 400 million US border crossings were recorded in 1996, and in 1998 more than 422,000 cargo-bearing aircraft were inspected on landing in the United States. This flood of people and goods has exacerbated the already difficult job of controlling who and what enters and exits the nation. Each incoming passenger and cargo load could harbor new and deadly diseases or pests. With the increasing globalization of American food sources, including snow peas from Guatemala, apples from Chile, and mangoes from India, the threat from diseases and pests to American crops and people is growing. According to the Department of Commerce, farm imports into the United States increased 65 percent between 1991 and 1999, and that trend is expected to continue as the food supply becomes more global.

In addition, invasive species – both plant and animal – that are controlled or balanced in their native environments increasingly threaten indigenous species in the United States. Conservation researchers cited by the Agriculture Department have found that invasive alien plant infestations cover more than 100 million acres in the United States and are spreading at the rate of 14 percent a year. The department estimates that its agents intercept more than 1.8 million illegal agricultural products a year, stopping more than 52,000 plant and animal pests and diseases from entering the United States. But inspecting bags and cargo and destroying their contents may not keep out viruses and bacteria. Carried by humans, animals, plants, soil, foodstuffs, water, and the very planes and ships that bring foreign people and products to the United States, some diseases do not wait to pass inspection.

Are diseases gaining the upper hand?

Scientists working on human, animal, and plant diseases all agree that the number of new diseases, the increasing resistance of known diseases, and the rapid geographic spread of both are on the rise. What they do not agree on is why. Theories include climate changes, human manipulation of plant and animal food and genetics, increasing travel of humans and some animals (especially animals used for food), as well as deliberate introduction. No one theory has been proven or eliminated, but policymakers must take seriously the threat posed by the spread of disease to human, plant, and animal health, as well as the implications for economies and food security. Putting in place prevention, mitigation, and disaster-response systems now may help avoid a catastrophe later.

Is the United States prepared?

What would happen to America's economy and health care infrastructure if a virulent and communicable human, animal, or plant disease entered the United States and gained a foothold? The worst-case scenario would be the introduction of a devastating disease by a terrorist group.

In May 2000, three mid-size US cities (Portsmouth, New Hampshire; Denver, Colorado; and Washington, DC) took part in a large-scale exercise spanning several days to see how local, state, and national emergency systems would respond to three potential disasters – nuclear, biological, and chemical attacks by terrorists. The biological attack scenario, played out in Denver, showed that most local and regional authorities, even those who had been specially trained, were underprepared to deal with a large communicable disease outbreak and were overwhelmed by the complex coordination, decisionmaking, and management needed to contain and control the spread of disease. When the scenario ended (after four days), between 950 and 2,000 people had "died" and the disease had spread throughout the United States and to other countries.

While being prepared for a possible terrorist attack is important, the more insidious threat to the American economy and the safety of its citizens is the daily, routine transportation of goods, products, and people, along with the diseases and pests they carry, across borders. Constructing robust, multi-agency systems to identify, eliminate, and control "normal" disease and pest outbreaks will lower that quotidian threat, while at the same time building a foundation of skilled individuals and systems to help prevent and respond rapidly to a potential biological terrorism event.

What needs to be done?

Recognizing and assessing US vulnerabilities in protecting against, containing, and treating diseases is the first step toward building a comprehensive system to lower the risk of disease outbreaks. The Denver exercise, for example, was part of an ongoing training effort that exposed the need for greater coordination in decision-making, communication, and emergency relief efforts. The West Nile virus has likewise proved the value of increased training and coordination among health, animal, and plant disease authorities. After people started falling sick from a mysterious encephalitis infection, animal control authorities began investigating increased crow deaths in the same region. They discovered that crows also die from the West Nile virus and may facilitate its spread. The Agriculture Department has begun to assess its own infrastructure and training gaps, and its Animal and Plant Health Inspection Service is now constructing an emergency management center to handle disease outbreaks in US plants and animals.

These efforts, however, are but the first steps to put in place a strengthened system to detect and deter both deliberate terrorist attacks and unintentional transmission. Increased training in diagnostic techniques, better communication networks between and among health and emergency response personnel and the scientific community, and increased resources for enforcement, protection, prevention, and education programs are needed.

Beyond America's borders

The threat to the United States does not, however, end at the border. Many diseases originate overseas. The EU, the United States, and other concerned nations should begin to work with international organizations on a range of efforts to identify, contain, and control new and drug-resistant diseases in humans, animals, and plants, and to mitigate the damage they cause. In the long term, an international effort should include agreements on disease identification, containment, and treatment, and standard protocols and cost-sharing structures to ensure that poor and rich countries alike can control outbreaks of the most deadly diseases. A global surveillance network to help identify and eliminate diseases in their countries of origin should also be considered. Cooperative efforts must also be undertaken to construct functioning primary health care systems and infrastructure in developing countries so that diseases originating in the tropics can be identified and eradicated before they spread. Such an effort, through improving access to primary care and vaccinations, would improve the health of children and their chances of obtaining an education. Better education, better health, and other opportunities could spur development and economic growth over the long term.

Short-term international efforts should focus on immediate threats and build foundations for long-term efforts. World health leaders could set up internationally recognized and endorsed standard protocols for human vaccine development and testing for HIV/AIDS, malaria, and other killer diseases, along with systematic plans for comparative trials of multiple vaccines against them. They should commit to the rapid eradication of diseases that have not yet developed resistance to standard treatments, including polio, measles, river blindness, and Guinea worm. (Polio cases have fallen 99 percent in the past 13 years since the launch of the Global Polio Eradication Initiative, but polio must be eliminated in the 20 countries where it still exists.) Public–private partnerships could accelerate development of new disease treatments. (Some possibilities include tax incentives to encourage companies to manufacture medications for diseases that affect primarily poor countries, and trust funds to guarantee a profit for the manufacturers of medicines to treat Third World diseases.) International intellectual property rights regimes should be reformed to ensure that essential drugs and medicines are more affordable for all people. Genetically diverse plant and animal species should be preserved to increase the genetic pool on which researchers can draw to find disease-resistant qualities. Scientists, medical professionals, and disease specialists should have better access to distance learning, training, and exchange programs to increase understanding of and best treatments for diseases.

The fight against diseases was largely considered over as recently as the 1970s, but, as fast as health professionals learn to treat them, diseases are fighting back. Increased travel and trade are accelerating these trends. Winning the fight against disease and protecting the world's health, economies, and food supplies will require coordination, cooperation, and resources. As has been shown time and again during vaccination campaigns in war zones, even people trying to kill each other will agree to a temporary cease-fire to save their children from disease. If the world can build on that model of cooperation, perhaps there is a chance to win this war – and in the process create the hope of cooperation in other areas as well.

Chapter 24

Mary E. Wilson

TRAVEL AND INFECTIOUS DISEASES

M**ANY FACTORS CONTRIBUTE** to the emergence of infectious diseases. Those frequently identified include microbial adaptation and change, human demographics and behavior, environmental changes, technology and economic development, breakdown in public health measures and surveillance, and international travel and commerce. This paper will examine the pivotal role of global travel and movement of biologic life in the emergence of infectious diseases. It will also examine the ways in which travel and movement are inextricably tied at multiple levels to other processes that influence the emergence of disease.

Travel is a potent force in disease emergence and spread. The current volume, speed, and reach of travel are unprecedented. The consequences of migration extend beyond the traveler to the population visited and the ecosystem. Travel and trade set the stage for mixing diverse genetic pools at rates and in combinations previously unknown. Massive movement and other concomitant changes in social, political, climatic, environmental, and technologic factors converge to favor the emergence of infectious diseases.

Disease emergence is complex. Often several events must occur simultaneously or sequentially for a disease to emerge or reemerge (Table 1). Travel allows a potentially pathogenic microbe to be introduced into a new geographic area; however, to be established and cause disease a microbe must survive, proliferate, and find a way to enter a susceptible host. Any analysis of emergence must look at a dynamic process, a sequence of events, a milieu, or ecosystem.

Movement, changing patterns of resistance and vulnerability, and the emergence of infectious diseases also affect plants, animals, and insect vectors. Analysis of these species can hold important lessons about the dynamics of human disease.

To assess the impact of travel on disease emergence, it is necessary to consider the receptivity of a geographic area and its population to microbial introduction. Most introductions do not lead to disease. Organisms that survive primarily or

From Mary E. Wilson, "Travel and the Emergence of Infectious Diseases," *Emerging Infectious Diseases*, vol. 1, no. 2 (April–June 1995), available from www.cdc.gov/ncidod/eid/vol1no2/downwils.htm.

entirely in the human host and are spread through sexual contact, droplet nuclei, and close physical contact, can be readily carried to any part of the world. For example, AIDS, tuberculosis, measles, pertussis, diphtheria, and hepatitis B are easily carried by travelers and can spread in a new geographic area; however, populations protected by vaccines resist introduction. Organisms that have animal hosts, environmental limitations, arthropod vectors, or complicated life cycles become successively more difficult to "transplant" to another geographic area or population. Epidemics of dengue fever and yellow fever cannot appear in a geographic area unless competent mosquito vectors are present. Schistosomiasis cannot spread in an environment unless a suitable snail intermediate host exists in that region. Organisms that survive only under carefully tuned local conditions are less likely to be successfully introduced. Even if an introduced parasite persists in a new geographic area, it does not necessarily cause human disease. In the United States, humans infected with Taenia solium, the parasite that causes cysticercosis, infrequently transmit the infection because sanitary disposal of feces, the source of the eggs, is generally available. In short, the likelihood of transmission involves many biological, social, and environmental variables.

Historical perspective

Human migration has been the main source of epidemics throughout recorded history. William McNeill, in his book *Plagues and Peoples*, describes the central role of infectious disease in the history of the world. Patterns of disease circulation have influenced the outcome of wars and have shaped the location, nature, and development of human societies. Trade caravans, religious pilgrimages, and military maneuvers facilitated the spread of many diseases, including plague and smallpox. A map in Donald Hopkins' book, *Princes and Peasants: Smallpox in History*, traces the presumed spread of smallpox from Egypt or India, where it was first thought to have become adapted to humans sometime before 1000 BC. Smallpox spread easily from person to person through close contact with respiratory discharges and, less commonly,

Table 1. Basic concepts in disease emergence

Emergence of infectious diseases is complex.

Infectious diseases are dynamic.

Most new infections are not caused by genuinely new pathogens.

Agents involved in new and reemergent infections cross taxonomic lines to include viruses, bacteria, fungi, protozoa, and helminths.

The concept of the microbe as the cause of disease is inadequate and incomplete.

Human activities are the most potent factors driving disease emergence.

Social, economic, political, climatic, technologic, and environmental factors shape disease patterns and influence emergence.

Understanding and responding to disease emergence require a global perspective, conceptually and geographically.

The current global situation favors disease emergence.

---

through contact with skin lesions, linens, clothing, and other material in direct contact with the patient. Because patients remained infectious for about 3 weeks, many opportunities for transmission were available. Even in this century, until the 1970s, smallpox continued to cause epidemics. A pilgrim returning from Mecca was the source of a large outbreak in Yugoslavia in the early 1970s that resulted in 174 Yugoslav cases and 35 deaths. The pilgrim apparently contracted the infection in Baghdad while visiting a religious site. Because his symptoms were mild, he was never confined to bed and was able to continue his travels and return home.

For most of history, human populations were relatively isolated. Only in recent centuries has there been extensive contact between the flora and fauna of the Old and New Worlds. Schoolchildren hear the rhyme "Columbus sailed the ocean blue, in fourteen hundred ninety-two," but may learn little about the disaster brought upon the native populations of the Americas by the arriving explorers. By the end of the fifteenth century, measles, influenza, mumps, smallpox, tuberculosis, and other infections had become common in Europe. Explorers from the crowded urban centers of Europe brought infectious diseases to the New World, where isolated populations had evolved from a relatively small gene pool and had no previous experience with many infections. The first epidemics following the arrival of Europeans were often the most severe. By 1518 or 1519, smallpox appeared in Santo Domingo, where it killed one-third to half of the local population and spread to other areas of the Caribbean and the Americas. The population of central Mexico is estimated to have dropped by one-third in the single decade following contact with the Europeans.

Travel across the Atlantic Ocean transformed the flora and fauna of the New World as well. Some of the transported materials became important sources of food (plants), clothing, and transportation (animals). Other transfers were less welcome: Japanese beetles, Dutch elm disease, and chestnut tree fungus. A.W. Crosby, exploring these exchanges between the Old and the New Worlds, sounds a pessimistic note: "The Columbian exchange has left us with not a richer but a more impoverished genetic pool."

The explorers also paid a price in loss of lives from disease. Philip Curtin provides a quantitative study of "relocation costs," the excess illness and death among European soldiers in the nineteenth century when they lived or worked in the tropics. Until the most recent armed conflicts, infectious diseases claimed more lives than injuries during wars. [. . .]

Movement of people

Travel for business and pleasure constitutes a small fraction of total human movement. People migrating individually or in groups may be immigrants, refugees, missionaries, merchant marines, students, temporary workers, pilgrims, or Peace Corps workers. Travel may involve short distances or the crossing of international borders. Its volume, however, is huge. In the early 1990s more than 500 million persons annually crossed international borders on commercial airplane flights. An estimated 70 million persons, mostly from developing countries, work either legally or illegally in other countries. Movement may be temporary or seasonal, as with nomadic populations and migrant workers who follow the crops. Military maneuvers worldwide employ and move huge populations. The consequences of armed conflict and political unrest displace millions. In the early 1990s, there were an estimated 20 million refugees and 30 million displaced persons worldwide. [. . .]

Although social, economic, and political factors push people from an area or draw them to another, environmental resources and their impact on food and water supplies are behind many conflicts leading to displacement of populations. Acute disasters, such as flooding, earthquakes, and hurricanes often force populations to seek shelter and sustenance in new lands. Chronic changes, such as drought, depletion of soil, and disappearance of fish from streams, lakes, and oceans, draw people to new territories, or, more frequently, to the fringes of large urban centers.

Another type of travel relevant to disease emergence is the shift of populations to urban areas. It is estimated that by the year 2010, 50 percent of the world's population will be living in urban areas. It is projected that by the year 2000, the world will comprise 24 "megacities," sprawling metropolitan areas with populations exceeding 10 million. These areas will have the population density to support persistence of some infections and contribute to the emergence of others. Many of these areas are located in tropical or subtropical regions, where the environment can support a diverse array of pathogens and vectors. Also developing are huge peri-urban slums, populated with persons from many geographic origins. Poor sanitation allows breeding of arthropod vectors, rodents, and other disease-carrying animals. Crowded conditions favor the spread of diseases that pass from person to person, including sexually transmitted infections. Travel between periurban slum areas and rural areas is common, paving the route for the transfer of microbes and disease. Transfer of resistance genes and genetic recombination may also occur in and spread from crowded environments of transients.

Acute disturbances, whether climatic or political, lead to interim living arrangements, such as refugee camps and temporary shelters, that provide ideal conditions for the emergence and spread of infections. Temporary living quarters often share similarities with periurban slums: crowding, inadequate sanitation, limited access to medical care, lack of clean water and food, dislocation, multiethnic composition, and inadequate barriers from vectors and animals. An example is the movement of 500,000–800,000 Rwandan refugees into Zaire in 1994. Almost 50,000 refugees died during the first month as epidemics of cholera and Shigella dysenteriae type 1 swept through the refugee camps. [. . .]

Shipping and commerce

The biomass of humans constitutes only a fraction of the matter moved about the earth. Humans carry and send a huge volume of plants, animals, and other materials all over the face of the globe. Much of this movement results from the planned transport of goods from one place to another, but some is an unintended consequence of shipping and travel. All has an impact on the juxtaposition of various species in different ecosystems. "Hitchhikers" include all manner of biologic life, both microscopic and macroscopic. Animals can carry potential human pathogens and vectors. The globalization of markets brings fresh fruits and vegetables to dinner tables thousands of miles from where they were grown, fertilized, and picked. Tunnels, bridges, and ferries form means to traverse natural barriers to species spread. The roads built to transport people often speed the movement of diseases from one area to another. Mass processing and wide distribution networks allow for the amplification and wide dissemination of potential human microbes. [. . .]

Confluence of events

Massive global travel is taking place simultaneously with many other processes that favor the emergence of disease. For example, the human population is more vulnerable because of aging, immunosuppression from medical treatment and disease (such as AIDS), the presence of prostheses (e.g. artificial heart valves and joints), exposure to chemicals and environmental pollutants that may act synergistically with microbes to increase the risk of diseases, increased poverty, crowding and stress, and increased exposure to UV radiation. Technological changes, while providing many benefits, can also promote disease dissemination. Resistance of microbes and insects to antimicrobial drugs and pesticides interferes with the control of infections and allows transmission to continue. Changes in land use can alter the presence and abundance of vectors and intermediate hosts.

Microbes are enormously resilient and adaptable. They have short life spans, which allow rapid genetic change. Humans, by comparison, are slow to change genetically but can change their behavior. People move and construct barriers to prevent contact with microparasites, macroparasites, and the extremes of the environment. Technology fosters a perception of human invincibility but actually creates new vulnerabilities, as it enables us to go deeper, higher, and into more remote and hostile environments. Studies show that no place on earth is devoid of microbes. Their range and resiliency are truly phenomenal. Only a fraction of the existing microbes have been characterized. Travel and exploration provide a greater opportunity for humans to come into unsampled regions with these uncharacterized microbes.

Summary and conclusions

Global travel and the evolution of microbes will continue. New infections will continue to emerge, and known infections will change in distribution, severity, and frequency. Travel will continue to be a potent factor in disease emergence. The current world circumstances juxtapose people, parasites, plants, animals, and chemicals in a way that precludes timely adaptation. The combination of movement at many levels and profound change in the physical environment can lead to unanticipated diseases spread by multiple channels. In many instances, the use of containment or quarantine is not feasible. Research and surveillance can map the global movement and evolution of microbes and guide interventions. Integration of knowledge and skills from many disciplines – the social, biological, and physical sciences – is needed. The focus should be system analysis and the ecosystem rather than a disease, microbe, or host.

PART XIII

Terrorism

TERRORISM, LIKE DISEASE, is one of the unfortunate aspects of an increasingly interdependent and inter-penetrable world. We should recognize, however, that terrorist attacks on political and other leaders have a long history. In the United States alone, four presidents were murdered by assassins (in 1865, 1881, 1901, 1963). In Europe, the Russian czar was assassinated in 1881, the Hapsburg empress in 1898, and the heir apparent in 1914. Japanese prime ministers were likewise killed in 1878, 1921, 1932, and 1936. In addition, we must recall mob violence such as the Boxers' indiscriminate assault on foreigners in China (1900) and the anti-Chinese attacks in Colorado during the 1880s. In the twentieth century, ethnic and nationalistic insurrections in colonial and post-colonial societies were commonplace, and terrorists in those cases frequently became "freedom fighters." Moreover, some states, such as Nazi Germany and Stalinist Russia, practiced organized mass terrorism, victimizing ethnic minorities and political dissidents.

Terrorism in the recent decades can nevertheless be seen as a distinctive phenomenon, as an important aspect of the global age. Terrorists make use of global technology, global capital, global travel, and the global migration of people. It has become much easier for terrorists to travel across national boundaries, communicate with one another electronically, raise and store funds in huge amounts, and to create trans-national organizations. Often terrorists are anti-globalizers. They view globalization as deracination; by creating trans-national links and developing a global culture, they assert, globalization has served to weaken traditional identities and loyalties. Some terrorist organizations, especially religious groups that are often referred to as "fundamentalists," seek to challenge the material culture as well as the intermingling of civilizations that have developed through globalization. Fundamentalists abhor an ideological vacuum and seek to fill it with rigid conceptions of right and wrong, often to the detriment of a more tolerant human community. Lastly, terrorism in the global age is inherently opposed to the authority of the state. Inasmuch as the sovereign state has been weakened due to cross-national movements of people, goods, capital, and organizations, terrorists take advantage of it and serve further to weaken the state's capacity to defend itself.

So terrorism provides an excellent topic through which to examine many, and contradictory, aspects of globalization. In the excerpts that follow, Bruce Hoffman (Acting Director of the RAND Center for Middle East Public Policy) provides a useful definition and history of terrorism, while Lawrence Freedman (Professor of War Studies at King's College, London) discusses the implications of the September 11, 2001, terrorist attacks on the United States.

Chapter 25

Bruce Hoffman

WHAT IS TERRORISM?

WHAT IS TERRORISM? Few words have so insidiously worked their way into our everyday vocabulary. Like "Internet" – another grossly over-used term that has similarly become an indispensable part of the argot of the late twentieth century – most people have a vague idea or impression what terrorism is, but lack a more precise, concrete, and truly explanatory definition of the word. This imprecision has been abetted partly by the modern media, whose efforts to com-municate an often complex and convoluted message in the briefest amount of air-time or print space possible have led to the promiscuous labeling of a range of violent acts as "terrorism." Pick up a newspaper or turn on the television and – even within the same broadcast or on the same page – one can find such disparate acts as the bombing of a building, the assassination of a head of state, the massacre of civilians by a military unit, the poisoning of produce on supermarket shelves, or the deliber-ate contamination of over-the-counter medication in a chemist's shop all described as incidents of terrorism. Indeed, virtually any especially abhorrent act of violence that is perceived as directed against society – whether it involves the activities of anti-government dissidents or governments themselves, organized crime syndi-cates or common criminals, rioting mobs or persons engaged in militant protest, individual psychotics or lone extortionists – is often labeled "terrorism". [. . .]

Terrorism, in the most widely accepted contemporary usage of the term, is fundamentally and inherently political. It is also ineluctably about power: the pursuit of power, the acquisition of power, and the use of power to achieve political change. Terrorism is thus violence – or, equally important, the threat of violence – used and directed in pursuit of, or in service of, a political aim. With this vital point clearly illuminated, one can appreciate the significance of the additional definition of "terrorist" provided by the *OED*: "Any one who attempts to further his views by a system of coercive intimidation." This definition underscores clearly the other fundamental characteristic of terrorism: that it is a planned, calculated, and indeed systematic act.

From Bruce Hoffman, *Inside Terrorism* (New York: Columbia University Press, 1998), pp. 13–16, 20–4, 23–33, 36–40.

Given this relatively straightforward elucidation, why, then, is terrorism so difficult to define? The most compelling reason perhaps is because the meaning of the term has changed so frequently over the past two hundred years.

The changing meaning of terrorism

The word "terrorism" was first popularized during the French Revolution. In contrast to its contemporary usage, at that time terrorism had a decidedly *positive* connotation. The system or *régime de la terreur* of 1793–4 – from which the English word came – was adopted as a means to establish order during the transient anarchical period of turmoil and upheaval that followed the uprisings of 1789, as it has followed in the wake of many other revolutions. Hence, unlike terrorism as it is commonly understood today, to mean a *revolutionary* or anti-government activity undertaken by non-state or subnational entities, the *régime de la terreur* was an instrument of governance wielded by the recently established revolutionary *state*. It was designed to consolidate the new government's power by intimidating counter-revolutionaries, subversives and all other dissidents whom the new regime regarded as "enemies of the people." The Committee of General Security and the Revolutionary Tribunal ("People's Court" in the modern vernacular) were thus accorded wide powers of arrest and judgment, publicly putting to death by guillotine persons convicted of treasonous (i.e. reactionary) crimes. In this manner, a powerful lesson was conveyed to any and all who might oppose the revolution or grow nostalgic for the *ancien régime*.

Ironically, perhaps, terrorism in its original context was also closely associated with the ideals of virtue and democracy. The revolutionary leader Maximilien Robespierre firmly believed that virtue was the mainspring of a popular government at peace, but that during the time of revolution must be allied with terror in order for democracy to triumph. He appealed famously to "virtue, without which terror is evil; terror, without which virtue is helpless," and proclaimed: "Terror is nothing but justice, prompt, severe, and inflexible; it is therefore an emanation of virtue". [. . .]

On the eve of the First World War, terrorism still retained its revolutionary connotations. By this time, growing unrest and irredentist ferment had already welled up within the decaying Ottoman and Habsburg Empires. In the 1880s and 1890s, for example, militant Armenian nationalist movements in eastern Turkey pursued a terrorist strategy against continued Ottoman rule of a kind that would later be adopted by most of the post-Second World War ethnonationalist/separatist movements. The Armenians' objective was simultaneously to strike a blow against the despotic "alien" regime through repeated attacks on its colonial administration and security forces, in order to rally indigenous support, as well as to attract international attention, sympathy, and support. Around the same time, the Inner Macedonian Revolutionary Organization (IMRO) was active in the region overlapping present-day Greece, Bulgaria, and Serbia. Although the Macedonians did not go on to suffer the catastrophic fate that befell the Armenians during the First World War (when an estimated one million persons perished in what is considered to be the first officially implemented genocide of the twentieth century), IMRO never came close to achieving its aim of an independent Macedonia and thereafter degenerated into a mostly criminal organization of hired thugs and political assassins.

The events immediately preceding the First World War in Bosnia are of course more familiar because of their subsequent cataclysmic impact on world affairs. There, similar groups of disaffected nationalists – Bosnian Serb intellectuals, university students, and even schoolchildren, collectively known as Mlada Bosna, or Young Bosnians – arose against continued Habsburg suzerainty. While it is perhaps easy to dismiss the movement, as some historians have, as comprised of "frustrated, poor, dreary and maladjusted" adolescents – much as many contemporary observers similarly denigrate modern-day terrorists as mindless, obsessive, and maladjusted – it was a member of Young Bosnia, Gavrilo Princip, who is widely credited with having set in motion the chain of events that began on June 28, 1914, when he assassinated the Habsburg Archduke Franz Ferdinand in Sarajevo, and culminated in the First World War. Whatever its superficially juvenile characteristics, the group was nonetheless passionately dedicated to the attainment of a federal South Slav political entity – uniting Slovenes, Croats, and Serbs – and resolutely committed to assassination as the vehicle with which to achieve that aim. In this respect, the Young Bosnians perhaps had more in common with the radical republicanism of Giuseppe Mazzini, one of the most ardent exponents of Italian unification in the nineteenth century, than with groups such as the Narodnaya Volya – despite a shared conviction in the efficacy of tyrannicide. An even more significant difference, however, was the degree of involvement in, and external support provided to, Young Bosnian activities by various shadowy Serbian nationalist groups. [. . .]

By the 1930s, the meaning of "terrorism" had changed again. It was now used less to refer to revolutionary movements and violence directed against governments and their leaders, and more to describe the practices of mass repression employed by totalitarian states and their dictatorial leaders against their own citizens. Thus the term regained its former connotations of abuse of power by governments, and was applied specifically to the authoritarian regimes that had come to power in Fascist Italy, Nazi Germany, and Stalinist Russia. In Germany and Italy, respectively, the accession to office of Hitler and Mussolini had depended in large measure on the "street" – the mobilization and deployment of gangs of brown- or black-shirted thugs to harass and intimidate political opponents and root out other scapegoats for public vilification and further victimization. "Terror? Never," Mussolini insisted, demurely dismissing such intimidation as "simply . . . social hygiene, taking those individuals out of circulation like a doctor would take out a bacillus." The most sinister dimension of this form of "terror" was that it became an intrinsic component of Fascist and Nazi governance, executed at the behest of, and in complete subservience to, the ruling political party of the land – which had arrogated to itself complete, total control of the country and its people. A system of government-sanctioned fear and coercion was thus created whereby political brawls, street fights, and widespread persecution of Jews, communists and other declared "enemies of the state" became the means through which complete and submissive compliance was ensured. The totality of party control over, and perversion of, government was perhaps most clearly evinced by a speech given by Hermann Goering, the newly appointed Prussian minister of the interior, in 1933. "Fellow Germans," he declared,

My measures will not be crippled by any judicial thinking. My measures
will not be crippled by any bureaucracy. Here I don't have to worry

about Justice; my mission is only to destroy and exterminate, nothing more. This struggle will be a struggle against chaos, and such a struggle I shall not conduct with the power of the police. A bourgeois State might have done that. Certainly, I shall use the power of the State and the police to the utmost, my dear Communists, so don't draw any false conclusions; but the struggle to the death, in which my fist will grasp your necks, I shall lead with those there – the Brown Shirts.

The "Great Terror" that Stalin was shortly to unleash in Russia both resembled and differed from that of the Nazis. On the one hand, drawing inspiration from Hitler's ruthless elimination of his own political opponents, the Russian dictator similarly transformed the political party he led into a servile instrument responsive directly to his personal will, and the state's police and security apparatus into slavish organs of coercion, enforcement, and repression. But conditions in the Soviet Union of the 1930s bore little resemblance to the turbulent political, social, and economic upheaval afflicting Germany and Italy during that decade and the previous one. On the other hand, therefore, unlike either the Nazis or the Fascists, who had emerged from the political free-for-alls in their own countries to seize power and then had to struggle to consolidate their rule and retain their unchallenged authority, the Russian Communist party had by the mid-1930s been firmly entrenched in power for more than a decade. Stalin's purges, in contrast to those of the French Revolution, and even to Russia's own recent experience, were not "launched in time of crisis, or revolution and war . . . [but] in the coldest of cold blood, when Russia had at last reached a comparatively calm and even moderately prosperous condition." Thus the political purges ordered by Stalin became, in the words of one of his biographers, a "conspiracy to seize total power by terrorist action," resulting in the death, exile, imprisonment, or forcible impressments of millions. [. . .]

Following the Second World War, in another swing of the pendulum of meaning, "terrorism" regained the revolutionary connotations with which it is most commonly associated today. At that time, the term was used primarily in reference to the violent revolts then being prosecuted by the various indigenous nation-alist/anti-colonialist groups that emerged in Asia, Africa, and the Middle East during the late 1940s and 1950s to oppose continued European rule. Countries as diverse as Israel, Kenya, Cyprus, and Algeria, for example, owe their independence at least in part to nationalist political movements that employed terrorism against colonial powers. It was also during this period that the "politically correct" appellation of "freedom fighters" came into fashion as a result of the political legitimacy that the international community (whose sympathy and support were actively courted by many of these movements) accorded to struggles for national liberation and self-determination. Many newly independent Third World countries and communist bloc states in particular adopted this vernacular, arguing that anyone or any move-ment that fought against "colonial" oppression and/or Western domination should not be described as "terrorists," but were properly deemed to be "freedom fighters." This position was perhaps most famously explained by the Palestine Liberation Organization (PLO) chairman Yassir Arafat, when he addressed the United Nations General Assembly in November 1974. "The difference between the revolutionary and the terrorist," Arafat stated, "lies in the reason for which each fights. For whoever stands by a just cause and fights for the freedom and liberation of his land from the invaders, the settlers and the colonialists, cannot possibly be called terrorist . . . ."

Although the revolutionary cum ethno-nationalist/separatist and ideological exemplars continue to shape our most basic understanding of the term, in recent years "terrorism" has been used to denote broader, less distinct phenomena. In the early 1980s, for example, terrorism came to be regarded as a calculated means to destabilize the West as part of a vast global conspiracy. Books like *The Terror Network* by Claire Sterling propagated the notion to a receptive American presidential administration and similarly susceptible governments elsewhere that the seemingly isolated terrorist incidents perpetrated by disparate groups scattered across the globe were in fact linked elements of a massive clandestine plot, orchestrated by the Kremlin and implemented by its Warsaw Pact client states, to destroy the Free World. By the middle of the decade, however, a series of suicide bombings directed mostly against American diplomatic and military targets in the Middle East was focusing attention on the rising threat of state-sponsored terrorism. Consequently, this phenomenon – whereby various renegade foreign governments such as the regimes in Iran, Iraq, Libya, and Syria became actively involved in sponsoring or commissioning terrorist acts – replaced communist conspiracy theories as the main context within which terrorism was viewed. Terrorism thus became associated with a type of covert or surrogate warfare whereby weaker states could confront larger, more powerful rivals without the risk of retribution. [. . .]

Why is terrorism so difficult to define?

Not surprisingly, as the meaning and usage of the word have changed over time to accommodate the political vernacular and discourse of each successive era, terrorism has proved increasingly elusive in the face of attempts to construct one consistent definition. At one time, the terrorists themselves were far more cooperative in this endeavor than they are today. The early practitioners didn't mince their words or hide behind the semantic camouflage of more anodyne labels such as "freedom fighter" or "urban guerrilla." The nineteenth-century anarchists, for example, unabashedly proclaimed themselves to be terrorists and frankly proclaimed their tactics to be terrorism. The members of Narodnaya Volya similarly displayed no qualms in using the same words to describe themselves and their deeds. However, such frankness did not last. The Jewish terrorist group of the 1940s known as Lehi (the Hebrew acronym for Lohamei Herut Yisrael, the Freedom Fighters for Israel, more popularly known simply as the Stern Gang after their founder and first leader, Abraham Stern) is thought to be one of the last terrorist groups actually to describe itself publicly as such. It is significant, however, that even Lehi, while it may have been far more candid than its latter-day counterparts, chose as the name of the organization not "Terrorist Fighters for Israel," but the far less pejorative "Freedom Fighters for Israel." Similarly, although more than twenty years later the Brazilian revolutionary Carlos Marighela displayed few compunctions about openly advocating the use of "terrorist" tactics, he still insisted on depicting himself and his disciples as "urban guerrillas" rather than "urban terrorists." Indeed, it is clear from Marighela's writings that he was well aware of the word's undesirable connotations, and strove to displace them with positive resonances. "The words 'aggressor' and 'terrorist,'" Marighela wrote in his famous *Handbook of Urban Guerrilla War* (also known as the "Mini Manual"), "no longer mean what they did. Instead of arousing fear or censure, they are a call to action. To be called an aggressor or a terrorist in Brazil is now an honor to any citizen, for it means that he is fighting, with a gun in his hand, against the monstrosity of the present dictatorship and the suffering it causes."

This trend towards ever more convoluted semantic obfuscations to side-step terrorism's pejorative overtones has, if anything, become more entrenched in recent decades. Terrorist organizations almost without exception now regularly select names for themselves that consciously eschew the word "terrorism" in any of its forms. Instead these groups actively seek to evoke images of:

- freedom and liberation (e.g. the National Liberation Front, the Popular Front for the Liberation of Palestine, Freedom for the Basque Homeland, etc.);
- armies or other military organizational structures (e.g. the National Military Organization, the Popular Liberation Army, the Fifth Battalion of the Liberation Army, etc.);
- actual self-defense movements (e.g. the Afrikaner Resistance Movement, the Shankhill Defense Association, the Organization for the Defense of the Free People, the Jewish Defense Organization, etc.);
- righteous vengeance (the Organization for the Oppressed on Earth, the Justice Commandos of the Armenian Genocide, the Palestinian Revenge Organization, etc.);
- or else deliberately choose names that are decidedly neutral and therefore bereft of all but the most innocuous suggestions or associations (e.g. the Shining Path, Front Line, al-Dawa ("the Call"), Alfaro Lives – Damn It!, Kach ("Thus"), al-Gamat al-Islamiya ("The Islamic Organization"), the Lantero Youth Movement, etc.). [. . .]

On one point, at least, everyone agrees: Terrorism is a pejorative term. It is a word with intrinsically negative connotations that is generally applied to one's enemies and opponents, or to those with whom one disagrees and would otherwise prefer to ignore. "What is called terrorism," Brian Jenkins has written, "thus seems to depend on one's point of view. Use of the term implies a moral judgment; and if one party can successfully attach the label *terrorist* to its opponent, then it has indirectly persuaded others to adopt its moral viewpoint." Hence the decision to call someone or label some organization "terrorist" becomes almost unavoidably subjective, depending largely on whether one sympathizes with or opposes the person/ group/cause concerned. If one identifies with the victim of the violence, for example, then the act is terrorism. If, however, one identifies with the perpetrator, the violent act is regarded in a more sympathetic, if not positive (or, at the worst, an ambivalent) light; and it is not terrorism.

The implications of this associational logic were perhaps most clearly demonstrated in the exchanges between Western and non-Western member states of the United Nations following the 1972 Munich Olympics massacre, in which eleven Israeli athletes were killed. The debate began with the proposal by the then UN Secretary-General Kurt Waldheim, that the UN should not remain a "mute spectator" to the acts of terrorist violence then occurring throughout the world but should take practical steps that might prevent further bloodshed. While a majority of the UN member states supported the Secretary-General, a disputatious minority – including many Arab states and various African and Asian countries – derailed the discussion, arguing (much as Arafat would do two years later in his own address to the General Assembly) that "people who struggle to liberate themselves from foreign oppression and exploitation have the right to use all methods at their disposal, including force."

The Third World delegates justified their position with two arguments. First, they claimed that all bona fide liberation movements are invariably decried as "terrorists" by the regimes against which their struggles for freedom are directed. The Nazis, for example, labeled as terrorists the resistance groups opposing Germany's occupation of their lands, Moulaye el-Hassen, the Mauritanian ambassador, pointed out, just as "all liberation movements are described as terrorists by those who have reduced them to slavery." Therefore, by condemning "terrorism" the UN was endorsing the power of the strong over the weak and of the established entity over its non-established challenger – in effect, acting as the defender of the status quo. [. . .]

The opposite approach, where identification with the victim determines the classification of a violent act as terrorism, is evident in the conclusions of a parliamentary working group of NATO (an organization comprised of long-established, status quo Western states). The final report of the 1989 North Atlantic Assembly's Subcommittee on Terrorism states: "Murder, kidnapping, arson and other felonious acts constitute criminal behavior, but many non-Western nations have proved reluctant to condemn as terrorist acts what they consider to be struggles of national liberation." In this reasoning, the defining characteristic of terrorism is the act of violence itself, not the motivations or justification for or reasons behind it. This approach has long been espoused by analysts such as Jenkins who argue that terrorism should be defined "by the nature of the act, not by the identity of the perpetrators or the nature of their cause." But this is not an entirely satisfactory solution either, since it fails to differentiate clearly between violence perpetrated by states and by non-state entities, such as terrorists. Accordingly, it plays into the hands of terrorists and their apologists who would argue that there is no difference between the "low-tech" terrorist pipe-bomb placed in the rubbish bin at a crowded market that wantonly and indiscriminately kills or maims everyone within a radius measured in tens of feet and the "high-tech" precision-guided ordnance dropped by air force fighter-bombers from a height of 20,000 feet or more that achieves the same wanton and indiscriminate effects on the crowded marketplace far below. This rationale thus equates the random violence inflicted on enemy population centers by military forces – such as the Luftwaffe's raids on Warsaw and Coventry, the Allied firebombings of Dresden and Tokyo, and the atomic bombs dropped by the United States on Hiroshima and Nagasaki during the Second World War, and indeed the countervalue strategy of the post-war superpowers' strategic nuclear policy, which deliberately targeted the enemy's civilian population – with the violence committed by substate entities labeled "terrorists," since both involve the infliction of death and injury on noncombatants. Indeed, this was precisely the point made during the above-mentioned UN debates by the Cuban representative, who argued that "the methods of combat used by national liberation movements could not be declared illegal while the policy of terrorism unleashed against certain peoples [by the armed forces of established states] was declared legitimate". [. . .]

The reporting of terrorism by the news media, which have been drawn into the semantic debates that divided the UN in the 1970s and continue to influence all discourse on terrorism, has further contributed to the obfuscation of the terrorist/"freedom fighter" debate, enshrining imprecision and implication as the lingua franca of political violence in the name of objectivity and neutrality. In striving to avoid appearing either partisan or judgmental, the American media, for example, resorted to describing terrorists – often in the same report – as variously guerrillas, gunmen, raiders, commandos, and even soldiers. A random sample of American newspaper reports of Palestinian terrorist activities between June and December 1973, found in the terrorism archives and database maintained at the University of St Andrews in Scotland, provided striking illustrations of this practice. Out of eight headlines of articles describing the same incident, six used the word "guerrillas" and only two "terrorists" to describe the perpetrators. An interesting pattern was also observed whereby those accounts that immediately followed a particularly horrific or tragic incident – that is, involving the death and injury of innocent persons (in this instance, the attack on a Pan Am airliner at Rome airport, in which thirty-two passengers were killed) – tended to describe the perpetrators as "terrorists" and their act as "terrorism" (albeit in one case only in the headline, before reverting to the more neutral terminology of "commando," "militant," and "guerrilla attack" in the text) more frequently than did reports of less serious or non-lethal incidents. One *New York Times* leading article, however, was far less restrained than the stories describing the actual incident, describing it as "bloody" and "mindless" and using the words "terrorists" and "terrorism" interchangeably with "guerrillas" and "extremists." Only six months previously, however, the same newspaper had run a story about another terrorist attack that completely eschewed the terms "terrorism" and "terrorist," preferring "guerrillas" and "resistance" (and "resistance movement") instead. The *Christian Science Monitor*'s reports of the Rome Pan Am attack similarly avoided "terrorist" and "terrorism" in favor of "guerrillas" and "extremists"; an Associated Press story in the next day's *Los Angeles Times* also stuck with "guerrillas," while the two *Washington Post* articles on the same incident opted for the terms "commandos" and "guerrillas." [. . .]

The cumulative effect of this proclivity towards equivocation is that today there is no one widely accepted or agreed definition for terrorism. Different departments or agencies of even the same governments will themselves often have very different definitions for terrorism. The US State Department, for example, uses the definition of terrorism contained in Title 22 of the United States Code, Section 2656f(d):

> premeditated, politically motivated violence perpetrated against non-combatant targets by subnational groups or clandestine agents, usually intended to influence an audience,

while the US Federal Bureau of Investigation (FBI) defines terrorism as

> the unlawful use of force or violence against persons or property to intimidate or coerce a Government, the civilian population, or any segment thereof, in furtherance of political or social objectives . . .

It is not only individual agencies within the same governmental apparatus that cannot agree on a single definition of terrorism. Experts and other long-established scholars in the field are equally incapable of reaching a consensus. In the first edition of his magisterial survey, *Political Terrorism: A Research Guide*, Alex Schmid devoted more than a hundred pages to examining more than a hundred different definitions of terrorism in an effort to discover a broadly acceptable, reasonably comprehensive explication of the word. Four years and a second edition later, Schmid was no closer to the goal of his quest, conceding in the first sentence of the revised volume that the "search for an adequate definition is still on." Walter Laqueur despaired of defining terrorism in both editions of his monumental work on the subject, maintaining that it is neither possible to do so nor worthwhile to make the attempt. "Ten years of debates on typologies and definitions," he responded to a survey on definitions conducted by Schmid, "have not enhanced our knowledge of the subject to a significant degree." Laqueur's contention is supported by the twenty-two different word categories occurring in the 109 different definitions that Schmid identified in his survey. [. . .]

At the end of his exhaustive exercise, Schmid asks "whether the above list contains all the elements necessary for a good definition. The answer," he suggests, "is probably 'no'." If it is impossible to define terrorism, as Laqueur argues, and fruitless to attempt to cobble together a truly comprehensive definition, as Schmid admits, are we to conclude that terrorism is impervious to precise, much less accurate definition? Not entirely. If we cannot define terrorism, then we can at least usefully distinguish it from other types of violence and identify the characteristics that make terrorism the distinct phenomenon of political violence that it is.

Chapter 26

Lawrence Freedman

WAR WITH TERRORISM

At war with terrorism

THE SEVERITY OF THE HUMAN, material and economic pain
caused by the September 11 attacks – and their sophistication, audacity, ruth-
lessness, and scale – focused attention on the terrorist methodology of the al-Qaeda
network, with Osama bin Laden at its head. The terrorism theme was reinforced
by a subsequent attack using anthrax, directed against a few political leaders and
media outlets. These had considerable and possibly unintended collateral effects. As
the spores were delivered by mail, some seeped out, contaminating facilities of the
US postal service and other letters. Although the casualties remain few, the disruption to American life has been substantial, and they had the effect of exposing US
vulnerabilities to a much wider range of terrorist attacks using biological or chemical agents. There appears to be no link between those responsible for hijacking
aircraft and turning them into guided missiles, and the dispatch of anthrax – the
combination of the two reinforced the view that the prime contemporary security
challenge comes from terrorism. From the start, President George W. Bush asserted
that the enemy in this war was "terrorism."

Declaring a war against terrorism is warranted to the extent that there is a
normative element in any war, so that success should confirm that certain types of
behavior are unacceptable and that the perpetrators can expect to see their efforts
thwarted and eventually punished. The problem with the designation is that it takes
the war beyond the immediate cause and raises questions of what is to be included
and excluded. Many acts can be described as "terrorism" and they might be undertaken in the name of many causes. There are also political implications in damning
a cause solely by reference to the methods used by some of its proponents, or for
that matter favoring the conventionally strong simply because they are in a position
to eschew such methods.

From Lawrence Freedman, "The Third World War?", *Survival* vol. 43, no. 4 (Winter 2001–2),
pp. 61–88.

"Our war on terror begins with al-Qaeda, but it does not end there," asserted President Bush, addressing Congress on September 20. "It will not end until every terrorist group of global reach has been found, stopped or defeated." This makes the distance over which the attack is mounted the critical feature, thus playing down motives and actual effect, and reinforcing the criticism that the real priority is terrorists who can hit the US homeland. At the same time, Bush's statement risked setting an almost unlimited challenge, and later allegations of contradiction should the US fail to take on other states accused of state-sponsored terrorism, notably Iraq, and begin to court others, such as Iran and Syria, that had denounced the September 11 outrages. Wars are fought between opposing political entities and not against tactics.

Al-Qaeda does not claim to be fighting a war for terrorism, but one that pits true Islam against Christianity and Judaism, in terms that echo Samuel Huntington's "clash of civilizations." President Bush, along with British Prime Minister Tony Blair, put in considerable effort to deny this claim, correctly asserting that Osama bin Laden does not speak for Islam. However, speaking for Islam is bin Laden's objective, so this *is* a war about the future of Islam, and therefore about the governance of all states with Muslim populations, and all conflicts in which Muslim groups are directly involved. These conflicts occupy much of the current international agenda, taking in the Middle East, the Gulf, the Balkans, Central and East Asia, and parts of Africa. North American and Western European countries have large Muslim populations, many drawn from these troubled regions, and the current conflict has highlighted the sensitive position of these communities, especially as members of the al-Qaeda network hid themselves within them as they planned and mounted operations. According to al-Qaeda and its ideological fellow travelers, the United States has become a target because it is an overweening, hegemonic and profoundly decadent power, and from this position has acted internationally on behalf of the enemies of Islam or apostates. Afghanistan has provided al-Qaeda's base, because many of its activists learned their trade during the war against Soviet occupation and because of the coincidence of interests and coordination of efforts with the Taliban regime.

Osama bin Laden's claim that only Afghanistan under the Taliban was a true Islamic country highlighted his challenge to the legitimacy of the Saudi Arabian and Egyptian governments, and the vulnerability of Pakistan. If only the US could be persuaded to disengage, then Iraq would recover its strength and Israel could be vanquished. The involvement of Muslim communities in so many contemporary conflicts and the importance of American policies, active and passive, to their course and eventual resolution, meant that they were all given added salience.

This was all very different from the third world war that, in prospect, had dominated strategic discourse throughout the Cold War period. This assumed the same cast of great powers that had dominated the international system since the start of the twentieth century. Having rationalized themselves into two grand coalitions, each disposing of unlimited destructive power, they would clash in the ultimate confrontation. In the event, instead of the remorseless logic of power politics working itself through to this grim conclusion, those involved balked at the prospect, and the underlying conflict was resolved as a result of the internal ideological demise of one of the coalitions in 1989. From this point, international politics began to be dominated by conflicts that could be traced to a century of falling empires, which culminated with the collapse of the Soviet Empire in Europe, and the implosion of multinational states hitherto bound together by communism. All the struggles upon which al-Qaeda had fed were by-products of the processes of decolonization, set in motion by previous world wars, and the creation of numerous new states, many of which turned out to be extremely weak and conflict-ridden. The chaotic ends to the Austro-Hungarian and Ottoman empires after the First World War can still be felt in the Balkans and the Persian Gulf. The conflicts in Kashmir and the Arab–Israeli dispute began as Britain retreated after the Second World War from the most controversial parts of its empire. The turmoil in Central Asia results from the last acts of the Cold War and the sudden collapse of Soviet power.

In contrast to great-power conflicts, which naturally spread to take in allies and clients, these weak-state conflicts might have been expected to remain contained in their scope and effects. That is how they have been treated by the Western world and the UN: as suspects for individual acts of intervention and conflict-resolution. Tests have been established for intervention, to be applied on a case-by-case basis. Yet during the 1960s, the US had no trouble claiming that a series of discrete counter-insurgency campaigns, waged within individual states, were part of an international struggle against communism. Then the links were identified through a Cold War filter, often at the risk of obscuring the distinctive features of individual conflicts and the more parochial motives of many of the participants.

Now the links have been identified by the enemies of the United States, and while the individual conflicts still have their critical distinctive features, a global struggle of sorts is emerging as a common factor. President Bush has shown himself ready to take up the challenge. Speaking in November to leaders from the states of Central and Eastern Europe, he linked this war quite explicitly to the great ideological challenges of the past:

> Like the fascists and totalitarians before them, these terrorists – al Qaeda, the Taliban regime that supports them, and other terrorist groups across our world – try to impose their radical views through threats and violence. We see the same intolerance of dissent, the same mad, global ambitions: the same brutal determination to control every life and all of life.

In this way, an alternative third world war could be constructed as an armed struggle underway for high political stakes and with global ramifications. It follows both a line of development from the previous two world wars, and a pattern they established, in which the core confrontation acts as a vortex, drawing in these other conflicts and in the process transforming their characters. In such circumstances, active engagement and even military intervention in Third Word conflicts ceases to be a matter of choice and becomes a strategic imperative.

Symmetrical and asymmetrical wars

To use the now-familiar terminology, while a third world war as previously envisaged would have been the ultimate in destructive symmetry, the war now being conducted is completely asymmetrical. The ideal type of a symmetrical war involves two belligerents of similar capabilities, with the outcome determined by the creation of a decisive advantage through superior training, tactical prowess, strategic imagination, technical innovation, and mobilization of national resources during the course of the war. If the symmetry runs deep enough, the victor is likely to emerge only through attrition, when mutual destructiveness has reached a point where small margins of staying power can make the difference. In the classic model for a third world war, the possibility of something that might count as a victory relied upon either a technological breakthrough achieved during the course of an arms race or else a greater capacity for risk taking, so that when matters came to a head it was the enemy's nerve that collapsed first. Whether mutual destruction really was so assured, and post-nuclear attack recovery so unlikely, became a matter of controversy, and deterrence relied upon a residual possibility that under certain circumstances, and despite the evident irrationality of the exercise, a nuclear war might nonetheless be waged. Regardless, the consequences of a superpower war were so obviously dire that every effort was made to prevent it occurring and the danger eventually passed with the end of the Cold War.

The Second World War started for the United States with a surprise attack, and the likelihood that the third might also start in such a fashion was a commonplace of American strategic literature throughout the Cold War, as was the possibility that the surprise would be directed against one or more major cities, almost certainly including New York and Washington. The links with these earlier nightmares could be found in the dust cloud ascending above Manhattan on September 11 and the designation of the World Trade Center site as "ground zero," a term first used by those measuring the possible effects of nuclear explosions. The anthrax attack in itself hardly constituted an act of "mass destruction," although its impact demonstrated how even a small attack could have a "mass effect" by raising fears about a more substantial biological attack. Warnings about al-Qaeda's eagerness to gain access to means of mass destruction, and its lack of qualms about using them, soon became a prominent theme of statements by coalition leaders. After the Taliban had evacuated Kabul, evidence was found of interest in nuclear and biological devices. Osama bin Laden was ready to encourage this view of this group's capabilities.

In most respects, however, the striking feature of this alternative third world war was its almost complete asymmetry. The ideal type of an asymmetrical war is of two belligerents of quite different capabilities with the outcome determined by one side's superior ability to find counters to the capabilities of the other. In this case, the remaining superpower, with superiority in every form of military capability, finds itself pitted against a non-state entity of modest means. The US had hoped to achieve an invincible position through the full exploitation of the proclaimed "revolution in military affairs," so that its wars would henceforth be those of the "third wave," dependent on the artifacts of the information economy, as the wars of earlier periods depended upon the artifacts of the first, agricultural, wave and the second, industrial, wave.

Instead the United States found itself contemplating exactly the opposite of the sort of war it wanted to fight, against an enemy able to find sanctuary by merging into a mountainous and inaccessible terrain for defensive purposes and possessing the ability to merge with global civil society to mount attacks against enemy assets, including in its homeland. The extremity of its weakness in conventional military terms is matched by the extremity of its dependence on terrorism. Low technology was used to turn the West's own high technology against itself. The box cutters used to capture the hijacked aircraft served as advanced versions of the knife, the weapon of choice for street brawlers throughout the centuries. Estimates for the direct cost of the September 11 operations suggest $100,000. For this outlay, al-Qaeda was able to impose immediate costs at least a million times higher, accelerate an international economic downturn, with airlines and tourism particularly shaken, and generate a requirement for massive additional expenditure on internal security – as well as on the subsequent military operations to close down the threat. This was in addition to severe human costs.

Al-Qaeda's readiness to take the initiative, and accept the certain death of its own militants in operations, meant that the US government found itself pondering how to defend a country where millions of people live and work close together in dense urban conurbations, reliant on complex and sophisticated systems of energy, transportation, and communication. When the tactical objective is to kill large numbers of people in spectacular fashion and cause panic and disruption, the United States constitutes a "target-rich environment," with many choices even if individual buildings and facilities turn out to be well protected. The choice of targets did not have to be confined to the homeland United States.

When the US responded with its standard coercive air campaign, the minimal results it achieved during the first month reinforced the image of a great power disoriented by a tiny power offering few "strategic" targets worth hitting, but still able to exploit every stray "precision" weapon that hit a civilian site to maintain the propaganda offensive. Columnist Maureen Dowd captured the frustration: "We're sophisticated; they're crude. We're millennial; they're medieval. We ride B-52s; they ride horses. And yet they're outmaneuvering us." A nation that invented the art of public relations and dominated the world media was being bested by a group that communicated only through melodramatic statements dispatched from a country that banned television. Nik Gowing, noting the challenge to "the complacent assumption of information supremacy," observed how "Low-cost video cameras and mobile phones can nimbly upstage billion-dollar information-processing systems and hierarchical command-and-control structures." When the strategy shifted to supporting local allies on the ground, key supplies turned out to be horse-feed. Many of the tactics and weapons employed would not have been out of place in the imperial wars of the nineteenth century and indeed, in their reliance on betrayal and defection, in much earlier times.

US Secretary of Defense Donald Rumsfeld had been anxious to explain from the start that this was going to be a new type of war, "like none other our nation has faced." Yet, while this war had many unique qualities, in many respects it was quite familiar. The core issues were those that have to be addressed in countless civil conflicts over the past half-century in which insurgent groups have sought to undermine the foundations of an established state. Terrorism is an obvious tactic for the weak to employ against the strong. Instead of taking on directly the military and police organizations responsible for protecting the states they wish to challenge, the weak seek to circumvent them by attacking the more vulnerable elements of civil society. This can cover a wide range of activities, from the assassination of senior political figures to indiscriminate assaults against civilians, with or without warning, to the sabotage of critical infrastructure. Unlike traditional armies, guerrilla groups and terrorists do not expect to hold territory. They need time more than space, for it is their ability to endure while mounting regular attacks that enables them to grow while the enemy is drained of patience and credibility. As with more conventional military action, success must be marked by the creation of desired political effects and this will depend on such factors as the ambition of the objective, the capacity to sustain a campaign rather than mount isolated incidents, the balance of popular support, and the ability to shift this balance through successful operations.

If there is a model for al-Qaeda's campaign, it is the old anarchist notion of the "propaganda of the deed." This notion justified acts of terrorism (usually assassinations) as a means of undermining the old order by demonstrating that those who claimed to be all-powerful were in fact vulnerable. Dramatic deeds would cause the ruling classes to lose their nerve while at the same time inspiring the masses. Part of this strategy assumed that the ruling classes would lash out to preserve their position. In the process, so the theory went, they would diminish themselves further. Every punitive attack would open the eyes of the masses and feed their clamor for justice and an end to oppression. The global scope of the media meant the "deed" of September 11 had the largest-ever audience for a deliberate act of war. The political impact of this, and the images resulting from the subsequent unfolding drama, would be felt in all those individual conflicts that al-Qaeda is seeking to influence.

The weak can only defeat the strong if they can survive sufficiently to mount hurtful campaigns, thereby turning latent and inchoate support into a political movement that cannot be turned off by military or other coercive means. This sets the terms for the response of the strong. [. . .]

The conduct of asymmetric war

The United States had taken on board the notion of asymmetric war but had geared it to the dominant scenarios that were guiding all American force planning. These still pointed to "proper" wars between the armed forces of major powers, with far less attention being given to those lesser types, previously dismissed as being "other than war" and now merely "small-scale." These were generally judged to be an inappropriate use of armed forces, apt to tie them down. US forces could become caught in vicious cross-fire while conducting largely political business that did not even touch on the nation's most vital interests. The military superiority of the United States created risks that in fighting major wars the opponents might resort to super-terrorism. While there was some understanding that the lesser types might also encourage terrorism, it seemed unlikely that this would be of the worst kind. Even after September 11, there was concern that once bin Laden and his coterie were hiding in the Afghan mountains, they would be devilishly difficult to find. Moreover, Afghanistan was notably inhospitable to foreign armies, and finding the prey would require confronting hardened and vicious fighters.

These would be the sort of "warriors" described by Ralph Peters, based on his observations in Central Asia, as "erratic primitives of shifting allegiances" who preferred to "snipe, ambush, mislead, and betray, attempting to fool the constrained soldiers confronting them into alienating the local population or allies, while otherwise hunkering down and trying to outlast the organized military forces pitted against them." Yet the use of Afghanistan as a sanctuary and the gradual integration of al-Qaeda fighters with those of the Taliban regime in their defensive operations against a much-depleted Northern Alliance, meant that al-Qaeda could not fully accept the logic of asymmetry and take to the mountains, but felt obliged to defend the land they held. Their forces were geared to a conventional battle, albeit one that at times bore more resemblance to the nineteenth than the twenty-first century, complete with cavalry charges. Nor was there much evidence that the shock of September 11 had changed the American way of warfare. The State Department put considerable effort into forging new relationships with regional powers, including Pakistan and India, but the Pentagon preferred to win the war while incurring as few obligations as possible to others. To avoid excessive dependence on any particular Afghan faction or member of the international coalition, a quick military fix was sought through strategic bombing and special-forces operations. It was hoped that this would undermine Taliban resistance and encourage defections. As the Taliban collapsed, the Americans would install a new, broad-based, UN-sponsored government into Kabul, possibly even including ex-Taliban "moderates," while their own forces, supported only by the reliable British, would start the search for Osama bin Laden's mountain redoubt.

So, for all the talk of a new war requiring new thinking, the American default strategy of air attacks against military targets was soon at play. In October 2001, the allied air campaign against Afghanistan bore similarities to that against Bosnia in 1995 (*Deliberate Force*) and Serbia in 1999 (*Allied Force*), with a focus on air defenses, command networks and arms dumps, and occasional "leadership" targets. Given the scarcity of appropriate targets, the scale was smaller, but there was still the same problem of meeting pre-war promises to avoid civilian casualties. It soon became apparent after one, largely unsuccessful, commando-type raid that these required far better logistics and intelligence than available, and that the air raids, after the few genuinely important targets had been struck, were doing more harm than good. It appeared that the Afghan people were angry with the Americans because of civilian deaths, while the Taliban fighters, who had largely survived unscathed, were even more confident. If American troops came, as "creatures of comfort," they would provide no match to fighters who had seen off much tougher Soviet soldiers. Meanwhile, coalition partners were becoming irritated by their assigned role – essentially cheerleading – and attempts to forge a new political order for Afghanistan were thwarted by a combination of traditional rivalries and uncertainty over the seriousness of the American intent.

In late October, the US resorted to a lower-risk military strategy. The air campaign became focused rather than speculative and geared to land operations, with a prominent role for B-52s dropping "dumb" bombs on the Taliban's forward positions. This required close cooperation with the Northern Alliance, putting to one side misgivings about the alliance's combat capability and the narrowness of its political base. The results were impressive. Almost as soon as the northern city of Mazar-e-Sharif fell, the fighting spirit of the Taliban appeared to evaporate. A series of sharp advances by Northern Alliance troops, backed by betrayals and defections, did the rest. Despite Western pleading for a more orderly progression, Kabul fell soon after and the Taliban retreated to Kandahar for a last stand. Many al-Qaeda fighters had been killed in the fighting and the conditions appeared propitious to the declared aim of "smoking out" Osama bin Laden himself, although at the time of writing this had not been achieved.

Strategically, this was comparable to the Kosovo War when NATO ended up relying on the Kosovo Liberation Army (KLA) to draw out Serbian forces sufficiently so that they could be targeted by allied aircraft. As the only presence on the ground, the KLA gained a considerable political initiative, but this was limited by the speed with which NATO ground forces, which had been waiting for such a moment, moved into fill the vacuum left by the retreating Serb units. In the case of Kabul, the vacuum was filled by the Northern Alliance and, while it said the right things about the need for a broad-based government, it showed little interest in the presence of substantial foreign armies in a peace-keeping role, actively discouraging British forces who were ready to move in.

The US showed no interest in participating in a peacekeeping force, even as the risks grew that the new victors would take the opportunity to settle old scores, and that Afghanistan would fragment further into warring factions. Before the start of the air strikes, the Pentagon had seemingly understood that a substantial number of ground forces might be required; however, in the event there was clear relief that they had not been necessary and that the US could chalk up, at least in its initial stage, another war virtually free of combat casualties. Nor had they become much obligated to allies, many of whom had assigned forces but were only required for marginal roles.

A third world war?

Might the campaign still be characterized as a third world war? That would certainly be the view of al-Qaeda, which has presented itself as a global focal point for a political movement seeking to influence and feed upon many regional conflicts involving Muslim people. It had operated militarily in areas where small numbers of well-trained and highly motivated militants can make a difference, and politically by appealing to disaffected sections of Muslim opinion over a much wider area. Its successes, including acts of spectacular terrorism, potentially add to its political appeal. This could be enhanced further by disproportionate Western responses, leading to the activation of many latent conflicts as well as the aggravation of those already in being.

By contrast, Western countries have not seen these various conflicts as linked but rather as separate processes, each with its own international dynamic and characteristics, so that the international response must also vary according to the circumstances. Yet the attitude and behavior of the leading international players, especially the United States, has a critical influence on all these conflicts, and the response to any one tends to impact upon the subsequent responses to the other. As American policy during the 1990s became one of strictly limited liabilities, then all involved, and not just radical activists, had an interest in just how strictly these liabilities would be set.

The challenge for al-Qaeda has been to sustain a campaign, demonstrating its ability to strike at American assets in a way that Washington would find both frustrating and humiliating. With every success, the "greatness" of the United States as a global power would be diminished, and its evident inclination to disengagement reinforced. Those governments that had looked to it for support would feel increasingly vulnerable. The radicals would gradually gain the upper hand, and, in the

Muslim world, conservative regimes would stumble and fall. This would be guerrilla warfare on a global scale.

This campaign did not begin on September 11, 2001. There is now evidence that al-Qaeda provided military training to Somali tribes fighting UN forces in 1993, which then included a substantial American contingent. In Somalia, the American military followed the tenets of the AirLand battle, with attempts to use offensive power at the local level to produce decisive results against local militias. The main target was General Aideed and this led, on October 3, 1993, to a raid on two of his lieutenants which went badly wrong. Al-Qaeda operatives participated in the subsequent engagement, which left 18 US Army Rangers dead. As warfare, this might be considered no more than a skirmish, yet politically this was a moment of great significance. Soon President Clinton had ordered *Operation Restore Hope* to be concluded, and the frequent references to "Mogadishu" thereafter in discourse on intervention indicates just what a profound affect it had on American thinking. Later, bin Laden remarked on how those who had fought in Somalia had been surprised by the "low spiritual morale" of the Americans. He noted how "the largest power on earth" left "after some resistance from powerless, poor, and unarmed people." The Somali episode soon influenced other adversaries of the United States. That same October, an American ship carrying US and Canadian soldiers and flying the UN flag turned around as it was about to dock at Haiti because of the presence of a hostile crowd shouting "Somalia! Dead American soldiers!" The Serbs also took note of this preoccupation with the safety of US forces in their strategies.

Thus, the size of a military event need not be a guide to its wider political importance. This skirmish did make a difference in the overall development of international politics. The flaw in al-Qaeda's strategy was to move beyond hurting American forces whenever they intervened in Third World conflicts. This clearly could bring results, as Beirut and Somalia both demonstrated, and had brought about a long-term change in American military philosophy, in the form of setting strict conditions for any intervention and "force-protection fetishism." They wished, however, to punish the Americans for their meddling and hurt them so much that they would abandon all idea of international engagement. There is evidence that the attack on the US embassies in Africa in August 1998 was some sort of retribution for the Somali intervention, although by this time it had no immediate or obvious coercive purpose. A group which claims such a strong religious inspiration may not always conform to the model of a Western rational actor. Retribution can appear important for its own sake.

A successful asymmetric strategy requires that the weak convince the strong that it is not in their interests to persist. The higher motivation of the weak, so long as it can endure the responses of the strong, should over time work to its advantage. For this reason, it has been argued that the archetypal asymmetric actor wants to achieve a "Mogadishu, not a Pearl Harbor." The advantages are likely to be reduced if the strong is hurt so badly that the defeat of the weak becomes a vital interest. In a judgment that may well be validated, Kenneth McKenzie argued that "When US national will has been mobilized, the strong will prevail." This was the response to the events of September 11, and opinion polls were soon recording an unreservedly robust national response and a readiness to do whatever necessary to defeat those responsible.

While it would be wrong to exaggerate what might be achieved if the al-Qaeda presence in Afghanistan is obliterated, it would also be wrong to overstate the ease with which its activities can be transferred to another country or left dependent upon a loosely connected network of activists. The successful campaign in Afghanistan should puncture the aura surrounding al-Qaeda. Wholly eradicating this political force may still be an unreal objective, for the beliefs that animate it are deeply and widely held; but it can be frustrated and demoralized. If, on the other hand, the current US campaign fails to break al-Qaeda, or future targets such as Iraq prove to be more resistant, disengagement from global politics and a retreat into a "Fortress America" posture may well be perceived by both the American government and people as the only way to avoid the indignity and pain of regular terrorist outrages.

Prior to September 11, US engagement had become increasingly conditional, leading to criticisms of American unilateralism, or at least a readiness to act multilaterally only on America's own terms. The Bush administration was even more of this view than its predecessor that involvement in distant Third World civil wars, requiring external help with constabulary duties and nation building, was a luxury it could not afford. The broad thrust of its military preparations was focused on decisive battles against regular armed forces. If the shock of September 11 leads to a reversal of course, then this would truly be an important moment in international history.

On this basis, instead of gearing up its security policy to deal with strong, but for the moment, hypothetical "peer competitors," the US must take more seriously the problems of weak states and the conflicts they engender. The dangers of allowing deep grievances to fester while insidious ideologies are being promoted have been highlighted.

That this should be the case has been argued, especially by Tony Blair, who has claimed that the shock provides a real opportunity as it has "opened the world up":

> Countries are revising their relations with others, pondering the opportunities for realignment. New alliances are being fashioned. New world views formed. And it is all happening fast. There is a shortcut through normal diplomacy. So we should grasp the moment and move, not let our world slip back into rigidity.

Blair had held this activist and interventionist view from the start of his premiership, but there is no evidence as yet that this is now heard by the Bush administration. Despite the assumption that it must become more engaged, in order to deny terrorists favorable political conditions and prevent the destabilization of vulnerable regimes, a successful and not too difficult campaign against the Taliban and al-Qaeda in Afghanistan could just as easily lead to the opinion that American foreign and defense policy is about right.

There is now a more multilateral tone to foreign policy, but this has yet to manifest itself in a greater appreciation of binding treaties, peacekeeping and nation-building. The stress on the lack of middle ground in the war against terrorism as fought by the United States suggests that instead of a "large discontinuity in Washington's external behavior," unilateralist tendencies might be reinforced. One report has referred to the doctrine for the use of force emerging out of Afghanistan as one "unrestrained by borders or allies." Clear signals have been sent out to other, more established, opponents and, in particular, Iraq, that they have now good reason to be uncomfortable about their future prospects. The US war on terrorism has yet to run its course and there is no reason to suppose that future stages will be easier than the first. A drive of this sort cannot but shake up local and global political structures, often in quite surprising and unintended ways. Whether or not international politics will be so transformed at the end of this process that it can be described as the third world war remains to be seen. A key test will be exactly how the United States emerges from this as an international actor.

PART XIV

Syntheses and conclusions

THE TWENTY-SIX ESSAYS THAT YOU HAVE READ, comprising thirteen separate but interrelated topics, represent only a fraction of the literature on global history. One could have added many more topics to the list. Still, you will have gained an understanding of the richness and diversity, the promise as well as many challenges, which together make up the history of humankind in the recent years.

In this concluding section, we consider the impact of globalization on today's world. One of the most important questions is the impact of globalization on inter-state affairs. Is an increasingly globalized world more conducive to peace, or to war? How can such a world be best provided with some order? Through the United Nations and other organizations? Through the European Union and similar regional entities? Through a small number of militarily and economically powerful states? Or through the most powerful of them, namely the United States? If so, is the United States becoming an empire? In the economic realm, is globalization proving to be equally beneficial to all parts of the world, or is disparity between rich and poor countries increasing? If so, what can be done to rectify the situation? Politically, has globalization been conducive to democratization? Can we expect that as global-ization proceeds there will be many more democratic states than today? Or, to the contrary, would globalization foster forces of extremism as a reaction?

These are all fascinating questions. In the following two pieces, however, the authors primarily focus on the cultural dimension of globalization. Arjun Appadurai (Professor of International Studies at Yale University) predicts that globalization will ultimately strengthen cultural forces across national boundaries and bring about the attenuation of sovereign states. Anthony Giddens (Director of the London School of Economics and Political Science) notes that globalization amounts to the global spread of modernization, political, economic, and social. Both authors foresee an uncertain future, but both see the present circumstances as deeply rooted in the past. Hence the need to put globalization in historical context, a perspective that also governs the editors' approach to global history.

Chapter 27

Arjun Appadurai

CULTURAL DIMENSIONS OF GLOBALIZATION

The global now

ALL MAJOR SOCIAL FORCES have precursors, precedents, analogs, and sources in the past. It is these deep and multiple genealogies that have frustrated the aspirations of modernizers in very different societies to synchronize their historical watches. This [essay], too, argues for a general rupture in the tenor of intersocietal relations in the past few decades. This view of change – indeed, of rupture, needs to be explicated and distinguished from some earlier theories of radical transformation.

One of the most problematic legacies of grand Western social science (August Comte, Karl Marx, Ferdinand Toennies, Max Weber, Émile Durkheim) is that it has steadily reinforced the sense of some single moment – call it the modern moment – that by its appearance created a dramatic and unprecedented break between past and present. Reincarnated as the break between tradition and modernity and typologized as the difference between ostensibly traditional and modern societies, this view has been shown repeatedly to distort the meanings of change and the politics of pastness. Yet the world in which we now live – in which modernity is decisively at large, irregularly self-conscious, and unevenly experienced – surely does involve a general break with all sorts of pasts. What sort of break is this, if it is not the one identified by modernization theory [. . .]?

Implicit in this [essay] is a theory of rupture that takes media and migration as its two major, and interconnected, diacritics and explores their joint effect on the *work of the imagination* as a constitutive feature of modern subjectivity. The first step in this argument is that electronic media decisively change the wider field of mass media and other traditional media. This is not a monocausal fetishization of the electronic. Such media transform the field of mass mediation because they offer new resources and new disciplines for the construction of imagined selves and imagined worlds. This is a relational argument. Electronic media mark and reconstitute a

From Arjun Appadurai, *Modernity at Large: Cultural Dimensions of Globalization* (Minneapolis: University of Minnesota Press, 1996), pp. 2–7, 9, 11–13, 15–16, 18–23.

much wider field, in which print mediation and other forms of oral, visual, and auditory mediation might continue to be important. Through such effects as the telescoping of news into audio-video bytes, through the tension between the public spaces of cinema and the more exclusive spaces of video watching, through the immediacy of their absorption into public discourse, and through the tendency to be associated with glamour, cosmopolitanism, and the new, electronic media (whether associated with the news, politics, family life, or spectacular entertainment) tend to interrogate, subvert, and transform other contextual literacies. [. . .] Electronic media give a new twist to the environment within which the modern and the global often appear as flip sides of the same coin. Always carrying the sense of distance between viewer and event, these media nevertheless complete the transformation of everyday discourse. At the same time, they are resources for experiments with self-making in all sorts of societies, for all sorts of persons. They allow scripts for possible lives to be imbricated with the glamour of film stars and fantastic film plots and yet also to be tied to the plausibility of news shows, documentaries, and other black-and-white forms of telemediation and printed text. Because of the sheer multiplicity of the forms in which they appear (cinema, television, computers, and telephones) and because of the rapid way in which they move through daily life routines, electronic media provide resources for self-imagining as an everyday social project.

As with mediation, so with motion. The story of mass migrations (voluntary and forced) is hardly a new feature of human history. But when it is juxtaposed with the rapid flow of mass-mediated images, scripts, and sensations, we have a new order of instability in the production of modern subjectivities. As Turkish guest workers in Germany watch Turkish films in their German flats, as Koreans in Philadelphia watch the 1988 Olympics in Seoul through satellite feeds from Korea, and as Pakistani cabdrivers in Chicago listen to cassettes of sermons recorded in mosques in Pakistan or Iran, we see moving images meet deterritorialized viewers. These create diasporic public spheres, phenomena that confound theories that depend on the continued salience of the nation-state as the key arbiter of important social changes.

Thus, to put it summarily, electronic mediation and mass migration mark the world of the present not as technically new forces but as ones that seem to impel (and sometimes compel) the work of the imagination. Together, they create specific irregularities because both viewers and images are in simultaneous circulation. Neither images nor viewers fit into circuits or audiences that are easily bound within local, national, or regional spaces. Of course, many viewers may not themselves migrate. And many mass-mediated events are highly local in scope, as with cable television in some parts of the United States. But few important films, news broadcasts, or television spectacles are entirely unaffected by other media events that come from further afield. And few persons in the world today do not have a friend, relative, or coworker who is not on the road to somewhere else or already coming back home, bearing stories and possibilities. In this sense, both persons and images often meet unpredictably, outside the certainties of home and the cordon sanitaire of local and national media effects. This mobile and unforeseeable relationship between mass-mediated events and migratory audiences defines the core of the link between globalization and the modern. In the [pages] that follow, I show that the work of the imagination, viewed in this context, is neither purely emancipatory nor entirely disciplined but is a space of contestation in which individuals and groups seek to annex the global into their own practices of the modern. [. . .]

There is growing evidence that the consumption of the mass media throughout the world often provokes resistance, irony, selectivity, and, in general, *agency*. Terrorists modeling themselves on Rambo-like figures (who have themselves generated a host of non-Western counterparts); housewives reading romances and soap operas as part of their efforts to construct their own lives; Muslim family gatherings listening to speeches by Islamic leaders on cassette tapes; domestic servants in South India taking packaged tours to Kashmir; these are all examples of the active way in which media are appropriated by people throughout the world. T-shirts, billboards, and graffiti as well as rap music, street dancing, and slum housing all show that the images of the media are quickly moved into local repertoires of irony, anger, humor, and resistance.

Nor is this just a matter of Third World people reacting to American media, but it is equally true of people throughout the world reacting to their own national, electronic media. On these grounds alone, the theory of media as the opium of the people needs to be looked at with great skepticism. This is not to suggest that consumers are *free* agents, living happily in a world of safe malls, free lunches, and quick fixes [. . .] consumption in the contemporary world is often a form of drudgery, part of the capitalist civilizing process. Nevertheless, where there is consumption there is pleasure, and where there is pleasure there is agency. Freedom, on the other hand, is a rather more elusive commodity. [. . .]

This theory of a break – or rupture – with its strong emphasis on electronic mediation and mass migration, is necessarily a theory of the recent past (or the extended present) because it is only in the past two decades or so that media and migration have become so massively globalized, that is to say, active across large and irregular transnational terrains. Why do I consider this theory to be anything more than an update of older social theories of the ruptures of modernization? First, mine is not a teleological theory, with a recipe for how modernization will universally yield rationality, punctuality, democracy, the free market, and a higher gross national product. Second, the pivot of my theory is not any large-scale project of social engineering (whether organized by states, international agencies, or other technocratic elites) but is the everyday cultural practice through which the work of the imagination is transformed. Third, my approach leaves entirely open the question of where the experiments with modernity that electronic mediation enables might lead in terms of nationalism, violence, and social justice. Put another way, I am more deeply ambivalent about prognosis than any variant of classical modernization theory of which I am aware. Fourth, and most important, my approach to the break caused by the joint force of electronic mediation and mass migration is explicitly transnational – even postnational. [. . .] As such, it moves away dramatically from the architecture of classical modernization theory, which one might call fundamentally realist insofar as it assumes the salience, both methodological and ethical, of the nation-state. [. . .]

The eye of anthropology

Anthropology is my archive of lived actualities, found in all sorts of ethnographies about peoples who have lived very different sorts of lives from my own, today and in the past. The archive of anthropology is a shadow presence in all the [pages] that follow. That is not because it is inherently better than some other disciplinary archive. Indeed, critiques of this archive have been trenchant and untiring in the past fifteen years. But it is the one I best know how to read. As an archive, it also has the advantage of reminding one that every similarity hides more than one difference, and that similarities and differences conceal one another indefinitely, so that the last turtle is always a matter of methodological convenience or stamina. This archive, and the sensibility that it produces in the professional anthropologist, predisposes me strongly toward the idea that globalization is not the story of cultural homogenization. This latter argument is the very least that I would want the reader to take away from this [essay]. But anthropology brings with it a professional tendency to privilege the cultural as the key diacritic in many practices (that to theirs might appear simply human, or stupid, or calculating, or patriotic, or something else). Because this [essay] claims to be about the *cultural* dimensions of globalization, let me spell out the special force that this adjective carries in my usage.

I find myself frequently troubled by the word *culture* as a noun but centrally attached to the adjectival form of the word, that is, *cultural*. When I reflect on why this is so, I realize that much of the problem with the noun form has to do with its implication that culture is some kind of object, thing, or substance, whether physical or metaphysical. This substantialization seems to bring culture back into the discursive space of race, the very idea it was originally designed to combat. Implying a mental substance, the noun *culture* appears to privilege the sort of sharing, agreeing, and bounding that fly in the face of the facts of unequal knowledge and the differential prestige of lifestyles, and to discourage attention to the worldviews and agency of those who are marginalized or dominated. Viewed as a physical substance, culture begins to smack of any variety of biologisms, including race, which we have certainly outgrown as scientific categories. Alfred Kroeber's term *superorganic* nicely captures both sides of this substantialism, something with which I am not in sympathy. The efforts of the past few decades, notably in American anthropology, to escape this trap by looking at culture largely as a linguistic form (understood mainly in Saussurean structuralist terms) only partly avoids the dangers of such substantialism.

If *culture* as a noun seems to carry associations with some sort of substance in ways that appear to conceal more than they reveal, *cultural* the adjective moves one into a realm of differences, contrast, and comparisons that is more helpful. This adjectival sense of culture, which builds on the context-sensitive, contrast-centered heart of Saussurean linguistics, seems to be one of the virtues of structuralism that we have tended to forget in our haste to attack it for ahistorical, formal, binary, mentalist, and textualist associations.

The most valuable feature of the concept of culture is the concept of difference, a contrastive rather than a substantive property of certain things. Although the term *difference* has now taken on a vast set of associations (principally because of the special use of the term by Jacques Derrida and his followers), its main virtue is that it is a useful heuristic that can highlight points of similarity and contrast between all sorts of categories: classes, genders, roles, groups, and nations. When we therefore point to a practice, a distinction, a conception, an object, or an ideology as having a cultural dimension (notice the adjectival use), we stress the idea of situated difference, that is, difference in relations to something local, embodied, and significant. This point can be summarized in the following form:

Culture is not usefully regarded as a substance but is better regarded as a dimension of phenomena, a dimension that attends to situated and embodied difference. Stressing the dimensionality of culture rather than its substantiality permits our thinking of culture less as a property of individuals and groups and more as a heuristic device that we can use to talk about difference. [. . .]

We rarely encounter the word *culturalism* by itself: It is usually hitched as a noun to certain prefixes like *bi*, *multi*, and *inter*, to name the most prominent. But it may be useful to begin to use *culturalism* to designate a feature of movements involving identities consciously in the making. These movements, whether in the United States or elsewhere, are usually directed at modern nation-states, which distribute various entitlements, sometimes including life and death, in accordance with classifications and policies regarding group identity. Throughout the world, faced with the activities of states that are concerned with encompassing their ethnic diversities into fixed and closed sets of cultural categories to which individuals are often assigned forcibly, many groups are consciously mobilizing themselves according to identitarian criteria. Culturalism, put simply, is identity politics mobilized at the level of the nation-state.

[. . .] What appears to be a worldwide rebirth of ethnic nationalisms and separatisms is not really what journalists and pundits all too frequently refer to as "tribalism," implying old histories, local rivalries, and deep hatreds. Rather, the ethnic violence we see in many places is part of a wider transformation that is suggested by the term *culturalism*. Culturalism, as I have already suggested, is the conscious mobilization of cultural differences in the service of a larger national or transnational politics. It is frequently associated with extraterritorial histories and memories, sometimes with refugee status and exile, and almost always with struggles for stronger recognition from existing nation-states or from various transnational bodies.

Culturalist movements (for they are almost always efforts to mobilize) are the most general form of the work of the imagination and draw frequently on the fact of possibility of migration or secession. Most important, they are self-conscious about identity, culture, and heritage, all of which tend to be part of the deliberate vocabulary of culturalist movements as they struggle with states and other culturalist focuses and groups. It is this deliberate, strategic, and populist mobilization of cultural material that justifies calling such movements culturalist, though they may vary in many ways. Culturalist movements, whether they involve African-Americans, Pakistanis in Britain, Algerians in France, native Hawaiians, Sikhs, or French speakers in Canada, tend to be counternational and metacultural. In the broadest sense, [. . .] culturalism is the form that cultural differences tend to take in the era of mass mediation, migration, and globalization. [. . .]

Social science after patriotism

The final part of the here and now is a fact about the modern world that has exercised some of the best contemporary thinkers in the social and human sciences: It is the issue of the nation-state, its history, its current crisis, its prospects. [. . .] I have come to be convinced that the nation-state as a complex modern political form is on its last legs. The evidence is by no means clear, and the returns are hardly all in. I am aware that all nation-states are not the same in respect to the national imaginary, the apparatuses of the state, or the sturdiness of the hyphen between them. Yet there is some justification for what might sometimes seem like a reified view of *the* nation-state [. . .]. Nation-states, for all their important differences (and only a fool would conflate Sri Lanka with Great Britain), make sense only as parts of a system. This system (even when seen as a system of differences) appears poorly equipped to deal with the interlinked diasporas of people and images that mark the here and now. Nation-states, as units in a complex interactive system, are not very likely to be the long-term arbiters of the relationship between globality and modernity. That is why, in my title, I imply that modernity is at large.

The idea that some nation-states are in a crisis is a staple of the field of comparative politics and was in some sense the justification for much of modernization theory, especially in the 1960s. The idea that some states are weak, sick, corrupt, or soft has been around for several decades (remember Gunnar Myrdal?). More recently, it has become widely acceptable to see nationalism as a disease, especially when it is somebody else's nationalism. The idea that all nation-states are to some extent bedeviled by globalized movements of arms, moneys, diseases, and ideologies is also hardly news in the era of the multinational corporation. But the idea that the very system of nation-states is in jeopardy is hardly popular. [. . .] My persistent focus on the hyphen that links nation to state is part of an evolving argument that the very epoch of the nation-state is near its end. This view, which lies somewhere between a diagnosis and a prognosis, between an intuition and an argument, needs to be spelled out.

First, I need to distinguish between the ethical and the analytic components of my argument. On the ethical front, I am increasingly inclined to see most modern governmental apparatuses as inclined to self-perpetuation, bloat, violence, and corruption. Here, I am in mixed company, from the left and from the right. The ethical question I am often faced with is, if the nation-state disappears, what mechanism will assure the protection of minorities, the minimal distribution of democratic rights, and the reasonable possibility of the growth of civil society? My answer is that I do not know, but this admission is hardly an ethical recommendation for a system that seems plagued by endemic disease. As to alternative social forms and possibilities, there are actually existing social forms and arrangements that might contain the seeds of more dispersed and diverse forms of transnational allegiance and affiliation. [. . .] [However] I readily admit that the road for various transnational movements to sustainable forms of transnational governance is hardly clear. I prefer, however, the exercise of looking for – indeed, imagining – these alternative possibilities to the strategy of defining some nation-states as healthier than others and then suggesting various mechanisms of ideology transfer. The latter strategy replays modernization-cum-development policy all over again, with the same triumphalist underpinnings and the same unhealthy prospects.

If the ethical front of my argument is necessarily fuzzy, the analytic front is somewhat sharper. Even a cursory inspection of the relationships within and among the more than 150 nation-states that are now members of the United Nations shows that border wars, culture wars, runaway inflation, massive immigrant populations, or serious flights of capital threaten sovereignty in many of them. Even where state sovereignty is apparently intact, state legitimacy is frequently insecure. Even in nation-states as apparently secure as the United States, Japan, and Germany, debates about race and rights, membership and loyalty, citizenship and authority are no longer culturally peripheral. While no argument for the longevity of the nation-state form is based on these apparently secure and legitimate instances, the other argument is an inverse one and bases itself on the new ethnonationalisms of the world, notably those of Eastern Europe. Bosnia-Herzegovina is almost always pointed to in the United States as *the* principal symptom of the fact that nationalism is alive and sick, while the rich democracies are simultaneously invoked to show that the nation-state is alive and well.

Given the frequency with which Eastern Europe is used to show that tribalism is deeply human, that other people's nationalism is tribalism writ large, and that territorial sovereignty is still the major goal of many large ethnic groups, let me propose an alternative interpretation. In my judgment, Eastern Europe has been singularly distorted in popular arguments about nationalism in the press and in the academy in the United States. Rather than being the modal instance of the complex-ities of all contemporary ethnonationalisms, Eastern Europe, and its Serbian face in particular, has been used as a demonstration of the continued vigor of nationalisms in which land, language, religion, history, and blood are congruent, a textbook case of what nationalism is all about. Of course, what is fascinating about Eastern Europe is that some of its own right-wing ideologues have convinced the liberal Western press that nationalism *is* a politics of primordia, whereas the real question is how it has been made to *appear* that way. This certainly makes Eastern Europe a fascinating and urgent case from many points of view, including the fact that we need to be skeptical when experts claim to have encountered ideal types in actual cases.

In most cases of counternationalism, secession, supernationalism, or ethnic revival on a large scale, the common thread is self-determination rather than terri-torial sovereignty as such. Even in those cases where territory seems to be a fundamental issue, such as in Palestine, it could be argued that debates about land and territory are in fact functional spin-offs of arguments that are substantially about power, justice, and self-determination. In a world of people on the move, of global commoditization and states incapable of delivering basic rights even to their majority ethnic populations [. . .], territorial sovereignty is an increasingly difficult justifica-tion for those nation-states that are increasingly dependent on foreign labor, expertise, arms, or soldiers. For counternationalist movements, territorial sover-eignty is a plausible idiom for their aspirations, but it should not be mistaken for their founding logic or their ultimate concern. To do so is to commit what I would call the Bosnia Fallacy, an error that involves (a) misunderstanding Eastern European ethnic battles as tribalist and primordial, an error in which the *New York Times* is the leader, and (b) compounding the mistake by taking the Eastern European case to be the modal case of all emergent nationalisms. To move away from the Bosnia Fallacy requires two difficult concessions: first, that the political systems of the wealthy northern nations may themselves be in crisis, and second, that the emer-gent nationalisms of many parts of the world may be founded on patriotisms that are not either exclusively or fundamentally territorial. [. . .] In making the[se argu-ments], I have not always found it easy to maintain the distinction between the analytic and the ethical perspectives on the future of the nation-state, although I have tried to do so.

As the nation-state enters a terminal crisis (if my prognostications prove to be correct), we can certainly expect that the materials of a post-national imaginary must be around us already. Here, I think we need to pay special attention to the relation between mass mediation and migration, the two facts that underpin my sense of the cultural politics of the global modern. In particular, we need to look closely at the variety of what have emerged as *diasporic public spheres*. Benedict Anderson did us a service in identifying the way in which certain forms of mass mediation, notably those involving newspapers, novels, and other print media, played a key role in imagining the nation and in facilitating the spread of this form to the colonial world in Asia and elsewhere. My general argument is that there is a similar link to be found between the work of the imagination and the emergence of a postnational political world. Without the benefit of hindsight (which we do have with respect to the global journey of the idea of the nation), it is hard to make a clear case for the role of the imagination in a postnational order. But as mass mediation becomes increasingly dominated by electronic media (and thus delinked from the capacity to read and write), and as such media increasingly link producers and audiences across national boundaries, and as these audiences themselves start new conversations between those who move and those who stay, we find a growing number of diasporic public spheres.

These diasporic spheres are frequently tied up with students and other intellectuals engaging in long-distance nationalism (as with activists from the People's Republic of China). The establishment of black majority rule in South Africa opens up new kinds of discourse of racial democracy in Africa as well as in the United States and the Caribbean. The Islamic world is the most familiar example of a whole range of debates and projects that have little to do with national boundaries. Religions that were in the past resolutely national now pursue global missions and diasporic clienteles with vigor: The global Hinduism of the past decade is the single best example of this process. Activist movements involved with the environment, women's issues, and human rights generally have created a sphere of transnational discourse, frequently resting on the moral authority of refugees, exiles, and other displaced persons. Major transnational separatist movements like the Sikhs, the Kurds, and the Sri Lankan Tamils conduct their self-imagining in sites throughout the world, where they have enough members to allow for the emergence of multiple nodes in a larger diasporic public sphere.

The wave of debates about multiculturalism that has spread throughout the United States and Europe is surely testimony to the incapacity of states to prevent their minority populations from linking themselves to wider constituencies of religious or ethnic affiliation. These examples, and others, suggest that the era in which we could assume that viable public spheres were typically, exclusively, or necessarily national could be at an end.

Diasporic public spheres, diverse among themselves, are the crucibles of a postnational political order. The engines of their discourse are mass media (both interactive and expressive) and the movement of refugees, activists, students, and laborers. It may well be that the emergent postnational order proves not to be a system of homogenous units (as with the current system of nation-states) but a system based on relations between professional bodies, some nongovernmental organizations, some armed constabularies, some judicial bodies. The challenge for this emergent order will be whether such heterogeneity is consistent with some minimal conventions of norm and value, which do not require a strict adherence to the liberal social contract of the modern West. This fateful question will be answered not by academic fiat but by the negotiations (both civil and violent) between the worlds imagined by these different interests and movements. In the short run, as we can see already, it is likely to be a world of increased incivility and violence. In the longer run, free of the constraints of the nation form, we may find that cultural freedom and sustainable justice in the world do not presuppose the uniform and general existence of the nation-state. This unsettling possibility could be the most exciting dividend of living in modernity at large.

Chapter 28

Anthony Giddens

THE GLOBALIZING OF MODERNITY

M ODERNITY IS INHERENTLY GLOBALIZING – this is
evident in some of the most basic characteristics of modern institutions,
including particularly their disembeddedness and reflexivity. But what exactly is
globalization, and how might we best conceptualize the phenomenon? I shall
consider these questions at some length here, since the central importance of globalizing processes today has scarcely been matched by extended discussions of the
concept in the sociological literature. [. . .] The undue reliance which sociologists
have placed upon the idea of "society," where this means a bounded system, should
be replaced by a starting point that concentrates upon analyzing how social life is
ordered across time and space – the problematic of time–space distanciation. The
conceptual framework of time–space distanciation directs our attention to the
complex relations between *local involvements* (circumstances of co-presence) and
interaction across distance (the connections of presence and absence). In the modern
era, the level of time–space distanciation is much higher than in any previous period,
and the relations between local and distant social forms and events become corre-
spondingly "stretched." Globalization refers essentially to that stretching process, in
so far as the modes of connection between different social contexts or regions
become networked across the earth's surface as a whole.

Globalization can thus be defined as the intensification of worldwide social relations which link distant localities in such a way that local happenings are shaped by
events occurring many miles away and vice versa. This is a dialectical process because
such local happenings may move in an obverse direction from the very distanciated
relations that shape them. *Local transformation* is as much a part of globalization as the
lateral extension of social connections across time and space. Thus whoever studies
cities today, in any part of the world, is aware that what happens in a local neighborhood is likely to be influenced by factors – such as world money and commodity markets – operating at an indefinite distance away from that neighborhood itself.
The outcome is not necessarily, or even usually, a generalized set of changes acting
in a uniform direction, but consists in mutually opposed tendencies. The increasing

From Anthony Giddens, *The Consequences of Modernity* (Oxford: Blackwell, 1990), pp. 63–78.

prosperity of an urban area in Singapore might be causally related, via a complicated network of global economic ties, to the impoverishment of a neighborhood in Pittsburgh whose local products are uncompetitive in world markets.

Another example from the very many that could be offered is the rise of local nationalisms in Europe and elsewhere. The development of globalized social relations probably serves to diminish some aspects of nationalist feeling linked to nation-states (or some states) but may be causally involved with the intensifying of more localized nationalist sentiments. In circumstances of accelerating globalization, the nation-state has become "too small for the big problems of life, and too big for the small problems of life." At the same time as social relations become laterally stretched and as part of the same process, we see the strengthening of pressures for local autonomy and regional cultural identity.

Two theoretical perspectives

Apart from the work of Marshall McLuhan and a few other individual authors, discussions of globalization tend to appear in two bodies of literature, which are largely distinct from one another. One is the literature of international relations, the other that of "world-system theory," particularly associated with Immanuel Wallerstein, which stands fairly close to a Marxist position.

Theorists of international relations characteristically focus upon the development of the nation-state system, analyzing its origins in Europe and its subsequent worldwide spread. Nation-states are treated as actors, engaging with one another in the international arena – and with other organizations of a transnational kind (intergovernmental organizations or non-state actors). Although various theoretical positions are represented in this literature, most authors paint a rather similar picture in analyzing the growth of globalization. Sovereign states, it is presumed, first emerge largely as separate entities, having more or less complete administrative control within their borders. As the European state system matures and later becomes a global nation-state system, patterns of interdependence become increasingly developed. These are not only expressed in the ties states form with one another in the international arena, but in the burgeoning of intergovernmental organizations. These processes mark an overall movement towards "one world," although they are continually fractured by war. Nation-states, it is held, are becoming progressively less sovereign than they used to be in terms of control over their own affairs – although few today anticipate in the near future the emergence of the "world-state" which many in the early part of this century foresaw as a real prospect.

While this view is not altogether wrong, some major reservations have to be expressed. For one thing, it again covers only one overall dimension of globalization as I wish to utilize the concept here – the international coordination of states. Regarding states as actors has its uses and makes sense in some contexts. However, most theorists of international relations do not explain *why* this usage makes sense; for it does so only in the case of nation-states, not in that of pre-modern states. The reason here has to do with a theme discussed earlier – there is a far greater concentration of administrative power in nation-states than in their precursors, in which it would be relatively meaningless to speak of "governments" who negotiate with other "governments" in the name of their respective nations. Moreover, treating states as actors having connections with each other and with other organizations in the international arena makes it difficult to deal with social relations that are not between or outside states, but simply crosscut state divisions.

A further shortcoming of this type of approach concerns its portrayal of the increasing unification of the nation-state system. The sovereign power of modern states was not formed prior to their involvement in the nation-state system, even in the European state system, but developed in conjunction with it. Indeed, the sovereignty of the modern state was from the first *dependent upon the relations between states*, in terms of which each state (in principle if by no means always in practice) recognized the autonomy of others within their own borders. No state, however powerful, held as much sovereign control in practice as was enshrined in legal principle. The history of the past two centuries is thus not one of the progressive loss of sovereignty on the part of the nation-state. Here again we must recognize the dialectical character of globalization and also the influence of processes of uneven development. Loss of autonomy on the part of some states or groups of states has often gone along with an *increase* in that of others, as a result of alliances, wars, or political and economic changes of various sorts. For instance, although the sovereign control of some of the "classical" Western nations may have diminished as a result of the acceleration of the global division of labor over the past thirty years, that of some Far Eastern countries – in some respects at least – has grown.

Since the stance of the world-system theory differs so much from international relations, it is not surprising to find that the two literatures are at arm's distance from one another. Wallerstein's account of the world system makes many contributions, in both theory and empirical analysis. Not least important is the fact that he skirts the sociologists' usual preoccupation with "societies" in favor of a much more embracing conception of globalized relationships. He also makes a clear differentiation between the modern era and preceding ages in terms of the phenomena with which he is concerned. What he refers to as "world economies" – networks of economic connections of a geographically extensive sort – have existed prior to modern times, but these were notably different from the world system that has developed over the past three or four centuries. Earlier world economies were usually centered upon large imperial states and never covered more than certain regions in which the power of these states was concentrated. The emergence of capitalism, as Wallerstein analyzes it, ushers in a quite different type of order, for the first time genuinely global in its span and based more on economic than political power – the "world capitalist economy." The world capitalist economy, which has its origins in the sixteenth and seventeenth centuries, is integrated through commercial and manufacturing connections, not by a political center. Indeed, there exists a multiplicity of political centers, the nation-states. The modern world system is divided into three components, the core, the semi-periphery, and the periphery, although where these are located regionally shifts over time.

According to Wallerstein, the worldwide reach of capitalism was established quite early on in the modern period: "Capitalism was from the beginning an affair of the world economy and not of nation-states. [. . .] Capital has never allowed its aspirations to be determined by national boundaries." Capitalism has been such a fundamental globalizing influence precisely because it is an economic rather than a political order; it has been able to penetrate far-flung areas of the world which the states of its origin could not have brought wholly under their political sway. The colonial administration of distant lands may in some situations have helped to consolidate economic expansion, but it was never the main basis of the spread of capitalistic enterprise globally. In the late twentieth century, where colonialism in its original formulas has all but disappeared, the world capitalist economy continues to involve massive imbalances between core, semi-periphery, and periphery.

Wallerstein successfully breaks away from some of the limitations of much orthodox sociological thought, most notably the strongly defined tendency to focus upon "endogenous models" of social change. But his work has its own shortcomings. He continues to see only one dominant institutional nexus (capitalism) as responsible for modern transformations. World-systems theory thus concentrates heavily upon economic influences and finds it difficult satisfactorily to account for just those phenomena made central by the theorists of international relations: the rise of the nation-state and the nation-state system. Moreover, the distinctions between core, semi-periphery, and periphery (themselves perhaps of questionable value), based upon economic criteria, do not allow us to illuminate political or military concentrations of power, which do not align in an exact way to economic differentiations.

I shall, in contrast, regard the world capitalist economy as one of four dimensions of globalization, following the four-fold classification of the institutions of modernity mentioned above. [. . .] The nation-state system is a second dimension; as the discussion above indicated, although these are connected in various ways, neither can be explained exhaustively in terms of the other.

If we consider the present day, in what sense can world economic organization be said to be dominated by capitalistic economic mechanisms? A number of considerations are relevant to answering this question. The main centers of power in the world economy are capitalist states – states in which capitalist economic enterprise (with the class relations that this implies) is the chief form of production. The domestic and international economic policies of these states involve many forms of regulation of economic activity, but, as noted, their institutional organization maintains an "insulation" of the economic from the political. This allows wide scope for the global activities of business corporations, which always have a home base within a particular state but may develop many other regional involvements elsewhere.

Business firms, especially the transnational corporations, may wield immense economic power, and have the capacity to influence political parties in their home bases and elsewhere. The biggest transnational companies today have budgets larger than those of all but a few nations. But there are some key respects in which their power cannot rival that of states – especially important here are the factors of territoriality and control of the means of violence. There is no area on the earth's surface, with the partial exception of the polar regions, which is not claimed as the legitimate sphere of control of one state or another. All modern states have a more or less successful monopoly of control of the means of violence within their own territories. No matter how great their economic power, industrial corporations are not military organizations (as some of them were during the colonial period), and they cannot establish themselves as political/legal entities which rule a given territorial area.

If nation-states are the principal "actors" within the global political order, corporations are the dominant agents within the world economy. In their trading relations with one another, and with states and consumers, companies (manufacturing corporations, financial firms, and banks) depend upon production for profit. Hence the spread of their influence brings in its train a global extension of commodity markets, including money markets. However, even in its beginnings, the capitalist world economy was never just a market for the trading of goods and services. It involved, and involves today, the commodifying of labor power in class relations which separate workers from control of their means of production. This process, of course, is fraught with implications for global inequalities.

All nation-states, capitalist and state socialist, within the "developed" sectors of the world, are primarily reliant upon industrial production for the generation of the wealth upon which their tax revenues are based. The socialist countries form something of an enclave within the capitalist world economy as a whole, industry being more directly subject to political imperatives. These states are scarcely post-capitalist, but the influence of capitalistic markets upon the distribution of goods and labor power is substantially muted. The pursuit of growth by both Western and East European societies inevitably pushes economic interests to the forefront of the policies which states pursue in the international arena. But it is surely plain to all, save those under the sway of historical materialism, that the material involvements of nation-states are not governed purely by economic considerations, real or perceived. The influence of any particular state within the global political order is strongly conditioned by the level of its wealth (and the connection between this and military strength). However, states derive their power from their sovereign capabilities, as Hans J. Morgenthau emphasizes. They do not operate as economic machines, but as "actors" jealous of their territorial rights, concerned with the fostering of national cultures, and having strategic geopolitical involvements with other states or alliances of states.

The nation-state has long participated in that reflexivity characteristic of modernity as a whole. The very existence of sovereignty should be understood as something that is reflexively monitored, for reasons already indicated. Sovereignty is linked to the replacement of "frontiers" by "borders" in the early development of the nation-state system: Autonomy inside the territory claimed by the state is sanctioned by the recognition of borders by some states. As noted, this is one of the major factors distinguishing the nation-state system from systems of states in the pre-modern era, where few reflexively ordered relations of this kind existed and where the notion of "international relations" made no sense.

One aspect of the dialectical nature of globalization is the "push and pull" between tendencies toward centralization inherent in the reflexivity of the system of states on the one hand and the sovereignty of particular states on the other. Thus, concerted action between countries in some respects diminishes the individual sovereignty of the nations involved, yet, by combining their power in other ways, it increases their influence within the state system. The same is true of the early congresses which, in conjunction with war, defined and redefined states' borders – and the truly global influence of the UN (still decisively limited by the fact that it is not territorial and does not have significant access to the means of violence) is not purchased solely by means of a diminution of the sovereignty of nation-states – things are more complicated than this. An obvious example is that of the "new nations" – autonomous nation-states set up in erstwhile colonized areas. Armed struggle against the colonizing countries was very generally a major factor in persuading the colonizers to retreat. But discussion in the UN played a key role in setting up ex-colonial areas as states with internationally recognized borders. However weak some of the new nations may be economically and militarily, their emergence *as* nation-states (or, in many cases, "state-nations") marks a net gain in terms of sovereignty, as compared to their previous circumstances.

The third dimension of globalization is the world military order. In specifying its nature, we have to analyze the connections between the industrialization of war, the flow of weaponry and techniques of military organization from some parts of the world to others, and the alliances which states build with one another. Military alliances do not necessarily compromise the monopoly over the means of violence held by a state within its territories, although in some circumstances they certainly can do so.

In tracing the overlaps between military power and the sovereignty of states, we find the same push-and-pull between opposing tendencies noted previously. In the current period, the two most militarily developed states, the United States and the Soviet Union, have built a bipolar system of military alliances of truly global scope. The countries involved in these alliances necessarily accept limitations over their opportunities to forge independent military strategies externally. They may also forfeit complete monopoly of military control within their own territories, in so far as American or Soviet forces stationed there take their orders from abroad. Yet, as a result of the massive destructive power of modern weaponry, almost all states possess military strength far in excess of that of even the largest of pre-modern civilizations. Many economically weak Third World countries are militarily powerful. In an important sense there is no "Third World" in respect of weaponry, only a "First World," since most countries maintain stocks of technologically advanced armaments and have modernized the military in a thoroughgoing way. Even the possession of nuclear weaponry is not confined to the economically advanced states.

The globalizing of military power obviously is not confined to weaponry and alliances between the armed forces of different states – it also concerns war itself. Two world wars attest to the way in which local conflicts became matters of global involvement. In both wars, the participants were drawn from virtually all regions (although the Second World War was a more truly worldwide phenomenon). In an era of nuclear weaponry, the industrialization of war has proceeded to a point at which [. . .] the obsolescence of Clausewitz's main doctrine has become apparent to everyone. The only point of holding nuclear weapons – apart from their possible symbolic value in world politics – is to deter others from using them.

While this situation may lead to a suspension of war between the nuclear powers (or so we all must hope), it scarcely prevents them from engaging in military adventures outside their own territorial domains. The two superpowers in particular engage in what might be called "orchestrated wars" in peripheral areas of military strength. By these I mean military encounters, with the governments of other states or with guerrilla movements or both, in which the troops of the superpower are not necessarily even engaged at all, but where that power is a prime organizing influence.

The fourth dimension of globalization concerns industrial development. The most obvious aspect of this is the expansion of the global division of labor, which includes the differentiations between more and less industrialized areas in the world. Modern industry is intrinsically based on divisions of labor, not only on the level of job tasks but on that of the regional specialization in terms of type of industry, skills, and the production of raw materials. There has undoubtedly taken place a major expansion of global interdependence in the division of labor since the Second World War. This has helped to bring about shifts in the worldwide distribution of production, including the deindustrialization of some regions in the developed countries and the emergence of the "Newly Industrializing Countries" in the Third World. It has also undoubtedly served to reduce the internal economic hegemony of many states, particularly those with a high level of industrialization. It is more difficult for the capitalist countries to manage their economies than formerly was the case, given accelerating global economic interdependence. This is almost certainly one of the major reasons for the declining impact of Keynesian economic policies, as applied at the level of the national economy, in current times.

One of the main features of the globalizing implications of industrialism is the worldwide diffusion of machine technologies. The impact of industrialism is plainly not limited to the sphere of production, but affects many aspects of day-to-day life, as well as influencing the generic character of human interaction with the material environment.

Even in states which remain primarily agricultural, modern technology is often applied in such a way as to alter substantially preexisting relations between human social organization and the environment. This is true, for example, of the use of fertilizers or other artificial farming methods, the introduction of modern farming machinery, and so forth. The diffusion of industrialism has created "one world" in a more negative and threatening sense than that just mentioned – a world in which there are actual or potential ecological changes of a harmful sort that affect everyone on the planet. Yet industrialism has also decisively conditioned our very sense of living in "one world." For one of the most important effects of industrialism has been the transformation of technologies of communication.

This comment leads on to a further and quite fundamental aspect of globalization, which lies behind each of the various institutional dimensions that have been mentioned and which might be referred to as cultural globalization. Mechanized technologies of communication have dramatically influenced all aspects of globalization since the first introduction of mechanical printing into Europe. They form an essential element of the reflexivity of modernity and of the discontinuities which have torn the modern world away from the traditional.

The globalizing impact of media was noted by numerous authors during the period of the early growth of mass circulation newspapers. Thus one commentator in 1892 wrote that, as a result of modern newspapers, the inhabitant of a local village has a broader understanding of contemporary events than the prime minister of a hundred years before. The villager who reads a paper "interests himself simultaneously in the issue of a revolution in Chile, a bush-war in East Africa, a massacre in North China, a famine in Russia."

The point here is not that people are contingently aware of many events, from all over the world, of which previously they would have remained ignorant. It is that the global extension of the institutions of modernity would be impossible were it not for the pooling of knowledge which is represented by the "news." This is perhaps less obvious on the level of general cultural awareness than in more specific contexts. For example, the global money markets of today involve direct and simultaneous access to pooled information on the part of individuals spatially widely separated from one another.

Index